# THE LAW OF SCHOOLS, STUDENTS AND TEACHERS

## IN A NUTSHELL

### SECOND EDITION

By

**KERN ALEXANDER**

President and University Distinguished Professor,
Murray State University

**M. DAVID ALEXANDER**

Professor and Director of Law
Division of Administrative and Educational Services
Virginia Tech

ST. PAUL, MINN.
WEST PUBLISHING CO.
1995

*Nutshell Series,* In a Nutshell, the Nutshell Logo and the WP symbol are registered trademarks of West Publishing Co. Registered in the U.S. Patent and
Trademark Office.

COPYRIGHT © 1984 WEST PUBLISHING CO.

COPYRIGHT © 1995 By WEST PUBLISHING CO.
> 610 Opperman Drive
> P.O. Box 64526
> St. Paul, MN 55164-0526
> 1-800-328-9352

All rights reserved
Printed in the United States of America

**Library of Congress Cataloging-in-Publication Data**

Alexander, Kern.
    Law of schools, students, and teachers in a nutshell  /  by Kern
  Alexander, M. David Alexander. — 2nd ed.
        p.    cm. — (Nutshell series)
      Includes index.
      ISBN 0-314-05882-6
      1. Educational law and legislation—United States.    I. Alexander,
  M. David.    II. Title.    III. Series.
  KF4119.3.A43        1995
  344.73'07—dc20
  [347.3047]                                                    94-48764
                                                                      CIP

ISBN 0-314-05882-6

# OUTLINE

III

# APPENDICES

# TABLE OF CASES

References are to Pages

## A

# TABLE OF CASES

# B

# TABLE OF CASES

# C

# D

# E

# F

# G

## TABLE OF CASES

# H

# I

# L

# M

# TABLE OF CASES

Alexander,Law Schools NS 2E --2

# N

# O

## TABLE OF CASES

# P

# S

# T

# U

# V

# W

# Y

# Z

# THE LAW OF SCHOOLS, STUDENTS AND TEACHERS

## IN A NUTSHELL

### SECOND EDITION

*

# INTRODUCTION

Law is about fairness. The law pertaining to students, teachers and public schools is an elaboration of fairness and justice as applied to individuals in their various relationships with each other and with the state. The fact that there is such a great quantum of legal precedents in American education is strong evidence that Americans are not only a law abiding people but, as such, are well aware of their legal rights and are justly jealous and protective of them.

The justice sought in the courts in legal cases involving education is ultimately, in most instances, reduced to three core subjects, the breadth and scope of knowledge, the liberty, and the equality of those persons involved with public schools.

That the American public schools have long been admired and much emulated by many countries throughout the world is a strong testimony to the strength and vitality of the American public school system. Nations in Asia, South America and Europe have established educational systems either fully or in part after that of the United States. Even today, countries in Eastern Europe are busily studying every nuance of the American system attempting to capture its essence. Yet, though they may have created systems with the apparent organizational and structural manifestations of the system of this country, the resulting reality has often fallen short of the grand design.

There has been much conjecture as to why some systems fail and, in particular, why the U.S. system is so difficult to successfully clone. Much, of course, has to do with the social structure on which the educational system is built and the potential philosophy that prevails in the particular circumstance.

The organization and financial structure of the educational system means very little if governmental restraints stifle the pursuit of knowledge. Education, by its very nature, reflects the social and political context within which it finds itself. If that contextual condition is one of limitation, with inherent restraints, then the system may falter and founder or at least obtain only limited success. More specifically, though, the cornerstones of the American public school that appear to form the foundation of its success are found in the aforementioned three legal cornerstones: (1) expansion of knowledge, (2) protection of liberty, and (3) guarantee of equality. Each embodies an important philosophical concept or context that is carried to fruition by the legal precedents of the nation. Where public schools of other nations have failed, one or all three of these elements have gone unestablished by legislation or have been allowed to erode through judicial inaction or complicity. Until now, the United States has been able to maintain the sanctity of each cornerstone to a substantial and remarkable degree.

Students, teachers and schools in the United States are affected by the presence of all three, and this book is primarily devoted to the discussion of the legal aspects of the preservation of the expansion of knowledge, liberty and equality. Nearly every chapter has, in some respect, these legal issues at its core.

In examination of the curriculum, programs and activities of the school, the extent and breadth of the knowledge to be conveyed is paramount to the legal discussion. In this regard, in the U.S. the courts have nearly always held in favor of expansion of knowledge. Those forces that would seek to "contract the spectrum" of knowledge have been generally rebuffed. Broader access to more information has usually prevailed over reduction and repression of knowledge. Where educational systems have failed, artificial constraints have been placed on the pursuit of the knowledge by conservative forces, persons or groups, which have sought to expand and perpetuate their own particular dogmas. The legal precedents that have weighed and rejected efforts to contract knowledge are found in differing contexts throughout the book, but in most particular in chapters on curriculum, teacher rights and religious freedom. A complete understanding of these is essential.

Of course, liberty and equality constitute the basis of all law and both are integral to education law. Consideration of liberty, while touching on many and diverse aspects of education law, becomes especially apparent in consideration of fairness and justice when the state deals in adverse ways with either students or teachers. Due process of law, in both its substantive and procedural aspects, becomes the primary legal means to protect and assure that the control of the state will not become oppressive to the detriment of education. Many countries have, with some wonderment, failed to grasp the fundamental reliance of education on due process. Summary dismissal of students and teachers without due process of law, while outwardly fostering a neatness and orderliness of operation, may result in a more detrimental effect on the entire social circumstance. Countries that do not extend to students and teachers the broad substance of liberty cannot hope to have an effective public school system. This is a vital strength of the American system, and it's touched upon throughout the book.

Equality of opportunity, likewise, permeates considerations of education law throughout chapters of this book. Of course, the American dilemma of racial segregation in school attendance immediately comes to mind when the mention of equality is made. Yet, as the various chapters of this book indicate, the issues pertaining to equality may come into play not only in their social context, but occur in many matters of equal treatment in the school instructional program, athletics, finance, and education of the disabled, as well. Deficiency in equality is the Achilles' heel of an educational system, state or nation.

Thus, this book, notwithstanding its treatment of law in a brief nutshell, conveys not only the more apparent and obvious legal precedents, but further, of necessity, addresses the underlying base for the law. Knowledge expansion, liberty and equality as they form the parameters of the law, are discovered, described and embellished throughout the pages of this book. The more deeply that the reader delves into the many legal precedents, the more readily can be seen the fundamental premises that undergird and support the unique American public school system.

The authors are greatly indebted to Drs. Mary Jane Connelly, Mary Hughes, and Teressa Caldwell, as well as

Jennifer Stuart, for assisting in analysis of the law and editing the manuscript. We also owe a great debt of gratitude to Paulette Gardner who typed and formatted the manuscript. Paulette did an enormous amount of work and we will forever be beholden to her for this effort.

# CHAPTER 1

# ATTENDANCE IN PUBLIC SCHOOLS

## § 1.1 INTRODUCTION

Provisions for free public schools are found in the various state constitutions. Within the scope of these constitutional provisions legislatures enact laws which prescribe admission and attendance requirements. Education clauses of state constitutions may designate an age span, such as between six and twenty years of age, for which the state shall provide an education. These constitutional provisions are viewed by the courts as requiring state legislatures to provide for public education covering at least this age group, but do not prohibit the legislatures from expanding educational opportunity beyond the specified ages. For example, courts have held that a legislature has the implied authority to create kindergarten programs for children below the age of six years. In re Kindergarten Schools (Colo.1893). Similarly, expansion of vocational education programs for adults has been held to be within legislative prerogative, even though the state constitution defined public education as covering only ages four through twenty years. In this case, the Supreme Court of Wisconsin said that: "The constitutional provision [that] the Legislature shall provide for establishment of district schools and that such schools shall be free to all children between the ages of four and twenty years does not impliedly prohibit free education for persons beyond the age of twenty and under the age of four." Manitowoc v. Manitowoc Rapids (Wis.1939).

Courts have, generally, acceded to expansion of educational opportunity through reliance on broad implication of either the state constitution or statute. In the famous *Kalamazoo* case, the precedent which helped form public secondary schools in America, the court relied on broad implication of state policy, not explicit statute, to support its conclusion that a local school district could, with consent of the voters, expand its educational program to include high school. Stuart v. School District No. 1 of the Village of Kalamazoo (Mich. 1874).

## § 1.2 ADMISSION

As the educational program is expanded, all persons in the particular age group are entitled to attend the public school. A state cannot set up unreasonable attendance classifications for persons within the same age groups. For example, the public schools in one sector of the state cannot be closed down and vouchers from public funds given to students to attend private schools, with the result that schools are racially segregated. Griffin v. County School Board of Prince Edward County (S.Ct. 1964). When the state makes the decision to provide an educational program, it must do so uniformly and denial of attendance cannot be for a discriminatory purpose.

## § 1.21 Age

Statutes setting minimum ages below which a child cannot be enrolled are valid and cannot be construed as denial of a child's right to attend school. In an Illinois case where state statute required a child to be five years of age by September 1, the parents of a child who became five on September 4 filed suit seeking to compel admission by the local school board. The parents maintained that such a cut-off date was arbitrary and therefore unconstitutional. The court ruled that the school board was within its statutory authority to deny admission to the child. According to the court, it was the intent of the legislature to create and strictly enforce a cut-off age below which a child could not attend school. The law was found not to be arbitrary because the statute was based upon good rationale that the age of the child could be reasonably assumed to indicate the readiness of a child for success in school. Morrison v. Chicago Bd. of Educ. (Ill.App. 1st Dist.1989).

Even though the general rule is that a specified minimum attendance age will be upheld by the courts, there are exceptions. For example, a West Virginia court has held that a state statute requiring a child to attain the age of five years by September 1 implied that local school boards must exercise a reasonable degree of regulatory flexibility in accepting children to kindergarten. Such implied discretion delegated to the local level would require that local school boards give consideration to the intellectual maturity of the child and not rigidly adhere to an "arbitrary cut-off date." Blessing v. Mason County Bd. of Educ. (W.Va.1985).

However, if a child is not entitled to attend school and the parents misrepresent the child's age to the school board, then the school board may recover the costs of the education that had been received by the child under false pretenses. Board of Educ. v. Marsiglia (N.Y.A.D. 2d Dept. 1992).

## § 1.22  Restrictions

States can impose restrictions on admission to public schools which are reasonably related to the state's purpose of providing a free public education. Such restrictions have been upheld when related to the maintenance of the health and protection of the public welfare. Also, residence requirements for reasonable classifications of children have been upheld. Residence statutes which require children to attend school in one school district rather than in another have been dealt with liberally by the courts. A school district has a right to question the *bona fides* of the residency of its students. Where a student changes guardianship solely to attend school in another school district, the validity of the change in residence may be rejected by the receiving school board. In the Matter of Proios (N.Y.1981).

## § 1.23  Residence

Most state laws require children to attend school in the district in which the student resides with his parents or guardian or person having lawful control of him. If a child lives with a custodian, but his parents are in residence in another school district, he must attend school in the district where his parents reside. The United States Supreme Court has held that a *bona fide* residence requirement which is appropriately defined and uniformly applied furthers the state interest in assuring that educational services of the state are enjoyed only by the state's residents. Martinez v. Bynum (S.Ct.1983).

"Residence" generally requires both physical presence and an intention to remain. The Supreme Court of Maine provided the best definition over a century ago,

"When ... a person voluntarily takes up his abode in a given place, with intention to remain permanently, or for an indefinite period of time; or, to speak more accurately, when a person takes up his abode in a given place, without any present intention to remove therefrom, such place of abode becomes his residence." Inhabitants of Warren v. Inhabitants of Thomaston (Me.1857).

Some courts have resolved the residency issue by applying a so-called "best interest test." A case in point is where a fifteen-year-old student resided with her grandmother who lived in Arizona and she sought to attend school in the district where her grandmother lived. The grandmother, however, was not the girl's legal guardian. The inevitable question then arose as to whether the girl was to attend public school free or would be subject to a fee. The Arizona Court of Appeals ruled that the "best interest" of the girl was served by tuition-free placement with the relative who resides within the school district, regardless of whether the relative is the legal guardian. According to this court, the best interest rule should apply if the student does not move to the school district for the primary purpose of obtaining educational benefits. Sleeseman v. State Bd. of Educ. (Ariz.App.1988).

In a decision similar to the Arizona decision above, an appellate court in Illinois held that a student who resided permanently with a maternal aunt was entitled to attend public school tuition-free in the district of the aunt's residence. The court ruled that residence in the school district is sufficient to permit the child to attend school free of charge, so long as residence was not taken solely to enjoy the benefits of the free schools in that district. The court further found that while the child could be required to show that school attendance in the district was not the sole reason for residing there, the school district could not compel the child to prove by third party professional assessment that the parents suffered hardship or were so incapacitated that they could not care for the child. In requiring such a burden of proof, the school district had overstepped its authority. Israel S. v. Board of Education of Oak Park (Ill.App.1992). See also Major v. Nederland Ind. School District (E.D.Tex.1991).

## § 1.24  Domicile

The word "domicile" is derived from the Latin "domus" meaning home or dwelling house. The word may be defined by law as the true place of habitation; for example, a Washington statute which was upheld as constitutional by the United States Supreme Court defined "domicile" as "a person's true, fixed and permanent home and place of habitation. It is the place where he intends to remain, and to which he expects to return when he leaves without intending to establish a new domicile elsewhere." Sturgis v. Washington (S.Ct.1973). A *bona fide* residence requirement may have the same legal connotation as domicile. Domicile and residence are usually in the same place, but the terms are not identical. A person may have two residences, but can have only one domicile. Whether the term "residence" or "domicile" is used, the key is the "intention to remain."

## § 1.25  Constitutional Classification

Classification of persons by geographical boundaries does not constitute a "suspect" classification requiring strict scrutiny to show a compelling reason to so classify.

Domicile requirements are not unconstitutional if the classification is rationally related to a legitimate state purpose. The Supreme Court affirmed a lower federal court decision which held valid a state university regulation which declared that no student could be eligible for resident classification "... unless he had been a *bona fide* domiciliary of the state for at least a year immediately prior thereto...." The rule required that the student show permanent residence and that his presence in the state was not solely for the purpose of attending the state university. Starns v. Malkerson (S.Ct.1971).

## § 1.26  Irrebuttable Presumption

A Connecticut residence requirement for university students was held to be unconstitutional as violating due process because it created an "irrebuttable presumption" of nonresidency for all students whose legal addresses were outside the state before they applied for admission. This meant that nonresident students could not gain resident status so long as they were students because the law created a presumption of nonresidence for all those who attended the state university. The nonresident students could not rebut this presumption even though they intended to continue to live in the state after graduation. Vlandis v. Kline (S.Ct.1973).

## § 1.27  Validity of Residence

In *Martinez v. Bynum*, supra, the United States Supreme Court upheld a Texas statute which denied tuition-free admission to minors who live apart from their parent or guardian for the "primary purpose of attending public free schools." In this case, Roberto Morales, who

was born in McAllen, Texas, in 1969, a citizen of the
United States by birth, was denied tuition-free admission
in the McAllen Independent School District because his
parents no longer lived in Texas and now resided in
Mexico. He moved to McAllen where he lived with his
sister who was his custodian but not his legal guardian.
The Court held that denial of admission was not violative
of equal protection because the State of Texas had a
substantial interest in maintaining school quality by
imposing *bona fide* residence requirements. The Court
said that: "Absent residence requirements, there can be
little doubt that the proper planning and operation of the
schools would suffer significantly."

## § 1.28  Illegal Aliens

If, however, state law regarding residency works to
completely deny school attendance in all districts of a
state, the constitution may be violated. Children of
illegal aliens have been held to have a right to attend the
public schools of Texas when the alternative was that
they would receive no public education at all. Plyler v.
Doe (S.Ct.1982). In this case plaintiffs, illegal aliens,
challenged a state statute in Texas which withheld state
school funds for the education of children who were not
legally admitted into the United States and which authorized local school districts to deny their enrollment. The
plaintiffs claimed that the statute violated the Equal
Protection Clause of the Fourteenth Amendment which
states that no state shall "deny to any person within its
jurisdiction the equal protection of the laws." The state
of Texas in defense maintained that the provision in the
clause "within its jurisdiction" excluded consideration of
aliens and, further, contended that such a classification

was rational because it was in the state's interest to preserve its limited resources for education for those children who were legal residents of the state. In ruling on the first issue, the Court said that the phrase "any person within its jurisdiction" was meant to confirm the understanding that the protection of the Fourteenth Amendment extended to any person, whether they be citizen or not, who is subject to the laws of the state. Since illegal aliens were within the state's boundaries, they were subject to its laws. The Supreme Court pointed out that even though undocumented aliens are not a "suspect class" under the Constitution and that education is not a fundamental right, such a statute would result in a lifetime of hardship for those affected. The Court noted that the children could not be denied services because their parents were illegal aliens and to subject them to such deprivation could not be justified on rational grounds. In arriving at this conclusion, the Court went to great lengths to expound the importance and virtues of public education and, while not declaring it fundamental, apparently elevated it to a level of importance substantially greater than other governmental functions. The Court said that the deprivation of education was not the same as denial of other social benefits of government. Public education plays a pivotal role "in maintaining the fabric of our society and in sustaining our political and cultural heritage"; the denial of education takes an "inestimable toll on the social, economic, intellectual, and psychological well-being of the individual." For the state to impose such an obstacle on a child is to impose a lifetime handicap. In balancing the educational interest of the alien child against the interest of the state, the Court found little contest.

## § 1.3  COMPULSORY ATTENDANCE

An educated citizenry is of paramount importance to perpetuate a democratic society.  Experience throughout history has shown that those societies with high levels of illiteracy and ignorance among their people are most susceptible to domination and tyranny.  James Madison observed that no nation can expect to have a popular government without popular information and Jefferson in his *Preamble to a Bill for the More General Diffusion of Knowledge* (1779) admonished that the most effectual means of preventing tyranny is "to illuminate, as far as practicable, the minds of the people."

Mass education is not only the best and surest means of preservation of liberty, but it is also essential to the economic and social welfare of the people.  Horace Mann probably expressed it best in 1848 when he said that: "For the creation of wealth, then—for the existence of a wealthy people and a wealthy nation—intelligence is the grand condition....  The greatest of all arts of political economy is to change a consumer into a producer;  and the next greatest is to increase the producing power—an end to be directly attained, by increasing his intelligence."

On these grounds the legislatures and the courts have justified universal education for all the people.  To accomplish this, compulsory school attendance laws have been enacted throughout the nation.  Those who have advanced ideas which would result in deschooling society have been given little serious consideration by thoughtful and forward-looking leaders of society.

§ 1.31   Parens Patriae

Legal rationale for compulsory education is found in the common law doctrine of *parens patriae*, which means that the state is the father or guardian for minors or others "to the end that the health, patriotism, morality, efficiency, industry, and integrity of its citizenship may be preserved and protected." Strangway v. Allen (Ky. 1922). An Illinois court has explained *parens patriae* in this manner, "It is the unquestioned right and imperative duty of every enlightened government, in its character of *parens patriae*, to protect and provide for the comfort and well-being of such for its citizens .... The performance of these duties is justly regarded as one of the most important of governmental functions, and all constitutional limitations must be so understood as not to interfere with its proper and legitimate exercise." County of McLean v. Humphreys (Ill.1882).

This power of the state to protect and educate the populace, generally, supersedes the custodial authority of the parent over the child. Parents have undoubted inherent rights to rear and control their own children, but these rights may be legitimately restricted by the state when parental prerogatives are exercised to the detriment of the child. The courts have long recognized that parents may not always act in the best interest of their children. The United States Supreme Court pointed out in 1962 that "... experience has shown that the question of custody, so vital to a child's happiness and well-being, frequently cannot be left to the discretion of the parents." Ford v. Ford (S.Ct.1962).

The United States Supreme Court clearly enunciated the power of the state in upholding a Massachusetts child labor law in 1943 under which a parent was convicted of contributing to the delinquency of a minor. The parent had continued to force the child to work and would not permit the child to attend school, in spite of the law. In this case, Prince v. Massachusetts (S.Ct.1944), the Court said: "[T]he family itself is not beyond regulation in the public interest ... acting to guard the general interest in a youth's well-being, the state as *parens patriae* may restrict the parents' control by requiring school attendance, regulating or prohibiting the child's labor and in many other ways."

## § 1.32  Truancy

Compulsory attendance laws provide for enforcement by penalizing parents for their children's absences. When a child is declared a truant or a chronic or habitual truant, the school board may institute legal proceedings which may include criminal penalty of the parent. A typical definition of truant is found in an Illinois law which reads as follows: "A 'truant' is defined as a child subject to compulsory school attendance and who is absent without valid excuse from such attendance for a school day or portion thereof." Ill.—S.H.A. 105 ILCS 5/27–2a.

Compulsory attendance laws are enacted for the protection of children. The enforcement of such noncriminal laws is within the traditional authority of the police. Police officers may detain students who are suspected of being truant from school. Matter of Shannon B. (N.Y. 1987).

The technical question of whether parents can be punished for their children's failure to attend school has become a more difficult issue as the family structure has broken down and parents are, in many instances, unable to control their children's actions. Two women in Maryland claimed that a compulsory attendance law punishing parents for truancy of children was unconstitutional because it imposed "strict liability" on them for the actions of their children. The court in ruling against the parents explained that the compulsory attendance law imposed an affirmative duty on a person who has control over children to see that a child attends school on a regular basis. Such a requirement is within the proper concern of the state to maintain an educated citizenry. "Passive acquiescence in the child's nonattendance of school is no defense." Thus, where a parent cannot show that he or she attempted to make the child attend school, a conviction of the parent for violating compulsory attendance law will be upheld. In re Jeannette L. (Md.App.1987).

Too, parents who pay little heed to the importance of compulsory attendance laws or overtly ignore legal requirements may find themselves subject to prosecution. In a case where parents were rather obviously contemptuous of truancy prohibitions, children were withdrawn from school, without school permission, to take a trip to Europe. The parents had requested school permission for the trip but when the permission was denied, they ignored the denial, and departed for Europe anyway. A Superior Court in Pennsylvania upheld truancy conviction of the parents observing that school boards have the discretionary authority to determine the appropriateness of school absences. Commonwealth v. Hall (Pa.Super.1983).

Truancy charges, however, must be sustained by the evidence and the school board must be able to present the factual information necessary to enforce a conviction of parents. In one such case where the evidence failed, a Minnesota appellate court ruled that (1) truancy must be proved beyond a reasonable doubt and (2) the student had a right to confront and cross-examine witnesses against him. This court ruled that school attendance records were hearsay and could not be used in court in lieu of a school attendance officer's testimony. Moreover, in truancy cases, the burden of proof is on the state to prove beyond a reasonable doubt that no valid excuse existed for the student's absence from school. Students are not required to prove that their absences were excused, the state must prove that the absences were unexcused. Matter of Welfare of L.Z. (Minn.App.1986, reversed in part on other issues, Minn.1986). Valid causes for absences may be variously defined by statute as illness, death in the family, family emergency or situations beyond the control of the student.

The importance of a valid doctor's certification is illustrated in an Illinois case, where parents took their daughter to several doctors occasionally over a two-year period, but there was no evidence that any single doctor thought she was unable to attend school and no medical excuse was ever received by the school. Here, the court upheld conviction and fining of parents for permitting chronic truancy of their child. People v. Berger (Ill.App. 1982).

## § 1.33 Education as Compelling Public Interest

In keeping with *Prince*, education is usually given special constitutional status by the courts requiring a balancing of constitutional interests. Where parental religious interests conflicted with a compulsory attendance requirement, a Minnesota court found that education constitutes a "compelling interest." Matter of Welfare of T.K. & W.K. (Minn.App.1991).

The fact that education is a compelling "public interest" gives the state, in its sovereign power, the right to make reasonable laws with regard to education even though some parents may believe that such laws encroach on their religious freedom. In a Maine case, the state required information be submitted to the school board for prior approval before allowing home instruction. The parents refused for religious reasons. The court found that providing information to the local school board prior to approval of home instruction was reasonable. The court reasoned that even though the parents were motivated by sincerely held religious beliefs they still had to fulfill the state's prior approval requirements because the state's "public interest in education" outweighed the parents' private religious beliefs. The state's insistence that parents supply the local school committee with information was not unduly restrictive of religious freedom given the state's vital interests in education. Blount v. Department of Education & Cultural Services (Me.1988).

## § 1.34  Limitations on State Power

The legal competence of the state to compel children to attend school is well established, but the power of the state is not unlimited. The state, for example, cannot require attendance solely in public schools. In Pierce v. Society of Sisters (S.Ct.1925), the United States Supreme Court held an Oregon statute unconstitutional because it sought to compel all children between the ages of eight and sixteen years to attend public schools. Two private schools sued claiming that the law denied them their property without due process of law. The institutions claimed that they owned valuable buildings which were constructed for school purposes and that they acquired income from education programs, the success of which was dependent on long-term contracts with teachers and parents. The Supreme Court held that the law did, in fact, deprive the schools of property without due process. The Court agreed that "the right to conduct schools was property and that parents and guardians, as a part of their liberty, might direct the education of children by selecting reputable teachers and places." The Court further said that it was clear that the statute interfered with the liberty of parents to control their children. The "fundamental theory of liberty" the Court said "excludes any general power of the state to standardize its children by forcing them to accept instruction from public teachers only." *Pierce*, therefore, recognizes and guarantees the private school's property interest and acknowledges a parental liberty interest in education of the child in other than public schools.

## § 1.4  HOME SCHOOLING

Home schooling is not, generally, considered to fulfill the requirements of compulsory school attendance. Statutes which provide for private school instruction as fulfillment of compulsory attendance requirements, as they must under *Pierce v. Society of Sisters*, supra, have not been construed to permit home schooling. Authority to exempt home schooling from compulsory attendance laws must be given by express statutory provision. A statute in California which provided for exemption for those "being instructed in a private full-time day school by persons capable of teaching" was held not to implicitly permit home instruction. People v. Turner (Cal.App. 1953). The fact that there is no statutory regulation of private schools does not mean that parents can proclaim that their homes are schools in an effort to avoid enrolling their children in public schools. State v. M. M. (Fla.App.1981).

Some courts have observed that the attributes of school attendance go beyond merely the instruction of children and include social interaction with other students, appropriate facilities such as libraries, laboratories and other features generally found in formal school settings but absent in homes. Student interaction is an essential ingredient of school, thus, home instruction involving only one's own children cannot constitute the equivalent of a regular school program. Stephens v. Bongart (N.J.1937).

A state's refusal to allow home instruction as a valid exemption from compulsory attendance does not violate the Equal Protection Clause of the Fourteenth Amendment. A New Mexico court held that statutory exclusion of home instruction was subject to the rational relationship test of constitutionality. State v. Edgington (N.M.App.1983). This test requires that the state merely show that the purpose for the law is rational. Plaintiffs had argued that the more rigorous test of strict scrutiny must be applied which would require that the state bear the burden of showing a compelling interest to justify its action. This latter test is very difficult to sustain. In considering the two tests, the court concluded that because the United States Supreme Court had held that education was not a fundamental interest, San Antonio Independent School District v. Rodriguez (S.Ct. 1973), the lesser test was appropriate. Using this test, the court reasoned that requiring children to go to school with other children was a legitimate state interest. The New Mexico court said: "By bringing children into contact with some person, other than those in the excluded group, those children are exposed to at least one other set of attitudes, values, morals, lifestyles and intellectual abilities. Therefore, we hold that the statutory classifications presented in the attendance law rationally relates to a legitimate state interest."

However, compulsory attendance laws must be clear and unambiguous so as not to be unconstitutional because of vagueness in violation of due process of law. A Missouri compulsory attendance law was held to be unconstitutional because of the use of language that could be subject to differing interpretations. The Missouri statute allowed exemption from compulsory attendance in public schools where the child was to be given "substantially equivalent" instruction at home. Without guidelines to interpret what "substantially equivalent" meant, the court found that parents and school officials could only guess at its meaning. Ellis v. O'Hara (E.D.Mo.1985).

## § 1.41   Regulation of Home Schooling

Modifications of compulsory attendance statutes to allow for home schooling dramatically increased during the decade of the 1980s. In 1982, only two states, Nevada (1956) and Utah (1957), had statutes that specifically permitted home schooling. This number had, however, increased to thirty-two by the end of 1993. In addition, two other states, Maryland and New York, permit home school by state regulations. See William M. Gordon, Charles J. Russo, and Albert S. Miles, *The Law of Home*

*Schooling* (Topeka, Kansas, National Organization on Legal Problems of Education, 1994), p. 3.

Religion is the primary source of contention for parents who do not want their children to attend public schools. They generally object that their particular sectarian brand of religion is not taught and/or that the public schools are secular. The U.S. Supreme Court has, however, maintained that the interest of the state in having an educated citizenry is sufficient to override specific religious objections, save the lone instance of the Amish in the Yoder case. State of Wisconsin v. Yoder (S.Ct.1972). Accordingly, religion cannot be used as an excuse to defeat properly prescribed state regulation.

The state's interest in public education may be generally encompassed within two aspects—the attainment of knowledge and socialization. In this regard, states usually defend compulsory attendance laws by requiring some assurance of quality of education and by maintaining that attending public schools with other children from various walks of life promotes tolerance and understanding of others. The value of the public schools as an engine to promote commonality and community interest, as opposed to individual egoism or selfish group interest, has largely fallen by the wayside as legislatures have allowed much greater parental option in permitting children to opt out of public schools and avail themselves of only home or private schooling.

But legislatures, and courts, have been more reluctant to permit this opting out to be so complete as to deprive the affected children of access to substantive knowledge. To this end, the legislatures, with the courts acquiescence, have imposed and maintained certain education quality standards for home schooling. Such standards

are usually of two types—teacher certification requirements and testing or output measures. The requirement
that home school teachers be certified teachers is, however, tenuous at best.

## § 1.42  Certification

Gordon's research indicates that the majority of the
court decisions uphold state requirements that home
school teachers be certified. Yet, challenges on the religious grounds have been increasingly successful. However, in North Dakota, claims based on religious freedom
exercise rights have not prevailed. In upholding the
state's authority to require certification of home school
teachers, the North Dakota Supreme Court provided the
most definitive precedent. When parents challenged
home school certification as a violation of their free
exercise of religion, the Court pointed out the importance
and validity of certification requirements saying: "While
a teaching certificate is no guarantee that the holder is a
competent teacher, it does guarantee that the holder has
been exposed to the knowledge that a competent teacher
should have ... [the] certification requirement for instructors in public, non-public, or home schools is reasonably justified ... Teacher certification appears to us to
be among the least personally intrusive methods now
available to satisfy the state's prime interest in seeing
that its children are taught by capable persons." State
v. Patzer (N.D.1986).

In keeping with this rationale, the North Dakota Supreme Court has ruled that the interest of the state in
having an educated citizenry is a legitimate interest that
outweighs any perceived religious freedom denial claimed
by plaintiff parents in objecting to a certification require-

ment. State v. Shaver (N.D.1980); State v. Rivinius (N.D.1982); State v. Melin (N.D.1988); State v. Toman (N.D.1989). Agreement with the North Dakota court has come from an Alabama court. Required certification of home school instructors was upheld in Alabama to be a valid state interest. Jernigan v. State (Ala.Crim.App. 1982).

On the other hand, the Michigan Supreme Court has held that the requirement of state certification of home school teachers could not be justified as a compelling state interest. To overcome an exercise of religion claim by home schooling advocates, the state must show that it has a compelling reason for its action. In this light, certification is not of sufficient importance to outweigh the individual's interest in free exercise of religion. People v. DeJonge (Mich.1993). In a companion case, however, the Michigan Court held that such certification requirements did not violate the due process rights of parents. People v. Bennett (Mich.1993).

In Arkansas, a court found a requirement that parents conducting home instruction have college degrees did not violate free exercise. Accordingly, the state's requirement that home instruction be conducted by a qualified teacher did not burden the parent's religious beliefs and did not prevent the parents from otherwise providing religious instruction to their children. Burrow v. State (Ark.1984).

Requirement that home instruction teachers be qualified must be clear enough that the statute or regulation is not constitutionally deficient for vagueness. The words a "qualified tutor" is not so vague, State v. Buckner (Fla.App.1985), as to violate due process while a mandate that teacher qualifications for home instruction be "essentially equivalent" to public school teachers has been held to be invalid for vagueness. State v. Newstrom (Minn.1985).

Even though the precedents are by no means clear and unequivocal, the prevailing view appears to be that states can require instructors at home schools to meet qualification standards as long as the requirements encroach as little as possible on religious beliefs.

## § 1.43 Testing Requirements

The interest of the state in the quality of home instruction has been exhibited by legislation mandating various student assessment measures. Gordon reports that thirty-five states have requirements of student assessment; seventeen of which require standardized tests solely, fifteen states provide for optional assessments, including testing; and two states of the thirty-five do not provide for testing as an evaluation alternative. Gordon et al., supra, p. 45. Montana is unique in that it places sole responsibility on parents to evaluate their own home instructional program.

State requirements that children in home schools be tested to assess their academic progress have been generally upheld by the courts so long as the governing statutes are not too vague for reasonable interpretation. State v. Bowman (Or.App.1982).

Testing was upheld as a reasonable assessment measure in spite of parental objection in Massachusetts; the court there said: "... the superintendent or school committee may properly require periodic standardized testing of the children to ensure educational progress and the attainment of minimal standards." Care and

Protection of Charles (Mass.1987). The statute authorizing evaluations to be conducted by local school district officials is not invalid because of unconstitutional delegation.

Neither does a requirement of testing of children who were educated at home violate due process or equal protection. In upholding a West Virginia statutory provision making children ineligible for home schooling if their test scores fell below the 40th percentile, the court said: "The state's interest in education is subject to a balancing process when it impinges on fundamental rights and interests, such as those specifically protected by the Free Exercise Clause of the First Amendment ... (but) when no fundamental right is involved, and only a general Fourteenth Amendment liberty interest is at stake, then parents' liberty interest is subject to reasonable state regulation." Null v. Board of Education of the County of Jackson (S.D.W.Va.1993).

Thus, state requirements that children in home schools be tested as a means to monitor their educational progress serve as a legitimate state interest and will be upheld so long as the statutes and regulations are not vague and are reasonable.

## § 1.5  PRIVATE SCHOOLS

Exemption from compulsory attendance to attend private schools is a right of all parents as protected by due process as enunciated in *Pierce v. Society of Sisters*, supra. Litigation, though, frequently arises as to whether a school has the attributes which are required to qualify as a "private school" as contemplated by law. A Washington court in 1912 held that the words "to attend a private school" meant more than home instruction; it means, to be approved for exemption, the school must be "the same character of school as the public school, a regular organized and existing institution making a business of instructing children of school age in required studies and for the full time required by the laws...." State v. Counort (Wash.1912).

According to a New Jersey court, whether an instructional program constitutes a "private school" within the meaning of statute is dependent on three tests: first, the qualifications of the parent or instructor; second, the teaching material being used; and third, whether the educational program was commensurate with that provided in public schools. Knox v. O'Brien (N.J.Super.1950).

Parents and children may be allowed by statute to choose between a "home instruction" and a "private school" exception for exemption from compulsory attendance in public schools. Such choices are, however, normally contained by the specific provision of the applicable statutes. Birst v. Sanstead (N.D.1992). In the absence of a home instruction statute, the burden of proof is on the parent to show that the instructional program is a "private school" and to be so adjudged it must be commensurate with that of a regular public school program.

## § 1.51 Religious Exemption

The general rule of law is that religious objection to education is not a valid reason for keeping a child away from school. The great English jurist Blackstone noted that common law recognized that the most important duty of parents is to give their children "an education suitable to their station in life" and Blackstone further acknowledged the power of the state to take children from the parents to assure that the children's abilities could be developed to "the greatest advantage of the commonwealth." 1 Commentaries 451.

In 1839 the United States Supreme Court held that the right to control their own children is a parent's natural, but not an "unalienable right." Ex parte Crouse (S.Ct.1839). In justification of compulsory attendance, as a limitation on parental control, a Pennsylvania court has said that "it must be conceded by all right thinking persons, that enforcement of the compulsory school code is a matter of paramount importance, to which the views of the individual view must yield . . . ." Commonwealth v. Gillen (Pa.Super.1916).

Objection to compulsory attendance cannot be simply justified by parent's claims that they have an inherent right to control their child's religious upbringing. *Prince v. Massachusetts*, supra. In Commonwealth v. Bey (Pa.Super.1950), Mohammedan parents persistently refused to send their children to school on Fridays, the sacred day of that religion. The court found the parents in violation of the compulsory attendance law and said: "It [the law] permits attendance at private and parochial schools. All that it requires is continuous attendance at a day-school of the kind and character mentioned in the statute, or daily instruction by a private tutor. Since the parent may avail himself of other schools, including parochial or denominational schools, the statute does not interfere with or impinge upon the religious freedom of parents . . . ."

A number of states have enacted legislation which permits a child to be exempt from compulsory attendance for a *bona fide* religious belief.  This is the situation in Virginia where that state's Supreme Court ruled that a compulsory attendance law did not require the school board to state its reasons for denying the religious exemption.  Johnson v. Prince William County School Bd. (Va.1991).

## § 1.52  The Amish Exception

The most important exception to the general rule, that religious belief does not exempt one from compulsory attendance laws, is found in the United States Supreme Court's decision in State of Wisconsin v. Yoder (S.Ct. 1972).  In this case the Court held that Amish children could not be compelled to attend high school even though they were within the age range of Wisconsin's compulsory attendance statute.  The Amish maintained that higher learning beyond that which could be acquired in neighborhood elementary schools tended to develop values which alienated their children from God.  The Amish sect believes that its members should reject the competitive spirit, deemphasize material success and insulate its youth from the modern world.

The Supreme Court, in interpreting the sweep of the First Amendment's Free Exercise Clause, observed that protection of religious beliefs is a basic freedom of such magnitude that the state's interest must be of the "highest order" if it is to overbalance the individual's religious interest.  The Court placed the burden of proof on the state to show that universal compulsory education was not merely rational public policy, but, indeed, a compelling state interest.

In attempting to show a compelling interest, Wisconsin maintained that education is necessary to prepare citizens to participate effectively in our democratic system of government.  In response the Court observed that the Amish community is a unique and special case which has been "highly successful as a social unit within our society" and that its members had an exemplary record as productive and law-abiding citizens.  With regard to participation in the democratic process, the Court held that the brief period of education from ages fourteen to sixteen, the period in question when the Amish children would be compelled to attend high school, was not a period of time significant enough to justify "severe interference with religious freedom."  According to the Court, the Amish alternative to formal secondary education had enabled the Amish to function effectively in day-to-day life of contemporary society as a "separate and sharply identifiable and highly self-sufficient community for more than 200 years in this country."  Further, the Court noted that when Thomas Jefferson emphasized the need for an educated citizenry as a bulwark against tyranny, he did not necessarily have in mind education beyond a basic eighth-grade education.

In ruling for the Amish parents, however, the Court so narrowly defined the attributes of the Amish religion in exempting it from compulsory attendance that the use of *Yoder* as precedent by parents of other religions to gain similar exemptions has been generally unsuccessful. The Court set out three criteria for balancing the individual's religious interests against the public interests of the state.  The court must determine (1) whether the individual's beliefs are legitimately religious and if they are sincerely held;  (2) whether the state regulation unduly restricts the religious practices;  (3) whether the state has a compelling interest justifying the regulation and whether the compelling interest is of such importance as to overcome the right to free exercise of religion.

The primary importance of *Yoder* is that it elevates religion to a special constitutional status as a First Amendment right which must be given particular consideration by the courts when parents and students contest state action. Importantly, it requires that the state bear the burden of showing that it has a compelling reason to justify its denial of a religious belief. In the unique case of *Yoder* and the Amish religion, the state was unable to bear this burden.

## § 1.53 Regulation of Religious Schools

The state has a legitimate interest in the quality of the educational program performed in private schools, but as indicated in *Yoder* where freedom of religion is in question the courts will apply strict judicial scrutiny. The extent of the state regulation to be permitted by the courts will depend on the state's constitution and statutes and how they are applied to the private school.

In a 1979 case, the Kentucky Supreme Court held that the state could not prosecute parents for violation of the compulsory attendance law who enrolled their children in private schools which did not employ certified teachers nor use state approved textbooks. Kentucky State Board v. Rudasill (Ky.1979). The court decided the case purely on a state constitutional provision which stated in part: "nor shall any man be compelled to send his child to any schools to which he is conscientiously opposed...." This provision, the court observed, was more restrictive on the state than the Free Exercise Clause of the First Amendment of the United States Constitution. In examining the debate at the constitutional convention at which the provision was adopted, the court found the intent of this provision was to allow parents to choose any school for their children, as a matter of conscience. The court found nothing wrong with the state mandating that private schools have instruction in several branches of study as was required of public schools, but the court would not allow the state to require the same instruments of education, certified teachers, and state-approved textbooks, to be used by private schools.

Parents again prevailed in an Ohio case in which parents were convicted of violating compulsory attendance laws because they enrolled their children in a Bible-oriented Christian school which failed to "conform to the minimum standards prescribed by the state...." State v. Whisner (Ohio 1976). The private school had only twenty-three children who were taught by a certified teacher in one room. The state minimum standards in Ohio were highly restrictive regulating virtually to the minute what should be taught in private schools. These standards regulated "[t]he content of the curriculum that [was] taught, the manner in which it [was] taught, the person or persons who [taught] it, the physical layout of the building in which the students [were] taught, the hours of instruction, and the educational policies intended to be achieved through the instruction offered."

The court found these rules to be so excessive as to deny the parents their freedom of religion and the right to direct the education of their children as they saw fit. In following *Yoder* the court required that the state show a compelling reason to justify the encroachment on individual religious freedom. This burden the state was unable to sustain.

Conviction of parents for violating compulsory attendance laws has, however, been upheld in Nebraska and North Dakota. In Meyerkorth v. State (Neb.1962), the Supreme Court of Nebraska held that statutes requiring that private school instruction be "substantially the same" as that of public schools did not violate the religious freedom of private school parents or the students.

The North Dakota case set a precedent almost precisely opposite that of *Whisner*. State v. Shaver (N.D.1980). Here defendant parents were convicted of violating compulsory attendance laws for sending their children to a church-affiliated private school which was not approved by the state. The school had no certified teachers and employed a widely used self-study curriculum made up of a series of Bible-oriented learning packets. The school showed, as was the case in *Rudasill*, that the students of the private school scored higher on achievement tests than did their counterparts in public schools.

The court in applying the three-part test of *Yoder*, balancing the parents' interests against the state's, ruled against the parents. As to the tests: first, the court acknowledged that the defendants had a sincere religious belief; second, the court did not agree that the state rules placed an undue burden on the defendants' religious beliefs, but assumed arguendo that such a burden did exist in order to apply the third test, holding that the state had a "legitimate and compelling interest ... in educating its people" and the regulation of private schools was within state prerogative.

Therefore, a state may regulate private religious schools so long as the regulations are reasonable and are not so excessive or restrictive as to constitute unwarranted interference with the individual's religious freedom. Where parents, though, are able to show that the state's requirements are too specific, then private school parents may succeed in averting conviction for violation of compulsory attendance laws.

## § 1.6 MARRIAGE

Compulsory attendance laws do not generally apply to married persons. Courts have agreed that the nature and responsibilities of marriage are such that married persons of compulsory attendance age should be exempted. The view of the courts is best expressed in State v. Priest (La.1946), which said that: "The marriage relationship, regardless of the age of the persons involved, creates conditions and imposes obligations upon the parties that are obviously inconsistent with compulsory school attendance or with either the husband or wife remaining under the legal control of parents or other persons."

In the eyes of the law, then, marriage emancipates the minor from control by either the parent or the state, for purposes of compulsory education.

## § 1.7 VACCINATION

To protect the health and welfare of citizens, states have required school children to be vaccinated. Courts have generally held that, if a parent violates a statute requiring vaccination, the parent is subject to arrest or fine, even if he or she claims religious, conscientious, or scientific objections.

In 1905, the United States Supreme Court held that a board of health requirement that all persons in Cambridge, Massachusetts, be vaccinated did not violate personal liberties found under the Fourteenth Amendment. In this case, the Court noted that "the liberty secured by the Constitution of the United States to every person within its jurisdiction does not impart an absolute right on each person to be, at all times and in all circumstances, wholly free from restraint. There are manifold restraints to which every person is necessarily subject for the common good." Jacobson v. Commonwealth of Mass. (S.Ct.1905). See also Maricopa County Health Dept. v. Harmon (Ariz.App.1987).

Although this particular decision challenged the vaccination regulation rather than compulsory attendance laws, the Supreme Court, nevertheless, cited several state court decisions approving state statutes and making vaccination of children a condition of the right to attend public schools.

In Viemeister v. White (N.Y.1904), a turn-of-the-century New York decision, the appellant argued that vaccination not only did not prevent smallpox but tended instead to bring on other harmful diseases. The court, while not ruling that vaccination was a smallpox preventive, nevertheless maintained that laymen and physicians alike commonly believed that it did prevent smallpox. The court concluded that, even if it could not be conclusively proved that the vaccination was a preventive, in our republican form of government the legislature has the right to pass laws based on common belief and the will of the people to promote health and welfare.

When an epidemic is imminent, there is no doubt that the state has the power to protect the citizenry by requiring vaccination. However, when there is no evidence of the imminence of an epidemic, the courts may rule differently.  Can the state's requirement of vaccination be a reasonable and permissible restraint on constitutional rights in the absence of epidemic?

In Board of Education v. Maas (N.J.Super.1959), the defendant argued that compulsory vaccination and immunization were not needed because there had been no smallpox or diphtheria in the area for almost a decade. The court disagreed and ruled that the absence of an emergency does not warrant a denial of the exercise of preventive means.  The court said, "A local board of education need not await an epidemic, or even a single sickness or death, before it decides to protect the public. To hold otherwise would be to destroy prevention as a means of combating the spread of disease."

In summary, one can reasonably draw several conclusions regarding compulsory attendance and vaccination: (1) The legislature has power to enact a statute providing for vaccination and including a penalty for noncompliance.  (2) Neither the parent nor the child has a constitutional right to schooling without compliance with statutory requirements for vaccination.  (3) A parent cannot escape conviction for failing to have his or her child vaccinated by demanding that the child be admitted to school unvaccinated.  (4) Religious objection has not generally prevented enforcement of compulsory vaccination and attendance requirements.

# CHAPTER 2

# THE INSTRUCTIONAL PROGRAM

## § 2.1  INTRODUCTION

As a general rule school officials have the authority to prescribe the method of teaching, decide on what curriculum shall be offered, and what books shall be used in the school. Such authority is vested in public schools either expressly or implicitly by state law. However, this authority is not absolute and may be curtailed or modified by the courts if school officials proceed beyond the bounds of their legal authority or act arbitrarily in violation of the constitutional rights of students or teachers. The courts, however, will not intervene in resolution of conflicts which arise from the daily operation of the schools and which do not directly involve basic constitutional values. Pratt v. Independent School District No. 831 (8th Cir.1982).

## § 2.11  Judicial Deference

The judiciary is normally very reluctant to enter the realm of school curricular and instructional matters. Courts have traditionally been uneasy in exercising their authority with regard to nature and content of the curriculum, course offerings and requirements, and the evaluation thereof. By in large, the courts are respectful of the knowledge of professional educators and will give substantial latitude and weight to their opinions. A federal circuit court has stated the court's position in this way: "Decisions on evaluation of the academic performance of students as it relates to promotion are peculiarly within the expertise of educators and are particularly inappropriate for review in a judicial context." This court observed that an expanded judicial presence in the classroom could be deleterious to many of the beneficial aspects of the faculty-student relationship. Sandlin v. Johnson (4th Cir.1981).

## § 2.2  CURRICULUM

Local school boards have the power as delegated by statute to enforce reasonable rules prescribing a specific curriculum. State ex rel. Andrews v. Webber (Ind.1886). Power given to school authorities by state legislatures implies discretion to determine course content. This power may emanate from rules of general authority which allow the local school authorities to establish the curriculum as well as requirements for promotion and graduation. Such power, of course, may be retained by the legislature, and rather than delegating to local school boards, statute may specifically mandate prescribed curricula or graduation requirements.

A case in point is illustrated in Pennsylvania legislation where a local school board passed a rule requiring that all students complete sixty hours of community service during the four years of high school. The objective of the school board was to "help students acquire life skills and learn the significance of rendering services to the community . . . [and] gain a sense of worth and pride as they understand and appreciate the functions of community organizations." Parents challenged the requirement claiming it violated the students' First Amendment rights of freedom of speech and Thirteenth Amendment rights of "involuntary servitude" or slavery. The court upheld the requirement holding that it violated neither the First nor Thirteenth Amendments. Steirer by Steirer v. Bethlehem Area School District (3d Cir.1993).

## § 2.21 Reasonable Rules

The right of every student to attend school is subject to reasonable regulation. Rules have often been invalidated by the courts because they are arbitrary or capricious. By definition a reasonable rule is neither arbitrary nor capricious. So long, though, as the legal authority is appropriately delegated to local school boards, and the boards act in good faith in formulating and applying reasonable standards, boards' actions will not be overturned.

## § 2.22 The Spectrum of Knowledge

In deciding whether a statute or rule is constitutional, the courts will balance the interests of the parties involved. With regard to the school curriculum, students, parents, teachers, and the state all have interests which must be taken into consideration.

The student's interest is normally one of self-interest which must be accommodated if the educational process is served. As the guardian of the child, the parent has certain expectations for the type of education and the quality and quantity of knowledge his or her child is to acquire. The teacher has freedom to convey knowledge and to exercise those prerogatives which normally flow from being a teacher. Academic freedom bestowed by the First Amendment is part and parcel of the teacher's interests and protections in teaching. The state has an overarching political, social and economic interest in fully developing the abilities of its citizenry. No one rule of law can be prescribed which addresses the problems which may arise from these conflicting interests. The rule which may come nearest to being generally applicable is that the courts will hold in favor of the expansion of knowledge. The party which seeks to "contract the spectrum of knowledge," or restrain the full expanse of human understanding and inquiry will generally be rebuffed by the courts. Griswold v. Connecticut (S.Ct. 1965).

## § 2.23  Intellectual Marketplace

The courts have held that a reluctance on the part of the teacher to investigate and experiment with new ideas is an "anathema" to the idea of education. Imposition of an intellectual straitjacket on teachers or educational leaders would, according to Chief Justice Earl Warren, "imperil the future of our nation." Education is intended to be a marketplace of ideas through which society is best served when there is wide exposure to truths and an unlimited exchange of ideas. The classroom is, thus, viewed as an intellectual marketplace protected by law.

## § 2.24  Evolution and Creation Science

Charles Darwin's theory of evolution has always bothered some people including conservative legislators, parents, and some school administrators. Those who rigidly adhere to the strict constructionist Biblical account of creation express particular dissatisfaction toward school systems which teach science from an evolutionary point of view. Feelings regarding the teaching of evolution have been so strong that several years ago a few states enacted anti-evolution laws making it a criminal offense for a teacher to teach the Darwinian evolution. It was on this issue that the famous "Scopes monkey trial" of Dayton, Tennessee, was contested. This highly publicized confrontation between the great politician Williams Jennings Bryan and the equally outstanding lawyer Clarence Darrow ultimately resulted in the conviction (a small fine) of Scopes for teaching the theory of evolution. In the process, however, the Tennessee statute was held in such disdain that the issue lay dormant for over 30 years without a real test of the statute's constitutional validity.

Finally, in 1968 in an Arkansas case, the United States Supreme Court ruled that a 1928 anti-evolution statute making it unlawful for a teacher in a state-supported institution to teach science from an evolutionary perspective was unconstitutional. By 1968 only two states, Arkansas and Mississippi, had such "monkey laws" on their books. The Court found the law violated the First Amendment because it proscribed a respected scientific theory from the classroom for no other reason but that it was in conflict with a particular religious doctrine in the Book of Genesis. Even though the Arkansas statute was less candid than the original Tennessee "monkey law," in that the Arkansas statute did not explicitly state that the reason for the statute was that it denied the story of the divine creation of man, the Court found that state sanction of the Christian doctrine of creation was, nevertheless, implicit in the Arkansas law and therefore unconstitutional. Epperson v. State of Arkansas (S.Ct. 1968).

The issue in Arkansas did not, however, fade away. A mixture of religious beliefs and political conditions in the late 1970s and early 1980s led to a revival of the evolution question in public schools. On March 19, 1981, the Governor of Arkansas signed a bill which required balanced treatment of "creation-science" and "evolution-science" in the public schools. The federal court in Arkansas ruled that creation-science was not a science at all. Rather, the court said that it was a religious doctrine which was, in this case, imposed on the youth by the state statute. McLean v. Arkansas Board of Education (E.D.Ark.1982).

In a similar case, in 1981, the Louisiana legislature passed a law entitled, "Balanced Treatment for Creation–Science and Evolution–Science in Public School Instruction." No school was required to teach the "subject of origin" but if the school chose to teach about "evolution-science," it must give balanced treatment to "creation science." The United States Supreme Court in Edwards v. Aguillard (S.Ct.1987), ruled the Louisiana act unconstitutional. The court stated, "The Act impermissibly endorses religion by advancing the religious belief that a supernatural being created humankind. The legislative history demonstrates that the term 'creation science,' as contemplated by the state legislature, embraces this religious teaching. The Act's primary purpose was to change the public school science curriculum to provide persuasive advantage to a particular religious doctrine that rejects the factual basis of evolution in its entirety."

## § 2.25 Liberty to Teach and Learn

The power of the state to compel attendance at school and to require all students to take instruction in the English language has been long recognized. Yet, the courts have not condoned the states' overreaching their authority to prohibit the teaching of any other language. In a landmark case, rendered in 1923, Meyer v. Nebraska, a statute forbidding the teaching of foreign languages to students who had not completed the eighth grade in public, parochial, or private schools was challenged by an instructor in a parochial school who was retained by parents to give their child instruction in the German language. The statute was enacted in 1919 when the thoughts of the nation's legislators were still much influenced by World War I. Constitutional basis for the plaintiff's action was found in the Due Process Clause of the Fourteenth Amendment which provides that "No state ... shall deprive any person of life, liberty or property without due process of law." In holding for the teacher, the Court said that the state's power was limited where it infringed on the liberty interests of the teacher and the pupil. In so ruling the Court gave broad definition to the word liberty saying "the term ... denotes not merely freedom from bodily restraint but also the right of the individual to contract, to engage in any of the common occupations of life, to acquire useful knowledge, to marry, establish a home and to bring up children, to worship God according to the dictates of his own conscience, and generally to enjoy those privileges long recognized at common law as essential to the orderly pursuit of happiness of free men."

Where state statute infringes on an individual's liberty, the legislative action may be stricken by the courts.

In *Meyer,* the Court said that education of the young is regarded as a high calling, useful, honorable, and, indeed, essential to the public welfare. Becoming knowledgeable about the German language could not be regarded as harmful, meriting state proscription. The Court concluded that the teacher's right to teach and the right of parents to engage the teacher to instruct their children were liberty rights bestowed by the Fourteenth Amendment.

## § 2.26  English Language Instruction

State law or school board rule can require that the basic language of instruction in all schools be English. Some states have passed legislation requiring bilingual education. In 1981 Texas passed the Bilingual and Special Language Programs Act which compelled bilingual education in elementary school. See United States v. State of Texas (5th Cir.1982).

The issue of whether the school district may provide instruction exclusively in English was raised in Lau v. Nichols (S.Ct.1974). In *Lau,* the San Francisco school district provided special English instruction for 1000 of 2800 Chinese students. The remaining students were not served because of a lack of funding.

The United States Supreme Court maintained that failure to provide methods of bridging the language gap offended Title VI of the Civil Rights Act of 1964, 42 U.S.C.A. § 2000d. The 1964 Act bans discrimination "on the ground of race, color, or national origin" in "any program or activity receiving federal financial assistance." The San Francisco school district receives large amounts of federal funds. Pursuant to the Civil Rights Act, the Department of Health, Education and Welfare had issued guidelines which specified that "Where inability to speak and understand the English language excludes national origin-minority group children from effective participation in the educational program offered by a school district, the district must take affirmative steps to rectify the language deficiency ...." (35 Fed. Reg. 11595). The court did not address the issue of deprivation under the Equal Protection Clause of the Fourteenth Amendment. The litigation concerned only Title VI. The lower federal courts have held that denial of bilingual education does not violate equal protection and a number of these rulings have revolved around desegregation of public schools.

With the federal law and guidelines as the legal basis, the Supreme Court held for the plaintiff Chinese children, and in so doing observed that there can be no equality of treatment where the students do not understand English. The Court concluded that "Basic English skills are at the very core of what these public schools teach. Imposition of a requirement that, before a child can effectively participate in the educational program, he must already have acquired those basic skills is to make a mockery of public education. We know that those who do not understand English are certain to find their classroom experiences wholly incomprehensible and in no way meaningful."

## § 2.27 Academic Freedom

Whether a teacher may be disciplined or even dismissed for using a "dirty word" depends on the circumstances surrounding the situation. "Each case must be examined on an independent basis," with the court considering a number of factors, such as age of students, context and manner of presentation and whether a valid educational objective is being met. In a case where a teacher was dismissed because he gave his class copies of an article published in the *Atlantic Monthly* magazine in which the vulgar term for an incestuous son was used, and the teacher explained the word's origin to the class, its context, and why the author had used it, the teacher was subsequently suspended. The teacher sued to recover his position maintaining the article was a valuable discussion of "dissent, protest, radicalism, and revolt" and was in no way pornographic. The court agreed with the teacher in finding that the article was thoughtful and thought-provoking and to delete the offending word would have made it impossible to understand the article or the point of view of the author. Keefe v. Geanakos (1st Cir.1969).

While the court agreed that some measure of public regulation of classroom speech is inherent in every provision for public education, to deny the teacher use of such words when used in an educational context would be to demean the academic process. Whether language is offensive or inappropriate is dependent on the circumstances in the particular situation. Other circumstances which must also be considered include the educational information being conveyed, the reason for use of the words, and the educational level of the students involved.

Teachers may, however, go beyond their legal bounds in use of offensive terminology. Courts have pointed out that a teacher's academic freedom does not extend to protection of conduct which is "both offensive and unnecessary to the accomplishment of educational objectives ... such questions are matters of degree involving judgment on such factors as the age and sophistication of the students, relevance of the educational purpose, and context and manner of presentations." Brubaker v. Board of Education, School District 149, Cook County, Illinois (7th Cir.1974).

In a case where an economics instructor was dismissed for using profanities in class, prior to which he had been warned orally and in writing for using profanities such as "hell," "damn," "bullshit" and "God damn," the court said such use of profane language was not a protected First Amendment right. Martin v. Parrish (5th Cir. 1986).

## § 2.28    The Pall of Orthodoxy

School authorities, as public policy makers, have comprehensive powers and broad discretion in discharging their duties to provide public education. In commenting on the extent of these powers, the U.S. Supreme Court said in Epperson v. Arkansas that: "By and large, public education in our nation is committed to the control of state and local authorities. Courts do not and cannot intervene in the resolution of conflicts which arise in the daily operation of school systems and which do not directly and sharply implicate basic constitutional values."

School boards, however, do not have an absolute right to remove material from the curriculum. One of the great strengths of the public school in America has been its openness and expansiveness in the conveyance of knowledge. At various times throughout the history of public schools attempts have been made to limit knowledge or cast a spectre of restraint preventing the free flow of learning. Such restraints have ranged in form from the "red scare" communist hunts and mandatory oaths of the 1950s to parental challenges to curriculum content of the 1980s. In a loyalty oath case from New Hampshire in 1957 the U.S. Supreme Court said that: "Teachers and students must always remain free to inquire, to study and to evaluate" and the state cannot "chill that free play of the spirit which all teachers ought especially to cultivate and practice." Sweezy v. New Hampshire (S.Ct.1957). Later in another New York oath case the U.S. Supreme Court again inveighed against those forces that would "cast a pall of orthodoxy." Keyishian v. Board of Regents (S.Ct.1967).

Of late, there have been increasing attempts by some parents and citizens claiming negative impact on religious or family values to seek to restrict the public school curriculum. In rejecting a parental and student attempt to ban from school the film "The Lottery," a short story in which citizens of a small town select one of their members to be stoned to death each year, a federal circuit rejected the parents complaint and, again, couched the legal logic in the context of protecting the schools against a "pall of orthodoxy." Pratt v. Independent School Dist. No. 831 (8th Cir.1982).

## § 2.3 CENSORSHIP OF TEXTBOOKS

The 1988 Supreme Court decision in Hazelwood School Dist. v. Kuhlmeier (S.Ct.1988), although involving the school board's ability to control a school sponsored newspaper, has had an impact beyond student publications. This decision has been applied in a variety of areas inclusive of the school curriculum and academic freedom of teachers. The expansion of *Hazelwood* from a case involving editorial control over a school sponsored paper to broader application is tied to the following statements by the Supreme Court. "Educators do not offend the First Amendment by exercising editorial control over the style and content of student speech in school-sponsored expressive activities so long as their actions are reasonably related to legitimate pedagogical concerns" and "It is only when the decision to *censor* (emphasis added) a school-sponsored publication, theatrical production, or other vehicle of student expression has no valid educational purpose that the First Amendment is so directly and sharply implicated as to require judicial intervention to protect students' constitutional rights."

The principle enunciated in *Hazelwood* was later applied to a curriculum textbook decision in Virgil v. School Board of Columbia County (11th Cir.1989). In this case, a minister whose child was a student in an English class filed a complaint with the school board concerning two books used in the class, Aristophanes' *Lysistrata* and Chaucer's, *The Miller's Tale*. The school board voted to discontinue use of the books because of "sexuality" and "excessively vulgar ... language and subject matter." In upholding the school board's decision to ban the books, the Eleventh Circuit Court of Appeals stated, "Hazelwood established a relatively lenient test for regulation of expression which may fairly be characterized as part of the school curriculum. Such regulation is permissible so long as it is 'reasonably related to legitimate pedagogical concerns.'" Accordingly, when prescribing learning materials, the school district must take into account the emotional maturity of the audience and the nature and sensitivity of the topics involved.

In a California case, the court chose to interpret *Hazelwood* in a more narrow light. This court would not accept any pedagogical justification for removing books, and ruled the school board's motives should be examined before accepting their pedagogical reasons as legitimate. In this case the two books, *Grendel* and *One Hundred Years of Solitude*, were removed because of a student complaint based on religious grounds. The court noted that a school board has broad powers to remove and restrict the use of books that may be profane or contrary to the prevailing community moral standards, but ruled that educational unsuitability must be the real reason for excluding a book(s) and not a religious reason. McCarthy v. Fletcher (Cal.App.1989).

## § 2.31 Textbooks Challenged on Religious Grounds

Controversy surrounding textbook selection by public school boards has become more frequent and increasingly acrimonious in recent years. The primary cause of this increased dissension has been the rising political strength and activism of fundamentalist religious groups. Various sects have taken great pains to search through textbooks adopted by public schools and ferret out what they consider to be objectionable matter. An example of an attempt by parents to ban certain books because of religious objections is vividly illustrated in a Tennessee case. Here, the parents objected to the use of textbooks, a reading series published by Holt, Rinehart and Winston. The plaintiff, a mother of four children, objected to a story on mental telepathy and claimed that such material violated her religious beliefs as protected by the First and Fourteenth Amendments of the U.S. Constitution. She sought proscription of any teachings that were not circumscribed by the Biblical scriptures. The plaintiff parent, a Mrs. Frost, testified that she had found at least 17 categories of offensive materials in the books including evolution, pacifism, secular humanism, "futuristic supernaturalism," magic and false views of death. She strongly objected to many specific passages including one that described Leonardo de Vinci as a human with a creative mind that "came closest to the divine touch." The U.S. Court of Appeals, Sixth Circuit, upheld the school board's required use of the textbooks and pointed out the parent had testified that she would "not be tolerant" of religious views other than her own. According to the court, the school board's view and the content of the reading series conveyed a respect and tolerance for the beliefs of others. The court found that the school board had sought to acquaint students with a multitude of ideas and concepts. There was no evidence that the readings prescribed by the school board would lead the plaintiff's children to any conclusions that were contrary to the plaintiff parent's religious beliefs. Mozert v. Hawkins County Board of Education (6th Cir.1987).

While the *Mozert* case was litigated on the Free Exercise of Religion Clause of the First Amendment, another similar textbook case was based on a premised violation of the Establishment Clause. In Smith v. Board of School Commissioners of Mobile County (11th Cir.1987), a parent claimed that certain textbooks in home economics, history, and social studies violated the Establishment Clause because they were advancing the religion of secular humanism. The plaintiff further claimed that the textbooks inhibited theistic religion. The Sixth Circuit held that the textbooks were secular in nature and as such did not promote secular humanism or inhibit a theistic religion. The court in quoting Everson v. Board of Education (S.Ct.1947), said "The public schools in this country are organized: 'on the premise that secular education can be isolated from all religious teaching so that the school can inculcate all needed temporal knowledge and also maintain a strict and lofty neutrality as to religion. The assumption is that after the individual has been instructed in worldly wisdom he will be better fitted to choose his religion.' "

However, such efforts to control the adoption of textbooks by religious fundamentalists are not infrequent. In these cases the courts are prone to defer to the established authority of the school board, regardless of its political leanings. An illustration of the deference that courts have for school board authority is illustrated in an Illinois school district case where reading material used in an elementary school contained "scary" stories with ghosts, goblins and witches. A group of parents complained that the readings had the effect of advancing pagan religious views. The court upheld the school board's use of the books finding that the material did not foster any particular religious view. This federal district court noted that these matters were for the school board to decide and observed that the courts cannot sit as reviewers of "educational decisions" made by school boards. Fleischfresser v. Directors of School District 200 (N.D.Ill.1992).

In a similar case, Brown v. Woodland Joint Unified School District (E.D.Cal.1992), the court ruled that the textbook series titled "Impressions" did not endorse the religion of witchcraft and/or Neo-Paganism in violation of federal or state constitutions.

# § 2.4  CENSORSHIP OF LIBRARY BOOKS

School boards have a significant degree of discretion in the determination of the content of school libraries. That discretion, however, is not without limits and may be abused if exercised in a political or narrowly partisan manner.  Because each case must stand on its own factual merits, precedents regarding the authority of the school board to remove books from the school library have not been definitive.  The United States Court of Appeals for the Second Circuit held in 1972 that the school board had the discretion to remove books from the library simply because they were without merit either as works of art or science.  Presidents Council, Dist. 25 v. Community School Board (2d Cir.1972).  The court observed that administration of a school library "involves a constant process of selection and winnowing based not only on educational needs but financial and architectural realities.  To suggest that the shelving or unshelving of books presents a constitutional issue, particularly where there is no showing of a curtailment of freedom of speech or thought, is a proposition we cannot accept."

In a later case from another federal appellate court a ruling was rendered indicating school boards do not have authority, unfettered by the First Amendment, to remove books from the school library simply because they find them to be objectionable in content.  Minarcini v. Strongsville City School District (6th Cir.1976).  This court said that a school board could not "place conditions on the use of the library which were related solely to the social or political tastes of school board members."  Further, the court observed that the public school library is a valuable adjunct to classroom discussion, that the First Amendment's protection of academic freedom would protect both the student's right not only to participate in classroom discussion but also to find and read a book on the subject of discussion. Censorship of the school library would, thus, place a serious burden upon academic freedom as protected by the freedom of speech provision of the First Amendment. See also Salvail v. Nashua Bd. of Educ. (D.N.H.1979).

Whether and to what extent school boards can remove materials from libraries remains a source of contention. The U.S. Court of Appeals for the Second Circuit held in 1980 that books could be removed from the school library because of their vulgar nature. According to this court school boards could not remove books because of the ideas they contained, but could remove books in applying their own standards and tastes in determining what is vulgar and explicit sexual conduct. Bicknell v. Vergennes Union High School Bd. of Directors (2d Cir.1980).

On the other hand, other courts have been reluctant to allow the availability of library materials to be contingent upon the tastes and standards of board members. Such unlimited discretion on the part of board members may be so vague as to permit arbitrary administration in such a way to offend due process. Moreover, boards may possibly violate due process if they remove books without adopting procedural safeguards for considering the book's content. Sheck v. Baileyville School Committee (D.Me.1982).

The library censorship issue was addressed by the United States Supreme Court in 1982 in a case in which the school board had removed nine books from the school library. Board of Education, Island Trees Union Free School District No. 26 v. Pico (S.Ct.1982). The board's justification for removal of the books was that they were irrelevant, vulgar, immoral, and in bad taste, making them educationally unsuitable for junior and senior high school students.

The Supreme Court in *Pico* noted that "local school boards must be permitted to establish and apply their curriculum in such a way as to transmit community values, and there is legitimate and substantial community interest in promoting respect for authority and traditional values, be they social, moral, or political." The Court, however, went on to point out that school boards could not in exercise of their broad discretion "strangle the free mind" and limit youth in acquiring important information which will allow them to become responsible citizens. The Court reemphasized that neither the school board nor anyone else could "consistent with the spirit of the First Amendment contract the spectrum of available knowledge." In this context the student has the right to receive information and ideas and such a right is the logical corollary of the rights of free speech and press. Too, the Court observed that a school library is the principal locus at which the student can exercise the freedom to inquire, study, and evaluate. In Lamont v. Postmaster General (S.Ct.1965), the Supreme Court had previously held that "the dissemination of ideas can accomplish nothing if otherwise willing addressees are not free to receive and consider them."

According to the Supreme Court in *Pico*, the critical issue to be considered is the motivation behind a school board's actions. If the school board members intended the book removal to suppress certain ideas with which they disagreed, then the action was unconstitutional; on the other hand, if the board removed the books because they were "pervasively vulgar" or obscene or solely because they were "educationally" unsuitable, then no right was violated. The evidence in *Pico* showed that the board did not employ regular and unbiased procedures in reviewing the books as to their educational suitability and that, in fact, the books had been removed solely because they had been placed on a list of objectionable books by a conservative organization of parents who had prevailed on the school board for the removal. In ruling against the school board, the Court admonished that its decision was limited to the removal of books from the library and in no way affected a school board's discretion in adding books to the school library.

## § 2.5  COURSE  CONTENT  AND  TEACHING METHODS

The school district's authority to decide the course content and to determine the teaching methods to be employed is well established. The weight and importance of the school district's discretion has usually been demonstrated in cases where teaching materials contained matter that was considered to be obscene.

In such cases there has been little doubt about the authority of the school district to regulate the course content. Yet, the courts will examine each circumstance to determine if the magnitude of the teacher's offensive behavior is sufficient to warrant the specific sanctions taken against the teacher. The primary issue to be considered by the courts is the extent and severity of the redress taken against the teacher. Firing of a teacher for unwittingly allowing obscene poetry to be read by students has been held too severe, De Groat v. Newark Unified School District (Cal.App.1976), while a nine month suspension of a teacher for showing cartoons of

"Fritz the Cat" in various stages of undress has been held to be appropriate. DeVito v. Board of Educ. (W.Va. 1984).

Teaching methods may also be prescribed and regulated by the school district. Teachers do not have a constitutional right to use whatever teaching methodology that pleases them if it runs counter to policies of the district. In a case illustrative of this point, where two high school teachers claimed their First Amendment rights were violated when a school district refused to allow them to team-teach a history course, the students complained that the teaching technique affected the substance of the course. The Supreme Court of Washington held against the teachers pointing out that while some flexibility in teaching techniques may be employed by teachers, the teachers cannot be allowed to implement a particular technique that will detract from the effectiveness of the course. Millikan v. Board of Directors of Everett School District (Wash.1980).

## § 2.6 PROMOTION

Schools are empowered to establish a prescribed level of student performance. Reading attainment may be one criterion for measuring performance for promotion of students from grade-to-grade. In a case where only one student out of twenty-three second-graders was promoted to the third grade because the others failed to reach a third grade reading level on the Ginn Reading Test, the court in upholding the criterion said, "Decisions by educational authorities which turn on evaluation of the academic performance of a student as it relates to promotion are peculiarly within the expertise of educators and are particularly inappropriate for review in a judicial context." Sandlin v. Johnson (4th Cir.1981). Such academic requirements are invalid only if they illegally classify students in a way which is prohibited by statute or by the state or federal constitutions.

In a higher education decision which has implications for elementary and secondary schools, the United States Supreme Court refused to reinstate a medical student who failed to adequately complete the internship phase of the training program. The Court said "We decline to further enlarge the judicial presence in the academic community and thereby risk deterioration of many beneficial aspects of the faculty-student relationship." Board of Curators of University of Missouri v. Horowitz (S.Ct. 1978). See also Regents of University of Michigan v. Ewing (S.Ct.1985).

## § 2.61  Lack of Scholarship

School boards and teachers have substantial discretion in determining what level of academic attainment will be required of students. School boards set general course requirements and teachers evaluate the students in achieving the objectives. Seldom will courts intervene to overturn a teacher's academic evaluation of a student. Only where school boards or the teachers act in bad faith or are found to be arbitrary or capricious will their actions be overturned. Students, thus, may be placed in alternative classes or retained at a particular grade level depending on their academic performance. (See Student Testing, Chapter 14.)

## § 2.7 DIPLOMA

School boards are empowered to set academic standards required to obtain a diploma. Such requirements, however, cannot be unreasonable and the diploma cannot be withheld except for valid reasons rationally related to the state's interests in public education. By establishing and maintaining a public school system, the state creates an expectation, to be reasonably held by the student, that upon successful completion of required courses, he or she will be awarded a diploma. This expectation constitutes a "property interest" on the part of the student which cannot be arbitrarily taken away. The diploma as a property interest cannot be taken away except where the state's interest exceeds that of the individual. Even then the denial can only be valid after the student has had an opportunity to be heard and is provided procedural due process. Thus, to deny the high school diploma because students failed to pass a Florida high school functional literacy examination was held to deny property interests to the student without due process of law. The court found that a test administered at the eleventh grade level covered material which had not been taught to students in the public schools of Florida, thus denial of a diploma based on a newly applied standard, after students had completed all other requirements for graduation, was held to be unfair and violated due process. Debra P. v. Turlington (5th Cir.1981).

Nothing in federal or state law, however, stands in the way of school boards making reasonable rules to effectuate a legitimate educational purpose. A successful score on a minimal competency test can be required of all students before they can receive a diploma. Those who do not succeed in passing the test may receive only a certificate of program completion. Rankins v. State Board of Elementary and Secondary Education (La.App. 1994).

Where severely mentally retarded and autistic students could not pass a minimum competency test, the court held that the school district was not required to issue them diplomas. Schools are required by the federal legislation to make reasonable modifications in tests to minimize the detrimental effects of a student's handicap; however, the federal law does not require that the test be modified to offset a student's mental deficiency or lack of knowledge. What is required, for example, is that a blind child be given the test orally or in braille or a deaf child be given visual instead of oral exams in measuring their qualifications to receive a diploma. Brookhart v. Illinois State Board of Education (D.Ill.1982).

## § 2.8  HOMEWORK

It is generally assumed that teachers and/or school boards can require students to devote a certain amount of out-of-school time to their studies. In fact, many believe that too little homework is required in schools today. A legal question may, though, arise where a parent objects to homework as an encroachment on parental prerogative and, too, it may be contended that the child should not be held accountable at school for work done at home.

Only a few early cases have been rendered giving guidance on this issue, but the limited precedent available indicates that it is an appropriate exercise of school authority to require homework so long as the requirements are reasonable and are directly related to the student's achievement at school. Teachers may punish students for refusing to do homework assignments. Mangum v. Keith (Ga.1918). Rules, though, may not be so constrictive as to deprive parental control over the activities of their children. Thus, a school rule setting aside specific hours each night, say between 7 and 9 p.m., during which time the student must be home studying is unreasonable. On the other hand, a rule requiring a student to take math problems home, work them and return them completed to school the next day is a reasonable rule. Too much direction from the school regarding the time and place that the homework is to be performed is apparently the legal determinant. Required homework may be reasonable even though a parent contends that the student time is taken from home chores. Balding v. State (Tex.App.1887).

## § 2.9 SEX EDUCATION

During the last two decades boards of education have increasingly introduced sex education courses into the public school curriculum. While in most cases the implementation has gone smoothly, in some instances parents have challenged the efforts as encroachments on religious liberty and privacy. In each instance the courts have rejected the parental claims maintaining generally that such requirements are within the police power of the state.

The rationale for providing sex education is based on the state's interest in the health and welfare of its children. This has been sufficient reason for courts to hold in favor of boards of education establishing such courses. Aubrey v. School District of Philadelphia (Pa. Cmwlth.1981).

Mandatory sex education courses have been upheld where students and parents maintained that required sex education courses violated their religious beliefs. A federal district court held in a Maryland case that the interest of the state in "healthy, well-rounded growth of young people" is properly enforced through required sex education courses regardless of the parents' objections based on religious scruples. Cornwell v. State Board of Education (D.Md.1969). The prevailing view appears to be that sex education can be constitutionally defended as a required course of study.

A minority view of some courts is that the compulsory nature of sex education courses may, possibly, make them questionable as an invasion of privacy or an encroachment on the free exercise of religion. The Supreme Court of Hawaii upheld a sex education program promulgated by the state education agency, but in so doing appeared to base its approval on the fact that the program was not compulsory. Medeiros v. Kiyosaki (Hawaii 1970). No court has ruled, though, that sex education courses are unconstitutional and boards of education appear to be within their rightful authority when they require sex education, and there is little doubt that boards are acting constitutionally when the sex education courses are noncompulsory or have an "excusal" arrangement whereby parents may request that their children not be involved. A state board of education regulation requiring that local school districts develop and implement a family-life education course which included teaching about human sexuality did not violate a student's rights of freedom of religion where the regulation provided for the student to be excused from specific portions of the course which the student or parents found objectionable. Smith v. Ricci (N.J.1982).

# CHAPTER 3

# DUE PROCESS RIGHTS OF STUDENTS

## § 3.1 INTRODUCTION

To deny attendance at public school has always been a method of controlling disruptive student conduct. Although the practice has fallen in disrepute among some educators in recent years, to remove students from public schools remains a disciplinary alternative. Bearing on the issue of exclusion is whether education is of such importance to the individual as to be considered a constitutional interest under the Due Process Clause of the Fourteenth Amendment.

Until relatively recently, decisions to suspend or expel pupils were made on the convenient assumption that to attend public schools was a privilege which could be taken away at the discretion of the school authorities. Students who offended, or were thought to have offended, school rules could be summarily dismissed from school with no redress or opportunity to present their side of the story. This is not the prevailing view today.

The courts have generally held that children have a constitutional interest in attending public schools and cannot be deprived of that interest without due process of law. A state can only deny the benefit of a public school education with due process of law. Once the state extends the benefit of education to all persons it acquires the substantive constitutional status of liberty and property and is treated as having the accompanying constitutional due process protections. Education can be denied, but it can only be taken away after the requirements of procedural due process of law have been fully extended to the child who may suffer a deprivation of education. Thus, the state can take away education, as it can life, liberty or property, but it can only do so with strict observance of procedural due process.

## § 3.2  DUE PROCESS

There are two types of due process. One is called *substantive due process*. To satisfy this constitutional requirement, the state must have a valid objective and the means used must be reasonably calculated to achieve the objective. Early interpretations by the United States Supreme Court recognized only the procedural aspects of due process of law. It was not until 1923 that the Supreme Court defined due process of law as inclusive of "substantive" protections, Atkins v. Children's Hospital (S.Ct.1923). Substantive due process has been defined as: "The phrase 'due process of law,' when applied to substantive rights, means that the state is without power to deprive a person of life, liberty or property by an act having no reasonable relation to any proper governmental purpose, or which is so far beyond the necessity of the case as to be an arbitrary exercise of governmental power." Substantive due process may be implicated by the rules or regulations written by educators to regulate or control student behavior, such as the student handbook with rights and responsibilities.

A second aspect of due process is *procedural due process*. If a person is to be deprived of life, liberty, or property, a prescribed constitutional procedure must be followed. The Supreme Court of the United States has said that in order to give an individual procedural due process as required by the federal constitution, three basic factors must be present. The person must have proper notice, must be given an opportunity to be heard, and must be given a hearing that is conducted fairly.

## § 3.21 Substantive Due Process

In 1923 the U.S. Supreme Court created a nexus between acquisition of knowledge and an individual's liberty interest under the Due Process Clause of the Fourteenth Amendment. The due process clause says that "No state ... shall deprive any person of life, liberty or property without due process of law." According to the Court, the word liberty has a substantive aspect which invests each person with a protected interest in acquisition and conveyance of knowledge. Meyer v. Nebraska (S.Ct.1923). From 1923 until 1961 there was no further development of education as a substantive due process interest. Generally, during that period, the *Meyer* precedent was construed very narrowly, having little implication for education rights, generally.

An important case, however, emerged in 1961 which indicated that education was a substantive interest of such magnitude as to invoke procedural due process if it is to be denied. In Dixon v. Alabama State Board of Education (5th Cir.1961), a federal court held that attendance at a college was so essential that it could not be taken away without a hearing and attendant due process procedures. Without specifically saying so, this court implied that education was of such importance that it may be implied within the substance of the terms liberty or property under the Due Process Clause.

Then in Tinker v. Des Moines Independent Community School District (S.Ct.1969), the Supreme Court explicitly recognized the substantive nature of due process
rights of students. In spite of the impact of *Dixon* and
*Tinker*, the relationship between education and due process was not clearly defined until 1975 in Goss v. Lopez
(S.Ct.1975), at which time the Supreme Court pointed
out that denial of education for even a short period of
time could not be construed as inconsequential. In explaining that the individual's interest in education fell
within the substantive scope of "liberty and property,"
the Court said: "[n]either the property interest in education benefits temporarily denied nor the liberty interest in reputation, which is also implicated, is so insubstantial that suspensions may constitutionally be imposed by any procedure one school chooses, no matter
how arbitrary."

§ 3.21a  Property

Therefore, education has been determined to have a
substantive aspect within the context of property. Property encompasses those individual interests which are
created by state statutes and rules that entitle all citizens to a certain benefit. When a state creates a public
system of education to which all children are entitled to
benefit, each child is vested with a "property" interest.

The Supreme Court has explained the property interest in this way: "Property interests ... are not created
by the constitution. Rather they are created and their
dimensions are defined by existing rules or understandings that stem from an independent source such as state
law—rules or understandings that secure certain benefits
and that support claims of entitlement to those benefits." Board of Regents v. Roth (S.Ct.1972).

In this regard, the federal constitution does not create education as a fundamental right, but rather education becomes a "property" interest when state law establishes a public education system to which all children have a right to attend. Where the right of attendance in public school is extended to all children throughout a state, the state then cannot selectively deny education without procedural due process. Thus, when the state creates a public education system, education is effectively established as a property right or interest for all pupils.

### § 3.21b   Liberty

As observed above, due process also forbids arbitrary deprivation of liberty, or denial of those interests which are implied by that term. A person's liberty includes his or her "good name, reputation, honor, or integrity." The standard definitions of the substantive breadth of liberty was given in *Meyer v. Nebraska*, where the question arose as to whether a teacher in a private school had a liberty interest in teaching the German language, even though teaching German had been prohibited by state statute. The U.S. Supreme Court, in holding for the teacher, asserted the expansive nature of liberty, said: "While ... [the] Court has not attempted to define with exactness the liberty thus guaranteed, the term has received much consideration and some of the included things have been definitely stated. Without doubt, it denotes not merely freedom from bodily restraint but also right of the individual to contract, to engage in any of the common occupations of life, to acquire useful knowledge, to marry, establish a home and bring up children, to worship God according to the dictates of his own conscience, and generally to enjoy those privileges long recognized at common law as essential to the orderly pursuit of happiness by free men." Meyer v. Nebraska (S.Ct.1923). For government to take a person's liberty away requires due process of law. In *Goss v. Lopez*, where it was found that procedural due process had not been afforded, the recording of the suspensions in student permanent files effectively attached a stigma infringing on the students' liberty interests, the Supreme Court said: "If sustained and recorded, those charges could seriously damage the students' standing with their fellow pupils and their teachers as well as interfere with later opportunities for higher education and employment."

## § 3.22  What Process is Due?

When it is determined that due process applies, and that a substantive interest is in jeopardy, the question next arises as to what process is due. Morrissey v. Brewer (S.Ct.1972). The answer is that "The nature of the hearing should vary depending upon the circumstances of the particular case." Dixon v. Alabama State Board of Education (5th Cir.1961). The hearing should be fair and impartial in keeping with the nature and gravity of the charges. "The nub of the matter is that the student [be] given an opportunity to present his side of the case, including anything by way of denial or mitigation." McClain v. Lafayette County Board of Education (5th Cir.1982). "Basic fairness and integrity of the fact-finding process are the guiding stars." Boykins v. Fairfield Board of Education (5th Cir.1974). The principle of fairness, while flexible, requires that the state adhere to the following touchstones of procedural due process. First, notice should be given containing specific charges and grounds, which if proven would justify the prescribed penalty. Second, a hearing should be conducted which gives the school administration the opportunity to hear both sides of the story in considerable detail. The hearing should observe the rudiments of the adversarial process though full dress judicial hearing is not required. Third, the student should be given the opportunity to present his or her version of the facts. Fourth, the hearing's result and findings should be open for the student's inspection. Dixon v. Alabama State Board of Education (5th Cir.1961).

## § 3.23 The Penalty Imposed

The punishment meted out to the student must not be excessive and must be in keeping with the nature of the offense. A prescribed mandatory punishment referring to particular offenses are not unconstitutional simply because they are mandatory. Clinton Municipal Separate School Dist. v. Byrd (Miss.1985).

Expulsion may be an appropriate penalty for certain offenses, but in all such cases strict adherence to standards of procedural due process must be observed. Where a tenth grade student was expelled for leaving school grounds, consuming alcohol, and then returning to school intoxicated, and school regulations provided for suspension or expulsion for "good cause," defined to include use or possession of alcoholic beverages or drugs, the U.S. Supreme Court held that the school board clearly had the authority to suspend and expel the student and that it was beyond the purview of federal courts to substitute their judgment for that of the school board. Board of Education v. McCluskey (S.Ct.1982). See also Salazar v. Luty (S.D.Tex.1991). Expulsion does not violate the student's right of due process. Craig v. Selma

City School Board (S.D.1992). Thus, expulsion is a viable disciplinary option, but can only be instituted after full and careful adherence to requirements of procedural due process.

Another penalty that may be imposed, if permitted by state statute or regulation, is corporal punishment. The United States Supreme Court in Ingraham v. Wright (S.Ct.1977), ruled corporal punishment did not constitute cruel and unusual punishment under the Eighth Amendment. Because "there can be no deprivation of substantive rights as long as disciplinary corporal punishment is within the limits of common law privilege," procedural due process is not required. The extent and severity of corporal punishment necessary to invoke substantive due process is, however, not entirely clear.

The Supreme Court in *Ingraham* recognized that a child's substantive liberty interests against corporal punishment are not insubstantial and that the school's disciplinary process may not be totally accurate and unerring, thus there is risk of unjustified intrusion on the child's liberty interest. If the punishment is severe, the child has a "strong" interest in procedural safeguards to "minimize the risk of wrongful punishment." *Ingraham v. Wright*, supra. The following statement in *Ingraham* has been interpreted as holding "that, at some point, excessive corporal punishment violates the pupil's substantive due process rights." Garcia by Garcia v. Miera (10th Cir.1987). According to the *Garcia* court, "the concept of the substantive due process right is implicit in *Ingraham* " where excessive punishment is concerned. Accordingly, corporal punishment of students may violate due process if it amounts "to a brutal and inhumane abuse of official power...." See Milonas v. Williams (10th Cir.1982).

Other courts, however, have not read into *Ingraham* the extent of substantive due process interest as ascribed by *Garcia*. In Cunningham v. Beavers (5th Cir.1988), the court ruled that severe spankings, leaving black and blue marks, on two little girls for the offense of snickering, did not implicate substantive due process so as to require procedural due process. Extension of the *Ingraham* due process was seen to be implicitly limiting by the U.S. Court of Appeals, 5th Circuit, where it held that even though "the infliction of punishment may transgress constitutionally protected liberty interest," that "if the state affords the student adequate post punishment remedies (such as tort and criminal action alternatives such as assault and battery) to deter unjustified or excessive punishment" then the student receives all the process that is required. Woodard v. Los Fresnos Ind. School Dist. (5th Cir.1984).

## § 3.24  Immediate Temporary Suspension

The Supreme Court in *Goss v. Lopez* has explained that there "need be no delay between the time [when] 'notice' is given and the time of the hearing." The court found in *Goss* that "[s]uspension is considered not only to be a necessary tool to maintain order but a valuable educational device," therefore immediate suspension is sometimes appropriate to protect other students and to preserve the decorum of the school. "Students whose presence imposes a continuing danger to persons or property or [constitute] an ongoing threat of disrupting [the] academic process may be immediately removed from school." *Goss v. Lopez*, supra. In such circumstances oral notice, a hearing and immediate suspension pending more formal proceedings later comports with the requirements of due process. Tate v. Board of Education (8th Cir.1972); Vail v. Board of Education (D.N.H.1973).

The U.S. Court of Appeals for the Seventh Circuit has upheld an initial suspension prior to which the school principal discussed the incident with the student, informed him of the accusations, and provided him with the opportunity to present his version of the facts. Lamb v. Panhandle Comm. Unit School Dist. No. 2 (7th Cir.1987). Whenever there is an ongoing threat of disruption to the academic process no formal notice is required. Craig v. Selma City School Bd. (S.D.Ala.1992).

## § 3.3  PROCEDURAL DUE PROCESS

As noted above, to take away a substantive liberty or property interest requires procedural due process. Courts are wary of too much discretion residing in the hands of school officials, and have acted to limit this power by establishing standards to ensure due regard for fundamental fairness. Intervention by the courts in matters of justice and fairness is justified on the basis of the ancient concept of "natural justice" and the more modern "due process of law" under the United States Constitution. Judicial developments in this area have had an important impact on public education in the United States and will continue to do so.

## § 3.4  NATURAL JUSTICE AND DUE PROCESS

Due process finds its roots in the words of Clause 39 of *Magna Charta* of England, 1215, which expressed that:

"No freeman shall be seized, or imprisoned or dispossessed, or outlawed, or in any way destroyed; nor will we condemn him, nor will we commit him to prison, excepting by the legal judgment of his peers, or by the law of the land." This provision according to Blackstone "protected every individual of the nation in the free enjoyment of his life, his liberty and his property, unless declared to be forfeited by the judgment of his peers or the law of the land." W. Blackstone, *The Great Charter and Charter of the Forest* (1759). Clause 38 added to the protection by requiring credible witnesses to be produced against the accused before he could be convicted. See Ray Stringham, *Magna Charta Foundation of Freedom* 63–65 (1966). Effectively, these provisions protected a citizen against arbitrary action by the King or his agents and guaranteed a minimal level of procedural due process.

Due process itself emerges from the concept of natural justice. Natural justice presupposes certain rules of judicial procedure established through legal precedent which compel government and its agents to treat individuals with minimal standards of fairness. In the United States the term due process does precisely the same. Essentially the concepts of natural justice and their progeny, due process, encompass two elements:

    (a) The rule against bias: No man shall be a judge in his own cause, or *nemo judex in causa sua*, and

    (b) The right to a hearing: No man shall be condemned unheard, or *audi alteram partem*.

The rule against bias is the first and most fundamental principle. Accordingly, it is of prime importance that justice should not only be done but should manifestly and undoubtedly be seen to be done.

*Audi alteram partem* requires that the accused know the case against him and have an opportunity to state his own case. Each party must have the chance to present his version of the facts and to make submissions relevant to his case. Fairness is the hallmark of this process and though the extent of process required is sometimes in question, the basic principle that "no one should be condemned unheard" prevails.

The Fifth and Fourteenth Amendments of the United States Constitution provide that neither the federal government nor a state shall "deprive any person of life, liberty or property, without due process of law." Originally, these provisions were interpreted to apply to judicial proceedings only, and not to quasi-judicial or administrative proceedings conducted by governmental ministers or by educational agencies. In early precedents, educators in the United States, by virtue of their standing *in loco parentis*, were not required to adhere to any particular standards of fair play when sitting in judgment over actions of students. Only since the landmark case of *Dixon v. Alabama*, supra, has this changed. *Dixon* manifestly established that procedural due process applied to schools and other governmental agencies and deviations from the minimal fairness required therein may void any disciplinary action taken.

## § 3.5  IMPARTIALITY: NEMO JUDEX IN CAUSA SUA

Impartiality is the essence of fair judicial treatment. Justinian stated the rule in his *Institutes* and numerous old English cases establish the precedent. *Institutes of Justinian*, Book 4, Title 5, Law 1 (R. W. Lee translation 1956). In 1614, in *Day v. Salvadge*, it was held that protection against bias was so fundamental that even the English Parliament could not enact a law contrary to the principle. The court said that "even an Act of Parliament made against natural equity, as to make a man judge in his own cause, is void in itself."

A judge must come to the case with an open mind without previous knowledge of the facts or preconceived notions of the outcome. No connection can exist between the judge and one of the parties involved so as to create a conflict of judicial interest.

Bias in the school setting may not always be so readily recognizable. Seldom do students or teachers sit in judgment over their own cases. If they did, obvious bias would be present. Bias may be charged, though, where an administrator or officer sits in review of challenged policies which he formulated, or in review of executive action which he carried out. Further, it may be that school officers may be forced to sit as tribunals at different levels, possibly reviewing their own decisions on appeal.

A fair trial by an impartial tribunal is a basic tenet of due process, In re Murchison (S.Ct.1955), just as it is with natural justice, and this applies to administrative agencies as well as to the court. Gibson v. Berryhill (S.Ct.1973). The United States Supreme Court rejected a teacher union claim that bias of the school board invalidated board action to dismiss teachers. As a party to the dispute, the school board was alleged to have a prejudicial interest in the proceedings. Hortonville Joint School District No. 1 v. Hortonville Education Association (S.Ct.1976).

In this case, the school teachers as a result of impasse over contract negotiations with the school board decided, illegally, to go out on strike. The school board instituted dismissal actions against the teachers and conducted a hearing prior to their dismissal. On appeal before the Supreme Court, the attorney for the teachers claimed *inter alia* that the board was not sufficiently impartial and free from bias to exercise judgment over the striking teachers. Plaintiff teachers argued that individual board members had a personal or official stake in the decision. Because of the strike, and the difficult negotiations, the teachers alleged that board members harbored personal bitterness toward the teachers. No actual proof of this was presented other than the fact that the board had dismissed the teachers in the first place.

The Supreme Court in holding against the teachers said that mere familiarity with the facts of the case by an agency in performance of its statutory responsibility does not disqualify the decision maker. "Nor is the decision maker disqualified simply because he has taken a position, even in public, on a policy issue related to the dispute, in the absence of a showing that he is not 'capable of judging a particular controversy fairly on the basis of its own circumstances.'" To merely show that a public board is "involved" in events preceding a decision is "not enough to overcome the presumption of honesty and integrity in policymakers with decisionmaking power."

In *Hortonville*, the board members were clearly parties to the dispute and were quite obviously sitting in judgment in a dispute in which they had an official interest. Yet, even in light of this, the Supreme Court found that bias must be shown to exist, in fact, and could not be established merely by virtue of the board members being judges in their own cause. A school board having executive, quasi-legislative and quasi-judicial functions must, according to the United States Supreme Court, frequently sit in judgment over certain of its own decisions, but this, in and of itself, did not create a presumption of bias. Simply to show that an administrative agency has a dual role, without more, does not constitute a due process violation.

## § 3.6  FAIRNESS: AUDI ALTERAM PARTEM

The right to be heard as a basic principle of fairness has long been accepted as a tenet of Anglo–American law. Although the right to be heard is a spontaneously acceptable idea, it is not settled as to what it entails or where it applies.  Demara Turf Club v. Phang (Sup.Ct. of British Guiana 1963).  Does it require a notice for a hearing, if so what should the notice include?  Is there a right to an oral hearing?  Can the accused confront witnesses and cross-examine?  Can the accused demand legal counsel? Can the hearing be conducted by one body and the decision be rendered by another?  Is there a right to remain silent?  All of these questions define the parameters of fairness in provision of due process.  The discussion below elucidates some of the considerations of fairness.

## § 3.7  ELEMENTS OF PROCEDURAL DUE PROCESS

A hearing is useless if the defendant does not know the charges against him and does not have time to prepare a defense.  Where a party is completely unaware of the proceedings, fairness cannot be achieved.  Consequently, it is rudimentary that notice is required.

## § 3.71  Notice

Fundamental fairness requires that notice give the specific ground or grounds on which the accused is being charged and the nature of the evidence against him. Due v. Florida Agricultural and Mechanical University (N.D.Fla.1963). According to *Dixon*, supra, the landmark case, no rigid procedural guidelines are required, but notice should contain a statement of specific charges and grounds which if proven could lead to the appropriate disciplinary action.

A notice of charges so vague "that men of common intelligence must necessarily guess at its meaning and differ as to its application" violates the first principle of due process. Dickson v. Sitterson (M.D.N.C.1968). Vagueness is primarily objectionable because it tends toward arbitrary and discriminatory enforcement and fails to provide explicit standards for those who apply them. Grayned v. City of Rockford (S.Ct.1972). Justice Black observed in Epperson v. Arkansas (S.Ct.1968), that: "It is an established rule that a statute which leaves an ordinary man so doubtful about its meaning that he cannot know when he has violated it denies him the first essential of due process...." Quite obviously then, if a vague charge is brought against a student or the charge is based on a vague rule or statute, elementary fairness cannot be served.

### § 3.71a  Miranda Warning

A student is not entitled to a *Miranda* warning prior to being questioned by school authorities. Boynton v. Casey (D.Me.1982); see Baxter v. Palmigiano (S.Ct.1976).

## § 3.72   Opportunity to be Heard

The courts have generally held that an accused student must have the opportunity to present evidence in his own behalf. S. (Charles) v. Board of Education (Cal.App. 1971). The courts have more or less implicitly assumed that such hearings will be oral in nature. The Superior Court of New Jersey has held that witnesses adverse to the accused student must be present and be compelled to testify. Tibbs v. Board of Education (N.J.Super.1971). Of course, this assumes that school boards have subpoena power which is true in New Jersey and a few other states, but is not uniformly the case in all states. If witnesses may be compelled to appear, then almost certainly one could conclude that the accused himself has a right to appear and testify. In 1914 the United States Supreme Court said that: "[T]he fundamental requisite of due process of law is the opportunity to be heard." Grannis v. Ordean (S.Ct.1914). Here, the court was referring to actual physical appearance and oral testimony. In its most important due process case involving students, the Supreme Court found that an oral hearing was possibly the only way which school officials in some situations could dismiss a student while allowing for fundamental fairness. Goss v. Lopez (S.Ct.1975). To say that the student could only convey his side of the story in writing would quite obviously fly in the face of procedural due process.

While due process is a flexible doctrine, it cannot be construed to be so lax as to deny a student an oral hearing, particularly where the facts are in dispute or where they may be subject to more than one interpretation.

## § 3.73 Access to Evidence

Due process requires that every individual have an opportunity to know the evidence against him or her. The general rule requiring evidence be released to the accused is directly in keeping with the due process standard of *Dixon*. *Dixon v. Alabama State Board of Education*, supra. See also *Goss v. Lopez*, supra; Esteban v. Central Missouri State College (8th Cir.1969); Soglin v. Kauffman (7th Cir.1969); and Sullivan v. Houston Independent School District (5th Cir.1973). The Court in *Dixon* put it succinctly: "The student should be given the names of the witnesses against him and an oral or written report on the facts to which each witness testifies." In *Mills*, a federal court in Washington, D.C., required the school board to inform parents of their right to examine the child's school records before a hearing, including tests, reports, medical, psychological and educational information. Mills v. Board of Education of District of Columbia (D.D.C.1972).

## § 3.74 Cross–Examination

Cross-examination of witnesses is fundamental to the criminal trial, but, in school administrative hearings, its status is less definitive. In *Esteban v. Central Missouri State College*, supra, the United States Eighth Circuit Court of Appeals set out procedural safeguards for student disciplinary actions but it excluded cross-examination as a general requirement. *Mills*, supra, contrarily, specifically required that schools provide the parent or guardian the opportunity to confront and cross-examine witnesses.

The United States Supreme Court in *Goss* did not go so far as to require the confrontation and cross-examination of witnesses for short-term suspensions. The Court said "[w]e stop short of construing the Due Process Clause to require ... that hearings ... [or] suspensions must afford the student the opportunity ... to confront and cross-examine witnesses...." The issue in *Goss* was short-term suspensions but the court left open that for more serious offenses a more formal procedure might be required. It has always been recognized that the more important the rights at stake, the more formal the procedural safeguards. S. (Charles) v. Board of Education (Cal.App.1971).

Therefore, for a more serious offense, such as expulsion, fundamental fairness may require cross-examination. Too, the right of cross-examination may be required for an administrative hearing if the testimony of one witness is the critical factor in determining the outcome of the hearing.

A problem with requiring witnesses to be present is that all school boards do not have subpoena power. With no subpoena power, the student and school officials may ask the witnesses to attend but cannot compel them to do so.

The U.S. Court of Appeals for the Sixth Circuit held in 1988 that protecting student witnesses in testifying against fellow students was of paramount importance if order and discipline are to be maintained in the school. The court said a student did not have a due process right to learn the identity of student accusers. The court further discussed in some detail the rationale for differing standards of cross-examination between the criminal courts and public schools. The court stated: "The value of cross-examining student witnesses in school disciplinary cases, however, is somewhat muted by the fact that the veracity of a student account of misconduct by another student is initially assessed by ... the school principal—who has, or has available to him, a particularized knowledge of the student's trustworthiness. The school administrator generally knows firsthand (or has access to school records which disclose) the accusing student's disciplinary history, which can serve as a valuable gauge in evaluating the believability of the student's account. Additionally, the school administrator often knows, or can readily discover, whether the student witness and the accused have had an amicable relationship in the past. Consequently, the process of cross-examining the student witness may often be merely duplicative of the evaluation process undertaken by the investigating school administrator. The value of cross-examining student witnesses in pre-expulsion proceedings must be set against the burden that such practice would place upon school administration. Today's public schools face severe challenges in maintaining the order and discipline necessary for the impartation of knowledge." Newsome v. Batavia Local School District (6th Cir.1988); Davis v. Alaska (S.Ct.1974).

## § 3.75  Hearsay

The courts have generally held that hearsay evidence is admissible in a formal school disciplinary hearing. In the leading case on the subject, a school principal read before the school board statements made by teachers regarding a student's conduct. Boykins v. Fairfield Board of Education (5th Cir.1974). The board in using this evidence ultimately suspended eight students for a week and expelled eight for their part in a school boycott. The students maintained that the information was hearsay and could not be used as a basis for dismissal. The court disagreed saying: "There is a seductive quality to the argument—advanced here to justify the importation of technical rules of evidence into administrative hearings conducted by laymen—that, since a free public education is a thing of great value, comparable to that of welfare sustenance or the curtailed liberty of a parolee, the safeguards applicable to these should apply to it.... In this view we stand but a step away from the application of the *strictissimi juris* due process requirements of criminal trials to high school disciplinary processes. And if to high school, why not to elementary school? It will not do.... Basic fairness and integrity of the factfinding process are the guiding stars. Important as they are, the rights at stake in a school disciplinary hearing may be fairly determined upon the 'hearsay' evidence of school administrators charged with the duty of investigating the incidents. We decline to place upon a board of laymen the duty of observing and applying the common-law rules of evidence." *Boykins*, supra.

Similarly, hearsay has been allowed in hearings where students have committed serious offenses, Tasby v. Estes (5th Cir.1981), and has been allowed by implication in a case involving expulsion. Linwood v. Board of Education (7th Cir.1972); and Whiteside v. Kay (W.D.La.1978).

*Goss* did not address the hearsay question directly, the only guidance it provided was the general admonishment that "[l]onger suspensions or expulsions for the remainder of the school term, or permanently, may require more formal procedures." Too, the Supreme Court emphasized in Board of Curators of University of Missouri v. Horowitz (S.Ct.1978), that due process should provide a "meaningful hedge against erroneous action." This language leaves substantial discretion to the school board in determining the extent of formality to be used in a hearing.

The Supreme Court's intent in *Goss* and *Horowitz* has been interpreted by a Wisconsin court as allowing hearsay statements from teachers or staff members in an expulsion hearing before the school board. Racine Unified School District v. Thompson (Wis.App.1982). This appears to represent the prevailing view of the courts.

## § 3.76  Legal Counsel

Presence of legal counsel is not a fundamental element of fairness but it may well be invoked by the courts if the issues are legally complex or the interests of the accused are of great magnitude. Legal counsel was not required by the United States Supreme Court in *Goss* for suspensions of less than ten days, but as with cross-examination, the Court implied that where more severe penalties could be invoked against a student, counsel may be required. *Goss v. Lopez*, supra.

Counsel, then, may probably be denied by tribunals adjudicating relatively minor student disciplinary cases, but, where major detriment may result for the accused, counsel may be elevated to a more important aspect of fairness. On balance, however, representation by legal counsel cannot be said to be, at this time, a fundamental or basic element of due process in the school setting.

## § 3.77  Appropriate Tribunal

Whether the tribunal or hearing committee is an appropriate one depends on at least three issues, (a) the make-up of membership, (b) the *ultra vires* doctrine, and

(c) due process. Courts are not concerned with whether a tribunal has representation of administrators, teachers or students; the only legal concern is that no conflict of interest or bias exists.

An administrative agency cannot delegate away its quasi-judicial or discretionary functions provided it statutorily by a state legislature. Games v. County Board of School Trustees (Ill.1958); see also State ex rel. School District No. 29 v. Cooney (Mont.1936). Likewise, a local school board cannot delegate its discretionary powers to a subordinate. This does not mean that an administrative committee cannot delegate to a subcommittee the responsibility to collect information, facts, and evidence to be presented to the full official committee for consideration and judgment.

It would be *ultra vires*, though, for the statutorily constituted school board to delegate to a subordinate committee or individual, the power to actually hand down a decision in a matter which statute required it, alone, to exercise. Similarly, it would contravene due process for a subcommittee to render a decision from a hearing it conducted and then have the superior or full committee to reverse the lower decision in the absence of full and complete hearing documentation. Due process requires, unequivocally, that the decision cannot be made by anyone other than the appropriate tribunal.

In general then it may be said that he who hears the case must also decide it. It is a breach of due process for a member of a judicial tribunal to participate in a decision if he has not heard the evidence presented in the case. Rulings by administrative bodies have been frequently quashed because decisions were given affecting individual rights where oral presentations were made before hearing officers other than those who actually rendered the decision. Bias and ignorance alike preclude fair judgment upon the merits of a case.

## § 3.78 Self–Incrimination

In the United States Constitution, the Fifth Amendment protects the individual against self-incrimination in a criminal proceeding. The Fifth Amendment states in part: " ... nor shall [*any person*] be compelled in any criminal case to be a witness against himself...."

There is very little case law addressing whether a student in elementary, secondary or post-secondary may invoke the self-incrimination provision of the Fifth Amendment. But where the courts have ruled they have generally held that this provision of the Fifth Amendment does not apply in educational disciplinary hearings. In Boynton v. Casey (D.Me.1982), the court said that the student did not have a right to prior advice or right to remain silent before questioning by school authorities. The court in *Boynton* said that since this was for determination of whether an expulsion should take place and not "custodial interrogation" the Miranda warning also was not required.

In Picozzi v. Sandalow (E.D.Mich.1986), the court ruled the law school dean did not deprive a student of his Fifth Amendment privilege against self-incrimination by offering the student a choice of either a polygraph test or a hearing. The court stated "even though a person may assert the privilege against self incrimination during a civil proceeding, the privilege protects a person from only criminal exposure." See Kastigar v. United States (S.Ct. 1972); Baxter v. Palmigiano (S.Ct.1976).

A complicating factor is added where the charge against the student may also be of such a nature as to violate a criminal statute. Frequently, the student wants to assert the privilege of self incrimination and postpone the disciplinary hearing until the court determines guilt or innocence in the criminal proceedings, since the testimony may be used against the student in the ensuing criminal trial. In Gabrilowitz v. Newman (1st Cir.1978), the court said, "[T]he hearing procedures do not place appellee between the rock and the whirlpool. He can, if he wishes, stay out of the stream and watch the proceedings from dry land. But, if he does so, he forfeits any opportunity to control the direction of the current. Appellee must decide whether or not to testify at the hearing with the knowledge that, if he does, his statements may be used against him in the criminal case.... Although the choice facing him is difficult, that does not make it unconstitutional."

Other courts have held that there is no constitutional necessity to postpone a disciplinary hearing until after criminal proceedings. These courts rely on the U.S. Supreme Court decision of Garrity v. New Jersey (S.Ct. 1967). In *Garrity*, the court said the state may not fire police officers for invoking their privilege against self-incrimination during a civil or administrative hearing regarding their conduct, nor may the state use the administrative hearing evidence in a later criminal trial. A school or university may proceed with a disciplinary hearing and not violate a students' privilege of self incrimination.

At this time, the general rule of law appears to preclude student access to the Fifth Amendment privilege against self-incrimination in a school hearing. Due process does not require it and the school administrator is unaffected by its strictures.

## § 3.79 Double Jeopardy

Under English common law a second trial and a second punishment for the same offense was prohibited whether the accused was acquitted or convicted. Ex parte Lange (S.Ct.1874). This is the general rule followed by American courts today. Kepner v. United States (S.Ct.1904); United States v. Oppenheimer (S.Ct.1916). The U.S. Supreme Court has, though, held that where the same act is an offense against both state and federal statutes, its separate prosecution and punishment by both governments is not double jeopardy.

The double jeopardy prohibition does not prevent public schools from holding a hearing for the same offense for which the criminal courts have already prosecuted a student. The courts view public school disciplinary matters as issues separate and apart from criminal prosecutions and punishments. A federal court in Texas has explained that "state laws defining criminal conduct and authorizing its punishment are intended to indicate public justice" while a public school board or a public university rule mandating suspension or expulsion is intended to protect "the education goals of the institution from such adverse influence as the offender may wield if he is allowed to remain a student. Thus the two sanctions imposed by the state upon plaintiffs have sufficiently different underlying purposes to permit characterization of the first as 'criminal' or 'punitive' and the second as 'civil,' 'remedial' or 'administrative.'" Paine v. Board of Regents of University of Texas System (W.D.Tex.1992).

See also Clements v. Board of Trustees of Sheridan County School Dist. No. 2 (Wyo.1978).

The double jeopardy prohibition was held not to apply in an Arkansas case where a student killed a man off school grounds and then claimed double jeopardy when expelled from school for the offense. Smith v. Little Rock School Dist. (E.D.Ark.1984). Similarly, suspension from school was deemed to be proper where a student in New York assaulted and attempted to stab a person during school vacation period. The court found that off-school grounds offenses were within the cognizance of school authorities and that prosecution in criminal courts did not foreclose school action to suspend for the same charges during the period when the criminal charges were pending. Pollnow v. Glennon (S.D.N.Y.1984).

## § 3.8 IN–SCHOOL SUSPENSION

Is procedural due process required for in-school suspension? Temporary isolation used in school "timeout" has been held to be a *de minimus* punishment not interfering with property or liberty interests. Dickens by Dickens v. Johnson County Board of Education (E.D.Tenn.1987).

## § 3.9 IMPACT OF PROCEDURAL DUE PROCESS

With the evolution of procedural due process as a potent force in the quasi-judicial administrative processes, school boards and school officials are required to formulate guidelines which will protect students. Due process balances the child's interest against corresponding and sometimes contrary school interests. At very least, due process requires school officials to provide the child with a hearing which is impartial and free of bias, and, secondly, to guarantee the student that fairness will prevail. Minimal due process requires that the administrator give the student adequate notice of what is proposed, allow the student to make representations on his own behalf, and/or appear at a hearing or inquiry, and to effectively prepare his case and answer allegations presented.

Courts have maintained that "The touchstones in this area are fairness and reasonableness." Due v. Florida Agricultural and Mechanical University (N.D.Fla.1963); see also Jones v. State Board of Education (N.D.Tenn. 1968). The precise boundaries of fairness must be kept reasonably flexible to ensure freedom for school districts to operate. The United States Supreme Court has reminded us that: "Due process is an elusive concept, its exact boundaries are undefinable, and its content varies according to specific factual contexts.... Whether the Constitution requires that a particular right obtain in a specific proceeding depends upon a complexity of factors. The nature of the alleged right involved, the nature of the proceeding, and the possible burden on that proceeding, are all considerations which must be taken into account." Hannah v. Larche (S.Ct.1960). But, flexibility cannot be an excuse for denial of proper procedure. Minimal fairness in the words of *Dixon* requires that (a) notice should be given containing a statement of the specific charges and grounds, (b) a hearing should be conducted affording the administrator or board with opportunity to hear both sides in considerable detail, (c) the student should be given the names of the witnesses against him, and an oral or written report on the facts, (d) the student should be given the opportunity to present his own defense against the charges and to produce either oral testimony or written affidavits in his own behalf, and (e) if the hearing is not before the Board empowered to make the decision, the results and findings of the hearing should be presented in a report open to the student's inspection. *Dixon v. Alabama State Board of Education*, supra.

Beyond these rudiments of "fair play" various judicial precedents add specificity reducing the school administrator's boundaries of discretion. The following guidelines are suggestive of such boundaries.

## § 3.91 Guidelines: Due Process

### § 3.91a Bias

1. The judge must come to the hearing with an open mind without preconceived notions of the ultimate outcome.

2. No connection can exist between the parties involved and the administrator except through his *ex officio* position as an officer of the school. No decisionmaker should be disqualified simply because of a position he has taken on a matter of public policy.

3. Intercommittee membership, although not illegal, should be avoided where possible in order to prevent any impression of bias. Committee membership should not be permitted to even approach offending the "real likelihood" of bias standards.

### § 3.91b Fairness

1. Every student has a right to be heard when punishment for an offense is severe enough to deprive him of schooling, even for a few days.

2.   Notice should be given conveying the specific ground or grounds with which the student is being charged citing rules or regulations which have been broken.   Notice must not be vague or ambiguous.

3.   Notice should be delivered to the student, in writing, in sufficient time to ensure ample opportunity to prepare a defense to the allegations.

4.   It goes without saying that the burden of proof should bear on the school and not the student.

5.   The student should be given the opportunity to testify and present evidence and witnesses in his or her own behalf.

6.   The tribunal should make its decision only on the information presented at the hearing.

7.   With the possible exception of evidence which could be harmful to the child or the parent, all evidence should be made available to the accused child, parent, and legal counsel.   *In re Gault*, supra.

8.   To confront and cross-examine witnesses is apparently not basic to due process, however, cross-examination may be required for more serious offenses or to maintain fundamental fairness.

9.   To have legal counsel present is not looked upon by the courts as being essential to fairness.   The rule appears to be that the "right to have legal counsel present is a function of the complexity of the case" and the potential loss to the student.

10.   Due process requires that the administrator with the quasi-judicial responsibility for rendering a judgment must both hear the case and make the decision.   Delegation of decision-making authority is

*ultra vires*. An administrator or a board, nevertheless, may delegate the collection of evidence, to a subordinate so long as the final decision is made by the lawful authority based on the evidence presented.

11. Students appear to have no right to remain silent to avoid self-incrimination in a school hearing. This is true even where the student claims that evidence given may tend to incriminate him in a later criminal proceeding on the same charge.

12. Hearsay may be admissible in either suspension or expulsion hearings.

# CHAPTER 4

# FREEDOM OF SPEECH AND EXPRESSION

## § 4.1  INTRODUCTION

Courts assume that rules and regulations are valid unless there is a clear abuse of power and discretion on the part of the school. A rule or regulation may be challenged on several grounds, the most common are that it is (1) *ultra vires*, beyond the board's legal authority, and (2) vague or overly broad, or (3) violative of one of several constitutional prohibitions such as freedom of expression, religion, privacy, due process, or equal protection.

To raise the *vires* issue simply means that the student maintains that the regulation is beyond the legal power vested in the school board by state law. A rule of a residential public high school that required all students to wear khaki uniforms while at school and while visiting public places within five miles of school was held not to be *ultra vires* when the students are in the custody of the school, but the rule became *ultra vires* as school officials sought to apply it to children on holidays or weekends when in the custody of their parents. The question becomes how far does the school's authority extend before it encroaches on the parent's and student's personal prerogatives.

Two different common law principles may render school disciplinary actions invalid, (1) ambiguity or vagueness of rules, and (2) arbitrary or capricious application of rules. The two principles are akin to each other because ambiguous or vague rules may give such broad latitude that administration of the rules may be based on the personal whim or fancy of either the administrator or teacher. Vagueness and overbreadth, a lack of specificity, delegates excessive authority in application of rules. These common law principles which govern all governmental agencies have, in recent years, been incorporated into constitutional law, as the rights and freedoms of students have become more clearly defined. For example, vagueness of rule and arbitrary administration may well invoke questions of both substantive and procedural due process under the Fourteenth Amendment of the U.S. Constitution.

School rules and regulations will not stand if they deny individual rights or freedoms which are protected by federal or state constitutions. This does not mean that rights and freedoms are without limitation. It does mean, however, that school authorities must have a very good reason to deny a student his or her rights and freedoms. If a school rule is to prevail, there must be a rational relationship between the rule and the purpose for which it is designed. In some instances where a fundamental interest such as race is concerned, the courts have held that the school authorities must have a compelling reason to support rules promulgated to control or categorize students.

## § 4.2 BALANCING THE INTERESTS

At one time it was believed that to attend school was a privilege and that virtually any school rule or regulation constraining a student's conduct was valid. Today, the privilege doctrine is no longer valid and the courts recognize that students do not "shed their constitutional interests when they enter a schoolhouse door." Having constitutional rights does not mean that a student's conduct can go unregulated. All members of society are subject to reasonable restraints, without which a society cannot adequately function. An environment for learning requires that student conduct be regulated. It is obvious that a student cannot be permitted the personal freedom to come and go at will or to ignore reasonable rules such as to be quiet in a library. In order to balance the constitutional rights of pupils against the necessity for order, peace and quiet, the courts have promulgated the "balance of interests" test. The interests of the school are weighed against the student's loss of a particular freedom or right. This balancing test is the heart of the United States Supreme Court's decision in Tinker v. Des Moines Independent Community School District (S.Ct.1969). *Tinker* established that school rules and regulations should be based on a determination of the school's legitimate interests. If the purpose for a rule or regulation is unclear or nonexistent, then there should be no rule. Teachers and administrators must examine their policies to determine their legitimacy.

## § 4.3  FORECAST OF DISRUPTION

In *Tinker*, the Supreme Court explained the balance of interests in terms of potential for disruption of the school. If a student's exercise of free speech or expression justifies a "reasonable forecast of substantial disruption," then it can be curtailed.

In *Tinker*, certain students and their parents decided to publicize their objections to hostilities in Vietnam, and to indicate their support for a truce by wearing black armbands to school.  School principals in Des Moines became aware of the plan to wear armbands and two days before the protest passed a rule prohibiting students from wearing an armband to school.  Students who refused to remove their armbands would be suspended from school.  Students did wear armbands and were subsequently suspended.

After holding that armbands were a manifestation of free speech falling under the ambit of the First Amendment, the Court stated: "School officials do not possess absolute authority over their students.  Students are 'persons' under our Constitution.  They are possessed of fundamental rights which the State must respect, just as they themselves must respect their obligations to the State.  In our system, students may not be regarded as closed-circuit recipients of only that which the State chooses to communicate.  They may not be confined to the expression of those sentiments that are officially approved.  In the absence of a specific showing of constitutionally valid reasons to regulate their speech, students are entitled to freedom of expression of their views."

With this as the *constitutional* basis of students' rights, the Court then sought to determine if the wearing of a black cloth around the arm could in fact interrupt school activities or intrude on the lives of other students.  The Court, in holding for the students, found that the record demonstrated no facts which could have been reasonably construed by school officials as evidencing a "forecast of substantial disruption" or of constituting "material interference" with school activities.

The Supreme Court's words were carefully chosen. For a student activity to be proscribed, the school officials must be able to reasonably forecast disruption, and the disruption must be more than minimal, it must be substantial. Too, the disruption must be physical, and be deleterious to the intellectual environment of the school program.

Reasonableness of forecast must be for more than mere vague apprehension of disruption, or an "undifferentiated fear or apprehension." There must be evidence to support the expectation of substantial disruption.

## § 4.31   Limitations on Students' Rights

After reading *Tinker*, one may ask what controls, if any, can reasonably be placed on students' conduct? The U.S. Supreme Court in 1986 provided additional clarification of the *Tinker* standard. In Bethel School District No. 403 v. Fraser (S.Ct.1986), conflict had arisen after a student made a lewd speech of sexual innuendos at a student assembly and the school responded by suspending him. The Court drew a line between the "political message" of the arm bands in *Tinker* and the sexual content of the speech in *Bethel*. The school's sanctions in *Bethel* were unrelated to any political viewpoint and were not unconstitutional. The Court said that: "The schools, as instruments of the state, may determine that the essential lesson of civil, mature conduct cannot be conveyed in a school that tolerates lewd, indecent, or offensive speech and conduct...." With this case as a new guide, the strictures of *Tinker* were substantially clarified.

In 1988, the Supreme Court further enunciated the rights of student expression in Hazelwood Sch. Dist. v. Kuhlmeier (S.Ct.1988) (discussed later in Chapter 6,

Student Publications).  The Court ruled that educators do not offend student expression by exercising editorial control over school sponsored activities, as long as there is a reasonably related pedagogical concern.  In other words, should a school have educational concerns about activities involving student expression it need not lend its name or resources to that activity.  Thus, freedom of expression in school controlled student newspapers is not controlled by the requirements of the "material and substantial disruption" language of *Tinker*.

Thus, because of *Tinker*, *Bethel*, and *Hazelwood*, freedom of expression in school can be described as follows: "First, 'vulgar' or plainly offensive speech (*Bethel*-type speech) may be prohibited without showing ... disruption or substantial interference with the schoolwork.  Second, school-sponsored speech (*Hazelwood*-type speech) may be restricted when the limitation is reasonably related to legitimate educational concerns.  Third, speech that is neither vulgar nor school-sponsored (*Tinker*-type) may only be prohibited if it causes a substantial and material disruption of the school's operation."  Pyle v. South Hadley School Committee (D.Mass.1994).

In recent cases, the courts have used all three cases, *Tinker*, *Bethel*, and *Hazelwood*, in determining the appropriateness of student expression.  Where a middle school student came to school with a T-shirt emblazoned with the eight inch high words "Drugs Suck," the court followed *Bethel* and found that speech need not be sexual to be prohibited by school officials.  Speech that is lewd, indecent, or offensive may be regulated.  What is constitutionally permissible outside of school is not necessarily constitutional within the school.  Broussard by Lord v. School Board of City of Norfolk (E.D.Va.1992).

In another illustrative case the teachers went on strike and the school board employed replacement teachers. Children of the striking teachers arrived at school with buttons and stickers stating "I'm not listening scab" and "Do scabs bleed," and were threatened with discipline. The court used *Hazelwood* to interpret *Bethel* and *Tinker* and ruled that in the absence of disruption, wearing of the emblems was constitutionally protected because the students' actions were related to a matter of public concern and therefore fell under the protection of *Tinker*. Chandler v. McMinnville School District (9th Cir.1992).

## § 4.32  Wearing Insignia and Gang Attire

The foregoing precedents establish the guidelines that schools must follow in addressing the disorder and accelerating violence in the schools today. Keeping order in schools has never been easy, but with the increase in drugs, weapons, and gangs, maintenance of a proper educational environment has become increasingly difficult. One of the most persistent areas of concern that touches on free expression is the regulation of gang symbols and dress. Because such emblems have an intimidating effect on non-gang members, schools have developed student dress codes that attempt to temper their use. One district, the San Jacinto Unified School District, school board adopted a dress code which prohibited clothing identifying any professional sport team or college. When the rule was challenged, the court found the policy violated the free speech rights of elementary, but not of high school students. Evidence indicated that the presence of gangs in the high school resulted in intimidation which could lead to disruption of school activities. Jeglin II v. San Jacinto Unified Sch. Dist. (C.D.Cal.1993).

In another case, a school board passed a rule which prohibited all gang symbols including jewelry and emblems. A student who claimed his earring was to attract girls was suspended. The court, in upholding the policy, held that schools have a responsibility not only to teach subjects but also to foster a democratic society. These lessons include not only self rights but also the rights of others. In this case the court deferred to the judgment of the school board indicating in matters of conduct and instruction, the courts were unprepared to intervene unless an obvious constitutional deprivation is at stake. Olesen v. Board of Ed. of Sch. Dist. No. 228 (N.D.Ill. 1987).

## § 4.4   SIT–INS/PROTESTS

The precedent set out by the U.S. Supreme Court in *Tinker* has been followed in other federal court decisions that remain as guideposts for school administrators. For example, prohibition of student sit-ins and nonattendance at classes have been upheld by the courts because they were obviously disruptive of the schools. A case in point is illustrated by a situation where a group of students assembled on school grounds outside the principal's office to protest an earlier suspension of eight students. After refusing to return to class, thirty-five were arrested for unlawful trespassing. In upholding the conviction, the court noted that students have constitutional rights as enunciated by *Tinker*, but such rights do not extend if they disrupt the school. According to the court, the principal " ... had the right and duty to take reasonable measures to restore order." The material and substantial disruption was obvious in this circumstance. Pleasants v. Commonwealth (Va.1974).

## § 4.5 FLAGS

School prohibitions of the Confederate flag have been upheld where racial tension was fueled by use of the flag. Smith v. St. Tammany Parish School Board (5th Cir. 1971). Yet, in a northern state where no *de jure* segregation had previously existed, the courts have declined to force school districts to remove the Confederate flag as a symbol of the school. Banks v. Muncie Community School (7th Cir.1970).

## § 4.6 PERSONAL APPEARANCE

Under the general principle that school authorities may make reasonable rules and regulations controlling student conduct, student dress and personal appearance may be regulated. It has been said that it is in the interest of the school to divert the students' attention from the hemline to the blackboard, or from beards to books. Whether or not a particular mode of dress or appearance detracts from the learning environment has a great deal to do with the acceptable standards of a particular community. That which is not acceptable in a rural midwestern town may be quite normal in a major eastern metropolis. If dress or personal appearance is so different and noticeable that it takes away from the ongoing educational program, school authorities have a valid interest in intervening.

Some early courts held that it is a proper function of the school to require students to wear uniforms to school, and to prohibit the wearing of cosmetics, certain types of hosiery, low-necked dresses, or any style of clothing which may tend, according to community norms, to be immodest. Pugsley v. Sellmeyer (Ark.1923).

Dress codes have been stricken by the courts when it has been shown that the rules were too broad, vague, ambiguous, or did not relate to legitimate educational purpose. A school board dress regulation is valid only to the extent necessary to protect the safety of the wearer, male or female, or to prevent disruption or distraction which interferes with the education of other students.

## § 4.61  Other Manifestations of Expression

In a case where a student drew a caricature of three administrators depicting them in an alcoholic stupor and then transferred the image to t-shirts, the court held against the student reasoning that "the student was not entitled to First Amendment protection for falsely accusing administrators of committing a misdemeanor, namely, consuming alcoholic beverages [he] would suffer little harm in being prevented from falsely accusing administrators from being drunk." Gano v. School District 411 of Twin Falls County, Idaho (D.Idaho 1987).

In another case the school board policy was litigated. One section of the policy stated that students were not to wear clothing which had comments, pictures or designs that were obscene, profane, lewd or vulgar. The second section prohibited clothing that "Harasses, threatens, intimidates, or demeans an individual or group of individuals because of sex, color, race, religion, handicap, national origin, or sexual orientation." A student wore t-shirts with slogans stating "Coed Naked Band; Do it to the Rhythm" and "See Dick Drink. See Dick Drunk. See Dick Die. Don't Be a Dick." which administrators determined to be prohibited under section one of the policy. The court ruled that section one of the policy was constitutional and stated " ... on the question of when the pungency of sexual foolery becomes unacceptable, the school board of South Hadley is in the best position to weigh the strengths and vulnerabilities of the ... high school students." On the second aspect of the policy which concerned harassment the court said the school could only ban the t-shirts if they created "a substantial risk of material and substantial disruption to the daily operations of the school...." Pyle v. South Hadley School Committee (D.Mass.1994).

## § 4.62 Hair Codes

At last during the 1980s the number of hair cases declined, but this decline only occurred after a decade when the courts were deluged with student long hair questions. Historically, the style of hair has been a contentious issue between schoolmasters and students. Students with generally more radical behavior have tended to deviate from what the teachers thought was acceptable in hair styles. The law is not well settled, in fact, the federal courts of appeals are split on the issue. The First, Third, Fourth, Seventh, and Eighth Circuits have held that students have a constitutionally protected right to choose their own hair style, while the Fifth, Sixth, Ninth, and Tenth Circuits have held that personal appearance is not a fundamental interest and that schools may reasonably regulate hair styles.

In those states where the students have prevailed, the courts have elevated personal appearance to a fundamental interest, and have placed the burden on school boards to show why the school's interest is of such magnitude as to restrain this basic freedom.  Several United States constitutional provisions have been used in these cases, the First Amendment's guarantee of free expression, the Fourth Amendment's guarantee of the right to privacy, and the Fourteenth Amendment's guarantee of due process and equal protection.  Each has been used to successfully strike down various hair codes.  In jurisdictions where personal appearance is elevated to a fundamental interest, school systems must present evidence to show that long hair creates "substantial and material disruption" in the school, or causes health or safety hazards, or, in some other way impinges on the educational program and other students' freedoms.  Such evidence is usually very difficult to obtain and in these jurisdictions the students usually prevail.

In the circuits where personal appearance has not been held to be a fundamental interest, the school systems need only show that hair code is rationally related to a legitimate educational purpose.  For example, in the Fifth Circuit, school grooming codes are presumed to be *prima facie* constitutional.  The burden is placed on the student to state a cause of action designed to show that the code is discriminatory and is arbitrarily or capriciously enforced.  In a recent case where the school had established a dress code which prohibited having long hair beyond the bottom of the collar, the rationale for the policy was "... [to] teach grooming and hygiene, instill discipline, prevent disruptions, avoid safety hazards and teach authority," the court in upholding the policy pointed out that judicial deference was the best policy in trivial matters of this sort.  Colorado Independent School District v. Barber (Tex.App.1993).

Another court upheld the prohibition of all facial hair worn by athletes during the competitive season. The rationale was that the rule promoted "total discipline." Humphries v. Lincoln Parish School Board (La.App. 1985).

There is no U.S. Supreme Court precedent generally applicable to the fifty states on hair cuts and it is impossible to reconcile the conflicting decisions of the lower federal courts. The best advice for teachers and school boards is to ascertain the rule of law governing hair cuts for their own jurisdictions and follow the precedents of those courts specifically.

## § 4.7  MEMBERSHIP IN STUDENT SOCIETIES

School systems and states have, in many instances, found it to be educationally necessary to prohibit student fraternities, sororities and secret societies on public school campuses. It is reasoned that these organizations create undesirable divisions among students, and, in so doing, greatly harm the morale of the school. Where states have enacted laws against such groups, the courts have uniformly upheld them. Such statutes have either prohibited such organizations outright, or have required school boards to expel students who are members. Students have usually challenged these statutes as a denial of equal protection under the Fourteenth Amendment, but have not succeeded in their efforts to invalidate such statutes.

In one case, the court upheld a school board regulation made pursuant to statute which proscribed fraternities, sororities, and secret societies, including charity clubs, but excluding the Boy Scouts, Hi-Y, and a few other clubs, to be held within the discretion of the school board. Passel v. Fort Worth Independent School District (Tex.Civ.App.1970). Such a regulation did not constitute discrimination against members of charity clubs who claimed their Fourteenth Amendment equal protection rights were violated.

The courts have also held that, in statutory prohibitions against societies, the word "secret" extends to exclusive social clubs whose memberships are determined by its own members. Societies or organizations, regardless of what they call themselves, may be prohibited under the aegis of secret societies if their membership is not open to all students. Robinson v. Sacramento City Unified School District (Cal.App.1966).

Just as these statutory and regulatory prohibitions do not violate equal protection, neither do they collide with the United States Constitution's First Amendment freedoms guaranteeing freedom of assembly or Fourteenth Amendment due process interests. As far as freedom of assembly is concerned, the courts have clearly maintained that adults have a complete and unrestrained right to form and maintain private, secret, or nonsecret clubs, whether for snobbish or more legitimate social reasons, but the public schools are a different setting entirely. Here the school systems have a definite interest in weighing the good of such clubs against their more inimical aspects. Where the school board, in the exercise of its judgment, feels that the harm outweighs the good, then the clubs, regardless of what they are called, can be banned. The students' rights in the school setting are subject to limitation.

It should also be noted that adult rights are not unlimited and cannot be because people do not exist in a political and social vacuum, and their acts may be, at times, harmful to others. In explaining the distinction between adults and students, secret clubs and societies, the California court, in *Robinson*, stated the rule of law in this manner: "Here the school board is not dealing with adults, but with adolescents in their formative years. And it is not dealing with activities which occur only within the home, and which, therefore, might be said to relate exclusively to parental jurisdiction and control. It is dealing under express statutory mandate with activities which reach into the school and which reasonably may be said to interfere with the educational process, with the morale of high school student bodies as a whole, and which also may reasonably be said not to foster democracy but to frustrate democracy." Such prohibitions, of course, in no way prohibit clubs or organizations whose memberships, activities, and function are decided by academic or athletic merit, such as French clubs, Latin clubs, letter-person clubs, etc.

## § 4.8 STUDENT PREGNANCY

In earlier years when unmarried students became pregnant the school rid itself of the issue by simply suspending or even expelling the girl. Usually, pregnancy for an unmarried student meant that her formal education was at an end. This was the unfortunate situation until the early 1970s, at which time more enlightened school administrators began to wonder about the consequences of such exclusions. At the same time, the courts became involved when a legal right to attend school was claimed by pregnant girls. Courts in a series of cases concluded that such exclusion violated the Equal Protection Clause of the Fourteenth Amendment. Perry

v. Grenada Municipal Separate School District (N.D.Miss.1969).

This issue was further statutorily addressed when the U.S. Congress passed Title IX of the Education Amendments of 1972. Title IX prohibits discrimination based on sex. 20 U.S.C.A. § 1681(a). Regulations promulgated pursuant to Title IX prohibited gender discrimination on the basis of pregnancy, parental status, and marital status and prohibited discrimination against any student. The Act also prohibited exclusion of girls from extracurricular activities when affected by childbirth, false pregnancies, or termination of pregnancy.

In *Wort v. Vierling*, the U.S. Court of Appeals, Seventh Circuit, held that Title IX and Equal Protection were violated when a student was dismissed from the National Honor Society because of her pregnancy. On the other hand, in Pfeiffer v. Marion Center Area School Dist. (3d Cir.1990), the Third Circuit Court upheld the dismissal of a student from the National Honor Society because she had engaged in premarital intercourse. The premarital sexual intercourse was deemed to be sufficient grounds for dismissal because it was determined to be contrary to qualities of leadership and character required by the school. The court in *Pfeiffer* distinguished *Wort*, saying that in *Wort* the dismissal from the NHS was for pregnancy, while *Pfeiffer* was premarital sex, therefore the action in *Wort* violated Title IX and Equal Protection. The court in *Pfeiffer* remanded the case to hear evidence that a male student who was a member of the Honor Society had had premarital sex. The court said "We are troubled ... that ... testimony of a male" concerning his premarital sex was excluded. The issue of sex discrimination was a spectre that concerned the court. Wort v. Vierling (7th Cir.1985).

Thus, it appears that exclusion from school benefits can be justified on the grounds that such conduct is contrary to the qualities of character that are advanced by the school, but exclusion for pregnancy *per se* will not be condoned by the courts.

## § 4.9  IMMORALITY

Immorality is a broad term, encompassing wickedness, lying, cheating, stealing, sexual impurity, or unchastity. Immorality is not necessarily confined to sexual matters, instead, it may be acts which are *contre bonos mores*, that which is considered to be inconsistent with the moral rectitude of the community. Synonyms are corrupt, indecent, depraved, dissolute, while its antonyms are decent, upright, good, and right. A student who so flagrantly violates the norms of the school and community as to be immoral under these definitions can be dismissed from school. Also, the selling of drugs or liquor to other students, fraud or plagiarism, sexual promiscuity and lascivious conduct may all constitute immorality.

Pregnancy of an unwed student is not necessarily immoral, but how the pregnancy occurs may be. Sexual intercourse at school may certainly be considered immoral conduct. For a minor to undress for another student or for an adult for the purpose of satisfying sexual desires is immoral conduct violating not only school rules but may offend delinquency statutes as well. Holton v. State (Alaska 1979). Such activities on the part of students, in violation of school rules, may be punishable by dismissal from school.

## § 4.10  MARRIAGE

In early cases, courts were inclined to uphold school rules denying participation in extracurricular activities by married students. Today, because the courts do not view education as being merely a privilege, educational activities offered to one student must be offered to all students regardless of whether the student is married. As with all rules, there are some exceptions. For example, the United States Court of Appeals for the Tenth Circuit has held that school attendance could not be denied without necessary procedural safeguards, but that similar constitutional protections did not apply to each component of the educational process, indicating that participation in extracurricular activities may be denied without due process. Albach v. Odle (10th Cir.1976). The weight of authority, though, appears to support the position that both students' rights of marital privacy, Moran v. School District No. 7 (D.Mont.1972), and equal protection, Hollon v. Mathis Independent School District, 491 F.2d 92 (5th Cir.1974), are violated by prohibiting participation in extracurricular activities.

## § 4.11  DRUGS, TOBACCO, AND ALCOHOL

School authorities may prohibit drugs, alcohol, and guns (or other weapons) on school grounds or in off-campus activities which bear on the conduct of the school. Most states have statutes against the possession of drugs on school grounds, but in the absence of such laws school boards may promulgate their own regulations. Students may, of course, be expelled from school for violation of drug regulations. (See Chapter 7, Search and Seizure.)

Schools may, too, control or prohibit the use and possession of tobacco and alcoholic beverages in school. Dismissal has been held to be appropriate punishment even though spiking of punch at school was so light as to be barely chemically detectible. So long as procedural due process is properly carried out, dismissals have been upheld. Wood v. Strickland (S.Ct.1975).

In an illustrative case in point a student who attended an off-campus party where there was alcohol was suspended from extra-curricular swimming activities and pursuant to school board policy prohibiting possession of alcohol the student was disciplined. The court here had "... no difficulty concluding that illegal consumption of alcohol has direct affects on the welfare of the schools." Therefore, the regulation was determined to be rationally related to the school board's interest in deterring alcohol consumption among minor students. Bush v. Dassel–Cokato Board of Education (D.Minn.1990).

## § 4.12  WEAPONS

Weapons possession on school campuses has in recent years become a problem of daunting proportions. Weapons can, of course, be excluded from school but at times legal complications may occur. In one such instance, a student was charged with criminal possession of a switchblade knife found in her bag during an administrative search with metal detectors at a high school. The student sought to have the evidence suppressed. A team of special police officers from the Central Task Force for School Safety had posted signs at the high school announcing the search. "An administrative search is upheld when the intrusion involved in the search is no greater than necessary to satisfy the governmental interest underlying the need for the search." The court determined that the knife could be used as evidence and the search was minimally intrusive considering the compelling need for security in the schools. People v. Dukes (N.Y.1992).

# CHAPTER 5

# RELIGION IN PUBLIC SCHOOLS AND STATE FUNDING OF RELIGIOUS SCHOOLS

## § 5.1 INTRODUCTION

The teaching function is very important to virtually all religions. Doctrines and dogmas of religious groups are spread and church membership is increased by teaching to youth and nonbelievers. It is natural that as sectarian beliefs are advanced they will come in conflict with beliefs of other sects and with the nonsectarian purposes of the state. Very early in this country education was conducted almost exclusively by the churches for the purposes of advancing their religious beliefs. Where the state provided tax funds to support schools one of the justifications was to teach the youth to read the Bible. In fact, the first governmental effort to establish tax-supported schools in this country was in 1647 when the colony of Massachusetts provided by statute for general taxation for the purpose of keeping men knowledgeable of the Scriptures in order that they might not fall into the grip of the "old deluder, Satan."

The concept of public education "divorced from denominational control was foreign to the colonial mind." Leo Pfeffer, *Church, State and Freedom*, Boston: Beacon Press, 1967, p. 321. Later Justice Frankfurter in the *McCollum* case was to explain that: "Traditionally, organized education in the Western world was Church education. It could hardly be otherwise when the education of children was primarily the study of the Word and the ways of God. Even in Protestant countries, where there was a less close identification of Church and State, the basis of education was largely the Bible, and its chief purpose inculcation of piety. To the extent that the State intervened, it used its authority to further the aims of the Church."

"The immigrants who came to these shores brought this view of education with them. Colonial schools certainly started with a religious orientation." People ex rel. McCollum v. Board of Education (S.Ct.1948).

The pervasiveness of the early religious influence on public schools is illustrated by the primer used to teach public school pupils to read in New England in the latter part of the seventeenth century. The book entitled *The New England Primer* taught the alphabet using letters and pictures with Biblical connotations, for example: "A—in *Adam*'s fall we sinned or P—*Peter* denies His Lord and cries." Because of these origins of religious involvement in public education it has been difficult to keep public schools from becoming inundated with religious strife and discord.

Over the decades many conflicts have developed between the clergy and the proponents of public education. In the 1830s when Horace Mann provided the leadership in the establishment of the first state system of public schools in Massachusetts, his chief opposition came from clergymen who sought to prevent him from creating Godless institutions. Mann had insisted the public schools should have no sectarian religious motivations and the state should "abstain from subjugating the capacities of children to any legal standard of religious faith."

Later, contrary to Mann's beliefs, religious activities were permitted in public schools in most states, including prayer, Bible reading, and other religious exercises. By the twentieth century, all but a few states had regular morning religious services. The practices were generally supported by opinion of the state courts and were, except in a few states, held to be consistent with state constitutions.

The public school system envisioned by Mann was founded on three basic assumptions: "First, that the legislature has the power to tax all—even the childless and those whose children attend private schools—in order to provide free public education for all; second, that the legislature has the power to require every parent to provide for his children a basic education in secular subjects; third, that the education provided by the state in the free schools must be secular." *Pfeffer*, supra, p. 327.

Each of these basic premises of public education continues to be attacked today by those who seek to invest the public school teachings with their own particular brand of religiosity. Some parents of private school children maintain they are entitled to tax credits because of what they consider (erroneously) to be double taxation. A few parents contest compulsory attendance laws, state regulation of private schools, and home instruction (see Chapter 1); and continuing efforts are made by some to teach religious doctrines in the public schools ranging from religious exercises to teaching creation-science (see Chapter 2).

## § 5.2   FREE EXERCISE AND ESTABLISHMENT

The controversy between advocates of religious sectarianism and secularism in the public schools is a part of a larger conflict which tends to permeate most governments and societies, the unending struggle between Church and State. Today, a casual glance at a newspaper reminds one that the Middle East, with Christian against Muslim, Muslim against Muslim, and Jew against both, is a torrent of religious bigotry and persecution. Ireland, Azerbaijan, Armenia, Kazakstan, not to mention the problems of the Serbs, Croats and Muslims in the Balkans, are among the current conflicts with critical religious overtones. Today's religious conflicts are merely descendants of the great religious quarrels of Europe and Asia which resulted in millions of deaths from wars and persecutions.

The European experience of embattled Church and State was fresh on the minds of founding fathers in America when the First Amendment was drafted. The basic antecedents to the religion clauses of the First Amendment were found in James Madison's *Memorial and Remonstrance Against Religious Assessments* and Thomas Jefferson's *Act for Establishing Religious Freedom*. Both were documents written in response to attempts to establish religion in Virginia and to encroach on individual religious liberty. Madison admonished that all persons had a right to "free exercise of their religion according to the dictates of their conscience;" and Jefferson asserted that it was time to do away with the "impious presumption of legislators and rulers, civil and ecclesiastical who ... have assumed dominion over the faith of others"; and that a person's "civil rights should have no dependence on [his] religious opinions."

When finally promulgated and ratified in 1791, the religion provisions of the First Amendment of the Bill of Rights provided: "Congress shall make no law respecting an establishment of religion, or prohibiting the free exercise thereof; ..."

## § 5.3  WALL OF SEPARATION

John Adams interpreted the free exercise and establishment clauses of the First Amendment to mean that "Congress will never meddle in religion ..."; and Jefferson explained the intent was to create a "wall of separation between Church and State." It had been from Jefferson's urging, while serving in France in 1787, that Madison proceeded to champion the promulgation and ratification of the Bill of Rights (first ten amendments of the U.S. Constitution).

Interpretations of the meaning of the First Amendment have carried forward to today. Time and again the United States Supreme Court has delineated the boundaries between Church and State only to have legislatures and school boards open new cracks and fissures requiring further interpretation. To Justice William O. Douglas there was little debate over the intent of the Amendment. He said "... [T]here cannot be the slightest doubt that the First Amendment reflects the philosophy that Church and State should be separated." And so far as interference with the "free exercise" of religion and an "establishment of religion are concerned, the separation must be complete and unequivocal." Zorach v. Clauson (S.Ct.1952).

## § 5.4   CONSTITUTIONAL STANDARD, THE LEMON TEST

In the large number of religion and public school cases which have come before the United States Supreme Court over the years, the one principle of law which appears to be consistent throughout is that the state must be "neutral" toward religion. As stated in *Zorach*, the government should show "no partiality to any one [religious] group" and should let "each [group] flourish according to the zeal of its adherents and the appeal of its dogma." This neutrality of government means, according to Justice Black's opinion in *Everson*, that: "The establishment of religion clause of the First Amendment means at least this: 'Neither a state nor the Federal Government can set up a church. Neither can pass laws which aid one religion, aid all religions or prefer one religion over another.... No tax in any amount, large or small, can be levied to support any religious activities or institutions, whatever they may be called, or whatever form they may adopt to teach or practice religion.' "

The majority of the church-state cases in education have involved the Establishment Clause of the First Amendment while a few cases have had the Free Exercise Clause as the main issue. Prior to 1970 in measuring whether a state action had violated the Establishment Clause, the Supreme Court sought to determine state neutrality with a two-part test which required that: (1) the purpose of the action of the state not be to aid one religion or all religions and (2) the primary effect of the program be one that "neither advances nor inhibits religion." In 1970 the Supreme Court added a third prong to the test, that the state must not foster "an

excessive government entanglement with religion."
Walz v. Tax Commission (S.Ct.1970).

In 1971 the Supreme Court combined these three
standards and applied them in striking down salary
supplements to teachers in parochial schools and purchase of educational services from parochial schools in
Lemon v. Kurtzman (S.Ct.1971). Since *Lemon*, the
Court has applied this three prong test: (1) purpose, (2)
effect, and (3) excessive entanglement, to cases involving
the Establishment Clause.

Thus, stated in the negative, this three part constitutional standard for separation of church and state as
prescribed by the "Establishment Clause" of the First
Amendment actions by government means that: (1) Legislation or governmental action must not have a religious
purpose; (2) Legislation or governmental action must
not have the primary effect of either enhancing or inhibiting religion; and (3) Legislation or governmental action
must not create excessive entanglement between church
and state.

The *Lemon* test was used in all school cases in the
1980s and for all but two nonschool cases: Marsh v.
Chambers (S.Ct.1983) (here the so-called historical analysis was used); and Larson v. Valente (S.Ct.1982). Justice Rehnquist and other justices, primarily the Reagan–
Bush appointees, criticized the *Lemon* test. In the most
recent decisions, the Court has downgraded the importance of the *Lemon* Test. The test was described as a
"guideline" in Committee v. Nyquist (S.Ct.1973), and
then merely as "no more than [a] useful 'guideline' " in
Mueller v. Allen (S.Ct.1983). Later, in Lynch v. Donnel-
ly (S.Ct.1984), the Court stated that the *Lemon* Test has
never been binding on the Court. There was speculation

that the Supreme Court would overturn *Lemon* or establish a new test when *Lee v. Weisman* was litigated. But then, however, Justice Kennedy, writing for the majority, stated "... that the court will not reconsider its decision in *Lemon*...." Yet the Court did not apply *Lemon* in *Weisman*, but rather applied a coercion test. The Court stated: "The principle that government may accommodate the free exercise of religion does not supersede the fundamental limitations imposed by the Establishment Clause, which guarantees at a minimum that a government may not coerce anyone to support or participate in religion or its exercise, or otherwise act in a way which 'establishes a [state] religion or religious faith, or tends to do so.' "

The Supreme Court justice most critical of *Lemon* has been Judge Scalia. Justice Scalia, in the *Lamb's Chapel* case, in attacking the *Lemon* test, stated that "As to the Court's invocation of the *Lemon* test: Like some ghoul in a late-night horror movie that repeatedly sits up in its grave and shuffles abroad, after being repeatedly killed and buried. *Lemon* stalks our Establishment Clause jurisprudence once again, frightening the little children and school attorneys of Center Moriches Union Free School District. Its most recent burial, only last Term, was, to be sure, not fully six-feet under: our decision in *Lee v. Weisman*, ..., conspicuously avoided using the supposed 'test' but also declined the invitation to repudiate it. Over the years, however, no fewer than five of the currently sitting Justices have, in their own opinions, personally driven pencils through the creature's heart ..., and a sixth has joined an opinion doing so."

Scalia then went on: "The secret of the *Lemon* test's survival, I think, is that it is so easy to kill. It is there to scare us (and our audience) when we wish it to do so, but we can command it to return to the tomb at will.... When we wish to strike down a practice it forbids, we invoke it, ... when we wish to uphold a practice it forbids, we ignore it entirely.... Sometimes, we take a middle course, calling its three prongs 'no more than helpful signposts' ... Such a docile and useful monster is worth keeping around, at least in a somnolent state; one never knows when one might need him.... I will decline to apply *Lemon*—whether it validates or invalidates the government action in question—and therefore cannot join the opinion of the Court today." Justice Scalia's efforts, however, to lower Mr. Jefferson's Wall of Separation have not yet succeeded.

The Supreme Court has, though, lately avoided use of the *Lemon* test. Recently the Supreme Court did not use the *Lemon* test in deciding Board of Education of Kiryas Joel Village School District v. Grumet (S.Ct.1994), rather it applied a "neutrality" standard, saying "A proper respect for both the Free Exercise and the Establishment Clauses compels the State to pursue a course of 'neutrality' toward religion." In this case the state legislature created a separate special education school district for a religious educational enclave. "The New York Village of Kiryas Joel is a religious enclave of Satmar Hasidim, practitioners of a strict form of Judaism. Its local incorporation intentionally drew its boundaries under the state's general village incorporation law to exclude all but Satmars." The state then carved out a special school district exclusively for the Satmar Hasidic sect. In declaring the act unconstitutional, the Supreme Court stated: "Because this unusual act is tantamount to an allocation of political power on a religious criterion and neither presupposes nor requires governmental impartiality toward religion, we hold that it violates the prohibition against establishment."

In the aftermath of the *Joel* case, it now appears that some other standard in measuring the Establishment Clause cases will be forthcoming from the Supreme Court, as alternative to *Lemon* that is likely to lower or abolish the "wall."

With regard to the Free Exercise Clause it should be remembered that the Supreme Court has distinguished between the freedom of individual *beliefs*, which are absolute and the freedom of individual *conduct*, which is not. The Free Exercise Clause protects an individual "from certain forms of governmental compulsion; it does not afford an individual a right to dictate the conduct of Government's internal procedures." Maintaining an ordered or organized society that guarantees religious freedom to such a vast variety of religious beliefs, as are held in this country, requires some religious practices to yield to the common good. Religious beliefs must be accommodated, but accommodation of certain conduct may restrict the operation of government and encroach on others religious beliefs. In such instances such religious conduct must be restrained for the good of all.

The free exercise clause is violated when one is compelled to perform an act which violates one's religious beliefs or forego a benefit bestowed by the government. Mozert v. Hawkins County Board of Education (6th Cir.1987); Sherbert v. Verner (S.Ct.1963); Hobbie v. Unemployment Appeals Commission of Florida (S.Ct. 1987).

## § 5.5  RELIGIOUS   ACTIVITIES   IN   PUBLIC SCHOOLS

### § 5.51  Release Time

Many different schemes have been devised by religious groups for using the public schools as a supportive device for teaching religion.  A common practice, by the turn of the century, in many school districts, was for a portion of the school day to be set aside for religious instruction in the public school building.  This went on without serious challenge until the *McCollum* case, in 1948, a case in which the United States Supreme Court held unconstitutional a released time situation in which Protestant preachers, Catholic priests, and a Jewish rabbi taught religion classes in the school each week.  Students who wanted to attend religious classes were *released* from their regular classes and those students who did not went to another location in the public school building to pursue their secular subjects.  Attendance reports were kept and absences were reported back to the regular school teachers.  The school district defended the practice maintaining that the students were not compelled to attend the religious classes and that one religion was not favored over another.  People ex rel. McCollum v. Board of Education (S.Ct.1948).

The Supreme Court in striking down the practice said that state tax-supported facilities could not be used to disseminate religious doctrines whether it aided only one or all religions.  Too, the Court noted that the state's compulsory attendance law provided a valuable aid to religion in that it brought the children to a central location at which the churches could capture the students' attention.  According to the Court, there existed too close a cooperation in that (1) the weight and influence of the public school is cast behind a program for religious instruction; (2) public school teachers provide the attendance accounting and police the process; (3) the school kept track of students who are released; and (4) the normal classroom activities come to a halt. For these reasons the practice was held to violate the First Amendment.

Following *McCollum*, the City of New York devised another released time program in which students were released from public schools during the school day to attend religious services off school grounds. A period was set aside each week when students could leave the public school grounds to go to a church or church school to attend religious services. The program was entirely optional, the school authorities were neutral, and teachers did no more than release the students when so requested by parents. In upholding this plan the United States Supreme Court said that the state could accommodate religion without aiding religion and it would too severely "press the concept of separation of Church and State" to condemn this New York law where the state assistance was so minimal. Accordingly, in this instance, for government to fail to accommodate this type of released time plan would constitute a callousness toward religion which is not required by the First Amendment. Zorach v. Clauson (S.Ct.1952).

In 1990, a federal district court ruled that a release time program was constitutional using the *Zorach* model. But the court concluded that members of the religious organization in question could not enter the school. The facts of the case indicated that not only were the members of the organization entering the school, but they were offering bags of candy trying to recruit children to join the religious program.   Doe by Doe v. Shenandoah County School Board (W.D.Va.1990).

## § 5.52  Prayer and Bible Reading

Prior to 1962 some states required each school day to begin with a prayer and the reading of verses from the Bible.  This practice was contested when the New York State Board of Regents composed a prayer which they recommended be used in the public schools.  The prayer stated: "Almighty God, we acknowledge our dependence upon Thee, and we beg Thy blessings upon us, our parents, teachers, and our Country."  The United States Supreme Court determined that the prayer violated the Establishment Clause.  "[W]e think that the constitutional prohibition against laws respecting an establishment of religion must at least mean that in this country, it is no part of the business of government to compose official prayers for any group of the American people to recite as a part of a religious program carried on by government."  Engel v. Vitale (S.Ct.1962).

Then in 1963 came companion cases, School District of Abington Township v. Schempp and Murray v. Curlett (S.Ct.1963), that challenged state practices in Pennsylvania and Maryland school districts of having prayer and Bible reading at the beginning of each day.  Children who did not want to stay in the room were excused while the exercises proceeded.  The reading of the Bible and Lord's Prayer was challenged as a violation of the First Amendment.  The Supreme Court determined that the exercises violated the Establishment Clause of the First Amendment.  But the Court went on to say, "It certainly may be said that the Bible is worthy of study for its literary and historic qualities.  Nothing we have said here indicates that such study of the Bible or of religion, when presented objectively as a part of a secular program of education, may not be effected consistently with the First Amendment. But the exercises here do not fall into those categories." Therefore, the Bible may be used in appropriate study of history, civilization, ethics, and comparative religion; but such Bible study classes must be taught in a manner that is secular and does not promote religion. If the classes are not objectively taught in a secular manner as an academic subject, then they are unconstitutional. Wiley v. Franklin (E.D.Tenn. 1980).

## § 5.53 Silent Meditation

In an effort to circumvent the Supreme Court's proscription of state sponsored prayer in the public schools, some states have exercised exceptional creativeness. One such example is found in Alabama where in 1981 the legislature enacted a statute authorizing a period of silence "for meditation or voluntary prayer" in all Alabama public schools. When the Court examined the legislative history of the statute, it was found that the prime sponsor of the statute had stated the purpose of the Act to be "an effort to return voluntary prayer to our public schools...." The Supreme Court concluded this obviously did not constitute a "secular legislative purpose" and the Act therefore violated the Establishment Clause of the First Amendment. Wallace v. Jaffree (S.Ct.1985).

## § 5.54 Prayer at Graduation Ceremonies

Insistence by various religious groups that religious exercises be included in public schools has assumed many shapes and definitions over the years. Various interpretations of the law have concluded that the constitutional application is only pertinent to the classroom while ancillary activities, such as commencement exercises, baccalaureate, and athletic events, are beyond the scope of constitutional consideration. The United States Supreme Court has, however, not drawn such definitive lines between curricular and after-curricular activities. In one such case, the Supreme Court invalidated prayer at high school graduation ceremonies, here, in Lee v. Weisman (S.Ct.1992), the public school principals in Providence, Rhode Island, were permitted to invite the clergy to give invocations and benedictions at graduation ceremonies. The school principal invited a Rabbi to offer prayers and provided him with guidelines to follow in the composition of "public prayers" for civic ceremonies and advised him that the prayers should be nonsectarian. The Supreme Court concluded that "state officials [were] direct[ing] the performance of a formal religious exercise" which is prohibited by the First Amendment. This conclusion was based on the fact that a school official, the principal, decided (a) that an invocation and benediction should be given, (b) whom should be chosen to present the prayers, and (c) the content of the prayer. These conditions made it clear that the prayer was state sponsored and directed. The school district argued the prayer was acceptable to most persons, but the Supreme Court countered that the school's undertaking of the enterprise in the first place was to "produce a prayer to be used as a formal religious exercise which students, for all practical purposes, are obliged to attend." Thus, by so doing, the state was found not to be neutral but rather was in fact advancing religion. The Court rejected the argument that the prayer was a kind of "nonsectarian prayer" legitimately conveyed by the state to advance a "civic religion." The Court said that "While some common ground of moral and ethical behavior is highly desirable for any society, for the state to advance a Judeo–Christian religious doctrine under the mantle of some perceived civic religious motivation is clearly in conflict with the religious clauses." The Court explained the intent of the Religion Clauses of the First Amendment to mean that "religious beliefs and religious expression are too precious to be either proscribed or prescribed by the state."

## § 5.55 Prayer at Other School Activities

The variations on the prayer issue appear to be virtually unlimited. Where a high school band teacher created a "new tradition" of mandatory prayer sessions before rehearsals and performances, a federal circuit court found the practice in violation of the Establishment Clause of the First Amendment. The plaintiff was awarded attorney's fees and was granted an order forbidding the school from allowing such prayer sessions. Steele v. Van Buren Public School District (8th Cir. 1988). See also Breen v. Runkel (W.D.Mich.1985).

Prayers before and after athletic contests are common and often little is said about such exercises. But, where people's religious convictions are offended challenges may arise. In one such incident, a coach at a school in Texas began and ended practices and games with team recitation of the Lord's Prayer. One player, a girl, participated only because she felt her refusal would create dissention and would be harmful to team morale. When she was informed by her father that she did not have to participate, she was asked by the coach to stand apart from the team during prayers. Her father filed suit to enjoin the activity and a federal district court granted the injunction. The U.S. Court of Appeals for the Fifth Circuit affirmed the decision. Doe v. Duncanville Independent School District (5th Cir.1993). The Eleventh Circuit ruled that it violated the First Amendment to have invocation before a public high school football game. Jager v. Douglas County School Dist. (11th Cir.1989).

## § 5.56 Equal Access Act of 1984 (20 U.S.C.A. § 4071)

In 1984 the U.S. Congress passed the Equal Access Act. The constitutional rationale for the law emanated from Widmar v. Vincent (S.Ct.1984). In *Widmar*, the United States Supreme Court ruled that the University of Missouri's refusal to allow religious groups access to its public facilities while allowing other groups access to the same facilities violated the free speech provision of the First Amendment. In this case the Court ruled that the grounds and facilities of a public university were a "public forum," the use thereof was protected by constitutional free speech rights.

The Reagan administration in seeking ways to accommodate the religious right for its political support seized upon the *Widmar* precedent for its precedential value in extending the free speech, public forum concept to the secondary public schools. The *Equal Access Act* prohibited public school districts receiving federal money and allowing noncurricular activities and club meetings, to deny secondary school students the right to meet in public school facilities for religious and/or other purposes. The Equal Access Act states in pertinent part: "It shall be unlawful for any public *secondary* school

which receives Federal financial assistance and which
has a limited open forum to deny equal access or a fair
opportunity to, or discriminate against, any students who
wish to conduct a meeting within that limited open
forum on the basis of the religious, political, philosophical, or other content of the speech at such meetings"
(emphasis added). According to this statute, when a
school district allows clubs and organizations that are
not directly curriculum related to meet in school facilities
then the school has created a *limited open forum*. When
such a forum is created the school district cannot deny
other student initiated groups, whether religious, political, or philosophical, from holding meetings in the facilities of the public school.

## § 5.57 Limited Open Forum

The constitutionality of the Equal Access Act was
decided in the case of Board of Education of Westside
Community Schools v. Mergens (S.Ct.1990). Two questions were raised. The first was whether the Equal
Access Act prohibited the Westside High School from
denying a student religious group permission to meet on
school premises and, secondly, whether the Act violated
the Establishment Clause of the First Amendment. In
response, the Supreme Court held against the school and
for the student religious group and, further, ruled that
the federal statute was not violative of the First Amendment. According to the Court, a "limited open forum"
exists whenever a public school "grants an offering to or
opportunity for one or more noncurriculum related student groups to meet on school premises during noninstructional time." The statutory reference to "noninstructional time" means "time set aside by the school

before actual classroom instruction begins or after actual classroom instruction ends."

In this regard the Supreme Court found that the obligations under the Act are triggered even if the public secondary school allows only one noncurriculum related student group to meet. A "noncurricular related student group" was interpreted broadly to mean "any student group that does not directly relate to the body of courses offered by the school." A French or a Latin club would directly relate to a French or Latin course offered as a planned part of the curriculum. While a checkers club, chess club, or community service club would be noncurriculum related. If such noncurriculum clubs are permitted, then the school is considered to have a "limited open forum" and religious and other student initiated clubs have equal access to the school premises.

As to whether the *Equal Access Act* is itself constitutional, the Court held that it was. In so ruling, the Court referred back to *Widmar* where it had ruled that "an open forum policy" did not violate any of the three parts of the *Lemon* test; allowing religious speech did not "confer any imprimatur of state approval on religious sects or practices," thus the purpose test is not violated; to allow all to speak was an act of neutrality neither inhibiting nor advancing religion.

With regard to the third part of the *Lemon* test, excessive entanglement, the Court observed that the Act prohibits "school sponsorship" of religious meetings, meaning according to the Court that school officials could not "promote, lead, or participate" in such meetings. Neither is excessive entanglement created by the school assigning a teacher, administrator or other school employee to oversee religious meetings for custodial purposes, to ensure order and good behavior. Thus, the Act is constitutional.

Therefore, where the school creates a "limited open forum" for noninstructional activities, religious clubs and organizations can use the premises for meetings and activities as assured by the Equal Access Act.

For the public school to remain neutral, however, means that the noninstructional activity (1) must be voluntary on the part of the students; (2) have no sponsorship by the school, the government, or its agents or employees; (3) have no employees or agents of the public school or government present at religious meetings except in a nonparticipatory, custodial capacity, (4) must not materially or substantially interfere with the orderly conduct of educational activities within the school; and (5) nonschool persons may not direct, conduct, control, or regularly attend activities of student groups. 20 U.S.C.A. § 4071(c).

The rules as set out by the Act were found to be violated in a Pennsylvania case in which a Gospel Choir that had advertised itself as being sponsored by the high school and the school district, had an official of the school district as its sponsor, and was directed by another school employee (a school secretary), had a school employee attend all practices and meetings in a participatory capacity, not merely a custodial capacity, and whose meetings were regularly attended by non-school persons. This violated Sections 4071(c)(2), 4071(c)(3), and 4071(c)(5) of the Equal Access Act. The Gospel Choir could have been formed under the Equal Access Act but could not have appeared to represent the school or to have involved state employees actively in the functioning of the choir. Sease v. School District of Philadelphia (E.D.Pa.1993).

## § 5.58   Use of Facilities

After *Widmar* and *Mergens*, the courts began to use the free speech test more frequently when dealing with church-state issues. As noted in *Widmar* and *Mergens*, if the school allowed one group to use a facility, religious groups could not be denied equal use since it would violate free speech. The free speech test has recently been applied to the use of school facilities. In the past courts ruled that school boards could have policies that allowed different groups to use the facility. In other words, for example, the school board could allow use of facilities by the boy scouts and girl scouts but could deny religious groups access.

With the use of the public forum rationale applied to free speech, schools must now be "viewpoint neutral." An aspect of viewpoint neutrality was litigated by the U.S. Supreme Court in Lamb's Chapel v. Center Moriches Union Free School District (S.Ct.1993). In this case, Center Moriches School District in New York denied Lamb's Chapel Church the after-hour use of school facilities for showing a series of films concerning "child-rearing, family values, family relationships, abortion, pornography, and loving God." The school district had acted in accordance with New York state law that allowed after-hours use by all outside groups except religious groups. The state law excluded religious groups from school premises in order to reduce the possibility of school districts enhancing religion of a particular church in preference to another religious group. In this way the state sought to remain neutral.

The Supreme Court ruled such an exclusion effectively violated the church's freedom of speech because evidence was presented to show that the school district had created a "limited public forum" by opening the school premises for "social, civic, and recreational" purposes such as the Salvation Army Band, Center Moriches Quilting Bee, Center Moriches Drama Club, Girl Scouts, Boy Scouts, and Center Moriches Music Awards Association, among others. According to the Court, to open school premises for other groups but to close them to religious groups was not to remain viewpoint neutral. The Supreme Court reversed the lower federal court that had agreed with the school district's excluding all religious groups in the belief that the school district thereby remained neutral. What the lower court determined to be viewpoint neutrality, the Supreme Court interpreted as discrimination against religion. The Supreme Court said "there would have been no realistic danger that the community would think that the District was endorsing religion or any particular creed" by opening the school premises for church use. Accordingly, the Supreme Court dismissed the concern of the school district that permitting use of school premises for such religious proselytizing would violate the Establishment Clause of the First Amendment.

A result similar to that reached in the Lamb's Chapel case was rendered by the U.S. Court of Appeals, First Circuit, Grace Bible Fellowship v. Maine School Administrative #5 (1st Cir.1991). Here the Court determined that a school district had created a public forum and subsequent denial by the district of the weekend evening use of the high school cafeteria for a Christmas dinner, where a minister would urge the belief in Jesus Christ as lord and savior, violated the free speech rights of members of the organization. Additionally, the court found the religious clauses of the First Amendment did not bar such religious accommodation by the school district.

## § 5.59  Posting Ten Commandments

The Kentucky legislature passed a statute requiring the posting of the Ten Commandments on the wall of each classroom in the state. The posters were to be purchased with private donations. At the bottom of each poster the statute required the printing of the following statement: "The secular application of the Ten Commandments is clearly seen in its adoption as the fundamental legal code of Western Civilization and the Common Law of the United States." The United States Supreme Court ruled that this disclaimer at the bottom did not change the pre-eminent purpose of the Ten Commandments which was plainly not neutral but patently religious in nature. Therefore, the statute violated the Establishment Clause of the First Amendment. Stone v. Graham (S.Ct.1980).

## § 5.6  PUBLIC TAX FUNDS FOR RELIGIOUS SCHOOLS

The *Lemon* test, as discussed earlier, has been applied by the U.S. Supreme Court in striking down an array of state actions that has sought to provide public tax funds for church schools. In one such case, School District of the City of Grand Rapids v. Ball (S.Ct.1985), the Grand Rapids School District in Michigan adopted two programs in which classes for nonpublic school students were financed by the public school system. Most of the nonpublic schools in the program were sectarian religious schools. Two programs were contested; the first involved the public schools hiring of teachers and placing them in classrooms that were leased from the religious schools by the public schools. The second program involved a community education program in which classes for both children and adults were taught in nonpublic religious schools paid for by public schools from tax funds. In applying the *Lemon* test the United States Supreme Court said: "Every analysis in this area must begin with consideration of the cumulative criteria developed by the Court over many years. Three such guides may be gleaned from our cases. First, the statute must have a secular legislative purpose; second, its principal or primary effect must be one that neither advances nor inhibits religion, (and) ... finally, the statute must not foster 'an excessive entanglement with religion....' "

In applying the three parts of the *Lemon* test the Court let stand lower court determinations that the avowed purpose of the legislation was secular, but struck down the programs on the second prong of the test finding that 40 of the 41 schools where the programs were offered were religious schools, and therefore the primary or principal effect was to advance religion. The Court found that the instructors paid from public funds were also teachers in the religious schools and that it was the role and purpose of such teachers to "inculcate their students with the tenets and beliefs of their particular religious faiths." Having held the programs unconstitutional under the effect part of the *Lemon* test, the application of the excessive entanglement standard was unnecessary.

In Aguilar v. Felton (S.Ct.1985), in a companion case to *Grand Rapids*, Justice Brennan writing for a majority of the Court held that the City of New York's use of federal funds to pay salaries of public employees to teach in parochial schools violated the Establishment Clause of the First Amendment. The City of New York, since the inception of the federal Elementary and Secondary Education Act (ESEA), Title I, had utilized these funds to provide instructional services to parochial school students on the premises of parochial schools. At the time the litigation began in 1981–82, 13.2 percent of all children eligible for Title I funds were enrolled in private schools and of these 84 percent were in schools affiliated with the Roman Catholic Archdiocese of New York and the Diocese of Brooklyn. The programs offered in the parochial schools were carried out by public school employees (teachers, guidance counselors, psychologists, psychiatrists, and social workers). In defending the practice, New York City maintained that this assistance to parochial schools did not have a religious purpose and the effect was not to enhance religion because the services rendered were secular, provided by public school employees. The Supreme Court observed, however, that regardless of purpose and effect parts of the *Lemon* test, that the practice violated the third requirement that the state not be involved in excessive entanglement with the Church. The complex system created by New York to employ, supervise, inspect public school employees in the pervasively sectarian environment of the parochial schools too closely entangled church and state. In this regard, the Court said that "When the state becomes so enmeshed with a given denomination ... the freedom of those who are not adherents of that denomination suffers" and additionally "the freedom of even the adherents of the denomination is limited by the governmental intrusion into sacred matters."

## § 5.61 Textbooks

In 1928 the Louisiana legislature passed an act which allowed the purchase and supply of textbooks for school children throughout the state, including private school children. The United States Supreme Court upheld the act as not violative of the Fourteenth Amendment and based its reasoning on what became known as the "Child Benefit Theory." Cochran v. Louisiana State Board of Education (S.Ct.1930). Accordingly, the Court said that if the benefit could be justified as benefitting the child, then the law would be upheld.

The state of New York later passed legislation which allowed the lending of textbooks to parochial school children free of charge. In so doing, the New York legislature took constitutional refuge in the child-benefit concept. The United States Supreme Court in Board of Education of Central School District No. 1 v. Allen (S.Ct. 1968), determined that the Act was constitutional and did not violate the Establishment Clause of the First Amendment. Therefore the loaning of textbooks to private school children does not conflict with the First Amendment. Under the same theory, loans of textbooks were subsequently upheld in Meek v. Pittenger (S.Ct. 1975) and Wolman v. Walter (S.Ct.1977). Although a state legislative act providing textbooks to private school children may not violate the federal Constitution, it may very well violate a state's constitution. A number of states have more restrictive separation provisions in their constitutions than does the federal Constitution. See In re Advisory Opinion Re Constitutionality of 1974 Pa 242 (Mich.1975); California Teachers Association v. Riles (Wilson) (Cal.1981).

## § 5.62   Public Transportation of Parochial School Students

Transportation of parochial school students at public expense has been upheld by the Supreme Court under the rationale that a "public purpose" or "child benefit" is effectuated. In the leading case establishing this principle, the state of New Jersey authorized reimbursement of bus transportation expenses to parents of private school children and the practice was challenged as a violation of the New Jersey Constitution and the Federal Constitution. The New Jersey Supreme Court decided the provision violated neither the state nor Federal Constitution. The case was appealed to the United States Supreme Court contending a violation of the First Amendment. The Court ruled that there was no violation of the Establishment Clause. Since the statute was justified on the child benefit theory, the Court said " ... we cannot say that the First Amendment prohibits New Jersey from spending tax-raised funds to pay the bus fares of Parochial School pupils as a part of a general program under which it pays the fares of pupils attending public and other schools." Everson v. Board of Education (S.Ct.1947).

This New Jersey decision, the famous *Everson* case, established that the First Amendment is not offended if transportation aid is provided to private school children. Approximately thirty states now provide aid in a variety of ways, such as transportation expense reimbursement, or direct grants to private schools, for private school transportation.

Although public funding for transportation of parochial school students has been permitted in some states, because of health and safety factors of going to and from school, providing aid for field trips has been declared unconstitutional. In one instance, Ohio attempted to allocate funds to private schools for field trip activities. The Supreme Court declared the reimbursement for field trips to be unconstitutional because there was no way for public school authorities to adequately insure that the trip would have a secular purpose without close supervision of the nonpublic trips. Such close supervision would constitute excessive entanglement. Wolman v. Walter (S.Ct.1977).

## § 5.63 Public Financing of Standardized Testing and Scoring in Parochial Schools

The state of Ohio passed legislation "... [t]o supply, for use by pupils attending nonpublic schools within the district, such standardized tests and scoring services as were in use in the public schools of the state." The United States Supreme Court in *Wolman v. Walter* ruled the statute was constitutional because the state had a legitimate interest in insuring students in parochial schools have an adequate secular education. Since the standardized tests were obviously secular and for the purpose to benefit the state and the child, the statute was found not to be violative of the First Amendment. Therefore, financial assistance may be given to private schools by paying for standardized tests and the subsequent scoring of those tests provided such funding is not prohibited by state constitution.

## § 5.64 Reimbursement of Parochial Schools for Teacher–Made Tests

The state of New York passed a statute which provided reimbursement to church-sponsored schools for the expenses incurred by the schools when the parochial school teachers prepared tests for their classes. The Supreme Court ruled this statute violated the Constitution because there were "no means available, to assure that internally prepared tests were free of religious instruction." Another significant deficiency of the statute was that no means were established to audit the state-granted expenditures. The legislature had provided no requirement for such audits for fear of violating the excessive entanglement test, but had, thereby, inadvertently fallen prey to the effect test of *Lemon*. Levitt v. Committee for Public Education (S.Ct.1973).

After the *Levitt* decision, New York legislated payment for teacher-made tests but required an audit of the funds expended. In Committee for Public Education v. Regan (S.Ct.1980), the Supreme Court ruled the reimbursement for teacher-made tests now met all constitutional standards because the funds were audited by the state. In a dissenting opinion, Justice Blackman said that the mere audit did not correct the constitutional defect from the first *Levitt* case. He stated: "The court in this case, I fear, takes a long step backwards in the inevitable controversy that emerges when a state legislature continues to insist on providing public aid to parochial schools."

## § 5.65  Diagnostic and Therapeutic Services for Parochial School Students

The state of Ohio passed legislation, "[t]o provide speech and hearing diagnostic services to pupils attending nonpublic schools within the district." The law stated that: "Such service shall be provided in the nonpublic school attended by the pupil receiving the service" and also "[t]o provide diagnostic psychological services to

pupils attending nonpublic schools within the district."
Too, the statute said that such "services shall be provided in the school attended by the pupil receiving the
service." Although these services were to be performed
on nonpublic school property, the service had to be
provided by public school employees except where physicians were involved. In *Wolman v. Walter*, supra, the
United States Supreme Court stated, "[w]e conclude that
providing diagnostic services on the nonpublic school
premises will not create an impermissible risk of the
fostering of ideological views. It follows that there is no
need for excessive surveillance, and there will not be
impermissible entanglement. We therefore hold [the
statute] constitutional."

The State of Ohio also enacted legislation authorizing
the expenditure of funds to provide certain therapeutic
services, guidance, and remedial service, to students in
private schools. All services were to be performed on
public premises by public school or health department
employees. The Court ruled the services were to help
the child and not the religious institution. Because the
services were performed off the nonpublic school premises, they were found not to advance religion or create
excessive entanglement. *Wolman v. Walter*, supra.

## § 5.66   Public Funding of Instructional Materials and Equipment in Parochial Schools

State legislatures have also attempted to provide instructional materials and equipment to parochial schools.
Pennsylvania passed legislation authorizing the loaning
of instructional materials and equipment to nonpublic
schools, which were defined as periodicals, photographs,
maps, charts, sound recordings, films, projectors, and

laboratory equipment. The Act appeared to be neutral since instructional materials and equipment themselves are secular; but the Court declared the Act would result in "... direct and substantial advancement of religious activities, ... and thus constitute an impermissible establishment of religion." Since the equipment could be used for sectarian education within the school, there was no feasible monitoring system that would not violate the excessive entanglement standard. Meek v. Pittenger (S.Ct.1975). Ohio attempted to circumvent the *Meek* decision by loaning equipment to the parent or pupil who would then let the private school use it. The Supreme Court said, "[d]espite the technical change in legal bailee, the program in substance is the same as before [Meek] ...", therefore, it violated the Establishment Clause. *Wolman v. Walter*, supra.

## § 5.67 Tax Credits and Deductions for Students in Parochial Schools

The issue of aid to parochial schools in the form of tax credits or tax deductions is not a new idea. In 1972, a lower federal district court invalidated Ohio's Parental Reimbursement Grant, which provided a tax credit to nonpublic school parents, a decision that was summarily affirmed by the U.S. Supreme Court in 1973, Kosydar v. Wolman (S.D.Ohio 1972). The Supreme Court also addressed the tax benefit question in *Nyquist* and found a New York statute for nonpublic school parents was unconstitutional. Committee v. Nyquist (S.Ct.1973). Again, in 1979, the Supreme Court confronted the tax benefit issue, at which time it summarily affirmed the Third Circuit Court of Appeals decision invalidating a tax benefit program for nonpublic school parents in New

Jersey. This program allowed nonpublic school parents a $100 tax deduction for each dependent child's attendance at a tuition-charging nonpublic school. Public Funds for Public Schools v. Byrne (3d Cir.1979). In yet another case, the U.S. Court of Appeals, First Circuit, ruled in 1980 in *Norberg*, a Rhode Island case, that a statute allowing nonpublic school parents a state income tax deduction for textbooks and transportation expenses was unconstitutional, violating the Establishment Clause. Rhode Island Federation of Teachers AFL–CIO et al. v. Norberg (1st Cir.1980).

The leading case on the subject of tax credits resulted from a Minnesota statute that allowed all parent taxpayers to deduct from their income taxes a legislatively specified amount. In approving this scheme of aid to private schools, the U.S. Supreme Court appeared to chart a new direction of even greater leniency in provision of public monies for parochial schools. In validating the Minnesota plan, the Court distinguished its rejection of the earlier tax deduction or credit plans by noting that each of those limited tax benefits were available only to parents of private school children, while the Minnesota deduction was available to parents of all children in both private and public schools. The Court did not seem to be concerned that tax deduction benefits to public school parents for tuition, transportation fees and textbooks would be virtually nonexistent. The primary benefits did, of course, accrue largely to the advantage of parochial school parents. Justice Rehnquist, in applying the three-part *Lemon* test for the 5–4 majority, held that the statute had a secular purpose, because "A state's decision to defray cost of educational expenses ... regardless of the type of schools ... evidences a purpose that is both secular and understandable." The second prong of the *Lemon* test, the primary effect of advancing religion, was not violated since the tax deduction was available to all and therefore "facially neutral." The government entanglement standard was quickly dismissed by the Court. The Court stated "... we have no difficulty in concluding that the Minnesota statute does not 'excessively entangle' the state in religion." Mueller v. Allen (S.Ct.1983).

Following the lead of Minnesota, the legislature of Iowa passed a law allowing a tax credit or tax deduction for payment of elementary and secondary school tuition and purchase of textbooks. Since the statute was substantially structured the same as the Minnesota statute, the court upheld the constitutionality, citing *Mueller* as precedent. Luthens v. Bair (S.D.Iowa 1992).

# CHAPTER 6

## STUDENT PUBLICATIONS

### § 6.1 INTRODUCTION

During the decades of the 1960s, 1970s, and even into the early 1980s, numerous court decisions were rendered which dealt with student publications. To a large degree, this was attributable to student activism against the Vietnam War. The famous *Tinker* case had established students have constitutional rights and do not abandon those rights at the schoolhouse door. During these years, however, the issue of student rights in relationship to student publications was not well settled. The court decisions concerning school sponsored publications did not agree and those decisions that dealt with non-school or underground publications were similarly indecisive.

This uncertainty as to publications in schools as to the meaning of precedents, however, does not extend to the freedom of press generally. Freedom of press is a cornerstone of the basic freedoms found in a democracy. In the Pentagon papers case, the United States Supreme Court stated the importance of freedom of the press. "In the First Amendment the Founding Fathers gave free press the protection it must have to fulfill its essential role in our democracy, the press was to serve the governed, not the governors. The Government's power to censor was abolished so that the press would remain forever free to censure the Government." New York Times Co. v. United States (S.Ct.1971).

Accordingly, it would be unthinkable for government agencies to have the legal authority to censor the press; yet, school districts are government agencies and as such have been given special leeway to exercise limited controls over student publications. This authority derives from the historical special legal relationship between the school and the student. The Supreme Court in *Bethel* stated, "... [T]he First Amendment rights of students in the public schools are not automatically coextensive with the rights of adults in other settings and must be applied in light of the special characteristics of the school environment." Bethel School District No. 403 v. Fraser (S.Ct.1986).

## § 6.11 Types of Publications

In recent years, litigation concerning student publications and their distribution have fallen into three categories: (1) school sponsored newspapers; (2) non-school or underground newspapers written and distributed by students; and (3) materials distributed by students at school but written and published by non-students. The majority of cases in the third category concerned the distribution by students of non-student written religious materials. These actions have presented arguments of free speech versus Establishment Clause restrictions.

## § 6.12 Tinker Analysis v. Forum Analysis

As discussed in *Tinker v. Des Moines*, students have constitutional rights including freedom of expression. But as noted in *Bethel v. Fraser*, there is a distinction between the political "message" of the *Tinker* armbands and the sexual innuendo that was manifested in *Bethel*. A political message, which may be a matter of public concern may only be curtailed if it "materially or substantially" disrupts the conduct of the school. This "material or substantial" disruption standard has been applied to the distribution of non-school publications in school. In other words, students may express their viewpoints in publications unless there is disruption or the reasonable forecast of disruption can be predicted from their publication. More frequently, though, the courts are applying the Forum Analysis of free speech to student publications issues.

Since the Supreme Court identified the "public forum" in Hague v. C.I.O. (S.Ct.1939), the precedent has been subject to continuous refinement. Such refinement by the courts has enunciated three types of forums and the restrictions that may be imposed upon each. The three categories are: traditional public forum "... which [has] immemorially been held in trust for use of the public and ... [has] been used for the purposes of assembly, communicating thoughts between citizens, and discussing public questions." *Hague*, supra. This forum has generally been applied to areas such as sidewalks and parks. In this forum, a speaker's free speech may be withdrawn only because of a compelling state interest and the reason must be narrowly drawn and must pass muster under strict scrutiny analysis.

The second category is a "limited public forum." This type of forum is found where the state intentionally creates or opens its property for public use. A school is generally assumed to be a closed or non-public forum but the school may purposely be opened by school officials and therefore created as a limited public forum. A limited forum will not be found to exist in a public school unless (1) there is a government interest in creating such a forum or (2) outsiders seek access to the school and there is evidence that wide access has been otherwise granted. The state is not required to create this type of forum but once created it is subject to the same regulations as a public forum and must pass the strict scrutiny analysis.

The third forum is the non-public or closed forum. This forum exists when the state does not open public property for indiscriminate public expression. "Control over access to a non-public forum can be based on subject matter and speaker identity so long as the distinctions drawn are reasonable in light of the purpose served by the forum and are viewpoint neutral." In a non-public forum the only applicable regulations are time, place and manner of distribution. The government agency must apply the content neutral standard, in other words all content must be treated the same. Slotterback v. Interboro School District (E.D.Pa.1991). See also Gregoire v. Centennial School District (3d Cir.1990).

## § 6.13   School Sponsored Publications

In 1988, after years of litigation involving school's attempts to regulate and control school sponsored newspapers, the Supreme Court decided Hazelwood School Dist. v. Kuhlmeier (S.Ct.1988). The decision in *Hazelwood* reaches beyond school sponsored publications that were at issue in this case. The *Hazelwood* decision allows the school administration to control or censor a school sponsored paper but also gives greater constitutional latitude to non-school publications. Non-school publications may be regulated only by time, place and manner of distribution, but school officials may not regulate the content of such publications. The time, place and manner restrictions of student publications are contingent upon the school having created a limited public forum as opposed to a non-public forum.

*Hazelwood* was litigated challenging a high school principal's deletion of two articles written by students on the subjects of student pregnancy and divorce. One article described the pregnancy experience of three students while the other discussed the impact of divorce on students at the high school. The principal refused to allow the articles to be printed in the high school newspaper. "The court ... undertook a forum inquiry, [and] concluded that the newspaper was a non-public forum, and held that the school officials had reasonably regulated the contents of the newspaper, thus satisfying the standard of review for state regulation in a non-public forum."

The Court in *Kuhlmeier* concluded that the First Amendment is not offended if school administrators exercise control over *school-sponsored* publications or activities. Such include "... publications, theatrical productions, and other expressive activities ..." that may be considered to have the imprimatur of the school. The action to exercise editorial control must be "... reasonably related to [a] legitimate pedagogical concern."

## § 6.14  Underground Publications

*Hazelwood*, thus, determined that school authorities may control school-sponsored activities. At the same time, it distinguished between those publications that are not connected officially or appear not to be a school publication. While the school sponsored activities may be censored for educational reasons, nonschool publications enjoy greater freedom of speech or press.

If a school permits materials to be distributed, then a limited public forum has been created. When such a forum has been established, then restrictions must be content-neutral with appropriate time, place and manner of access to the school.

In Burch v. Barker (9th Cir.1988), students distributed a student written four-page newspaper entitled *Bad Astra*. The paper was critical of the school administration but included *no* profanity, obscenity, defamatory statements, etc. School policy required that all non-school publications be submitted to the principal for prior approval. Since this was not a school-sponsored publication, *Hazelwood* did not apply, therefore, the paper was "... not within the purview of the school's exercise of reasonable editorial control." Using *Tinker* as precedent, the court ruled that the prior approval aspect of the policy violated the Constitution by suppressing speech. "... [S]uppressing speech before it is uttered, as opposed to punishment of individuals after expression has occurred, is prior restraint, which generally comes before a court bearing a 'heavy assumption' of unconstitutionality." *Burch*, supra.

## § 6.15 Prior Restraint

A number of student publication cases have been litigated because of school policies that permit prior restraint. These policies usually require any student who wishes to distribute material to present that material to the principal for prior review. The Supreme Court has identified two "evils" which will not be tolerated when considering regulations with prior restraint provisions. "First, a regulation that places 'unbridled discretion' in the hands of a government official constitutes a prior restraint and may result in censorship." The second is prior restraint regulations that do not place time limits within which the official must make a decision as to whether the proposed publication is allowable. Normally prior restraint is not *per se* unconstitutional. In student publications, some courts have held prior restraint to be *per se* unconstitutional: Burch v. Barker (9th Cir.1988); Fujishima v. Board of Education (7th Cir.1972). Other courts have found prior restraint to be constitutional only if accompanied by specific standards and procedural safeguards. Bystrom v. Fridley High School (8th Cir. 1987); Quarterman v. Byrd (4th Cir.1971).

## § 6.16  Distribution of Religious Literature

A number of recent cases have concerned the distribution of religious material at school. In these cases, the students have attempted to distribute religious newsletters written by non-students. The courts have ruled students may not distribute the Gideon Bible in school, Berger v. Rensselaer Central School Corporation (7th Cir.1993), but other court decisions have not been uniform when it comes to distributing other religious materials such as newsletters. Such cases have juxtaposed free speech protections against Establishment Clause restrictions.

Certain of these cases were decided on the basis of the previously discussed limited public forum question. Such assume that schools are a closed forum. The Supreme Court in *Hazelwood* stated, "... school facilities may be deemed to be public forums only if school authorities have by policy or by practice opened those facilities for indiscriminate use...." Therefore, if students distribute other materials, then a limited public forum is created.

The Seventh Circuit Court of Appeals in Hedges v. Wauconda Community School Dist. No. 118 (7th Cir. 1993), ruled unconstitutional a school policy that allowed some materials to be distributed but prohibited the distribution of a religious publication, *Issues and Answers*. The school policy singled out religious materials as prohibited. Such designation, singling out religious publications is not content neutral.

## § 6.17 Conclusion

School officials may control school-sponsored publications. If there are non-school publications and the school has created a "limited public forum," then the school officials may control only time, place and manner of distribution, but not content. If a school policy requires that students submit materials before distribution, then strong due process procedures must be in place or the policy is vulnerable to prior restraint challenge.

# CHAPTER 7

# SEARCH AND SEIZURE

## § 7.1 INTRODUCTION

Teachers and principals have frequently found it necessary to search students and remove from their possession items which may be harmful to them or to others. Several years ago most searches were found to be necessary to remove slingshots or pocketknives from a student's possession, or to detect and retrieve the fruits of minor thievery. Such searches remained almost entirely an affair internal to the school and seldom, if ever, involved outside authorities. Today, however, the prevalence of drugs, handguns, bombs, and/or bomb threats have broadened the importance of school search and seizure to include offenses which may subject the student to criminal prosecution. A majority of the student search and seizure cases are initiated during criminal proceedings by students who are seeking suppression of evidence obtained at school. See Matter of Gregory M. (N.Y.1993). The constitutional basis for such challenges emanates from the Fourth Amendment.

## § 7.11 Right of Privacy

The courts have ruled that students have a right to privacy which is protected by the Fourth Amendment and this right cannot be invaded unless the intrusion can be justified in terms of the school's legitimate interests.

The right of privacy is not absolute but is subject to reasonable school regulation within the bounds of reasonable suspicion.

The right of privacy, itself, is predicated on two factors being present: first, whether the person in question "exhibited an actual (subjective) expectation of privacy," and, second, whether the "expectation of privacy be one that society is prepared to recognize as 'reasonable.'" The Supreme Court has said that: "The Fourth Amendment protects people, not places. What a person knowingly exposes to the public, even in his own home or office, is not a subject of Fourth Amendment protection.... But what he seeks to preserve as private, even in an area accessible to the public, may be constitutionally protected." Katz v. United States (S.Ct.1967).

A one-way mirror in a boys' restroom in a high school used to observe students buying marijuana did not violate students' right of privacy. Stern v. New Haven Community Schools (E.D.Mich.1981). The court reasoned that the community had a significant interest in school discipline and protection of students from drugs. The test according to the court is one of balancing the school's interests in the surveillance against the plaintiff's interest in privacy. Here the balance was in favor of the school.

## § 7.2 FOURTH AMENDMENT

The Fourth Amendment of the United States Constitution provides: "The right of people to be secure in their persons, houses, papers, and effects, against unreasonable searches and seizures, shall not be violated, and no warrants shall issue, but upon probable cause, supported by oath or affirmation, and particularly describing the place to be searched, and the persons or things to be seized."

The Fourth Amendment has five important components. First, it enunciates and protects the *right* of people "to be secure in their persons, houses, papers and effects." Second, it protects persons from *unreasonable* searches and seizures. Third, a search cannot be instituted without government showing *probable cause* or giving evidence that a search is necessary. Fourth, the search must be *specific*, describing the place to be searched and the articles to be seized. Last, a *magistrate* or *judge* is interposed between the individual and the government, requiring that the government justify with evidence the necessity of the search.

Application of three of these five components is easily made to student searches in public schools. Students have a right of privacy—to be secure in their persons, papers and effects—and this right protects them against unreasonable searches and seizures. Moreover, any search must be specific as to what is sought in the search and the location where it is secreted. The courts do not, however, require that school officials be able to provide evidence constituting probable cause or that they obtain a warrant from a judge justifying a search.

The Supreme Court in New Jersey v. T.L.O. (S.Ct. 1985), established the prevailing precedent regarding school searches and seizures. The Court held that the Fourth Amendment applies to schools and in order for searches to be constitutionally valid reasonableness must prevail. The Court stated that "the legality of a search of a student should depend on the reasonableness, under all circumstances, of the search." According to the

Court in *T.L.O.*, the constitutional validity of a search is to be determined at two levels. The first level involves consideration of whether the search is justified at its inception. The inception of the search is the point at which reasonable suspicion comes into play. Was the motivation for the search reasonable in light of the information obtained by the school official? The second level concerns the reasonableness of the search itself; the "measures adopted for the search must be reasonably related to the objectives of the search and not excessively intrusive in light of the age and sex of the student and the nature of the infraction." A search is not reasonable if it lacks specificity, or if it excessively intrudes on the student's privacy. (See Chapters 13 and 16.)

## § 7.21  Reasonable Suspicion

Reasonable suspicion is a standard less rigorous of proof than the requirement of probable cause. Probable cause requires more than mere suspicion or even reasonable suspicion. School officials need only have "reasonable suspicion," not the more stringent "probable cause." Reasonable suspicion is a belief or opinion based on the facts or circumstances.

Although the standard of "reasonable suspicion" is a lower standard than that of the "probable cause" required for police to obtain a warrant, it is not so unrestrictive as to place no constraints on school personnel.

A student's freedom from unreasonable search and seizure must be balanced against the need for school officials to maintain order and discipline and to protect the health and welfare of all the students. For example, in a case where a student's car was searched revealing cocaine, after an assistant principal observed that the student had glassy eyes, a flushed face, slurred speech, smelled of alcohol, and walked with an unsteady gait. The court found this condition to be ample evidence to support reasonable suspicion. Shamberg v. State (Alaska App.1988). "Reasonable suspicion of wrong doing is a common-sense conclusion about human behavior upon which practical people—including governmental officials—are entitled to rely." United States v. Cortez (S.Ct.1981).

## § 7.22 Inception of Search

The facts leading to the initiation of a search must indicate that the suspicion was reasonable from the inception. In a case where a student was observed in an office where items had been stolen and was also found to have unauthorized objects in his possession, the court concluded that reasonable suspicion was established for a search of the student's locker. R.D.L. v. State (Fla.App. 1986).

## § 7.23 Intrusiveness of Search

Whether a search is reasonable is a subjective determination and the court's decision will be based on the individual facts of each case. It is clear, though, that excessively intrusive searches must be supported by a strong degree of suspicion by the school officials. The courts will require a corresponding relationship between the extensiveness of grounds supporting reasonable suspicion and the degree to which a search intrudes on a student's privacy. A more extensive and intrusive search, however, may require more evidence to establish reasonable suspicion.

## § 7.24  Context of Search

Further, the courts have held that "what is reasonable depends on the context within which the search takes place." A context indicating a loosely articulated factual background that is not necessarily related to a specific violation is too nebulous to support "reasonable suspicion." The lack of specificity in a search of large groups of students without specific knowledge of rule violations by any particular student(s) is not reasonable. Individualized suspicion is essential as a prerequisite to a constitutional search. One court has cautioned that even though general searches are easier and may be more effective in finding illegal contraband, such searches will not survive the reasonableness test without individualized suspicion unless other safeguards are available to assure respect for individual privacy.

## § 7.25  Exclusionary Rule

School officials should be concerned with removing contraband from the school environment for the betterment of other students and not for use in the criminal prosecution of students. Because materials seized in public schools are frequently illegal and may be turned over to law enforcement officials, the "exclusionary rule" has often been raised where the student is ultimately tried in a court of law. The question, thus, arises, can illegal materials seized by school officials be used in criminal prosecutions?

In 1914, in Weeks v. United States (S.Ct.1914), the Supreme Court established that evidence seized without a warrant could not be used in federal courts for federal prosecution. This doctrine, the *Weeks Doctrine*, thereafter excluded evidence obtained illegally by federal officials from use in federal trials.

In Mapp v. Ohio (S.Ct.1961), the Supreme Court expanded the *Weeks Doctrine* or "exclusionary rule" to ban illegally seized evidence in state courts. This extension of the exclusionary rule has been litigated numerous times in public education cases.

The Supreme Court in *T.L.O.* noted the courts have "... split over whether the exclusionary rule is an appropriate remedy for Fourth Amendment violations committed by school authorities." The Court further stated the issue was not resolved by *T.L.O.* when it noted "... our determination that the search at issue in [*T.L.O.*] did not violate the Fourth Amendment implies no particular resolution of the question of the applicability of the exclusionary rule." A majority of the courts have ruled materials seized by school officials may be used as evidence in criminal prosecution.

## § 7.26   Liability for Illegal Search

One may wonder what the consequences are of an illegal search of students by teachers or school administrators. What redress is available for the student? As discussed above, if the search is illegal, its fruits may or may not be excluded from prosecution of the student should a criminal trial ensue. Beyond this, the student may conceivably bring an action under Title 42 U.S.C.A., Section 1983. (See Chapter 12, Civil Liability.) As discussed elsewhere in this book, a student may seek damages if school officials maliciously deny his or her constitutional rights. The Sixth Circuit in the *Williams* case, supra, noted "government officials performing discretionary functions, generally are shielded from liability for civil damages insofar as their conduct does not violate clearly established statutory or constitutional rights of which a reasonable person would have known." It is important to note that if school officials deny constitutional rights, but do so in the good faith fulfillment of their responsibilities and not in ignorance and disregard for established indisputable principles of law, then no liability will occur. This immunity is accorded only within the bounds of reason. When school officials, in *Doe v. Renfrow*, infra, strip searched a child "without any individualized suspicion and without reasonable cause," the court said: "We suggest as strongly as possible that the conduct herein described exceeded the 'bounds of reason' by two and a half country miles. It is not enough for us to declare that the little girl involved was indeed deprived of her constitutional and basic human rights. We must also permit her to seek damages from those who caused this humiliation...."

## § 7.27 Police Involvement

Because school officials may on the basis of reasonable suspicion search students without a search warrant, police will on occasion seek school assistance from a school principal or other school official in searching students. The stronger probable cause standard to which police must adhere makes it more advantageous and opportune for police to merely convince a school principal that a search is needed. If this is done, the court must decide whether the school official was, in fact, conducting the search based on his/her own initiation or whether the search was really conducted at the instigation of the police. A number of courts have ruled where police are involved, and in charge, that the full complement of Fourth Amendment rights apply, and the higher standard of probable cause must prevail, with Miranda warnings, and other trappings of a full-fledged police search. Simply because a student is on school grounds does not mean the police officers are not bound by appropriate constitutional duties. The lesser "reasonable suspicion" standard is not available to school officials if the search is carried out at the behest of the police. In interest of F.P. v. State (Fla.App.1988). If a school official does not act on his/her own initiative and follows the request of the police, then the school officials would be acting as an agent of the police. In this capacity they would need consent from the student or probable cause that the law had been violated to search a student.

## § 7.28  Consent

School authorities do not need the consent of the student in order to conduct a search. On the other hand, if the police participate in the search, they must have a warrant or obtain the student's consent. Consent, though, must be given freely and willingly without coercion. Accordingly, the police cannot ask a school official to influence the student's decision to permit a search. Students are under the control of the school and will in most instances respond positively to school authority, thus use of school authority may implicitly involve coercion. Thus, school authority cannot be used by police to acquire the student's consent.

## § 7.3  CANINE SEARCHES

In recent years, because of the use of drugs in public schools, officials have used dogs to sniff out contraband.

These canine searches have been viewed by the courts with mixed reactions.

The Tenth Circuit Court of Appeals in Zamora v. Pomeroy (10th Cir.1981), upheld the use of dogs in the exploratory sniffing of lockers. The court noted that since the schools gave notice at the beginning of the year that the lockers might be periodically opened, the lockers were jointly possessed by both student and school. With joint possession either party can effect entry. The court further stated that since the school officials had a duty to maintain a proper educational environment it was necessary for them to inspect lockers.

The Seventh Circuit Court in Doe v. Renfrow (7th Cir.1980), held that school officials stood *in loco parentis* and had a right to use dogs to seek out drugs because of the diminished expectations of privacy inherent in the public schools. School officials had a duty to maintain an educational environment that was conducive to learning. Although the court ruled in *Doe* that the dog search was constitutional, the subsequent strip search performed by school officials in this case was ruled to have violated the privacy rights of the child.

In a federal district court case, Jones v. Latexo Independent School District (E.D.Tex.1980), the decision was different from that in *Doe* and *Zamora*. The school district in *Jones* used dogs to sniff both students and automobiles. The court ruled, in the absence of individualized suspicion, that the sniffing of the students was too intrusive and not reasonable. Moreover, because the students did not have access to their automobiles during the school day, the school's interest in having dogs sniff the cars was minimal, and was therefore also unreasonable.

In another dog case, Horton v. Goose Creek Independent School District (5th Cir.1982), the court stated, "The problem presented in this case is convergence of two troubling questions. First, is the sniff of a drug-detecting dog a 'search' within the purview of the Fourth Amendment? Second, to what extent does the Fourth Amendment protect students against searches by school administrators seeking to maintain a safe environment conducive to education?" In response to the first question the court stated, "We accordingly hold that the sniff of the lockers and cars did not constitute a search and, therefore, we need make no inquiry into the reasonableness of the sniffing of the lockers and automobiles." Concerning the second question the court ruled that school officials may search students if they have "reasonable cause" but "the intrusion on dignity and personal security that goes with the type of canine inspection of the student's person involved in this case cannot be justified by the need to prevent abuse of drugs and alcohol when there is no individualized suspicion; and we hold it unconstitutional." It should be noted that all canine searches pre-date the U.S. Supreme Court case of *New Jersey v. T.L.O.* Using the standards in *T.L.O.* it would appear that individual suspicion or a very high risk to the health and safety of the student body would be required to justify a canine search.

## § 7.4 STRIP SEARCHES

The courts have allowed school officials to search students if they have reasonable suspicion that the student is in possession of something illegal, violating school regulations, or that which is secreted may be harmful to the health and safety of other students. During the

1980s the courts ruled in the majority of cases that a strip search was too intrusive. The courts reasoned that the more intrusive the search becomes the more necessary is a showing of probable cause. In Bellnier v. Lund (N.D.N.Y.1977), the court ruled that a teacher who strip searched the class trying to locate three dollars violated the Fourth Amendment. However, in *Bellnier*, the court noted that the relative slight danger of the missing money had to be considered and if something more dangerous were present, the result might be different. The only strip search upheld during the 1980s involved drugs. Rone By and Through Payne v. Daviess County Board of Education (Ky.App.1983).

It appears that recently the courts have been more lenient in allowing strip searches where drugs are involved. The Sixth Circuit Court of Appeals concluded in one case that a strip search was valid because school officials were searching for drugs. After talking with concerned parents and students, school officials believed a student possessed a "white powder substance," the student was requested to remove her t-shirt and lower her jeans to her knees. In spite of this high degree of intrusiveness the court held that the search complied with *T.L.O.* standards and was ". . . not unreasonable in light of the item sought (narcotics) in conducting a search so personally intrusive in nature." Williams by Williams v. Ellington (6th Cir.1991).

In another drug search case, a sixteen year old student who was enrolled in a behavioral disorder program was known to use drugs and to hide them in his crotch. School personnel observed that the student appeared "too well endowed" and reported this to school administrators. The following day two school administrators took the student to the boy's locker room and required him to remove his clothes. The administrators rejected the alternative of a pat down as excessively intrusive and ineffective in detecting drugs. The student was requested to change into gym clothes while the administrators stood approximately ten to twelve feet away and visually inspected him. Previously, the student told a teacher he crotched drugs, and a policeman told the Dean of Students earlier he had information the student was selling marijuana and had failed a urine test for cocaine, therefore reasonable suspicion was cumulative. Because these incidents were reported by various individuals, there was sufficient reasonable suspicion to conduct the strip search and, given the circumstances, the method of search was the least intrusive to confirm the suspicion. Cornfield by Lewis v. Consolidated High School District No. 230 (7th Cir.1993).

In a case of similar factual nature, but with different results because of the lesser danger involved, a West Virginia court ruled a strip search for missing money was unreasonable. The court stated that stealing "... should never be condoned or encouraged in our schools, but in evaluating the nature of the situation in terms of the danger it presents to other students, it does not begin to approach the threat posed by possession of weapons or drugs." State of West Virginia v. Mark Anthony B. (W.Va.1993).

## § 7.5  LOCKERS AND DESKS

Since the *T.L.O.* case, most courts have concluded that no expectation of privacy exists for school lockers. Lockers are made available to the students for limited purposes of storing legitimate materials needed for educational purposes. Some courts have held there is no reasonable expectation of privacy at all if school officials have stressed by policy that lockers are not private property. One court stated, "School administrators may adopt a locker policy retaining ownership and possessory control of school lockers and give notice of that policy to students." Such policy permits school searches. In Interest of Isiah B. (Wis.1993).

The school's control over lockers and desks was clearly justified by a New York court, which said that: "Indeed, it is doubtful if a school would be properly discharging its duty of supervision over students, if it failed to retain control over the lockers. Not only have the school authorities a right to inspect but this right becomes a duty when suspicion arises that something of an illegal nature may be secreted there." People v. Overton (N.Y.1967).

The Supreme Court of Wisconsin held constitutional a random search of student lockers. In this case, the school was having considerable problems with weapons. Guns on school buses, guns in school, and multiple gunshots at a school dance were found to be justifiable reasons to have a random search of lockers as a "preventive measure." Because of a written policy stating that the school retained ownership of the lockers, the court found that: "... students had no reasonable expectation of privacy in those lockers." The court further observed "our holding is an example or adaptation of constitutional principles to a modern crisis." *In Interest of Isiah B.*, supra.

## § 7.6 AUTOMOBILE SEARCH

Few cases are available to define the law governing searches of students' automobiles in school parking lots.

The precedents which do shed light on the subject suggest that there is no difference in the school official's prerogative in searching autos or in conducting locker searches. Reasonable suspicion is required before such a search can be undertaken.

In an illustrative case, a reliable student informant told the vice principal that a student was selling marijuana in the school parking lot, the student was searched, whereupon a large amount of cash and a telephone pager were found. The offending student's locker was then searched and nothing else was discovered. The school officials then searched his car and a locked briefcase inside the car. Marijuana was found. The court ruled the search was reasonable and observed that school officials were confronted with exigent circumstances that warranted an immediate search because the car could have been removed from school grounds. State v. Slattery (Wash.App.1990).

In another case, a student was intoxicated, his speech slurred, his eyes glassy, and he could not maintain his balance, and to make matters worse, if possible, his car was improperly parked. He, as may be expected, was evasive in answering questions regarding his car. As a result, his car was searched and cocaine was found. The court ruled that the school officials had "reasonable suspicion" to search the student's car. Shamberg v. State (Alaska App.1988).

In another case the court upheld the search of a student's car, and stated "... the suspicion that marijuana was to be sold to high school students justified the intrusiveness of the search of the [student's] person, locker and car." People in the Interest of P.E.A. (Colo. 1988).

In yet another case, a student who was attempting to "skip school" was stopped. He was patted down, made to remove his shoes and socks, and to pull his pants down to his knees. The court ruled that the principal "had reasonable grounds to investigate why [the student] was attempting to leave school and was justified in 'patting down' ... for safety reasons." The principal then searched the student's car. This, the court felt, went too far and was unreasonable because of excessive intrusion. The car search was not sufficiently connected to the inception of the search and therefore not justified. Coronado v. State (Tex.Crim.App.1992).

## § 7.7  FIELD TRIP SEARCHES

Many schools have established the practice of searching all the baggages of students who are participating on school field trips. The courts are currently split on such searches. The pre-*T.L.O.* ruling challenged school officials' rights to search student baggage before a band concert tour. The purpose of the search was to deter disruptive conduct. The court ruled the search was unreasonable because it was not "particularized with respect to each individual searched." Kuehn v. Renton School District No. 403 (Wash.1985).

On the other hand, in the post-*T.L.O.* case, the court ruled that hand luggage searched prior to a field trip was justified under the Fourth Amendment. This decision was based on the presence of a legitimate interest of school administrators to deter students from taking contraband on field trips. "The deterrent effect of the board's search policy advances a legitimate interest ... in preventing students from taking contraband...." The fact that this deterrence is not perfect, because students can hide some contraband, e.g., small quantities of drugs, does not render the search unconstitutional. Desilets v. Clearview Board of Education (N.J.Super.1993).

## § 7.8 DRUG TESTING

The private sector, beyond state and federal government agencies, is now resorting to drug testing as a means to deter drug use and ensure job health and safety. Where governmental agencies are concerned the collection and testing of urine constitutes a "search" within the meaning of the Fourth Amendment. Any procedure used to collect samples invades a personal function "traditionally shielded by great privacy."

The United States Supreme Court in 1989 ruled on two cases concerning search of governmental employees: one railway workers and the other customs officials. The Court upheld drug testing of these employees because the government was found to have a compelling interest in protecting the public's health and safety. Because customs officials carry firearms and railway workers operate dangerous machinery, they must always be alert and sharply cognizant of their immediate physical situation. The Court ruled individual suspicion was not required before drug testing. The Court did note that in the absence of health and safety of the general public, governmental officials must have reasonable individualized suspicion before testing. Skinner v. Railway Labor Executives Assoc. (S.Ct.1989); National Treasury Employees Union v. Von Raab (S.Ct.1989).

Although no cases involving elementary and secondary students have been litigated by the U.S. Supreme Court, lower court decisions are split. There have been four

cases, three involving the testing of students for extracurricular activities and one for testing of all students.
Three of the four elementary and secondary cases have
ruled that drug testing of students violates the Fourth
Amendment.

Where a school policy requiring all students to submit
urine samples for drug and alcohol analysis as a part of
the child's physical examination was ruled unconstitutional, the school official argued that this was no search,
because testing was a part of a medical procedure used
for the purpose of remedying a drug or alcohol problem
at school. The court ruled that the testing program did
not comport with the *T.L.O.* reasonableness standard.
The program, the court said, "violates [the student's]
right to be free of unreasonable search and seizure, ...
due process ... [and] the [student's] legitimate expectation of privacy and personal security." Odenheim by
Odenheim v. Carlstadt–East Rutherford Regional School
District (N.J.Super.1985).

Three other federal court cases have involved random
drug testing of students participating in extracurricular
activities. The Seventh Circuit ruled public schools
could randomly test students who participated in interscholastic athletic programs. Although the court found
that the search fell under the penumbra of the Fourth
Amendment, the testing conformed to the reasonableness
standard established in *T.L.O.* Schaill v. Tippecanoe
County School Corp. (7th Cir.1988).

Another court has strongly disagreed with the *Schaill*
holding. The Ninth Circuit Court of Appeals has ruled
that "participation in interscholastic sports does not
significantly diminish a high school athlete's reasonable
expectation that he will not be compelled to submit to

suspicionless drug testing by urinalysis." The court commented on the *Schaill* case, saying "... the Seventh Circuit has unduly minimized the privacy interests of students ... [and] we simply do not agree...." Acton v. Vernonia School District 47J (9th Cir.1994).

In yet another case involving drug testing of all students who participated in interscholastic programs, another federal court held that the students' constitutional rights were violated by the school district's requirement of urine tests administered to all participating students. This court also criticized the *Schaill* decision holding that the critical requirement of individualized suspicion was missing and said that random testing constituted an impermissible search. Brooks v. East Chambers Consol. Independent School Dist. (S.D.Tex.1989).

## § 7.9  METAL DETECTOR SEARCHES

In New York the Board of Education established guidelines for the use of metal detectors in high school that required a team of special police officers from the Central Task Force for School Safety to set up a scanning post in the school's main lobby. All students entering the school were subject to the search although the officers could choose to limit the search by any random formula if the waiting lines became too long. A student was searched with the metal detectors whereupon a switchblade knife was found with a 4 to 5 inch blade. She was charged with criminal possession of a weapon, a Class A misdemeanor. The student filed an action to suppress the knife from being used as evidence. The court stated that an administrative search is upheld as reasonable when the intrusion involved in the search is no greater than necessary to satisfy the governmental interest underlying the need for the search. In other words, in determining whether the search is reasonable, the courts balance the degree of intrusion, including the discretion given to the person conducting the search, against the severity of the damages posed. The court found the metal detector search satisfied the balancing test and was not unreasonable because the school had a compelling need for security. People v. Dukes (N.Y.1992). See also 75 Opinion California Attorney General 155, 1992 WL 469726.

# CHAPTER 8

# STUDENT DISCIPLINE

## § 8.1 INTRODUCTION

Courts have long recognized that if schools are to be properly conducted, teachers and principals must be given authority to maintain an orderly and responsible learning environment. This requires that students live and study in a relationship of mutual accord with other students and with the school faculty. Disruption of the school social setting will undoubtedly have deleterious effects on the quality of the educational program. Recognizing this, courts have uniformly held that student conduct is under the reasonable control of school officials.

Parents, by law, acquiesce in this control over their children when they place the child in the charge of the school. Thus, the teacher and principal are said to stand *in loco parentis*, in the place of the parent, in the performance and exercise of those functions necessary to operate the schools. "School discipline is an area which courts enter with great hesitation and reluctance—and rightly so. School officials are trained and paid to determine what form of punishment best addresses a particular student's transgression. They are in a far better position than is a black-robed judge to decide what to do with a disobedient child at school. They can best determine, for instance, whether a suspension or an after-school detention will be more effective in correcting a student's behavior. Because of their expertise and their closeness to the situation—and because we do not want them to fear court challenges to their every act—school officials are given wide discretion in their disciplinary actions." Donaldson v. Board of Educ. (Ill.App.1981). See also Smith v. School City of Hobart (N.D.Ind.1993).

## § 8.2　IN LOCO PARENTIS

To stand *in loco parentis* means that the teacher has the authority and the duty to guide, correct, and punish the child in the accomplishment of educational objectives. The teacher is the substitute for the parent while the child is in school and for those endeavors which bear directly on the school. The teacher, however, does not have unlimited control over the student and, of course, neither does the parent for that matter. Child abuse is prohibited whether it is committed by a parent or a teacher. To stand in the place of the parent, though, means that the teacher can control the conduct of the student in various ways, including corporal punishment where permitted by state statute. Blackstone, the great jurist, in summarizing the law of England in 1788 wrote that the schoolmaster had only that portion of parental powers necessary for the conduct of the school. Authority to control students is not necessarily vested in the teacher through affirmative school board policy; it, instead, is derived from the common law relationship between teacher and pupil. In other words, a teacher is assumed to stand *in loco parentis* unless state law or school board policy removes that authority. It has historically been held by the courts that there exists, on the part of students, the obligation of civil deportment, obedience to reasonable commands, and a respect for rights

of other pupils. Students must submit to these requirements and teachers have an inherent duty to see to it
that good order is carried out. These obligations on the
part of both students and teachers constitute the common law of the school.

Implicit in common law authority is the power of the
state to control student conduct for the welfare of the
school. Statutes or regulations may place limits on the
teacher's authority to discipline students. Where statute
or rule limits the teacher's discretion, the teacher must
act accordingly. The authority of school officials acting
within their state prescribed powers has been consistently reaffirmed by the courts. "School officials are afforded broad discretion in enforcement of school codes because of the important interests and responsibilities affiliated with school administration." Wiemerslage v.
Maine Township High School Dist. 207 (N.D.Ill.1993).

## § 8.21 Reasonable Rules

If students break school rules, they may be held accountable. The broken rule, though, must be a reasonable one. Courts are relatively vague as to what constitutes reasonableness, but have generally held that a rule
must, first, be motivated by reason and humanity premised on accomplishment of some desirable educational
result and second the teacher must act in good faith in
enforcing the rule. By standing *in loco parentis* teachers
have a legal presumption in favor of the correctness of
their actions. To exceed this presumption, a teacher
must have been motivated by malice and with disregard
for the pupil's welfare.

That which constitutes reasonableness is often litigated. For example, in a case where a student was expelled

for having approximately 100 pills that contained caffeine, and later claimed in court that the punishment was "arbitrary, unreasonable and excessive," the court said the punishment was neither arbitrary, unreasonable, capricious nor oppressive because rules prohibiting such conduct were in the best interest of the school. Wilson v. Collinsville Community Unit School District No. 10 (Ill.App.1983).

## § 8.3 CORPORAL PUNISHMENT

Corporal punishment for many years was a widely accepted medium for disciplining school children. This tradition has historic roots in Western culture. The great Samuel Johnson, the famous lexicographer, lamented the decline in corporal punishment in the English schools of the eighteenth century and said, "There is now less flogging in our great schools than formerly, but then less is learned there; so that what the boys get at one end they lose at the other."

During the last several decades there has been substantial debate about the appropriateness of corporal punishment in schools. During this period, the 1970s, two states prohibited corporal punishment, and during the decade of the eighties other states enacted legislation abolishing such punishment. It is reported that today approximately one-half of the states prohibit corporal punishment. Those states that have no statutes regarding corporal punishment are governed by the common law right of school personnel to reasonably punish students.

## § 8.31 Assault and Battery

Corporal punishment may invoke the charge against the teacher of assault and battery. Such actions may be brought either in criminal law or in tort. If the criminal action is successful against a teacher, the teacher may be subject to a fine or imprisonment. In a tort action, the unsuccessful defendant may suffer monetary damages. Torts are discussed in more detail in a later chapter of this book.

Actions against teachers for criminal assault and battery are relatively infrequent. One court has said that whether such an action is successful depends on the circumstances and the severity of the punishment. Some of the factors to be considered are: the prior conduct of the student, whether there was malice on the part of the teacher, the motivation for punishment, the pupil's size and strength and the effect of the pupil's conduct on other pupils in the school. People ex rel. Hogan v. Newton (N.Y.1945).

Prior conduct of the pupil is an important factor for the court to consider. Punishment may be permissibly more severe if the student has a long history of rule infractions. In a case where a teacher was convicted at trial of criminal assault and battery for whipping a pupil who had dropped a book from the school auditorium balcony, the state appeals court reversed the decision because the student's prior misbehavior had not been taken into account in considering the reasonableness of the punishment. People v. Mummert (N.Y.1944).

## § 8.32  Cruel and Unusual Punishment

The only United States Supreme Court case directed to corporal punishment is Ingraham v. Wright (S.Ct.1977). It involved an action by students who claimed corporal punishment constituted "cruel and unusual" punishment as proscribed by the Eighth Amendment. The case also addressed whether the Fourteenth Amendment required due process before paddling. In this case, the school principal and an assistant had whipped two students so severely that one suffered a hematoma requiring medical attention. The Court, while admitting that the punishment was possibly too severe, nevertheless, denied the students relief under the Eighth and the Fourteenth Amendments.

In commenting generally on corporal punishment, the Court said that even though professional and public opinion is sharply divided on the practice, at common law a single principle has governed the use of corporal punishment: "Teachers may impose reasonable but not excessive force to discipline a child.... The prevalent rule in this country today privileges such force as a teacher or administrator reasonably believes to be necessary for [the child's] proper control, training and education."

Further, the Court noted that to the extent that the force used by the teacher is unreasonable or excessive, virtually all states provide the student with a possible criminal law remedy and additionally a possible claim for damages may lie in a tort action.

With regard to tort, the Court said that among the important considerations are the "seriousness of the offense, the attitude and past behavior of the child, the nature and severity of the punishment, the age and strength of the child, and the availability of less severe but equally effective means of discipline." Noting that the law could provide redress to the student in both tort and criminal law, the Court refused to extend the Eighth Amendment to effectively prohibit use of corporal punishment in the schools nor the Fourteenth Amendment to require due process before paddling.

In considering the constitutional question, the Court gave a thorough analysis of the intent of the "cruel and unusual" provision of the Eighth Amendment finding that the prohibition was meant to apply to criminal cases where, historically, persons were punished by being maimed in various ways, including having their ears or hands cut off, or having been drawn and quartered before being put to death or crucified. Such historical antecedents to the Eighth Amendment led the Court to conclude that public school spankings were not envisioned as falling within the amendment's proscriptions. The Court concluded by saying "The openness of the public school and its supervision by the community afford significant safeguards against the kinds of abuses from which the Eighth Amendment protects the prisoner. In virtually every community where corporal punishment is permitted in the schools, these safeguards are reinforced by the legal constraints of common law. . . . We conclude that when public school teachers or administrators impose disciplinary corporal punishment, the Eighth Amendment is inapplicable."

With regard to a plaintiff's assertion that procedural due process must be given each student before punishment, the Court disagreed. Even though the Court found that physical punishment fell within the scope of "liberty" as a substantive due process interest, the need to have notice and a hearing prior to a spanking was obviated by the longstanding common law tradition which gives the teacher a privilege to administer moderate punishment.

## § 8.33  Substantive Rights

The federal Circuit Courts of Appeals have not been in agreement as to whether the U.S. Supreme Court in *Ingraham* meant to encompass protection against corporal punishment as a substantive constitutional right.

The U.S. Courts of Appeals for the Fourth and Tenth Circuits have sought definitive standards with regard to punishment. Both have maintained that punishment may be so severe as to constitute a denial of a substantive due process interest. The Appeals Court for the Fourth Circuit, in Hall v. Tawney (4th Cir.1980), said that the scope and magnitude was of a different level than commonly considered in tort law, whether "ten licks rather than five licks" is excessive; rather, the court observed that "substantive due process is concerned with violation of personal rights of privacy and bodily security of so different an order of magnitude" and that an overly simplistic application, such as counting of licks, is not necessarily appropriate.

The U.S. Court of Appeals for the Tenth Circuit, in Garcia v. Miera (10th Cir.1987), has followed the rationale of Hall v. Tawney. This court concluded "that grossly excessive corporal punishment may indeed constitute a violation of substantive due process rights."

The views expressed in *Hall* and *Garcia* have been followed and reinforced by precedents from the Third and Eighth Circuits. The Third Circuit said: "[A] decision to discipline a student, if accomplished through excessive force and appreciable physical pain, may constitute an invasion of the child's Fifth Amendment liberty interest in his personal security and a violation of substantive due process prohibited by the Fourteenth Amendment." Metzger v. Osbeck (3d Cir.1985).

The Eighth Circuit said we agree that "at some point the administration of corporal punishment may violate a student's liberty interest in his personal security and substantive due process rights."

Even though the nebulous nature of the U.S. Supreme Court's decision in *Ingraham* leaves the question in doubt, and the U.S. Courts of Appeals are not in agreement, it appears that the view enunciated in *Hall* and *Garcia* may suggest the emerging prevailing precedent whereby a substantive due process interest is implicated if corporal punishment is excessively immoderate, inhumane or brutal.

## § 8.4  CHILD ABUSE

While the phenomena of child abuse and neglect are ageless, only recently have they been given national attention. Commencing in 1962, state legislatures began enacting legislation designed to deal with problems of child abuse and neglect, and in 1974 a federal statute, the Child Abuse Prevention and Treatment Act was enacted. The purpose of this legislation was to provide federal financial assistance to the states that had implemented programs for identification, prevention, and treatment of instances of child abuse and neglect. Currently, all fifty states plus the District of Columbia, Puerto Rico, and the Virgin Islands have enacted various forms of child abuse and neglect statutes. A component of the 1974 act was the creation of the National Center of Child Abuse and Neglect, which developed the Model Child Protection Act (Model Act). The Model Act has been used extensively throughout the nation for development of individual state child abuse legislation.

## § 8.41 Corporal Punishment/Child Abuse

Corporal punishment, if excessive, may run counter to most child abuse statutes. This conflict between corporal punishment and child abuse statutes has not gone without litigation. In one such case, where an assistant principal paddled students for smoking, a parent reported the administrator's action to the appropriate state agency and charged child abuse. Since the child had marks from the paddling the case worker ruled the charges were "substantiated" because the child abuse law prescribed that markings after paddlings was evidence of abuse. The administrator's name was placed on the State Central Registry for Child Abuse. The administrator appealed to have her name removed, whereupon the court ruled the paddling was not abusive.

Reasonable paddling may be legal but excessive punishment may be abuse. This scenario has been played out numerous times in courts. Arkansas Dept. of Human Services v. Caldwell (Ark.App.1992).

Where allowed, punishment administered must be moderate, with a proper instrument taking into account the age, sex, size and overall physical strength of the child. Within these broad limits a teacher must balance the gravity of the offense with the extent of the punishment to be meted out. Because teachers are usually present when student mischief transpires and normally know the manner, look, tone, gestures, language, setting and general circumstances of the offense, courts will allow teachers considerable latitude in their exercise of discretion. Yet, punishment which is cruel and excessive will not be tolerated by the courts. Cruel and excessive punishment is evidence of malice which will forego the teacher's *in loco parentis* privilege.

Malice may be evidenced by showing that the instrument used to administer the punishment was improper. An important consideration, here, is whether the instrument is the type normally used and commonly accepted in the community or in other schools. For example, paddles are acceptable instruments, provided the size, shape and weight are reasonable.

## § 8.42 Child Abuse Definition

The federal Model Act included the following succinct definition of child abuse and neglect: "*[C]hild abuse and neglect* means the physical or mental injury, sexual abuse, negligent treatment, or maltreatment of a child under the age of eighteen by a person who is responsible for the child's welfare under circumstances which indicate that the child's health or welfare is harmed or threatened thereby, as determined in accordance with regulations prescribed by the Secretary."

Commonly contained within state child abuse and neglect statutes is a purpose statement that outlines the intent of the legislation. Typically, the primary purpose of child abuse and neglect statutes is to identify children who are being abused or neglected so that state protection may be provided. A commonly enunciated purpose of child abuse laws, as stated in the Virginia law, is the state's desire to preserve "the family life of the parents and children, where possible, by enhancing parental capacity for adequate child care."

Nearly all states have accepted the federal definition of a child as a person under the age of eighteen but such statutes vary widely in regard to definitions of abuse and neglect. Some states provide their own individualized definitions, yet a number of states attempt to distinguish between child abuse and child neglect.

## § 8.43  Child Abuse Reporting

An integral component of state child abuse and neglect statutes is the mandated reporting of suspected instances of child abuse and neglect. Statutes protect teachers who report parental abuse from counteractions in court.

All states have enacted legislation which grants immunity to persons who report child abuse and neglect from actions for criminal and civil liability if the report *is made in good faith*. For example, the Virginia immunity statute states: "A person making a report ... shall be immune from any civil or criminal liability in connection therewith unless it is proven that such person acted with malicious intent."

A 1985 Oregon case, McDonald v. State, By and Through CSD (Or.1985), serves to illustrate the effect of statutory immunity granted reporters of child abuse and neglect. In this case, a teacher observed scratches on the neck of one of her pupils and had him examined by a child development specialist. When questioned about how he had acquired the scratches, the child told two stories. One version attributed the scratches to his kitten, and the second version suggested that the child's mother had made the scratches by choking him, as the child said she had done on several occasions. The principal was informed, who in turn instructed the child development specialist to report the incident to the state's Children's Services Division. The child was removed from parental custody and placed in a foster home. Subsequently, the parents appeared in court where the allegations of child abuse were ruled groundless and the child was reinstated with his parents. The parents brought suit against Children's Services Division, principal, teacher, and others. The court dismissed the parents' complaint and indicated that although two versions of the derivation of scratches were told and that the principal relied only upon the opinion of the child development specialist, both the principal and teacher had acted in good faith and had reasonable grounds to report suspected child abuse.

## § 8.44 Child Abuse: Penalty for Failure to Report

In order to gain compliance from those persons, including teachers, who are required to report instances of child abuse and neglect, most states permit the assessment of penalties for knowing and willful failure to report. These states have enacted criminal penalties for those persons guilty of not reporting suspected cases of child abuse and neglect. Other states have legislated both criminal and civil penalties, and a few states have provided for only civil remedies.

States that have established criminal penalties for persons found guilty of not reporting instances of child abuse and neglect commonly classify such an offense as a misdemeanor. Punishments normally include fines up to $1,000, and/or jail sentences up to one year.

## § 8.45 Child Abuse: Defenses for Failure to Report

Included in child abuse statutes that provide criminal penalties for failure to report child abuse are terms such as "reasonable cause to believe," "cause to believe," or, as in the case of Oklahoma, "reason to believe." Within these terms rest the nucleus for a teacher's discretion in reporting or not reporting child abuse. These terms may also serve to defend a teacher who is accused of not reporting. Such terms are considered to provide an objective standard on which to determine compliance. Less rigorous terms, such as "knows or suspects" are considered to provide a subjective standard and one that may permit mandatory reporters to shield their own poor judgments. Regardless of whether the standard is objective or subjective, a teacher charged with failure to report suspected child abuse under the criminal code of a state will attempt to show that there was not "reasonable cause to believe" that child abuse and neglect had occurred. Too, in regard to possible civil liability for failure to report instances of suspected child abuse and neglect, the teacher may also be forced to defeat allegations of negligence.

## § 8.5 DISCIPLINE FOR OUT–OF–SCHOOL ACTIVITIES

The teacher has no general right of discipline over students after school hours and off school grounds, but this rule has its limitations. The school has the responsibility to discipline students going to and from school; such authority extends to any student misconduct which has a direct or immediate tendency to harm or subvert the proper performance of the educational function.

When children fight and misbehave it is likely that these actions will carry over to their performance in school. A classic case is where one boy intimidates another by announcing that he will "meet him after school" to settle affairs. In such instances, the welfare of the child and the school are intertwined.

In this regard, Mechem has summarized the rule of law as follows: "The authority of the teacher is not confined to the school room or grounds, but he may prohibit and punish all acts of his pupils which are detrimental to the good order and best interests of the school, whether such acts are committed in school hours or while the pupil is on his way to or from school or after he was returned home." Mechem on Public Officers, § 730.

The most explicit case demonstrating this point of law is O'Rourke v. Walker (Conn.1925), an old Connecticut case, wherein a principal administered moderate corporal punishment to two young boys for abusing and annoying two small girls while on their way home from school, after school hours. The mother of one of the boys sued the school principal maintaining that he had no legal right to administer punishment for any misconduct of the pupil which did not occur in school hours, or for misbehavior which did not take place in the school building or on the school grounds. The lower court concluded and the appellate court affirmed: "(1) that the conduct of the plaintiff boys had a tendency to demoralize the other pupils of the school and to interfere with the proper conduct of the same; (2) that the acts of the plaintiff were detrimental to the good order and best interests of the school; (3) that the defendant, as the principal of said school, in the absence of rules established by the school board or other proper authority, had a right to make and enforce all necessary and proper rules for the regulation of the school and pupils during school hours and afterwards; (4) that said punishment administered by the defendant was reasonable and proper."

In an illustrative case of punishment for off grounds offenses, students on a Sunday evening shouted at a teacher, "there's Stear," and another yelled, "He's a prick." The students were disciplined on Monday. The court, in upholding the school, stated "It is the opinion of the court that the First Amendment rights of the plaintiffs were not violated" and " ... it may be deemed a matter of discipline ... [and] ... to countenance such student conduct ... could lead to devastating consequences in school." Fenton v. Stear (W.D.Pa.1976). See also Clements v. Board of Trustees of Sheridan County School Dist. No. 2 (Wyo.1978), 53 A.L.R.3d 1124, 68 Am.Jur.2d, Schools §§ 256 and 266.

In another case where a school rule placed off-limits an area just off school property and students were punished for loitering there, the court ruled that the school was only exercising " ... its power *in loco parentis* to guide student behavior...." Wiemerslage v. Maine Township High School District 207 (N.D.Ill.1993).

## § 8.6 ACADEMIC DISCIPLINE

Challenges to school grading policies have usually been couched in due process of law. A Michigan court has said that a student has no vested interest in a particular grade and the school board has the authority to set grading policy. The court's rationale is based on the assumption that grading is to set academic standards and not a discipline measure.

Courts have generally held that grades cannot be reduced as a disciplinary measure for violation of school rules. Where a student, while on a school field trip, drank a glass of wine in violation of school rules, the school suspended her for five days, expelled her from the cheerleading squad and the National Honor Society, prohibited her participation in school activities during the days she was expelled from school, and, in addition, imposed a further penalty of grade reduction. The school policy called for the reduction of grades in all classes by two percentage points for each day of suspension. Upon challenge, the court held for the student and ruled that a school board may not impose a grade reduction sanction for infractions that are not related to education. To do so, the court maintained, was to misrepresent the student's true scholastic achievement for college entrance and other purposes.

In another instance of applicable judicial thinking, students who were attending an off-campus class drank alcohol on the way to class and were suspended for five days. School policy said that grades would be reduced by four percent for each day the student was not in attendance. The court ruled that the school rule violated constitutional substantive due process rights by reducing the grades as punishment for alcohol-related misconduct. Further, the court declared the rule that calls for a grade reduction to discipline nonacademic conduct illegal, and null and void. Smith v. School City of Hobart (N.D.Ind. 1993).

Yet, attendance at school and academic performance may be reasonably connected, and failure to attend school may affect the overall educational process. If a school board decides that attendance is essential to fulfill academic requirements and rules are so promulgated relating attendance to academic performance, then the courts are not likely to intervene. Slocum v. Holton Board of Education (Mich.App.1988). In *Slocum*, the court said, "School authorities may determine that attendance, class participation and similar factors are proper educational values bearing on a student's academic achievement."

Thus, while school authorities have broad authority in the evaluation of students, the exercise of the authority cannot be so broad and indiscriminate as to permit unreasonable or improper exercise of discretion. What constitutes appropriate use of discretion largely depends on how well the school documents its rationale and how closely that rationale relates to the desirable educational end that the rule is designed to achieve.

# CHAPTER 9

# RACIAL SEGREGATION

## § 9.1 INTRODUCTION

Governments have the inherent authority to classify persons in reasonable ways and for legitimate purposes. Reasonableness of classification and legitimate purposes are, however, difficult to define. The regretful history of racial discrimination in the United States and its moral consequences make all classifications in American society highly suspect. Racial discrimination is, as a result of that history, particularly noxious to American's sensitivities of right and wrong and justice and injustice. The American tradition of relying on mass public education as the means by which persons gained social and economic mobility naturally resulted in the public schools being a primary battleground on which the racial discrimination issue was to be contested. Thus, the most important court decisions involving the racial discrimination in American history have been educationally related.

## § 9.2 SEPARATE–BUT–EQUAL

The pernicious doctrine of separate-but-equal emanated from an 1850 Supreme Court of Massachusetts decision that legalized the concept in permitting racial segregation in the public schools of Boston. Roberts v. City of Boston (Mass.1850). In this case a Negro child was compelled by school board rule to attend an elementary

195

school designated for black children even though other elementary schools were closer to her home. The child's lawyer, Charles Sumner, the famous abolitionist, maintained that separate schools "exclusively devoted to one class must differ essentially, in its spirit and character, from that public school known to the law, where all classes meet together in equality." He argued that persons who were otherwise equal before the law should not be made unequal by discriminatory devices such as segregated schools. The Massachusetts court disagreed with Sumner, and in so doing, created the separate-but-equal doctrine and justified it by saying that the great principle of equality before the law did not warrant the assumption that all persons are clothed with the same civil and political powers and that such powers, and the benefits therefrom, may vary depending on the "infinite variety of circumstances" surrounding society. The court concluded that this infinite variety of circumstances which may justify school segregation can be found in societal standards which separate the races. Thus, according to this court, separation of races in schools was not discriminatory, so long as the school facilities were not unequal. The court made it clear that it did not consider segregation of the races to be unequal *per se*.

The *Roberts* case was decided under the Constitution of Massachusetts, because the United States Constitution, at that time, contained no prohibition against racial discrimination.

## § 9.21 Equal Protection Clause

It was not until 1868 when the American people enacted the Fourteenth Amendment that racial discrimination became impermissible at the federal level. The Fourteenth Amendment provided that "... No state shall ... deny any person within its jurisdiction the equal protection of the laws."

In spite of this amendment racial segregation persisted as courts failed to fully enforce its intent. Many states enacted Jim Crow laws which extended segregation to most aspects of public life, including separate waiting rooms in railroad stations, train cars, telephone booths, separate storage for textbooks used by black school children, separate elevators, and separate Bibles for swearing in Negro witnesses in some southern courts, and, of course, separate schools. The federal government's practices were as discriminatory as many of the southern states since federal laws and regulations also allowed and even provided for segregation, including the maintenance of racially separate schools in the District of Columbia.

Segregation gained legal credence through the adoption of "separate-but-equal" from the Roberts case in *Boston*, which was adopted by the United States Supreme Court in applying to the Fourteenth Amendment in the infamous case of Plessy v. Ferguson (S.Ct.1896).

Justice Harlan dissented in *Plessy* maintaining that the separate accommodations contributed to creation of a racial caste system excluding blacks from association with whites. Because whites held the prestige, wealth, and power in society, the doctrine of "separate-but-equal" condemned blacks to a permanently inferior position. *Plessy,* however, was the precedent that prevailed until 1954 when the Supreme Court, in Brown v. Board of Education (S.Ct.1954), held the separate-but-equal doctrine to be inherently unconstitutional.

## § 9.22  Demise of Separate-but-Equal

The United States Supreme Court was never able to clearly enunciate what constituted "equal" in the context of "separate-but-equal." It was, though, generally understood that the entire absence of facilities would violate equal protection. As a result, states made some provision, though in most cases quite modest, for black students to have some type of facility. Educational facilities at the graduate and professional school levels were, generally, not available in southern states for black students. Where this was the case, the state legislatures usually provided some type of tuition assistance for black students to attend colleges in other states. In Missouri ex rel. Gaines v. Canada (S.Ct.1938), a Negro plaintiff who did not want to attend law school in another state challenged the State of Missouri because it had no law school for black students. Justice Hughes, writing for the majority of the United States Supreme Court, ruled that Missouri must either permit plaintiff to attend the white law school or that the state must establish a black law school. At the next session of the Missouri legislature a statute was enacted to create a law school for blacks.

It was not until twelve years after *Gaines*, however, that the Supreme Court was asked to rule on the quality of the separate facilities. The inferiority of the black institutions was obvious, but no court decision had established a standard of comparison until 1950, when the Supreme Court in Sweatt v. Painter (S.Ct.1950), held that the black law school in Texas was so inferior to the University of Texas Law School that it could not be construed as a "separate-but-equal" facility. Separate-but-equal had by this time forced the Court into an untenable and unworkable position of justifying separate facilities when it was quite clear that the requirement of equal tradition, prestige and influence by definition denied the efficacy of the "separate-but-equal" doctrine, to say nothing of its moral and ethical shortcomings.

## § 9.3 THE BROWN CASE

A frontal attack was launched on the doctrine by the NAACP in the decade of between 1940 and 1950 led by Thurgood Marshall and a battery of black lawyers, law professors, historians, and sociologists who had analyzed both the legal and social ramifications of segregation. *Brown v. Board of Education of Topeka*, supra, was the first cited case of five cases which were carefully selected to present the complete issue of school segregation to the Supreme Court. Initial arguments were made on December 9, 1952, two and one-half years after the *Sweatt* decision, but the Court reached no decision based on these first briefs and arguments. The case was reargued on December 8, 1953, after which the *Brown* decision was rendered and the doctrine of "separate-but-equal" was nullified.

The basic legal issue propounded by the Court was whether the Fourteenth Amendment contemplated abolishment of school segregation. This was the essential question, whether the constitutional intent was to prohibit state statutory or regulatory segregation of the public schools. The Court rendered its decision saying: "We conclude that in the field of public education the doctrine of 'separate-but-equal' has no place. Separate educational facilities are inherently inequal."

The potential societal effects of *Brown* were so pervasive that the Court was forced to carefully evaluate alternative enforcement measures. Suddenly, the dual system of public education in seventeen states which had been legal under "separate-but-equal" was now unconstitutional. Because of these immense ramifications, on the rendering of the *Brown* decision, the Court charged plaintiffs, defendants and friends of the Court to return and present alternatives for implementation. The plan that was finally adopted by the Court in *Brown II* in 1955, said that the lower courts should act "with all deliberate speed" in desegregating the public schools. Brown v. Board of Education (S.Ct.1955).

Because *Brown* dealt only with state-enforced segregation no guidelines were established for the courts to follow in bringing about desegregation. *Brown* extended only to the erasure of state segregation laws and their enforcement, but did not provide guideposts for abrogation of the continuing effects of segregation.

## § 9.31  With All Deliberate Speed

A plethora of lower federal court decisions dominated the actions of school boards in the south during the fifteen years after *Brown*. Almost immediately, upon remand to a lower federal court, in a companion case to *Brown*, Briggs v. Elliott (E.D.S.C.1955), the issue of desegregation versus integration was addressed. Here the federal judge was asked to determine whether *Brown* merely meant to abolish state sanctioned segregation or did it intend that the courts force the states to act affirmatively to integrate the schools. The judge concluded that "all that is decided, is that a state may not deny to any person on account of race the right to attend any school that it maintains.... The Constitution, in other words, does not require integration. It merely forbids segregation." Accordingly, for several years thereafter, this case stood as precedent for school districts which did not want to take affirmative action to mix white and black children in the same schools.

## § 9.32 Interposition

In other instances the speed of desegregation was delayed by state officials interposing themselves and their offices between court decrees and the people. The most notorious example was that involving the public schools of Little Rock, Arkansas, where state officials sought to revive the Civil War doctrines of nullification and interposition to prevent integration of the Central High School in Little Rock. The constitutionality of the state officials' actions was finally decided by the United States Supreme Court when it said: "In short, the constitutional rights of children not to be discriminated against in school admission on grounds of race or color declared by this Court in the *Brown* case can neither be nullified openly or directly by state legislators or state executive or judicial officers, nor nullified indirectly by them through evasive schemes for segregation whether attempted 'ingeniously or ingenuously.' " Cooper v. Aaron (S.Ct.1958).

One device used to circumvent the effects of *Brown* was to close the public schools and to provide vouchers for students to attend private schools. When this method of maintaining segregation was challenged, the Supreme Court held that the ill effects of such a system bore more heavily on Negro students because the white students had access to accredited private schools while the Negro children did not. Thus the Court concluded that to close public schools and contribute tax funds for students to attend segregated private schools was a violation of equal protection. Griffin v. County School Board of Prince Edward County (S.Ct.1964).

## § 9.33  Freedom of Choice

Whether the Equal Protection Clause required that states merely eradicate state enforced segregation or act affirmatively to integrate, the issue addressed in *Briggs*, persisted as a major question.  The United States Office of Education (now U.S. Department of Education) in the mid–1960s issued guidelines for desegregation of school districts in southern states which, if not followed, could result in the withholding of federal funds.  The guidelines, initially, called for freedom of choice plans to be submitted in order to qualify for the federal funds, but, after a time, it was concluded that freedom of choice would not bring about desegregation in many districts. It was found that black parents for many reasons, including community coercion, would not choose to send their children to schools which were formerly all white.

When the "freedom of choice" issue finally reached the United States Supreme Court, the Court concluded that if freedom of choice plans actually worked to desegregate the schools, then they constituted acceptable legal alternatives; but if they failed to integrate the schools, then the state and school districts must devise new schemes that would place black children in schools with white children and vice versa.  According to the Court, a "freedom of choice" plan must "effectuate a transition" to a "unitary system."  Green v. County School Board of New Kent County (S.Ct.1968).

## § 9.34  Desegregate at Once

The "all deliberate speed" standard which was attributed to Justice Felix Frankfurter ultimately proved to be
unworkable.  After fifteen years of attempting to implement the standard, the United States Supreme Court
reconsidered the entire question in Alexander v. Holmes
County Board of Education (S.Ct.1969).  In exasperation
the Court concluded that the "all deliberate speed" terminology was a legalized term that allowed too much
discretion and resulted in action so deliberate that
schools would remain segregated indefinitely in many
districts of the South.  The Court concluded that "...
continued operation of segregated schools under a standard of allowing 'all deliberate speed' for desegregation is
no longer constitutionally permissible."  The Court ordered all school districts in the seventeen southern states
to "terminate dual school systems at once and to operate
now and hereafter only unitary schools."  From the date
of this decree, all school districts in the south were
required to become unitary without further delay.

## § 9.4  THE SWANN CASE

Even though *Alexander v. Holmes County Board of
Education* required that every school district operating
dual school programs for blacks and whites was to immediately terminate the practice and to establish unitary
schools, the Supreme Court did not clearly define what
unitary meant nor did it prescribe the standards to be
used by school authorities to disestablish dual school
systems.  This the Supreme Court undertook to accomplish in Swann v. Charlotte–Mecklenburg Board of Education (S.Ct.1971).  *Swann* addressed the issues in four

contexts—(1) the use of racial quotas, (2) the elimination of one-race schools, (3) racial gerrymandering of attendance zones, and (4) the use of busing for remedial purposes.

## § 9.41  Racial Quotas

Several earlier lower court decisions had used ratios of black to white in the total school population to establish racial quotas for each school.  A federal district court had established that racial imbalance could not be justified at substantial variance from a 71–29, white to black, ratio for schools in Charlotte–Mecklenburg County, and ruled that no school could be operated with an all black or predominately black student body.  The Supreme Court said that if it was, in fact, the lower court's intent to establish a "mathematical racial balance reflecting the pupil constituency of the system" then the approach would be disapproved and the lower court would be reversed.  The Supreme Court said: "The constitutional command to desegregate schools does not mean that every school in every community must always reflect the racial composition of the school system as a whole."  The Court did acknowledge, however, that "very limited use" of mathematical ratios was within the equitable remedial discretion of a district court and that "awareness of the racial composition of the whole system is likely to be a useful starting point in shaping a remedy to correct past constitutional violations."

## § 9.42  One–Race Schools

A second question necessary to define a unitary system is whether one-race schools are to be permitted at all.

The Court answered this question affirmatively, but admonished that such schools required close judicial scrutiny to determine whether the assignment of pupils was a part of state-enforced segregation. Where a school district's desegregation plan permits such schools to continue, the district has the burden of showing that pupil assignments are "genuinely nondiscriminatory."

## § 9.43 Remedial Altering of Attendance Zones

Racial gerrymandering of districts as required by courts is a permissible device to overcome segregation. Pairing, clustering, and grouping may also be validly required by the lower courts. The Supreme Court said that no rigid rules could be set because of varying local conditions such as traffic patterns and availability of good highways, but that pairing and grouping of noncontiguous school zones may be feasible alternatives. Mere administrative awkwardness or inconvenience is not to be allowed to stand in the way of such remedial actions. Concerning assignment of children to the nearest or neighborhood school the Court said: "All things being equal, with no history of discrimination, it might well be desirable to assign pupils to schools nearest their homes. But all things are not equal in a system that was deliberately constructed and maintained to enforce racial segregation." Thus, where *de jure* segregation has prevailed, the school district must reassign students to bring about integration whether or not the reassignments result in breaking up neighborhood school attendance patterns.

## § 9.44 Busing

The use of busing to alleviate segregation has long been a volatile issue. Until *Swann* the Supreme Court had not directly sanctioned busing as a remedial measure to effectuate integration. In *Green,* supra, the freedom of choice case, the Court had remained vague on the issue saying merely that measures must be taken which are "workable," "effective," and "realistic." With regard to busing, the Supreme Court said in *Swann* that: "Bus transportation has been an integral part of the public education system for years and its use is not novel nor are the people unaccustomed to use of buses." Further, the Court pointed out that in *Charlotte-Mecklenburg,* elementary pupils' bus trips averaged about seven miles; therefore, the present wide use of buses strongly supported the use of bus transportation as one tool for remedying school segregation. "Desegregation plans," the Court said, "cannot be limited to the walk-in school."

## § 9.5 DE FACTO AND DE JURE SEGREGATION

With the *Alexander* case, supra, it was well decided that school districts in states with legal segregation, *de jure,* before *Brown,* had an affirmative duty to integrate, but it had not been clearly decided whether schools that were *de facto* segregated because of housing patterns were required to integrate. President Nixon summarized the law in 1969 saying that "There is a fundamental distinction between so-called *'de jure'* and *'de facto'* segregation: *de jure* segregation arises by law or by the deliberate act of school officials and is unconstitutional; *de facto* segregation results from residential housing patterns and does not violate the Constitution."

Earlier, the United States Court of Appeals for the Seventh Circuit had said that "There is no affirmative United States constitutional duty to change innocently arrived at school attendance districts by the mere fact that shifts in population either increase or decrease the percentage of either Negro or White pupils." Bell v. School City of Gary (7th Cir.1963).

## § 9.51   Implicit Intent to Segregate

Thus, if segregation is *de facto* and not *de jure,* no affirmative duty exists to integrate. In the seventeen southern states all segregation was *de jure,* but in the North *de jure* segregation could only be present if the plaintiffs could show that states or local school boards had acted either explicitly or implicitly to bring about segregation. In explaining the requirement for northern states, the Supreme Court said in *Keyes,* a Denver case, that ". . . we have held that where plaintiffs prove that a current condition of segregated schooling exists within a school district where a dual system was compelled or authorized by statute at the time of our decision in *Brown* . . ., the state automatically assumes an affirmative duty to 'effectuate a transition to a racially nondiscriminatory school system.' " In states where dual systems of education did not exist, the plaintiffs must show that there was official purpose or intent to segregate. Keyes v. School District No. 1, Denver (S.Ct.1973).

*De jure* segregation has, though, been found to exist within several school districts in northern states. For example, both the Columbus and Dayton, Ohio, school systems were held to have been segregated by discriminatory acts of public officials and, thus, an affirmative duty was required to eradicate the vestiges of such *de jure* segregation. Columbus Board of Education v. Penick (S.Ct.1979); Dayton Board of Education v. Brinkman (S.Ct.1979). To desegregate, the court required that a "balanced" school system be attained; the court said:

"[T]he measure of the post-*Brown* conduct of a school board under an unsatisfied duty to liquidate a dual school system is the effectiveness, not the purpose of the actions in decreasing or increasing the segregation caused by the dual system." Thus, the school board must not only abandon its discriminatory practice, but it must establish policies and procedures which will integrate the schools.

## § 9.52  Single Standard

Although the prevailing view remains today that there is a legal distinction between *de facto* and *de jure* segregation, the trend is toward a single standard. The basic distinction is that in the states which had legal segregation before 1954, the burden is on the school district to overcome vestiges of past discrimination. If the effect is to segregate, then it must be addressed with affirmative action to erase the racial imbalance. On the other hand, in other states plaintiffs must show that there was an official intent to segregate before remedial measures will be required by the courts. Justice Powell in a concurring opinion in *Keyes* argued that such a dual standard is not now justified. He said "... The net result of the Court's language, however, is the application of an effect test to the actions of southern school districts and an intent test to those in other sections, at least until an initial *de jure* finding for those districts can be made. Rather than straining to perpetuate any such dual standard, we should hold forthrightly that significant segregated school conditions in any section of the country are a *prima facie* violation of constitutional rights...."

Justice Douglas, in dissent in *Keyes,* agreed with Powell maintaining that there should be no legal distinction made between *de facto* and *de jure* segregation. Douglas said, "The school board is a state agency and the lines that it draws, the locations it selects for school sites, the allocations it makes of students, the budgets it prepares are state action for Fourteenth Amendment purposes .... I think it is time to state that there is no constitutional difference between *de jure* and *de facto* segregation, for each is the product of state actions or policies ...."

## § 9.53 Northern De Jure Segregation Defined

A 1971 case involving the desegregation of the San Francisco school district dealt with the distinctions between *de jure* and *de facto*. The school district having a large racial minority and a great diversity of ethnic groups had substantial racial imbalance among its schools. Johnson v. San Francisco Unified School District (N.D.Cal.1971). Even though this decision was later vacated, Johnson v. San Francisco Unified School District (9th Cir.1974), it is instructive because of its discussion of the North–South and *effect-intent* issues. The school board defended its school boundaries by maintaining that the court decisions forbidding segregation applied only to those states "which at an earlier time, had dual school systems," therefore, the school board was not required to adopt affirmative measures where no dual system had previously existed. The district court rejected this argument refusing to draw a distinction between segregation in the North and South. The Court said that: "It is shocking, indeed, it is nonsensical, to assume that such practices are forbidden to school authorities in Florida or North Carolina, for example, but are permitted to school authorities in California.

Neither the United States Supreme Court nor any other court has drawn a Mason–Dixon line for constitutional enforcement."

The San Francisco school board further maintained that its actions were not unconstitutional because the district officials merely drew attendance lines without regard to racial or ethnic groups. In addressing this issue, the district court further defined the *de facto* and *de jure* distinction by explaining that any action by school authorities "which creates or continues or heightens racial segregation of school children is *de jure*." On appeal, the judgment of this district court was vacated because the U.S. Supreme Court had held in *Keyes,* supra, that the differentiating factor between *de jure* and *de facto* segregation is whether the purpose or intent is to segregate, not whether the effect is to segregate. When the district court used the words "creates," "continues" or "heightens" segregation, it was erroneously using the effect test. The appeals court could find no evidence to suggest that the San Francisco school officials had "intentionally discriminated against minority students by practicing a deliberate policy of racial discrimination." An excellent example of what constitutes *de jure* segregation in a northern state is found in a Pennsylvania case in 1982, Hoots v. Commonwealth of Pennsylvania (3d Cir.1982). Here the state had enacted a school district reorganization statute requiring each county board of school directors to prepare a plan of organization for school districts for review by the State Board of Education. The plan approved for Allegheny County called for creation of five school districts, four of which had 87 percent or more white students and a fifth district that had 63 percent black. A federal district court held the plan unconstitutional finding that action by both state and county boards had the intent to segregate the students of the school districts and, as such, "constituted an act of *de jure* discrimination in violation of the Fourteenth Amendment." According to the court, defendants could foresee the predictable effects of the reorganization and from that an inference of segregative intent could be drawn. Further, substantial evidence was presented that white parents and school officials sought to shield white students from attending school with nonwhites. Most damaging was testimony by a desegregation consultant that "race, indeed, was taken into consideration" by public officials "in recreating school districts" and that certain neighborhoods were excluded from the white districts because they were predominately black.

## § 9.6 A UNITARY SYSTEM

A dual school system becomes unitary when the vestiges of past legal (*de jure*) segregation are erased. The Supreme Court has defined a unitary system as the status a school system achieves "when it no longer discriminates between school children on the basis of race," Columbus Board of Education v. Penick (S.Ct. 1979), or when no person is "effectively excluded from any school because of race or color." Alexander v. Holmes County Board of Education (S.Ct.1969). In Flax v. Potts (5th Cir.1990), a federal circuit court ruled that a school district is unitary if schools are not identifiable by race and students and faculty are assigned in a manner that eliminates the vestiges of past segregation.

A quarter of a century ago the U.S. Supreme Court held in Green v. County School Board of New Kent County, Virginia (S.Ct.1968), that the courts must look to six areas of the educational program to determine whether a district is unitary: 1) student assignment, 2) faculty, 3) staff, 4) transportation, 5) extracurricular activities, and 6) facilities. Subsequently, as the courts applied these criteria, the question arose as to whether all measures had to be met at once or whether they could be achieved incrementally. Federal courts split over the issue. In Ross v. Houston Independent School District (5th Cir.1983), the U.S. Court of Appeals, Fifth Circuit, ruled that the Houston district was unitary even though it did not have a homogenous student population, and in Keyes v. School District No. 1 (10th Cir.1990), the U.S. Court of Appeals, Tenth Circuit, held the Denver system to be "unitary in certain aspects, even though other aspects remain nonunitary." This "incremental approach" did not, however, have a consensus among the federal courts. Another view advanced by the U.S. Court of Appeals for the Eleventh Circuit, Pitts v. Freeman (11th Cir.1989), added a potential seventh criterion, "quality of education," and ruled that all criteria had to be met simultaneously. This court said, "If the system fulfills all six factors *at the same time* for several years, the court should declare that the school system has achieved unitary status. If the school system fails to fulfill all six factors at the same time for several years, the federal district court should retain jurisdiction" (emphasis added). Finally, in 1992, the U.S. Supreme Court settled the question by upholding the "incremental approach." In so holding the Supreme Court reversed the lower *Pitts*, and held that a workable plan may be effectively achieved if some of the six criteria are successfully addressed and the others are left to further consideration. Thus, by this ruling the Court substantially reduced the strictures on school boards in accommodating conditions of unitariness. Freeman v. Pitts (S.Ct. 1992).

## § 9.61   Unitariness and Burden of Proof

How, though, can one know when this erasure has been achieved? Experience has shown that there may be substantial difficulty in ferreting out the causes of segregation, whether it is *de facto* or *de jure*. The U.S. Court of Appeals, Tenth Circuit, has summarized its own view of unitariness and how it is to be determined. "To determine whether a school district has become unitary, ... a court must consider what the school district has done or not done to fulfill its affirmative duty to desegregate the current effects of those actions or inactions, and the extent to which further desegregation is feasible. After a plaintiff establishes intentional segregation at some point in the past and a current condition of segregation, a defendant then bears the burden of proving that its past acts have eliminated all traces of the past intentional segregation to the maximum feasible extent.... The actual condition of the school district at the time of trial is perhaps the most crucial consideration in a unitariness determination. The plaintiff bears the burden of showing the existence of a current condition of segregation...."

"Once a plaintiff has proven the existence of a current condition of segregation, the school district bears the substantial burden of showing that that condition is not the result of its prior *de jure* segregation.... The school district must show that no causal connection exists between past and present segregation, not merely that it did not intend to cause current segregation.... In sum, when a school system was previously *de jure*, a plaintiff bears the burden of showing that there is a current condition of segregation. It may do so by proving the existence of racially identifiable schools. The school district must then show that such segregation has no causal connection with the prior *de jure* segregation, and that the district has in fact carried out the maximum desegregation practicable for that district." Brown v. Board of Education of Topeka (Brown III) (10th Cir. 1989).

In a sequel to the famous original Brown v. Board of Education (1954), a federal court ruled that the board of education of Topeka, Kansas, had not yet removed the vestiges of earlier illegal segregation. The federal court said that the Supreme Court in *Freeman* had made it clear that the school district bears the burden of showing the current racial imbalance is not traceable to the original *de jure* segregation. Accordingly, the plaintiff is not required to prove discriminatory intent on the part of the school district. Also, the plaintiff is not required to bear the burden of proof to show intentional discrimination on the part of the school district until after unitary status is achieved. Brown v. Board of Education (10th Cir.1989). See also Board of Education of Oklahoma City v. Dowell (S.Ct.1991).

Whether the vestiges of past discrimination have been eradicated and unitary status has been achieved is, thus, vital to an equal protection case. As noted above, after the declaration of unitariness, the burden of proof born by the plaintiffs to relitigate the case is much heavier in subsequent actions to prove that a school board actually had the underlying intent to discriminate. If unitariness has not been declared, discriminatory intent is presumed by virtue of the fact that earlier *de jure* segregation existed.

Resolution of the unitariness issue is so complicated that its pursuit and achievement has often taken a tortuous route of great time and legal expense through the hierarchy of the judicial structure. An example of such elongated judicial action was illustrated by an Oklahoma City case that reached the U.S. Supreme Court in 1991. In this case, a dispute arose over a reassignment plan for students. In 1972, a federal court had ordered a desegregation plan for Oklahoma City. By 1977, the court determined that the school district had reached unitary status. Later in 1984, as the number and percentage of black students increased, the school board adopted a new student reassignment plan. The plan assigned students K–4 to their respective neighborhood schools, but continued to bus students in grades 5–12. Plaintiffs objected to the plan claiming that it constituted a return to a segregated school system.

The primary issue was whether the court order which determined the school district to have achieved unitary status was still in effect and proper. The federal district court held that the 1977 unitariness decree prevented relitigation of the 1972 injunction. On appeal the U.S. Court of Appeals for the Tenth Circuit held that the 1972 desegregation order was still active and unitariness had not been achieved in spite of the 1977 unitary declaration. This court remanded the case back to the lower court for a decision consistent therewith. The lower court ruled that the 1984 student reassignment plan (SRP) had no discriminatory intent and ordered the 1972 court ordered desegregation plan lifted. The U.S. Court of Appeals reversed this decision and the school board of

Oklahoma City appealed to the U.S. Supreme Court. The U.S. Supreme Court ruled that the 1977 decision by the U.S. district court, that unitary status had been achieved, was too ambiguous to prevent parents from challenging the 1984 SRP. The U.S. Supreme Court then remanded the case back to the trial court for the purpose of determining whether the school district had complied in good faith with the original 1972 order and had eliminated "the vestiges of past discrimination." Board of Education of Oklahoma City Public Schools v. Dowell (S.Ct.1991).

On reconsideration of the question, the federal district court found that the Oklahoma City School Board had acted in good faith to eliminate the "vestiges" of past legal discrimination. The lower court examined the criteria of student assignments, faculty, staff, transportation, curriculum, extracurricular activities, facilities and the pattern of residential segregation. From this intensive inquiry, the lower court ruled that the school board had fulfilled the requirements of the original 1972 court-ordered desegregation and had obtained unitary status. Thus, the original 1972 decree was completely dissolved and the school board could implement the new SRP without a presumption of discriminatory intent. Dowell v. Board of Education of the Oklahoma Public Schools (W.D.Okla.1991). As can readily be seen, the legal intricacies of the desegregation cases have become increasingly complex as precedents on the issue have mounted. This trend will probably not subside in the near future.

## § 9.7 INTERDISTRICT DESEGREGATION

In reversing a lower court decision which had found that *de jure* segregation existed in Detroit and its suburbs, creating a constitutional requirement to integrate several of the suburban districts with the Detroit School System, the United States Supreme Court said that before boundaries of school districts can be changed to effectuate integration it must be shown that "racially discriminatory acts of the state or local school districts, or of a single school district have been a substantial cause of interdistrict segregation." Milliken v. Bradley (S.Ct.1974). The Supreme Court could not find in the record of the Detroit case any evidence that would suggest discriminatory acts, explicit or implicit, by the state of Michigan or by suburban districts that would cause the districts themselves to be segregated.

## § 9.8 STATE EQUAL PROTECTION

In 1970 the Supreme Court of California held that state school boards had a constitutional obligation to take reasonable steps to alleviate segregation in public schools whether it be classified as *de facto* or *de jure* in origin. Crawford v. Board of Education (Cal.1970). Accordingly, the Equal Protection Clause of the California Constitution was more forceful in compelling desegregation than equal protection of the Fourteenth Amendment. However, in 1979 the voters of California ratified Proposition I amending the Equal Protection Clause of the California Constitution providing that state courts shall not order mandatory pupil assignment or transportation to overcome racial imbalance unless a federal court so requires under federal case law. The effect of this amendment was to limit the sweep of the Equal Protection Clause in the California Constitution while not affecting the federal requirements. Crawford v. Los Angeles Board of Education (S.Ct.1982). The Court said we reject the contention that "once a state chooses to do 'more' than the Fourteenth Amendment requires, it may never recede."

## § 9.9 REMEDIES

During the later years of the 1960s and the decade of the 1970s the federal courts fashioned remedies for school segregation by moving students from school to school to achieve desegregation. The hypothesized social benefits from such integration have been very difficult to achieve or prove, however, because white flight to the suburbs and to private schools had rendered such integration largely ineffectual.

Because of the arguable failure of such efforts and because of the social tendency of the races to resegregate themselves, some courts have sought alternative remedies to achieve equality of educational opportunity. In the place of busing and reassignment of students by race, some courts have approved programs of remediation that include early childhood intervention, curriculum development, reduction in pupil-teacher ratios, counseling and career guidance, remedial reading and staff development. See Alexander and Alexander, *American Public School Law* (St. Paul, West Publishing Company, 1992), pp. 445–446.

Possibly the most definitive application of the various means of remediation are given in *Milliken II* in which the U.S. Supreme Court set out guidelines that must govern lower court consideration of remedial options. Milliken v. Bradley (S.Ct.1977). These guidelines enunciated are three: First, the remedy should be commensurate with the nature and scope of the constitutional violation. Second, the court's decree should be remedial in nature, fashioned as nearly as possible "to restore the victims of discriminatory conduct to the position they would have occupied in the absence of such conduct." Third, in formulating a decree, the courts "must take into account the interest of state and local authorities in managing their own affairs, consistent with the Constitution."

The lower courts in abiding with these strictures, however, have substantial latitude and more recent cases have seen new measures of substantial innovation. Moreover, these measures are relying less and less on student reassignment and more on educational program remedies, some of which, in addition to those referred to above, include reduction in class size, provision for summer school, full-day kindergarten, pre- and post-school day tutoring, early childhood education, magnet schools, and facilities improvements.

The major issue of costs and whether federal courts can require expensive programs to be instituted as remedies has been of great importance. Can the federal courts require the school district to levy taxes to raise sufficient revenues to implement such plans? Can the federal courts levy the taxes themselves? An array of alternatives, some requiring substantial expense, were implemented in Kansas City, Missouri, by order of the federal court in that district. The costs of such redress were very high, especially the costs associated with the creation of new magnet schools was quite high. The magnitude of the costs of remedy was originally estimated to exceed $88 million, a sum so large as to necessitate local and state sharing of the funding. Later, for 1991–92, this estimate was increased to over $142 million. Local tax levies in force at that time in Kansas City were

insufficient to raise the necessary revenues and to implement the plan. The federal district court, therefore,
imposed taxes on the Kansas City School District sufficient to pay the local share of the costs.

Ultimately the issue reached the U.S. Supreme Court
with the state claiming that the federal district court had
exceeded its authority by imposing the increase in local
taxation. The state argued that such action by a federal
court violated Article III, the Tenth Amendment, and the
principles of federalism defined as federal/state comity.
The U.S. Supreme Court agreed with the state's contention and held that the federal district court had overstepped its bounds in that it, the court, imposed the local
tax. The Supreme Court, though, pointed out that the
same result could be constitutionally achieved if the
district court had authorized or required the Kansas City
School District to levy the property tax rates, rather than
the court itself levying the rates. The Supreme Court
observed that the difference was "far more than a matter
of form. Authorizing and directing local government institutions to devise and implement remedies not only
protects the function of those institutions, but, to the
extent possible, also places the responsibility for solu-
tions to the problems of segregation upon those who have
themselves created the problems...." The district
court, thus, had abused its discretion in levying the tax
itself, however, the desired result of a higher tax levy
could be achieved in the future by ordering the school
district to levy the higher rates and enjoining the state
laws that limited the school district's ability to raise the
necessary local revenues. Thus, the end result was that
a federal district court could fashion remedies that had
substantial cost consequences and could require the

school district to levy the necessary taxes to achieve the desired end. Missouri v. Jenkins (S.Ct.1990).

Therefore, in answer to the general question as to whether federal courts have the authority to require costly remedial measures, the answer is in the affirmative. The courts can within their judicial prerogative require a whole range of alternative programs to erase the vestiges of racial discrimination, including very expensive ones. The courts, however, cannot usurp taxing authority and in fact levy taxes themselves to raise the revenues. The courts can, though, require the appropriate state statutory authorities to levy the taxes to raise the revenues. Thus, the same end is achieved, the courts can require additional expenditures to effectuate remedies.

# CHAPTER 10

# EDUCATION OF DISABLED CHILDREN

## § 10.1 INTRODUCTION

State provision for education of the disabled has historically been far from adequate. Until the mid to late 1960s, most states did not have uniform standards for education of the disabled and many states did not provide state financing for such purposes. Disabled students were systematically excluded from educational programs because their emotional or physical disabilities tended to disrupt the continuity of the everyday school program, or the costs of their education were beyond that which the taxpayers were willing to undertake.

Today the situation is much different, both state and federal statutes guarantee educational opportunity for the children with disabilities and court decisions have mandated that the civil rights of these children be protected.

## § 10.2 RIGHT TO ATTEND SCHOOL

Although a number of states already had statutes requiring educational services to disabled children, two cases provided impetus to other state legislatures and the Congress to form new legislation guaranteeing educational opportunity for disabled children. The first case, *Pennsylvania Association for Retarded Children* (PARC), was brought by the parents of seventeen children who claimed that Pennsylvania laws enacted prior to 1972 were unconstitutional. Pennsylvania Association for Retarded Children v. Commonwealth (E.D.Pa.1971) and Pennsylvania Association for Retarded Children v. Commonwealth (E.D.Pa.1972). The laws allowed for exclusion of disabled children from public school if they were certified by psychologists as "uneducable and untrainable." The parents claimed that: (1) the law did not provide for appropriate due process measures to be taken before exclusion, such as notice to parents and a proper hearing; (2) the children were denied equal protection because they were declared to be uneducable without a rational factual basis for such determination; (3) the state constitution guaranteed education for all children; and (4) the law which excluded handicapped children was arbitrary and capricious. The federal district court held that exclusion of handicapped children was, indeed, unconstitutional, that: "having undertaken to provide a free public education to all its children, including its exceptional children, the Commonwealth of Pennsylvania may not deny any mentally retarded child access to a free public program of education and training." The court gave the parties involved an opportunity to agree on procedures acceptable to both sides. A consent decree was issued which required a "free public program of education and training appropriate to the child's capacity, within the context of a presumption that, among the alternative programs of education and training required by statute to be available, placement in a regular public school class is preferable to placement in a special public school class i.e., a class for 'handicapped' children (only) and placement in a special public school class is preferable to placement in any other type of program of education and training...."

To determine the education and training appropriate for the "child's capacity," elaborate due process procedures were written into the decree so that an appropriate educational program could be established. From the due process procedure, the school was to determine if the child could be placed first in a regular class (mainstreamed), or in an alternative placement in a self-contained or special resource room. The last and least desirable alternative was placement in homebound or other setting outside the public school.

Shortly following *PARC* which required services to mentally retarded children, another court action, the *Mills* case, emerged which further accentuated the issue of educating the disabled. The *Mills* case extended the rights not only to mentally retarded children but also to all disabled children. Mills v. Board of Education of District of Columbia (D.D.C.1972). Because this case arose in Washington, D.C., it gained substantial notoriety having a great impact on both state and federal legislation. Here, parents challenged exclusionary practices which had resulted in nearly 18,000 disabled children going without public education in 1972–73. Law in the District of Columbia mandated a free public education for all children between the ages of 7 and 16. Parents of disabled children claimed that denial of education violated the constitutional right of due process. In defense, school officials argued that to educate the disabled children would cause a great financial burden for which there was not adequate funding.

The federal district court held that equal protection was implicit in the Due Process Clause of the Fifth

Amendment, applying to the District of Columbia, and that through this provision a right existed to attend public schools. While the substantive aspects of due process gave these students a right to attend public schools, the procedural aspects of due process entitled the students to a fair hearing before they could be excluded or placed in alternative classes within the school system.

In answer to the school district's financial concerns, the court bluntly stated that "If sufficient funds are not available to finance all of the services and programs that are needed and desirable in the system, then the available funds must be expended equitably in such a manner that no child is entirely excluded from a publicly supported education consistent with his needs and ability to benefit therefrom. The inadequacies of the District of Columbia Public School System, whether occasioned by insufficient funding or administrative inefficiency, certainly cannot be permitted to bear more heavily on the 'exceptional' or handicapped child than on the normal child." In the decree the court established due process procedures which included step-by-step detail on how notice was to be given to parents when placement of a child was contemplated, who should serve as hearing officers, and the requirements for the actual hearing. Many of these procedures were later adopted in state and federal legislation to protect the interests of disabled children.

## § 10.3  THE ORIGINAL PUBLIC LAW 94–142 AND SECTION 504

With an awareness created by *PARC* and *Mills* and emergent cases in other states, the Congress moved rapidly to provide federal legislation and funding which would assist in educating disabled children. The federal law entitled Education for All Handicapped Children Act of 1975, 20 U.S.C.A. § 1401, initially applied to all children between the ages of 3 and 21. In order to receive federal funds under the Act, states were required to abide by the Act and regulations made pursuant thereto.

Congress, a year earlier in 1973, had addressed the needs of disabled individuals when it had passed the Vocational Rehabilitation Act of 1973 which applies to all agencies receiving federal funds for any purpose. These funds may be forfeited if charges of agency discrimination against disabled people are sustained. Section 504 of this act states: "No otherwise qualified handicapped individual in the United States . . . shall, solely by reason of his handicap, be excluded from the participation in, be denied the benefits of, or be subjected to discrimination under any program or activity receiving Federal financial assistance."

Although § 504 is concerned with the discrimination of disabled individuals in work situations, it also addresses the problems encountered by disabled children in seeking equal educational opportunity. Five mandates are encompassed in § 504 that pertain directly to the educational needs of disabled children: "(a) location and notification, (b) free appropriate public education, (c) educational setting, (d) evaluation and placement, and (e) procedural safeguards." These provisions of § 504 have been used successfully in obtaining desirable school programs and services for disabled students. This Act has been successful in obtaining services for disabled children who do not meet the IDEA definition. Specifically, the provisions for a free appropriate public education in a proper educational setting enabled a child with cystic fibrosis to attend regular classes while receiving supportive services for a daily suctioning procedure and recently were instrumental in assisting children with Acquired Immunodeficiency Syndrome (AIDS) to remain in school. Also Section 504 is not as prescriptive as IDEA.

## § 10.31  Individuals with Disabilities Education Act (IDEA)

The original Act, the Education for All Handicapped Children Act (EAHCA), signed on November 29, 1975, by President Gerald R. Ford, was amended in 1978 and in 1986 and was finally incorporated into a new law in 1990, the Individuals with Disabilities Education Act (IDEA), 20 U.S.C.A. §§ 1400–1485. Little of substance was added in the 1990 legislation except a limited expansion of the definition of disabilities, such as inclusion of head trauma, autism, etc., and a provision to prevent states from using the Eleventh Amendment as a shield against liability in actions by disabled children.

The IDEA defines disabled children as those who are mentally retarded, hard of hearing, deaf, speech and language impaired, visually handicapped, seriously emotionally disturbed, orthopedically impaired, or otherwise health impaired. In addition, the definition includes children with specific learning disabilities who require special education and related services. As mentioned, the 1990 Act increased the listed disabilities to include autism, specifically, and traumatic brain injury. The 1990 amendment also requires the development of services for disabled students to ease their transition into the world of the adult. Provisions for such transitional services must be included in the IEPs of all students sixteen years of age and older.

One disability that is not recognized under IDEA is "attention deficit disorder" (ADD). A bill to amend IDEA to include ADD under the definition of "health impaired" was defeated. Although ADD children may be eligible for IDEA services if they are learning disabled, educationally disabled or other health impaired, ADD is not a listed category under IDEA. IDEA is much more prescriptive in outlining the services required to children than Section 504, therefore many parents and others would like to have ADD become a defined eligibility category under IDEA.

Most importantly, the Act assured that all disabled children would have access to "a free appropriate public education and related services designed to meet their unique needs." The appropriate educational program must be tailored to each disabled child's educational needs. Under the law, an "individualized education program" (IEP) must be designed for each child and reevaluation of the plan must be conducted annually. Another provision requires that disabled children be educated in the "least restrictive" environment appropriate to their needs. This requires disabled children be mainstreamed and included in regular classes where possible. A regular class with appropriate supplemental services is considered to be preferable to special classes, special classes are considered to be preferable to separate special schools, and special schools are considered to be preferable to homebound instruction. If no public facilities are available, then private schools may be used in the alternative and public funds may be used to defray the costs.

Some of the procedural safeguards provided for in the Act are: (1) access by parents to relevant school records, (2) prior notice to parents of any proposed change in their child's educational placement, (3) opportunity for a fair and impartial hearing, including right to be represented by a lawyer or advisor, right to present evidence, to subpoena, confront and cross-examine witnesses and obtain a transcript of the hearing and written decision, (4) opportunity to appeal to court, (5) right of child to remain in current placement during pendency of hearing proceedings, and (6) also parents may be eligible for legal fees if they prevail. See S-1 v. Spangler (M.D.N.C.1986).

## § 10.32 A Right to Special Education

By virtue of the IDEA a disabled child has a right to an education and does not need to show that he or she will benefit from an education in order to attend public school. Whether such a right exists was one of the primary issues emerging from the enactment of the Individuals with Disabilities Education Act (IDEA). The issue was whether the severity of handicap can be so great as to render the child incapable of benefitting from education. The theory is that if a child cannot benefit from the educational process then the state is not required to provide an educational service to the child. Indeed, the question as to whether a showing of benefit is required at all was the subject of litigation of primary importance for education of disabled children. The court answered very clearly and held that IDEA does not require a child to demonstrate a benefit from the education as a condition precedent to participation.

In the defining case on the subject, *Timothy W.*, the child had been born two months premature, with severe respiratory problems, and had shortly thereafter suffered intracranial hemorrhage, subdural effusions, seizures, hydrocephalus, and meningitis. As a result, the boy was multiple handicapped and profoundly mentally retarded. These extensive handicaps specifically included complex developmental disabilities, spastic quadriplegia, cerebral palsy, seizure disorder and cortical blindness. Expert testimony indicated that the boy had virtually no brain cortex and, therefore, had no capacity to learn. Other expert testimony was to the effect that he was aware of his surrounding environment, attempted on occasion purposeful movement, responded to tactile stimulation, recognized familiar voices and noises, and could part his lips when spoon fed.

In considering the extensiveness of the handicap and the intent of the federal statute, the court concluded the meaning of the law was that "*all* handicapped children should be included," and, in fact, the Act gives priority to the most severely handicapped. Furthermore, the Act does not in any provision place the burden on the child to demonstrate that he or she can "benefit" from the educational program. The court pointed out emphatically that the Act made it clear it intended a "zero-reject" policy, that is, no child, "regardless of the severity of his or her handicap," is to be deprived of education. This court summed up its opinion by saying: "Public education is to be provided to all handicapped children, unconditionally and without exception. It encompasses a *universal right* and is not predicated upon any type of guarantees that the child will benefit from the special education and services before he or she is considered eligible to receive such education." (emphasis added). Timothy W. v. Rochester, New Hampshire, School District (1st Cir.1989).

## § 10.33  Eleventh Amendment Immunity Abrogated

Importantly, too, the 1990 IDEA amendments abrogated state immunity for liability that could be claimed under the Eleventh Amendment. The amendments responded to a loophole in the original Act that had not specifically rendered states liable for reimbursement to parents of disabled children for tuition and other necessary costs they incurred in educating their children. The Supreme Court had ruled that even though the Congress had the authority under Section Five (5) of the Fourteenth Amendment to specifically abrogate state immunity under the Eleventh Amendment, the wording of the original 1975 legislation (P.L. 94–142) had not done so, thus depriving parents of the reimbursement. In *Dellmuth*, the U.S. Supreme Court had said that "Congress may abrogate the State's constitutionally secured immunity from suit in federal court only by making its intention unmistakably clear in the language of the statute." The IDEA legislation of 1990 provided this language in "unmistakably clear" terms. Dellmuth v. Muth (S.Ct. 1989). See also 20 U.S.C.A. § 1400.

## § 10.4  LITIGATION PURSUANT TO IDEA

Much litigation has emerged during the last several years which clarifies several of the provisions of the Act. Most of these cases have to do with interpretation of appropriateness of program, placement, and costs of treatment.

## § 10.41   Impartial Hearing

Implicit in the due process provision of the Act is that there should be an impartial tribunal (see Due Process, Chapter 3). The IDEA and the Handicapped Children's Protection Act of 1986 (HCPA) specifically provided for extensive procedural due process protections. These procedures must be strictly adhered to by the school district in evaluation and placement of disabled children. One aspect of the due process afforded a child is the "stay put" provision requiring that a child's status cannot change until the required due process procedures are completed. Then, and only then, can the child's placement be changed. With regard to the "stay put" requirement the U.S. Supreme Court has said: "The language of Subsection 1415(e)(3) (of IDEA) is unequivocal. It states plainly that during pendency of any proceedings initiated under the Act, unless the state or local educational agency and the parents or guardian of a disabled child otherwise agree, 'the child *shall* remain in the then current educational placement.'" § 1415(e)(3) (emphasis added). Honig v. Doe (S.Ct.1988).

## § 10.42   Least Restrictive Environment

An overriding objective of the IDEA is to normalize the education of disabled children and place them in the regular classroom setting whenever possible. Federal regulations promulgated pursuant to IDEA state "... that separate schooling, or other removal of handicapped children from the regular educational environment [should] occur only when the nature of severity of the handicap is such that education in regular classes with the use of supplementary aids and services cannot be achieved satisfactorily." 34 C.F.R. § 300.551; 20 U.S.C.A. § 1412(5)(B).

Under this regulation the disabled child is to be given the broadest educational opportunity available and the option with the "least restrictive environment" must be chosen in order to minimize to the greatest extent possible harmful effects on the child. In considering alternative placements a continuum is envisaged that has on one end the regular classroom, the least restrictive environment, and at the other end, the hospital, the most restrictive. See Laura F. Rothstein, *Special Education Law* (New York: Longman, 1990), p. 112.

"Integrating children with disabilities in regular classrooms is commonly known as 'mainstreaming.'" The least restrictive environment should result in mainstreaming the child as frequently as possible. Although mainstreaming is not always required, a number of courts have interpreted sections of IDEA, which relates to mainstreaming, as so requiring. The specific statement in IDEA that establishes mainstreaming is "procedures to assure that, to the maximum extent appropriate, children with disabilities, ... are educated with children who are not disabled, and that special classes, separate schooling, or other removal of children with disabilities from the regular educational environment occurs only when the nature of severity of the disability is such that education services cannot be achieved satisfactorily, ...." 20 U.S.C.A. § 1412(5)(B). Mavis v. Sobol (N.D.N.Y.1993). This provision appears to reflect Congress' strong preference in favor of including or integrating disabled children in regular classrooms.

In determining whether a child should be mainstreamed, the Third, Fifth and Eleventh Circuits have

used what is known as the *Daniel R.R.* test.  Daniel R.R.
v. State Board of Education (5th Cir.1989).  This test has
a two-part inquiry.  "First, we ask whether education in
the regular classroom, with the use of supplemental aids
and services, can be achieved satisfactorily for a given
child.... If it cannot and the school intends to provide
special education or to remove the child from regular
education, we ask, second, whether the school has mainstreamed the child to the maximum extent appropriate."

The Fourth, Sixth and Eighth Circuits apply the
*Roncker* Test.  The *Roncker* test provides "[W]here the
segregated facility is considered superior, the court
should determine whether the services which make the
placement superior could be feasibly provided in a non-
segregated setting.  If they can, the placement in the
segregated school would be inappropriate under the Act."
Roncker v. Walter (6th Cir.1983).

What constitutes the least restrictive environment is
yet so uncertain that litigation continues to proliferate.
The courts have generally held that where disputes arise
over appropriate educational methodology, the court will
defer to the judgment of school officials.  Lachman v.
Illinois State Board of Education (7th Cir.1988).  "The
primary responsibility for formulating the education to
be accorded a handicapped child, and for choosing the
educational program most suitable to the child's needs,
was left by the Act to state and local educational agencies
in cooperation with the parents and guardians of the
child."  Board of Education of Hendrick Hudson Central
School District v. Rowley (S.Ct.1982).

The court in *Lachman* concluded that parental discretion in the matter of placement must defer to the judgment of the professional educators of the public school

district. This court said that "... parents, no matter how well-motivated, do not have a right under EAHCA (IDEA) to compel a school district to provide a specific program or employ a specific methodology in providing for education of their handicapped child...." *Lachman v. Illinois State Board of Education*, supra. See also Kruelle v. New Castle County School District (3d Cir. 1981).

## § 10.43 Inclusion

The terms "inclusion," "full-inclusion," and "integrated services" are not found in Public Law 94–142 (EAHCA, 1975) or Public Law 101–476 (IDEA, 1991) or regulations for these acts. The inclusion movement came out of the U.S. Department of Education in the early 1980s under the "regular education initiative." Regular education initiative advocates criticized special and regular education because disabled children were not being placed in regular education frequently enough. Although not classified in the statute or regulations, these terms are now being used by the courts when addressing the child's "least restrictive environment." In Mavis v. Sobol (N.D.N.Y.1993), the court stated "... in recent years use of the term mainstreaming has not been favored by some educators, and instead use of the term 'inclusion' is now preferred in some educational circles. Despite that, the court will continue to use the term mainstreaming in this case...." In *Oberti*, the court also preferred to use mainstreaming rather than the currently in vogue term inclusion. The court stated, "Integrating children with disabilities in regular classrooms is commonly known as 'mainstreaming.' The Obertis [parents] point out that some educators and public school authorities have come to disfavor use of the term 'mainstreaming' because it suggests, in their view, the shuttling of a child with disabilities in and out of a regular classroom without altering the classroom to accommodate the child. They prefer the term 'inclusion' because of its greater emphasis on the use of supplementary aids and support services within the regular classroom to facilitate inclusion of children with disabilities. While 'inclusion' may be a more precise term, we will nonetheless use the term 'mainstreaming' because it is currently the common parlance. Moreover, ... 'mainstreaming' as required under IDEA does **not** mean simply the placement of a child with disabilities in a regular classroom or school program." Oberti by Oberti v. Board of Education of Borough of Clementon School District (3d Cir.1993). See also Sacramento City School District v. Rachel H. (9th Cir.1994).

## § 10.44  Free Appropriate Public Education

The key to meeting the requirements of IDEA is to determine what constitutes an appropriate education. In the most authoritative statement yet made in interpretation of IDEA, the United States Supreme Court in Board of Educ. of Hendrick Hudson Central School District v. Rowley (S.Ct.1982), ruled on the question "What is meant by the Act's requirement of a 'free appropriate public education?'" The case arose when parents of Amy Rowley, a deaf student, contested the appropriateness of the educational program provided her by the Hendrick Hudson School District. Amy had minimal residual hearing and was an excellent lipreader. After meeting with her parents, and prior to her entering school, it was decided to place her in a regular kindergarten class where she would have supplemental assistance. She was to be provided with a FM hearing aid which would amplify words spoken into a wireless receiver by the teacher and other students during classroom activities. Amy successfully completed kindergarten and per the law was prescribed a new IEP for her first-grade year. The Individual Education Plan (IEP) called for her to be mainstreamed in a regular classroom, continue to use the FM equipment and additionally receive instruction from a tutor for the deaf for one hour each day and from a speech therapist for three hours a week. Her parents agreed with the IEP but insisted that, additionally, Amy should be provided with a qualified sign-language interpreter, full time, in all her academic classes. The school district officials disagreed maintaining that the child did not need the interpreter.

In reviewing the evidence, the lower federal district court found that even though the child was performing better than the average child for her class; she understands much less of what transpires in class than if she were not deaf. Thus, she was not learning as much as she would have without her handicap. With this in mind, the lower court concluded that a "free appropriate public education" must be defined as "an opportunity to achieve her full potential commensurate with the opportunity provided other children." The federal Court of Appeals affirmed but the United States Supreme Court reversed and remanded the decision. The Supreme Court interpreted the Act as requiring that services for handicapped be sufficient to permit the child "to benefit" from instruction, but was not intended to prescribe a substantive standard prescribing a level of education.

In taking issue with the lower court's determinations that "the goal of the Act is to provide each handicapped child with an equal educational opportunity" and to "maximize" each child's potential "commensurate with the opportunity provided other children," the Supreme Court maintained that the lower courts had erred and that there was evidence that Congress "did not intend to achieve strict equality services for handicapped and non-handicapped children...." Rather, according to the Court, the intent was to merely provide "a basic floor of opportunity consistent with equal protection."

As to how and by whom the "basic floor" is to be defined, the Court said that the Act expressly charges states with the responsibility of providing teachers, administrators, and programs and practices appropriate for education of the handicapped. The Court concluded that it was "unlikely that Congress intended the courts to overturn a State's choice of appropriate educational theories ..." in treating the needs of handicapped children. The Act requires that state and local educational agencies in cooperation with the parents or guardian of the child would decide on the appropriateness of the educational services to be offered, but where there is disagreement the Act vests the authority for final determination in the State. The Supreme Court said "We previously have cautioned that courts lack the 'specialized knowledge and experience' necessary to resolve 'persistent and difficult questions of educational policy.' We think Congress shared that view when it passed the Act. As already demonstrated, Congress' intention was not that the Act displace the primacy of the States in the field of education, but the States receive funds to assist them in extending their educational systems to the handicapped. Therefore, once a court determines that the requirements of the Act have been met, questions of methodology are for resolution by the States." *Rowley*, supra.

Latitude of states, however, is limited by provisions of the Act which mandate preference be given to certain types of education. For example, the Act expressed and the Court in *Rowley* emphasized that "states 'to the maximum extent appropriate' must educate handicapped children 'with children who are not handicapped.'" This is the mainstreaming requirement. In this regard, following *Rowley*, the United States Court of Appeals for the Eighth Circuit held that the state of Arkansas could not require a deaf child to leave her local district school to attend the Arkansas School for the Deaf, the state residential school for deaf children. The state authorities had determined that the child could only acquire the best possible education by attending the state school. The appeals court, noting that *Rowley* did not require the state to "maximize" the educational opportunity, found that an overriding requirement of the Act was that the child should remain with other children in a regular school setting among nonhandicapped children. The court, therefore, invoked *Rowley* to overrule the state's placement of the child. Springdale School District #50 of Washington County v. Grace (8th Cir.1982).

The *Rowley* precedent is now relied on by lower courts in determining appropriate placement and the requirements of the child's IEP. However, to determine what constitutes the basic floor of opportunity as required by *Rowley*, as opposed to placement in programs of maximum service, has become a source of contention between school districts and parents. For example, in a case where parents rejected public school placement and sought to compel a school district to reimburse them for expenses they incurred in placing their severely retarded child in a private maximum service facility, the court ruled that the *Rowley* standard prevailed and the hearing officer's determination of appropriate placement in the public school should be given due consideration by the lower court. Kerkam v. McKenzie (D.C.Cir.1988).

## § 10.45 Procedural Safeguards

As indicated in the *Mills* and *Rowley* cases, proper procedures are a vital aspect in assuring that appropriate educational services are extended to handicapped children. The necessary due process specifications delineated in *Mills* were followed and embellished by the EAHCA in 1975. Section 1415 of that act contains procedures that are mandatory. Most importantly, the procedures specify that parents must be given notice and an opportunity to participate in the development of a child's education program. Inclusive is the requirement that parents be informed of all methods and procedures by which conflicts and grievances may be appealed and resolved. Implicit therein is the assurance that hearings regarding the child's placement will be impartial and unbiased. The law, § 1415, emphasizes this standard of fairness by giving the parent a right to have the hearing conducted by a person who is neither an employee of the school district nor of the state department of education.

As stated in *Rowley*, a reviewing court must make sure that procedures are followed by the district. A school district making a placement decision without reference to the IEP violates the requirements of the law and free appropriate education. On the other hand, if an insignificant procedural error is made not resulting in the child's loss of educational opportunity, the court will decline to "exalt form over substance" by enforcing a technical infraction from the act's procedural standards.

If the results of the hearing are not to the satisfaction of the parent or the school district, then appeal can be made to the state department of education. During the time in which appeals are taken, the child must remain or "stay put" in his or her "then current" program. As discussed later in this chapter, indefinite suspension during pendency of appeal violates this section of the law. Appeal to either state or federal courts may be taken after a decision has been rendered by the state department of education.

## § 10.46  Individualized Education Program (IEP)

The purpose, of course, of all these procedural safeguards is to ensure to the parent and child that an appropriate individualized educational program (IEP) will be provided. The IEP goes beyond merely providing a place for the child in the public schools, but, more extensively, must design and reduce to writing an educational plan that takes into account the identification of the child's educational needs, the annual instructional goals and objectives, the specific educational programs and services to be provided, and the necessary evaluation procedures to monitor the child's progress. An IEP is "more than a mere exercise in Public Relations," indeed it is the "centerpiece of the statute's education delivery system for disabled children." "The term 'individualized education program' means a written statement for each child with a disability developed in a meeting by a representative of the local educational agency or an intermediate educational unit who shall be qualified to provide, or supervise the provision of, specially designed instruction to meet the unique needs of children with disabilities...."

The IEP statement describing the child's educational goals and specifying required services is developed by a multidisciplinary team. For initial evaluation and placement the IEP team must have as members a school official, the child's teacher(s), parents and other person(s) qualified to interpret evaluation results. Because the IEP must be jointly prepared by school officials and parents and reviewed annually, a condition of possible contention is staged. Contests between parents and school districts over the nature of the IEP have created a plethora of handicapped litigation in recent years, all of which has begun to form a formidable body of case law.

## § 10.47   Related Services

The IDEA requires that school districts provide disabled students with supportive services that will meet their educational needs as prescribed by the Individualized Education Program (IEP). Such support services are called "related services" by the Act. A school district is required to provide "related services" to disabled children, but not "medical services." The courts though tend to give broad meaning to related services. See Antkowiak v. Ambach (2d Cir.1988). The Act defines related services as "transportation and such developmental, corrective, and other supportive services (including speech pathology and occupational therapy, recreation, and medical and counseling services, except that such medical services shall be for diagnostic and evaluative purposes only) as may be required to assist a handicapped child to benefit from special education...." 20 U.S.C.A. § 1401(17).

Federal regulations pertaining to this section of the Act have further defined each of the terms included in "related services." For example, "psychological services" are explained to be "planning and managing a program of psychological services, including psychological counseling for children and parents." 34 C.F.R. § 300.13(b)(8). "Counseling services" are defined as "services provided by qualified social workers, psychologists, guidance counselors, or other qualified personnel." 34 C.F.R. § 300.13(b)(2). Courts have further added their interpretation of other terms, psychotherapy, for example, T.G. v. Board of Education of Piscataway (D.N.J.1983); "transportation," Alamo Heights Ind. School District v. State Board of Education (5th Cir. 1986); and "free transportation," School District of Philadelphia v. Commonwealth, Dept. of Education (Pa. Cmwlth.1988); Filter v. Cape Girardeau School District (E.D.Mo.1993). See also School Board of Pinellas County v. Smith (Fla.App.1989). Metropolitan Government v. Tennessee Department of Education (Tenn.App.1989).

The leading case regarding "related services" was decided by the U.S. Supreme Court in 1984. Irving Independent School District v. Tatro (S.Ct.1984). The issue in *Tatro* was the scope of "medical services" that the school district is required to provide. The child requiring medical services had spina bifida orthopedic and speech impairments and a neurogenic bladder, which prevented her from emptying her bladder voluntarily. The child's parents maintained that the school was required to provide the necessary catheterization every three to four hours, while the school maintained that this was not the role of the school because it constituted "medical services." The specific question required the Court to interpret the meaning and statutory intent of Congress in requiring "medical and counseling services, except that such medical services shall be for diagnostic and evaluation purposes only as may be required to assist a handicapped child to benefit from special education...." The Court said "Congress plainly required schools to hire various specially trained personnel to help handicapped children, such as 'trained occupational therapists ... psychologists,' " etc. Thus, the Court concluded that "school nursing services are not the sort of burden that Congress intended to exclude as a 'medical service.' " The Court then set out guidelines that could be used by school districts pertaining to both health and educational needs that fall within the definition of "related services." First, the child must be classified as handicapped and entitled to related services. Second, only those services necessary to aid the handicapped child must be provided. Third, services are to be extended only if they can be provided by a school nurse or other qualified person and do not require the level of knowledge to be performed only by a physician. Fourth, the related service requires "services" and not the purchase of special equipment. Subsequent court decisions have held that "related services" do not extend to requiring the school to hire an in-school nurse to attend to the child's daily medical needs. Conditions so severe as to require constant nursing care go beyond "related services" and fall within the realm of the medical services that school districts are not required to provide. Detsel v. Board of Education (N.D.N.Y.1986).

## § 10.48  Placement

Proper placement of the student in a particular program or school is a most important aspect of the individualized educational program (IEP). There may be several options for placement of handicapped students in programs within the public school, but there is also the recognized alternative to placement in a nonpublic school which has special education facilities. A question arises as to whether the nonpublic school options must be taken into account when the student's IEP is devised and if failure to do invalidates the IEP. The United States Court of Appeals for the Fourth Circuit has held that such consideration of private services are not required to have a valid IEP. Hessler v. State Board of Education of Maryland (4th Cir.1983). The court said "While the federal and state statutory schemes clearly contemplate the use of nonpublic educational services under the circumstances, we think it clear that such resort is limited to those instances in which public educational services appropriate for the handicapped child are not available."

Further, the court said that just because parents may be able to show that the nonpublic school program is possibly more appropriate or better than the public school program, this does not mean that the public school program is necessarily inappropriate. Following the rationale of *Rowley*, this court emphasized that there was no obligation on the part of the school district to provide a handicapped child "all services necessary to maximize his or her potential commensurate with the opportunity provided to other children."

Where it is shown that a placement in a summer school program, in addition to the regular year-long program, prevents the handicapped child from retrogressing educationally, the school district may be required to provide a summer program. The requirement of the Act that personalized instruction be provided to meet individual needs of the handicapped child may possibly require an IEP with summer school as a requisite condition. Yaris v. Special School District of St. Louis County (E.D.Mo.1983). See also Alamo Heights Ind. School Dist. v. State Bd. of Educ. (5th Cir.1986).

In Johnson v. Independent School Dist. No. 4 of Bixby (10th Cir.1990), the court ruled that the regression recoupment problem should be applied not only to academic problems but also to non-academic ones as well. Non-academic problems such as behavioral and social needs are to be considered in determining extended school year needs.

## § 10.5  PRIVATE SCHOOL FOR CHILDREN WITH DISABILITIES

There are two categories of disabled children in private schools. The first are those disabled children who are placed in private schools following the appropriate IEP determination. These children are in private schools with specially designed programs to meet their educational needs. The facilities where children are placed by public agencies must be facilities that are state approved. The second category are those children with disabilities who have been placed in private schools by their parents. These private schools may or may not have appropriately designed education programs. The question is are children placed in private facilities by parent eligible for IDEA services? The IDEA requires a state's plan to have policies and procedures assuring that: "To the extent consistent with their number and location in the State provision is made for the participation of private school children with disabilities in the program assisted or carried out under this part by providing them with special education and related services."

Also according to the federal regulation, the local educational agencies are required to "... provide special education and related services designed to meet the needs of private school children with disabilities residing in the jurisdiction of the agency." The local educational agency is not required to pay for the child's education at the private school or facility unless the local educational agency cannot provide the services.

Recently, the U.S. Supreme Court in Florence County School Dist. Four, et al. v. Carter (S.Ct.1993), decided that if the court finds the educational placement is not reasonable, then the public school can be ordered by the court to reimburse the parents for costs. In this case, the state and local educational authorities found that the IEP developed for a child was adequate, the parents disagreed and enrolled her in a private academy. Subsequently the parents filed suit seeking reimbursement for tuition and other costs. The district court ruled the public school's proposed IEP and educational goals "were wholly inadequate" and failed to meet IDEA requirements. The Supreme Court stated: "This case presents the question whether a court may order reimbursement for parents who unilaterally withdraw their child from a public school that provides an inappropriate education under IDEA and put the child in a private school that provides an education that is otherwise proper under IDEA, ... We hold that the court may order such reimbursement, and therefore affirm the judgment of the Court of Appeals."

# § 10.6 DISABLED CHILDREN IN SECTARIAN SCHOOLS

In Zobrest v. Catalina Foothills School Dist. (S.Ct. 1993), the Supreme Court ruled that it does not violate the Establishment Clause of the First Amendment for a public school to pay for a sign language interpreter to accompany a student to classes at a Roman Catholic High School. The student was provided an interpreter while enrolled in a public school. When the student enrolled of his volition in a sectarian school, he requested the same services. The public school board refused to pay for the interpreter on the grounds that such assistance constituted aid to religion. The Supreme Court held that "the Establishment Clause does not prevent (the school board) from furnishing a disabled child enrolled in a sectarian school with a sign language interpreter in order to facilitate his education. Government programs that neutrally provide benefits to a broad class of citizens defined without reference to religion are not readily subject to an Establishment Clause challenge just because sectarian institutions may also receive an attenuated financial benefit."

The Supreme Court, however, did not reconcile Zobrest with Aguilar v. Felton (S.Ct.1985). Aguilar is discussed more fully in the chapter on religion in this book. In Aguilar, the Supreme Court held that use of public funds to pay for employees in sectarian schools violated the Establishment Clause. Perhaps related services may be delivered in the sectarian school but full-time special education teachers would come under the penumbra of Aguilar and therefore be unconstitutional. How the cases are distinguished must be determined by further litigation.

## § 10.7 DISCIPLINE

The mainstreaming of handicapped children has underscored the need for guidelines governing the discipline of handicapped students. Neither § 504 nor Public Law 101–476 (94–142) addresses the discipline issue, leaving it to the courts to decipher the legal ramifications involved.

Two provisions of the Individuals with Disabilities Education Act (IDEA) must be considered when disciplinary action is taken with a handicapped student: appropriate education and least restrictive environment. IDEA mandates that a disabled student must be provided a free appropriate education in the least restrictive environment. Acceptable environments for the placement of a disabled child range from least restrictive (a regular classroom) to highly restrictive (an institution). However, each environment can be termed "least restrictive" depending upon the seriousness of a particular disability, and the student's ability to cope within a specific environment.

Courts have consistently ruled that disabled students must be given special consideration in disciplinary proceedings. Earlier court decisions prohibited expulsion, noting that, under Public Law 94–142, services must be provided through alternative placement in one of the other educational environments offered.

In 1981, expulsion was at the forefront of a major case wherein nine mentally retarded students in Florida sued local districts and the state, claiming that their expulsion from school effectively denied them an appropriate education. The court upheld expulsion as a viable form of discipline. But, however, pointed out that cessation of all educational programs violated the rights of handicapped students. Thus, students could be removed, but could not be denied educational services, requiring the schools to make special provision to convey education to students after their dismissal. S–1 v. Turlington (5th Cir.1981).

Suspension has been viewed favorably by the courts as an appropriate disciplinary action for disabled students, when it has been determined that misconduct is not related to the student's disability. If it is related to the disabling condition, an alternate or more restrictive placement should be considered, rather than suspension or expulsion. Doe v. Koger (N.D.Ind.1979).

## § 10.71  Stay-put

The IDEA contains a pendency of review provision that prohibits school authorities from unilaterally excluding a disabled child from school during review proceedings to determine the placement of the student. Section 1415(e)(3) of the act states that "the child shall remain in the then current educational placement" until proper placement can be determined. This so-called stay-put provision raises the question as to whether a child can be excluded from school for an indefinite period of time for dangerous or disruptive conduct growing out of a disability. In Honig v. Doe (S.Ct.1988), the U.S. Supreme Court resolved the issue by making it clear that the EAHCA (1) confers a substantive right to education on disabled students, (2) prohibits school officials from unilaterally excluding a disabled student from the classroom for dangerous or disruptive conduct for an indeterminate period of time where conduct grows out of a disability, and (3) permits school officials to temporarily suspend a student for up to ten days to protect the safety of others and to provide a "cooling down." During a period of temporary suspension an IEP process can be initiated to review the child's placement.

If the school needs more than ten days to change the placement to a more restrictive environment, it may petition the court for an injunction. Yet, even though the "stay put" provision requires that the child remain in school, it does not forbid the use of reasonable measures to control an offending child who endangers himself or others. The school may employ methods such as study carrels, time-outs, detention or other restriction of privileges in the interest of the safety and decorum of the school. Such measures do not constitute a change of placement.

In Texas City Independent School District v. Jorstad (S.D.Tex.1990), the court issued an injunction allowing the school more time to find an appropriate placement for a child who was a danger to himself and others; he struck teachers and other students, tore a wooden door off its hinges and jumped out of a second floor window, among other things.

## § 10.8 ACQUIRED IMMUNODEFICIENCY SYNDROME (AIDS)

One of the many legal issues emerging from the dread of AIDS retrovirus is whether children so infected can be excluded from school. AIDS cases have been litigated under IDEA, the Rehabilitation Act of 1973, Section 504 (29 U.S.C.A. § 794), and under the Due Process and Equal Protection Clauses of the U.S. Constitution. A threshold question is whether an AIDS child may be defined as a "handicapped individual" under § 504 of the Rehabilitation Act of 1973. Under this law a person is handicapped if he or she has "a physical impairment" which substantially limits major life activities, has a record of impairment, or is regarded as having an impairment as provided in 29 U.S.C.A. § 707(7)(B). In Doe v. Dalton Elementary School District No. 148 (N.D.Ill.1988) the court said that AIDS constituted impairment under Section 504. The rationale supporting this conclusion was based on the U.S. Supreme Court ruling in *Arline*, wherein the Court said that handicapped individuals may include "not only those who are actually physically impaired but also those who are regarded as impaired and who as a result 'are substantially limited in a major life activity.' " Simply having the virus may be considered a handicapping condition, thus, any person infected with the AIDS virus may be handicapped under the meaning of Section 504.

Another issue with AIDS students is whether they are covered by the IDEA. In the case of AIDS students, the category that would most closely fit is "other health impaired children." AIDS is not listed as an example of an acute or chronic health problem by the IDEA. In October of 1984, the Department of Education addressed the applicability of EAHCA (IDEA) to AIDS victims. The department stated that AIDS is not considered to be "handicapped" as a term defined in EAHCA (IDEA), unless the child needs special education. The opinion states: "Children with AIDS could be eligible for special education programs under the category of 'other health impaired,' if they have chronic or acute health problems which adversely affect their educational performance."

The IDEA would apply to AIDS victims only if the virus adversely affects their educational performance. If a child is seropositive or a "healthy carrier," then he or she is not covered under IDEA, but if the child becomes an AIDS victim and this diminishes his or her educational performance, then the IDEA must be enforced to meet the needs of the child.

The courts have unanimously upheld the right of an AIDS child to attend school. A California court held that a child infected with the AIDS virus could not be excluded from regular school program because the school board could not prove that he was not "otherwise qualified." The school board was, also, unable to prove that the child could possibly spread the AIDS virus to other children even though the infected child had a record of aggressive behavior and had bitten another child. Thomas v. Atascadero Unified School District (C.D.Cal.1986).

## § 10.9 ATTORNEY'S FEES

Prior to 1986 there was no provision for attorneys' fees to be awarded to successful parents in litigation over provision of educational services for a disabled child. In that year Congress enacted the Handicapped Children's Protection Act (HCPA) (P.L. 99–372), amending the EAHCA to enable the courts to award attorney's fees. The act authorized the awards to be made for litigation that was either filed or still pending as of July 3, 1986.

The U.S. Court of Appeals for the Sixth Circuit has held that Section 1988 of HCPA establishes that the courts may award parents' attorney "reasonable fees" to be calculated according to the prevailing market rate in the relevant community, regardless of whether the plaintiff is represented by private or non-profit counsel. Eggers v. Bullitt County School District (6th Cir.1988).

Attorney's fees may be awarded by the court for legal work done even though the dispute ends in an out-of-court settlement, prior to trial, in which the school district assumes the special education obligation originally sought by the plaintiff parents. Masotti v. Tustin Unified School District (C.D.Cal.1992). Attorney's fees were awarded in an Ohio case where a dispute between parents and school district was settled prior to a hearing. Moore v. Crestwood Local School District (N.D.Ohio 1992).

## § 10.91 Monetary Damages

While "Congress did not intend the child's entitlement to a *free* education to turn upon her (or his) parent's ability to 'front' its costs," Miener v. State of Missouri (8th Cir.1986), nevertheless, federal legislation does not provide for money damages to be awarded to parents of disabled students when they prevail in court challenges. Where school officials do not violate any civil or equal protection rights, but merely fail to provide the student with an IEP under the IDEA, no money damages will be awarded for physical or emotional harm. Smith v. Philadelphia School District (E.D.Pa.1988). Disabled children, however, may seek recovery by bringing a civil rights suit against local school boards. Edward B. v. Brunelle (D.N.H.1986).

# CHAPTER 11

# STUDENT SEX DISCRIMINATION

## § 11.1 INTRODUCTION

Education in America reflects the norms of society; if society is unjust, then the educational system is likely to be also. Societal standards have historically assumed that women and men should play much different and carefully delineated roles in the work force. Societal stereotypes of males and females spilled over to the schools where boys played interscholastic athletics and girls were the cheerleaders or majorettes. Athletic participation by girls was generally confined to intramural sports or to physical education classes. In the classroom, boys were assumed to be more capable in mathematics and science and girls more adept at English grammar and foreign languages.

The women's rights movement of the 1970s has had an important influence on the schools; today women are advised to enter occupations which were formerly male enclaves and are being advised to enter colleges and graduate and professional schools once reserved for men only.

Court decisions and legislation have reinforced the equal treatment between women and men. Most important have been the expanding judicial interpretation of the intent of the Equal Protection Clause of the Fourteenth Amendment, Title VI of the Civil Rights Act of 1964 and Title IX of the Educational Amendments of

1972, each of which affects sexual equality among students. (See Chapter 18, Employee Discrimination).

## § 11.2  EQUAL PROTECTION OF SEXES

The first of the modern cases involving gender discrimination was Reed v. Reed (S.Ct.1971), in which the United States Supreme Court struck down a state statute because it gave preference to the male over the female and as such was held to violate the Equal Protection Clause. The Court, however, did not elevate sex classifications to the special category of constitutional classes, such as race, requiring strict judicial scrutiny of legislative actions when challenged under federal Equal Protection. Where race is concerned the state must show a compelling interest in classifications; where sex is concerned the state need only to show that its actions are not arbitrary or capricious. In fact, gender discrimination occupies a kind of in-between constitutional status which requires that the state bear the burden of showing that its acts are not arbitrary or irrational, but does not rise fully to the status of a fundamental right that would require that the state bear the burden of showing that its acts are, in fact, compelling and absolutely necessary to effectuate the common interests of all the people.

It was in a later case in which the Supreme Court appeared to add more significance to sex as a classification when it held, in Craig v. Boren (S.Ct.1976), "that classifications by gender must serve important governmental objectives and must be substantially related to achievement of those objectives." In this case it appears that the Court established a separated, albeit, intermediate category, of judicial scrutiny to cases involving sex discrimination. Instead of the state showing simply that its classification by sex is rational, it must now show that the classification "serves important governmental objectives." Thus, the state must bear a greater burden in justifying an act which classifies persons based on gender. What this means is that actions by a school district which treat students differently because of their sex must bear the burden of showing that the rule furthers an "important governmental objective." Whether the rule will stand depends on the interpretation of what constitutes an "important" objective.

## § 11.21 Admission of Females

Higher admission standards for female than for male applicants to a public preparatory high school violates the Equal Protection Clause. Berkelman v. San Francisco Unified School District (9th Cir.1974). In another case, a federal district court in Massachusetts held that the admission policy at the Boston Latin School violated equal protection because it set a different test cutoff score for boys and girls. Bray v. Lee (Mass.1972). Here the school in attempting to maintain a 50–50 balance in the number of boys and girls had established separate cutoff scores. The method used for each group was to simply count down from the highest test score in each of the two groups of applicants, boys and girls, until they had accepted the total number necessary to maintain a balanced enrollment. Girls, though, scored higher on the tests, thus, the cutoff for girls was 133 while it was only 120 for boys. Several girls who scored between 120 and 133 were not admitted. The court held that this type of admissions policy violated equal protection because it created "prejudicial disparities" based on sex.

## § 11.22  Athletic Teams

Gender classifications which deny participation to female students may violate equal protection. The courts have generally held the Equal Protection Clause requires high school females be allowed to compete in non-contact sports. Under Title IX regulations provide that a school must allow an individual to participate in a particular sport if no such sport is available to the individual or where athletic opportunities have been limited for that sex. Title IX also allows a school to deny participation in a contact sport, but some federal and state courts have ruled that denying a female the right to participate in a contact sport, such as football, violates the equal protection clause of the Fourteenth Amendment. One rationale has been that the exclusion of girls from contact sports in order to protect them from injury is not related to a justifiable government objective in relationship to the Fourteenth Amendment. Darrin v. Gould (Wash. 1975); Leffel v. Wisconsin Interscholastic Athletic Association (E.D.Wis.1978).

On the other hand, the courts have generally ruled that it does not deny equal protection to refuse to allow males to compete on female teams. Clark v. Arizona Interscholastic Assoc. (9th Cir.1992). See also Rowley v. Members of the Board of Education (10th Cir.1988). In *Clark*, the court considered the governmental reasons for denying males the right to compete on female teams. Among the objectives was the desire of the school to offer girls the opportunity to participate in interscholastic sports, an opportunity not previously extended with all male teams. To allow males to participate in female sports and to possibly crowd girls out of their own sports activities would have defeated the school's purposes in creating such opportunities for females. These objectives were legitimate and important, therefore they withstood the equal protection test as proffered in *Craig v. Boren*, supra, of serving important governmental objectives. In Kleczek v. Rhode Island Interscholastic League, Inc. (R.I.1992), the court denied a male student the opportunity to participate on a girl's field hockey team. The reason was that gender issues were to be reviewed under the intermediate scrutiny standard which requires a rational reason as opposed to the strict scrutiny standard which places an obligation on the government to have a compelling reason for the rule. The court accepted as reasonable that the rule excluding males from female sports was to promote safety and the preservation of interscholastic competition in high school athletics. Thus competition is determined by the innate physiological difference between boys and girls. See also B.C. v. Board of Educ., Cumberland Regional School District (N.J.Super.1987) denying male student's request to play on girl's hockey team.

In a Minnesota case, a state athletic association league rule was challenged because it forbade girls' participation in the boys' interscholastic athletic program either as a member of a boys' team or as a member of a girls' team competing against boys. Two girls where denied the opportunity to participate as members of boys' skiing and cross-country running teams. No teams in these sports were provided for girls by their schools. The court adopted the rational basis test and said that in evaluating state actions under the Equal Protection Clause, the courts were to consider three criteria: (1) the character of the classification, (2) the individual interest affected by the classification, and (3) the governmental interest asserted in support of the classification. In evaluating the facts of the case against these criteria, the court concluded, first, that the discrimination was based on sex and as such was subject to examination by the courts as a legitimate controversy. In this regard the court said that discrimination based on sex can no longer be justified by "reliance on outdated images ... of women as peculiarly delicate and impressionable creatures in need of protection from the rough and tumble of unvarnished humanity." Secondly, the interests denied were educational benefits that should be for all students. In particular, the court said, "discrimination in education is one of the most damaging injustices women suffer. It denies them equal education and equal employment opportunity, contributing to a second-class image.... Discrimination in high school interscholastic athletics constitutes discrimination in education." The court went on to point out that interscholastic activities are today recognized as an integral part of the educational process and that stereotyping of students in education has helped to perpetuate discrimination against females, generally. Thirdly, the court queried the high school athletic league in determining its interest in maintaining the separation of the sexes in the sports activities. The league maintained that physiological differences between males and females made it impossible for girls to equitably compete with males. The court refused to accept this rationale observing that evidence had been presented indicating that there was widely differing athletic ability within the classes of men and women, possibly as wide as between the classes of men and women. The record showed the schools had, in fact, adopted no cut policies allowing all male students, no matter how untalented, to participate in these same non-contact sports. On this basis the court had no alternative but to declare the rule unconstitutional. Brenden v. Independent School District 742 (8th Cir.1973).

However, another court ruled that the gender classifications must be analyzed under the strict scrutiny standard for purposes of the Massachusetts constitution. Using this higher standard, the court determined the male must be allowed to participate on the girl's team. Attorney General v. Massachusetts Interscholastic Athletic Association (Mass.1979).

## § 11.3 TITLE IX

The Education Amendments of 1972, 20 U.S.C.A. §§ 1681–1683, contained Title IX, the popular law that forbade discrimination based on sex. Title IX prohibits discrimination not only for athletics and other extracurricular activities but also for financial aid, testing, curricular offerings, pregnancy and marital status. In 1984 in Grove City College v. Bell (S.Ct.1984), the U.S. Supreme Court interpreted the section of Title IX which states "any education program or activity receiving federal financial assistance" to mean that the specific program must be receiving federal funds for Title IX to apply. In other words, federal funds provided to an education program would be subject to Title IX restrictions only if the discrimination alleged occurred in the specific program that actually received the federal funds. This program specific approach obviously excluded interscholastic athletic programs because they do not receive federal funding.

In response to *Grove City*, Congress passed the Civil Rights Restoration Act of 1987. This Act specified that Title IX applied to the entire institution if any program within the institution was a recipient of federal funding. Also in North Haven Board of Education v. Bell (S.Ct. 1982), the Supreme Court determined Title IX not only includes students but also employees and that Title IX is enforceable through the Office of Civil Rights (OCR) in the Department of Education. Further, in Franklin v. Gwinnett County Public Schools (S.Ct.1992), the court interpreted Title IX to cover sexual harassment based on the same standards that sexual harassment is covered under Title VII, 1964 Civil Rights Act. Title VII prohibits sexual harassment based on "quid pro quo" harassment, involving conditioning of benefits based on sexual favors and "hostile environment" which relate to an abusive environment.

In Cannon v. University of Chicago (S.Ct.1979), the United States Supreme Court held that Title IX created a private remedy under which an individual could challenge discriminatory acts. Before *Cannon*, Title IX had been interpreted as establishing legal redress resulting only in termination of federal funds. The Supreme Court said: "Title IX was patterned after Title VI of the Civil Rights Act of 1964. Except for the substitution of the word 'sex' in Title IX to replace the words 'race, color, or national origin' in Title VI, the two statutes use identical language to describe the benefitted class." Therefore, an individual had a right to litigate under Title IX to seek enforcement of the Act. As will be noted later, punitive damages were not available under *Cannon*, these would come later by court interpretation in the *Franklin* case.

A rule of an athletic association or a high school may violate Title IX but not be offensive to the Equal Protection Clause. The statute itself provides in Section 901(a)

"No person in the United States shall, on the basis of sex, be excluded from participation in, be denied the benefits of, or be subjected to discrimination under any education program or activity receiving Federal financial assistance...." Certain exceptions are noted including religious schools if the act is contrary to religious tenets, United States military schools, or institutions of higher education that have historically admitted students of only one sex.

## § 11.31  Enforcement of Title IX

Until 1992 if there was sex discrimination in a school district, the plaintiff could request that the federal funding be removed or suit could be filed under a private right of action as per *Cannon*. There were no damages available for the first twenty years of Title IX and there was a paucity of litigation. In 1992 in *Franklin v. Gwinnett County Public Schools*, supra, the Supreme Court drastically changed the enforcement of Title IX and other anti-discrimination statutes by unanimously allowing monetary damages for intentional violations of Title IX.

In *Franklin* a female student was sexually harassed by a teacher. The student said the teacher "... engaged in sexually-oriented conversations ... forcibly kissed her on the mouth ... [and] subjected her to coercive intercourse" among other things. School officials were aware of the sexual harassment but took no action. The student filed an action against the school board for monetary damages and the Supreme Court held damages were available under Title IX for intentional violations of the law. The Court noted that without damages, Ms. Franklin would basically have no remedy for her grievous injury.

## § 11.32  Comparability

Regulations pursuant to Title IX permit institutions to offer separate team sports, but are not intended to require boys' teams be opened to girls.  Teams, however, must be offered on a "comparable" basis for students of both sexes taking into account the interests and abilities of both sexes; "an institution would be required to provide separate teams for men and women in situations where the provision of only one team would not 'accommodate the interests and abilities of both sexes.'" *O'Connor v. Board of Education of School District 23*, supra.

Some of the standards that are reviewed to determine if the teams are comparable are:

1.  Whether the selection of sports and levels of competition effectively accommodate the interests and abilities or members of both sexes;

2.  A provision of equipment and supplies;

3.  Scheduling of games and practice times;

4.  Travel and per diem allowances;

5.  Opportunity to receive coaching and tutoring;

6.  Assignment and compensation of coaches and tutors;

7.  Provision of locker rooms, practice and competitive facilities;

8.  Provision of medical and training facilities and services;

9. Provision of housing and dining facilities and services;

10. Publicity.

## § 11.33 One Sex Teams

Regulations under Title IX (§ 86.41) provide for operation of separate sports where selection of teams is based on "competitive skill or the activities involved is a contact sport." Where a team is offered for one sex but not for the other, members of both sexes must be allowed to try out for the team offered unless the sport involved is a contact sport. In Colorado a high school girl sued because she was denied a chance to participate on a boys' soccer team, a contact sport. A court found that denial of the girl's request violated the Equal Protection Clause even though it may not have violated Title IX. Hoover v. Meiklejohn (D.Colo.1977). In this case, the court said that "the failure to establish any physical criteria to protect small or weak males from injurious effects of competition with larger and stronger males destroys the credibility of the reasoning urged in support of the sex classification ... and there is no rationality in limiting this patronizing protection to females."

# CHAPTER 12

# CIVIL LIABILITY

## § 12.1 INTRODUCTION

One of the most frequently expressed concerns of teachers and school administrators is their potential liability. When can they be sued and, if so, what are the chances of having to pay substantial damages out of their own meager earnings? In addressing these questions, this chapter is divided into two sections: (1) common law torts and (2) constitutional torts. The first section deals with common law torts, since they more commonly come into play with school litigation in which teachers are involved.

## § 12.2 WHAT IS A TORT?

Tort is a term applied to a wide variety of civil wrongs for which a court will afford a remedy to the injured party in the form of money damages. Torts are civil wrongs of person against person as opposed to person against the state, as in a crime. In a tort action, the injured party brings an action in law to recover compensation for damage suffered, while with a crime the state brings criminal proceedings to protect the interests of the public against the wrongdoer. A tort is to be distinguished from a breach of contract in that no special agreement exists between the parties. With a tort the person's rights are created by common law and not by the condition of a contract.

The word "tort" is a French term derived from the Latin "torquere," meaning twisted, which in English became a common synonym for "wrong." A tort may be committed by either an act or an omission to act which violates a person's right as created by law. While most are aware that to directly harm someone is deserving of damages, the more indirect nature of harm caused by an omission or failure to act creates a less discernible action. At school, the teacher and the student are placed in a special legal relationship where, if danger occurs, the teacher may, by virtue of this special relationship, be required to act to prevent harm to the student. Failure to act accordingly may result in a tort of omission.

Torts may be classified into three basic groups: (1) intentional interference, (2) strict liability, and (3) negligence. Virtually all of tort law in schools can be divided into actions for injuries caused by intentional acts and those for negligence.

## § 12.3  INTENTIONAL INTERFERENCE

Intentional torts come about as a result of voluntary action by the defendant. The defendant must intend to bring about a certain result which invades the interests of another. In schools, the most common types of intentional torts are assault and battery. Assault and battery brought as a tort is a civil action, a corresponding criminal action of assault and battery may be brought for the same incident. This section deals with assault and battery as a civil tort.

## § 12.31  Assault and Battery

Technically, a defendant may be liable if the plaintiff is placed in fear and apprehension of immediate physical contact. To hold a weapon in a threatening position, to chase in a hostile manner, or shake a fist under another's nose may all constitute assault. The key to establishing assault is the intent of the defendant and the knowledge of imminent harm by the plaintiff. No assault exists if the defendant did not intend to harm the plaintiff; there is no such thing as negligent assault. On the other hand, there is no assault if the plaintiff is not aware of the physical threat. If a person brandishes a gun over the head of a sleeping person, there is no assault.

In order for an assault to exist, there must be an unequivocal appearance of an attempt to do some immediate physical injury to the person of another. The act must be a display of force or menace of violence of such a nature as to cause reasonable apprehension of immediate bodily harm. For example, where a man said were you not an old man I would knock you down, the court held there was no assault. There was no assault because the old man had no reason to expect immediate harm.

Therefore, the intentional tort of assault may be consummated by an act which, while not involving physical contact, places a person in immediate fear of physical attack.

While assault is apprehension, battery is the actual physical contact. Assault and battery generally go together, but it is possible for each to exist without the other. For example, if a plaintiff is struck from behind and was not aware of the impending attack, battery is present, but not assault.

In a very old English case involving the meeting of two individuals in a narrow passageway, the judge explained assault and battery in this fashion. "First, the least touching of another in anger is a battery. Second, if two or more meet in a narrow passage, and without any violence or design of harm, the one touches the other gently, it will be no battery. Thirdly, if any of them use violence against the other, to force his way in a rude inordinate manner, it will be a battery; or any struggle about the passage to that degree as may do hurt will be a battery." Cole v. Turner (Eng.1704).

Assault and battery in schools are most often found in actions for excessive punishment of pupils. As discussed elsewhere in this book, teachers and school administrators have the authority by virtue of the doctrine of *in loco parentis* to administer reasonable corporal punishment where permitted by state statute or regulation. If, though, such punishment is excessive, malicious, or in violation of school regulations, then the teacher or administrator may be subject to an assault and battery action by or on behalf of the pupil. The school's authority extends to all pupil offenses which directly affect the decorum and conduct of the school, whether on school property or not.

To be guilty of assault and battery, the teacher must not only inflict on the child immoderate chastisement, but must do so with legal malice, wicked motives or the punishment must be the cause of permanent injury. The fact that a teacher administers several licks with a board fourteen to fifteen inches long, five inches wide, and one-half to two inches thick, producing reddish purple discoloration of the buttocks does not constitute excessive punishment to justify damages. LeBlanc v. Tyler (La.App.1980). (See Chapter 8, Student Discipline—Child Abuse.)

This same court observed that minor bruises could be expected from a hit or a swat on the posterior and that discoloration of the skin or soreness was not sufficient to establish excessiveness to constitute assault and battery. A teacher, however, should not be misled into believing that the courts will tolerate any degree of severity. (See Chapter 8, Student Discipline—Child Abuse.)

Where a teacher took a student alone into a vacant schoolroom and claimed to have given the student a "severe shaking," bruises on the student's chest and stomach, apparently fist marks, belied the teacher's testimony and the teacher was held to be liable for battery. Thomas v. Bedford (La.App.1980).

The Supreme Court of the United States has observed that tort actions for battery of students are viable legal remedies when it can be clearly shown that a teacher exceeded bounds of propriety in punishing a child.

Technically, assault is not a very practical action for a student to bring against a teacher. It is conceivable that a teacher could so intimidate or humiliate a student as to cause such mental anguish as to justify an assault action, but proof of cause and effect would be very difficult to establish.

On the other hand, the effects of physical punishment are easier to show, through photographs of the affected part of the body or by medical records; yet such evidence must clearly establish excessiveness in order to sustain an action for battery.

## § 12.32  False Imprisonment

A teacher may wonder if a student could institute an action for false imprisonment for staying after school or being confined to a certain schoolroom or space as punishment. False imprisonment is an unlawful restraint of one's physical liberty by another. A cause of action for false imprisonment must be sustained by the plaintiff showing two things: first, that detention or restraint was against his or her will and, second, that the detention or restraint was unlawful.

The key word here is "unlawful." Certain persons are immune from liability because they have a special legal relationship with the person who is restrained. Judicial officers, attorneys, physicians, parents, and school teachers, generally, have such legal status. School teachers, acting *in loco parentis*, have the authority to place reasonable restraints on students' physical liberty. The word reasonable is a necessary qualifier since the teacher and even the parent could restrict a child's freedom to an extent exceeding the bounds of their special privilege. Certainly, the teacher cannot chain the child in the dark basement of the school for two days and justify such action as reasonable. To be reasonable, detention must be relatively brief, in terms of minutes or a very few hours, and such infliction must be in good faith, without malice, for the best interests of the student and/or the school. Fertich v. Michener (Ind.1887). The belief that detention after school is an unjustified or injudicious exercise of authority on the part of the teacher does not in itself establish malice as to overcome the teacher's privilege.

In a Michigan case the court said, "[The] principal was engaged in [a] discretionary act in keeping students in his office, and had individual governmental immunity from action for false imprisonment resulting in keeping student in [the] office, absent allegations that [the] principal was not acting in [the] course of [his] employment or that he maliciously or intentionally falsely imprisoned student." Willoughby v. Lehrbass (Mich.App.1986).

## § 12.4 STRICT LIABILITY

Cases of strict liability are almost nonexistent in public school litigation. Strict liability may, though, occur where injury is done yet there is the inability to establish "fault." An establishment of fault requires that a causal connection be proven between an act and the injury. Where, however, there is no specific act, *per se*, or definable chain of events causing the injury, damages for the traditional negligence tort cannot prevail. This problem is particularly acute where hazards or ultrahazards to individuals or the public have been created. In such instances, on occasion, courts have allowed the claim of strict liability in the theory that "he who breaks must pay" or that the person (or corporation) best able to pay for an injury must bear the burden. Within the schools, it is conceivable that hazards subject to strict liability could be found in inherently dangerous activities.

A rare example of such a claim was litigated in Illinois in 1986 where a child was injured at school while jumping on a trampoline. The plaintiff alleged that "the trampoline was an *abnormally dangerous* instrumentality" (emphasis added). Illinois state law provides you must be held strictly liable under two theories (1) unreasonably dangerous defective products and (2) ultrahazardous activities. The trampoline met neither of these standards and the injury was caused by the manner of its use. Fallon v. Indian Trail School (Ill.App.1986). Strict liability is an area of tort law that has very little impact on teacher or school administrator liability.

## § 12.5 NEGLIGENCE

The most common tort action against teachers and school administrators is negligence. Negligence torts are neither expected nor intended as opposed to the intentional tort whose result is contemplated at the time of the act. Negligence is conduct falling below a legally established standard which results in injury to another person. It is failure to exercise due care when subjecting another to a risk or danger which causes harm.

An accident is by definition unavoidable and thus does not constitute negligence, but in many instances what first appears to be an accident may be traced to someone's negligent act. Children are well known for their accident propensities and courts are well aware of this, yet teachers must be on constant guard to prevent avoidable injuries to students. Where an injury could have been prevented by a teacher or an administrator, what may appear to be an accident becomes the tort of negligence.

## § 12.51 Standard of Conduct

That which is negligence in one circumstance may not be in another. No definite result can be predicted in an action for negligence. Each case must stand on its own set of facts as applied to a rule of law. The basic rule, which is the key to negligence, is the standard of conduct of the defendant. The appropriate standard of conduct is determined by a balancing of the risks, in light of the social value of the threatened interest, and the probability and extent of harm, against the value of the interest which the actor is required to protect. *Restatement of Torts*, pp. 291–293.

This balance between the threatened harm and the utility of the actor's conduct is not, in most cases, easy to determine. In attempting better definition, the courts have developed the reasonableness theory requiring that for negligence to exist injury must have occurred from the exposure of another to "unreasonable risk." The reasonableness test has been personified in the "reasonable person."

## § 12.52 The Reasonable Person

The reasonable person is hypothetical, a community ideal of human behavior, whose conduct under the same or similar circumstances is regarded as the measure of reasonable behavior, "a fictitious person who never has existed on land or sea." William L. Prosser, *Law of Torts* (West Publishing Company, 1955), p. 124.

The reasonable person has been portrayed by different courts as a prudent person, a person of average prudence, a person of ordinary sense using ordinary care and skill, and as a reasonably prudent person. He or she is an ideal, a model of conduct and a community standard. The nature of the reasonable person, although a community ideal, varies in every case. His or her characteristics are (1) the physical attributes of the defendant, (2) normal intelligence, (3) normal perception and memory with a minimum level of information and experience common to the community, and (4) such superior skill and knowledge as the actor has or holds himself or herself out as having. As can be seen, the reasonable person formula changes with different factual situations because of the attributes or deficiencies of the defendant and because of peculiarities of beliefs, values, and customs of the individual community.

The reasonable person then has the same physical characteristics as the actor himself and the acts in question are measured accordingly. Correspondingly, the man who is crippled is not held to the same standard as the man with no physical infirmities. The courts have also made allowances for the weaknesses or attributes connected with the sex and age of the individual. The courts have not, however, been so lenient with individuals who have mental deficiencies. The courts have traditionally held that a person with lower mental ability than an average person must adjust and conform to the rules of society. Where a person is actually insane, a more convincing argument can be made for allowing for the particular incapacity but that also depends on the situation.

One such case illustrating this point occurred when a junior high pupil entered school and shot and killed the principal and wounded a teacher and two students. The student was ruled criminally insane, but the wounded teacher and student filed a civil action in tort. The court found that although a person was criminally insane, civil liability in damages was an appropriate remedy. The court said that "American courts have unanimously chosen to impose liability on an insane person rather than leaving the loss on the innocent victim." Williams v. Kearbey (Kan.App.1989).

## § 12.53   A Reasonably Prudent Teacher

Teachers are specially educated and trained to teach and work with children and young adults. Teachers hold college degrees and are certified in educational methodologies. As such, teachers hold themselves out to the public as possessing superior skills and understanding of educational processes. By virtue of these attributes teachers may be held to a higher standard of conduct than the ordinary person without commensurate education and training. The teacher's required conduct in tort law may be that of a reasonably prudent teacher in the same or similar circumstances rather than the lesser standard of merely a reasonably prudent person.

Too, the teacher has the additional responsibility of standing *in loco parentis*; a Vermont court has said that a teacher's "relationship to the pupils under his care and custody differs from that generally existing between a public employee and a member of the general public. In a limited sense the teacher stands in the parents' place in his relationship to a pupil ... and has such a portion of the powers of the parent over the pupil as is necessary to carry out his employment. In such relationship, he owes his pupils the duty of supervision...." Eastman v. Williams (Vt.1965).

This view is apparently taken by most courts. Some, though, hold that a teacher should not bear this additional burden. Where this view prevails the teacher is required to exercise only the reasonable prudence of any normal person.

# § 12.6　ELEMENTS OF NEGLIGENCE

The nature of negligence is best explained in four component parts. These are: (1) a duty on the part of the actor to protect others against unreasonable risks, (2) a failure on the part of the actor to exercise a standard of care commensurate with the risks involved, and (3) the conduct of the actor must be the proximate or legal cause of the injury. A causal connection must exist between the act and the resulting injury. The fourth is that there must be an injury, actual loss, or damage that resulted from the act.

## § 12.61　Duty

A person has a duty to abide by a standard of reasonable conduct in the face of apparent risks. The courts generally hold that no duty exists where the defendant could not have reasonably foreseen the danger of risk involved. A duty owed by one person to another intensifies as the risk increases. In other words, the duty to protect another is proportional to the risk or hazard of a particular activity. In school functions, where risks are greater to school children, a teacher has an increased level of obligation or duty to the children. For example, whenever a teacher has children perform a dangerous laboratory experiment, he or she has a greater obligation for the childrens' safety than where he or she is merely supervising a study hall. One judge has explained the duty requirement in this way. "Every person is negligent when, without intending any wrong, he does such an act or omits to take such a precaution that under the circumstances he, as an ordinary prudent person, ought reasonably to foresee that he will thereby expose the interest of another to an unreasonable risk of harm. In determining whether his conduct will subject the interest of another to an unreasonable risk of harm, a person is required to take into account such of the surrounding circumstances as would be taken into account by a reasonably prudent person and possess such knowledge as is possessed by an ordinary reasonable person and to use such judgment and discretion as is exercised by persons of reasonable intelligence under the same or similar circumstance." Osborne v. Montgomery (Wis.1931).

A person is negligent when, by affirmative act, he injures another. However, the question often arises as to whether a person can be liable for failure to act at all. Generally the law holds that a person is not liable for an omission to act where there is no definite relationship between the parties. In other words, no general duty exists to aid a person in danger. For example, even though there is a moral duty, no legal duty exists for a bystander to aid a drowning person.

Where teachers and students are concerned, however, the situation is quite different. The greater duty of the teacher invested by the *in loco parentis* standard compels the teacher to take affirmative actions to protect students. Thus, teachers may be liable for an omission to act as well as for a negligent affirmative act.

An example of an action raised because of an alleged omission was litigated in a case where a student told several friends that she intended to kill herself and the information was relayed to a guidance counselor. The counselor questioned the girl who denied the statement. Yet, later the girl committed suicide in a murder suicide pact with another thirteen year old. There had earlier been much discussion at school about teen suicides. The question before the court was whether the counselor owed a duty to inform the parents of the suicidal statements. The court said, "We hold that school counselors have a *duty* to use reasonable means to attempt to prevent a suicide when they are on notice of a child or adolescent student's suicide intent." The case was remanded to the lower court to determine if the counselor had breached her duty. Eisel v. Board of Education (Md.1991).

## § 12.62  Standard of Care

A standard of care must be exercised commensurate with the duty owed. A legally recognized duty or obligation requires the actor to conform to a certain standard of care as the foreseeable risk involved in an act increases. The standard of care of auto mechanics shop teachers for protection of youngsters is generally greater than that of the school librarian. This is, of course, true because the risk of injury involved in handling power tools, machinery, and electrical equipment is much greater than the risk of being injured while reading a book.

The standard of care which a teacher owes a student assumes an extra duty to keep the children secure from injury. Teachers have a "special responsibility recognized by common law to supervise their charges." Miller v. Griesel (Ind.1974). It is further well settled that the amount of care which the teacher owes the student increases or decreases with the relative maturity or immaturity of the student. One court has commented that even with students of seventeen or eighteen years of age, a teacher's care must be quite high, particularly where students are in groups "where the herd instinct and competitive spirit tend naturally to relax vigilance." Satariano v. Sleight (Cal.App.1942).

While standards of care may differ among teachers, differences may also be found among other persons in society. Children and aged persons have generally been given substantially more leeway in their activities than is allowed a normal adult. While both children and aged persons are liable for their torts, they are not held to the same standard as are others without impairments of age. While it is difficult to pinpoint precise standards to determine the reasonableness of a child because of the great variations in age, maturity and capacity, the courts nevertheless have established a rough standard as a guideline. This subjective test for negligence in children is what it is reasonable to expect of children of like age, intelligence, and experience. As the age, intelligence, and experience of the child increases, a commensurate increase in the standard of care is required of the child. A child is generally held to a standard of care of a reasonable child of the same age, intelligence, and experience in the same or similar circumstances.

Some courts have established an arbitrary cutoff age below which a child cannot be held liable for tort. Authorities generally agree though that such arbitrary limits are not the best standard. No one can deny that, under certain circumstances, a child of six or even five years could conceivably be guilty of negligence. Some courts have said that the rule providing for a specific age cutoff, usually at six or seven years of age, is arbitrary and open to objection because one day's difference in age surely cannot determine whether a child is capable of negligence.

At any rate, children of school age are almost always capable of negligence. Thus, each child at school, as well as the teachers and administrators, may be negligent if their standard of conduct falls below that of a reasonably prudent person, of their age, physical attributes and knowledge, in the same or similar circumstances.

## § 12.63 Proximate or Legal Cause

"Proximate cause" or "legal cause" is the sequential connection between the actor's negligent conduct and the resultant injury to another person. The *Restatement of Torts* explains the necessity of adequate causal relation in this way: "In order that a negligent actor shall be liable for another's harm, it is necessary not only that the actor's conduct be negligent toward the other, but also that the negligence of the actor be a legal cause of the other's harm."

In order for proximate or legal cause to exist, there must first be a duty or obligation on the part of the actor to maintain a reasonable standard of care. In such cases, the courts require that the defendant's conduct be the legal or proximate cause of the injury. In most negligence cases, however, the courts will not refer to proximate cause but will rely solely on the duty or obligation of the defendant and the standard of conduct required to avoid liability. Proximate cause as a criterion of liability has been used most often where some doubt is present as to whether the injured person was within the zone of obvious danger.

Courts require that the negligence of the defendant must be the "substantial" cause of the harm to the plaintiff, substantial enough to lead a reasonable person to conclude the act is indeed the cause of injury. There must be an unbroken chain between the act and the resulting injury. If the negligence is not a substantial factor in producing the harm, then there is no liability.

The actor's negligent act must be in continuous and active force up to the actual harm, and the lapse of time must not be so great that contributing causes and intervening factors render the original negligent act to be an insubstantial or insignificant force in the harm.

Therefore, a teacher may be relieved of liability where an intervening act results in a pupil's injury. In a case illustrating this point, a teacher went home after school leaving three young boys unsupervised in her classroom. The student found a small knife left in the unlocked teacher's desk drawer and one student was cut rather severely. The teacher's leaving the boys alone in the room was adjudged not to be the proximate cause of the injury. Richard v. St. Landry Parish School Board (La. App.1977).

Proximate cause tends to overlap with the question of duty and serve in some cases as a corollary to an intervening act. Courts will sometimes say that an act is not the proximate cause of injury when what they mean is that the defendant is not negligent in the first place. Or, a court may say that an act was not the proximate cause of injury when, in fact, it meant that another's act intervened to cause the injury. Prosser has noted the elusive nature of proximate cause, thusly: " 'Proximate cause' ... has been all things to all men. Having no integrated meaning of its own, its chameleon quality permits it to be substituted for any one of the elements of a negligence case when decision on that element becomes difficult...." Prosser, § 42.

## § 12.64  Injury or Actual Loss

A defendant is not liable for injury unless he has, in fact, caused the injury. Similarly, a defendant is not liable for damages unless the plaintiff shows that he has actually suffered an injury or can show actual loss or damages resulting from the act. Nominal damages cannot be obtained where no actual loss can be shown or has occurred.

Damages for an injury may be assessed against one or more persons. If the harm suffered was caused by more than one person, then damages may be apportioned among the feasors. Also, if more than one harm is present and the harms and damages can be distinguished, there will be apportionment among the defendants.

## § 12.7  DEFENSES FOR NEGLIGENCE

Teachers or school administrators may employ one or more of several defenses if an action is brought against them in tort. In all cases involving negligence, the defendant may seek to show that the plaintiff's injury was caused by mere accident and not by anyone's fault. It may be to show, too, that no duty was owed or that there was an intervening act which broke the causal chain between the act and the injury. Or, it may be maintained that the plaintiff simply could not foresee the injurious result. These, though, are not strictly speaking defenses, but instead are elements of the tort which the plaintiff must establish in order to have a case. Assuming that foreseeability, duty, standard of care, and so forth are established by plaintiff, then defendant must respond with what are classically known as tort defenses;

they are: (1) contributory negligence, (2) comparative negligence, (3) assumption of risk, (4) act of God, (5) immunity, and (6) last clear chance. Of these, contributory negligence and assumption of risk are most common in school cases where the teacher is the defendant.

## § 12.71 Contributory Negligence

Contributory negligence involves some fault or breach of duty on the part of the injured person, or failure on his or her part to exercise the required standard of care for his or her own safety. The injured party through personal negligence and fault contributes to his/her injury. In other words, contributory negligence is conduct on the part of the injured party which caused or contributed to the injury and which would not have been done by a person exercising ordinary prudence under the circumstance. This is sometimes referred to as the "all or nothing" rule meaning that if the plaintiff is shown to be negligent at all, then defendant is completely absolved from liability. *The Law of Torts*, William L. Prosser (West Publishing, 1971), defines contributory negligence as "... conduct on the part of the plaintiff ... which falls below the standard to which he is required to conform for his own protection.... [A]lthough the defendant has violated his duty, has been negligent, and would otherwise be liable, the plaintiff is denied recovery because his own conduct disentitles him to maintain the action. In the eyes of the law both parties are at fault ...."

As previously pointed out, a child is capable of negligence and his failure to conform to a required standard of conduct for a child of his age, physical characteristics, sex, and training will result in the court assigning fault to his actions.  If an injured child is negligent and his or her negligence contributes to the harm, then a defendant teacher, who is also negligent, may be absolved from liability.

However, since a child is not expected to perform with the same standard of care as an adult, teachers have more difficulty in showing contributory negligence than if the plaintiff were an adult.  A child is by nature careless and often negligent, and knowing this, a teacher should allow for an additional margin of safety when dealing with students.  This is especially true with younger children.  Contributory negligence is much less reliable as a defense when dealing with children than it is with adults.  In fact, courts have said that where a child is concerned, the test to be employed is whether the child has committed a gross disregard of safety in the face of known, perceived, and understood dangers.

In older cases, if a plaintiff's negligence or fault contributed to his or her injury, the court will bar recovery of any damages at all.  This rule, which prevents recovery no matter how "slight" the plaintiff's negligence, has more recently been almost entirely abandoned by the "substantial factor" rule.  That is, plaintiff's negligence must be a substantial factor in causing his or her own injury or defendant will be liable anyway.  Some courts have held that complete barring of any damages because of contributory fault is perhaps a little drastic and have, therefore, sought to prorate damages based on the degree of fault of each of the parties.  This results in what is known as damages for comparative negligence, discussed below.

# § 12.72 Comparative Negligence

As previously pointed out, where contributory negligence on the part of the plaintiff is shown, the defendant is often absolved from all liability. This, some courts and legislatures have felt, works a hardship on the negligent plaintiff who suffers injury but can recover nothing from the negligent defendant. This concern for the injured party has led legislatures in some states to enact statutes to determine degrees of negligence and allow recovery based on the relative degree of fault. While the specific provisions of "comparative negligence" statutes vary from state to state, the concept works this way: If the plaintiff's fault is found to be about equal to the defendant's, then the plaintiff will recover one-half the damages and must bear the remainder of the loss. If the plaintiff's negligence amounted to one-third of the fault and the defendant's two-thirds, then the plaintiff could recover two-thirds of the damages, or damages may be apportioned more than two ways. For example, where a six year old child was killed by an automobile while crossing an intersection where a guard was normally posted, the court ruled that the percentage of comparative fault of the automobile driver was fifty percent, for Orleans Parish School Board it was twenty-five percent, and the City of New Orleans Police Department was twenty-five percent. Barnes v. Bott (La.App.1993). In all states with "comparative negligence" statutes, the idea is carried forth that the plaintiff, even though he is partly to blame for his own harm, will not be totally barred from recovery. Today, over one-half the states have adopted comparative negligence in some form.

In some instances courts have not waited for legislatures to shift from contributory to comparative negligence. For example, the Florida Supreme Court in 1973 decided that it was within the province of judicial authority to make the change. In so doing the court said: "Whatever may have been the historical justification for it [contributory negligence], today it is almost universally regarded as unjust and inequitable to vest an entire accidental loss on one of the parties whose negligent conduct combined with the negligence of the other party to produce the loss." Hoffman v. Jones (Fla.1973).

## § 12.73   Assumption of Risk

Another defense against negligence is assumption of risk which, if pleaded and proved by the defendant, will absolve the defendant from liability. The theory here is that the plaintiff in some manner consents to relieve the defendant of his duty or obligation of conduct. In other words, the plaintiff by expressed or implied agreement assumes the risk of the danger and thereby relieves the defendant of responsibility. The defendant is simply not under any legal duty to protect the plaintiff from normal risks. The plaintiff with knowledge of the danger voluntarily enters into a relationship with the defendant, and by so doing agrees to take his own chances.

Important to this defense is the plaintiff's knowledge and awareness of the danger. Basically, assumption of risk is plaintiff's voluntary consent to encounter a known danger. Unlike contributory negligence, which requires only unreasonable conduct on the part of the plaintiff, assumption of risk requires voluntary consent or a showing that plaintiff's state of mind was such that the danger was known to him.

The courts have generally established that the participant in athletic events, whether intramural or interscholastic, assumes the risk of the normal hazards of the game when he participates. This also applies to spectators attending sports or amusement activities. Spectators assume all the obvious or normal risks of being hurt by flying balls, fireworks explosions, or the struggles of combatants.

For example, where a boy playing basketball was injured when his arm went through a glass pane in a door immediately behind the basketball backboard, the court said that the boy had not assumed the risk of such an injury because he did not know the glass in the door was not shatterproof. Stevens v. Central School District No. 1 (N.Y.1966). However, another court held that a boy had assumed the risk when he suffered a broken neck in a football game. "Assumption of risk in competitive athletics is not an absolute defense but a measure of the defendant's duty of care." Players who voluntarily participate in extracurricular sports assume the risks to which their roles expose them but not risks which are concealed or unreasonable. Benitez v. New York City Board of Ed. (N.Y.1989)

Essential to the doctrine of assumption of risk is that the plaintiff have knowledge of the risks; if he or she is ignorant of the conditions and dangers, then risk is not assumed. If plaintiff does not take reasonable precautions to determine the hazards involved, the risk is not assumed, and contributory negligence may be present instead. However, neither a participant nor a spectator assumes the risk for negligence or willful or wanton conduct of others. For example, a spectator at an athletic contest does not assume the risk of the stands falling down at a football game nor is risk assumed by attending a baseball game, where a player intentionally throws a bat into the stands and injures a spectator. Only those hazards or risks normally associated with the activity are assumed.

## § 12.74 Act of God

Man cannot, of course, be held responsible for injuries caused by natural elements or acts of God. No liability will ensue if the injury caused to a student is the result of a tornado, lightning, earthquake, volcano, etc. One should be very sure, however, that sufficient precautions are taken to protect students if natural calamities are foreseen. Slippery roads due to snowfall may result in school bus accidents, thus, school officials should exercise reasonable care in judging whether school should be held when poor road conditions exist.

When games or practices are conducted out-of-doors, coaches should be especially cognizant of weather conditions, such as thunderstorms. A coach is not normally liable if a child is struck by an unexpected burst of lightning, but liability may well result if the weather conditions are ignored and students are allowed to continue to play when lightning strikes repeatedly in the vicinity.

## § 12.75 Immunity

Immunity from tort liability is used in different contexts. Immunity is generally conferred on (1) national and state governments unless abrogated by statute; (2) public officials performing judicial, quasi-judicial, or discretionary functions; (3) charitable organizations granted immunity in some states; (4) infants under certain conditions; and (5) in some cases, insane persons.

Governmental or sovereign immunity is an historical and common law precedent which protects a state agency against liability for its torts. The defense of immunity may be invoked to protect the public school district against liability.

Teachers as well as others are liable for their own torts; in most states, however, school districts, as state entities, are not subject to liability for an action in tort.

A general rule of law is that government is immune from tort liability unless the legislature or the courts specifically abrogate the immunity. In other words, common law theory maintains that government cannot be sued without its consent. A school district is an arm of the state and as such has immunity. The doctrine of governmental immunity originated with the idea that "the King can do no wrong" and manifests itself today in the sovereign immunity of government in general.

Legal historians claim that sovereign immunity, as it applied to torts of the King, did not become common law until the sixteenth century. At that time, it was maintained that the King was not liable for his torts or for the torts of his ministers. Most agree that the transition was made from "the King can do no wrong" to "the government can do no wrong" in 1788 in the case of Russell v. The Men Dwelling in the County of Devon (Eng.1788). Governmental immunity evidently crossed the ocean to Massachusetts and became American law in 1812 in the case of Mower v. The Inhabitants of Leicester (Mass.1812).

The courts in the United States that have sustained the immunity principle with regard to school districts have relied primarily on five criteria: (1) school districts have only those powers granted by the legislature; if the legislature has not given the school district authority to be sued in tort, then it is beyond the district's legal powers; (2) payment of tort claims is an illegal expenditure of public funds since the public receives no benefit; (3) abolition of immunity would cause a multiplicity of cases putting a financial burden on the school; (4) the doctrine of *respondeat superior*, where the master is liable for acts of his servant, does not apply to public school districts; and (5) immunity must be abolished by the legislature, not the courts.

The doctrine of governmental immunity has been severely criticized by many courts. The leading case attacking the concept is an Illinois case where a pupil was injured in a school bus accident and sued the school district. Molitor v. Kaneland Community Unit District No. 302 (Ill.1959). School districts in Illinois had, prior to the case, been immune from liability. The court, in a sweeping opinion, abrogated immunity in Illinois and, thereby, set in motion a trend toward abrogation which has been followed by about one-half the states.

In *Molitor*, the court said: "The whole doctrine of governmental immunity from liability for tort rests upon a rotten foundation. It is almost incredible that in this modern age of comparative sociological enlightenment, and, in a republic the medieval absolutism supposed to be implicit in the maxim, 'the King can do no wrong,' should exempt the various branches of the government from liability for their torts, and that the entire burden of damage resulting from the wrongful acts of the government should be imposed upon the single individual who suffers the injury, rather than distributed among the entire community constituting the government, where it could be borne without hardship upon any individual, and where it justly belongs."

## § 12.76  Last Clear Chance

The doctrine of "last clear chance" is sometimes discussed under the heading of and as a part of contributory negligence.  It amounts to a defense for plaintiff against a countercharge of contributory negligence by defendant. What the doctrine of "last clear chance" does, in effect, is shift the fault or legal cause of an injury from a contributorily negligent plaintiff back to the negligent defendant.  If the defendant has a "last clear chance" to avoid the harm and does not, then the plaintiff's negligence is not the legal cause of the result.  Therefore, the "last clear chance" concept can probably best be explained as a counterattack against the defense of contributory negligence.  As such, then, it cannot be classified as a defense for the defendant, but as a device which may be used by the plaintiff in overcoming the defense of contributory negligence.

Most courts will allow the use of the "last clear chance" doctrine where the plaintiff is either helpless or inattentive and the defendant discovers the peril in time to avoid it but does not.  Last clear chance was apparently first used in 1842 where the plaintiff left his ass tied in the roadway and the defendant drove a wagon into it. The court pointed out that the plaintiff could recover, notwithstanding his own negligence, if he could show that the defendant had a last clear chance to avoid injuring the animal.  Prosser says that as a result of this case, the last clear chance rule is sometimes referred to as the " 'jackass doctrine' with whatever implications that nickname may carry."  Davies v. Mann (Eng.1842).

Although the use of this doctrine is not common in tort cases involving teachers, its applicability may be easily seen. For example, where a child is injured and both he and the teacher are negligent, the child may well claim that the sequence of events leading to the accident gave the teacher a superior opportunity or a last clear chance to avoid the harm.

Courts, basically, take two variables into account: (1) the nature of plaintiff's circumstance and (2) the alertness or attentiveness of the defendant. Last clear chance, though, is not readily applicable to the school setting where the teacher has a relatively high duty to protect the student. Courts will generally assume that children are most times inattentive and that teachers are expected to be observant. As such, the higher duty would probably make the teacher liable even though the "last clear chance" doctrine could conceivably apply, as well.

## § 12.77 Save Harmless Laws

This view has been slowly adopted by several state legislatures as well as by the courts. In Florida, for example, the state legislature abolished immunity of school districts and municipalities and, secondarily, enacted a save harmless provision which protects teachers and other school and governmental employees against liability up to a specified limit of damages.

Certain other states along with Florida have enacted save harmless laws; these include Connecticut, Iowa, Massachusetts, New Jersey, Oregon, New York, and Wyoming. The wording of the New York statute is typical; it reads in part: "... it should be the duty of each board of education, trustee or trustees ..., to save harmless and protect all teachers, practice or cadet teachers, and members of supervisory and administrative staff or employees from financial loss arising out of any claim, demand, suit, or judgment by reason of alleged negligence or other act resulting in accidental bodily injury to any person within or without the school building, provided such teacher, practice or cadet teacher, or member of the supervisory or administrative staff or employee, at the time of the accident or injury was acting in the discharge of his duties within the scope of his employment...."

Such provisions are tantamount to liability insurance policies against personal liability of teachers, administrators and others, including student teachers, so long as they are acting within the scope of their employment. Where the amount of damages which a school district is authorized to pay is limited by statute, as it is in Florida at $100,000, then the teacher or other school employee is well advised to supplement the state efforts by obtaining personal liability insurance. This is particularly true where the teaching takes place in high risk areas such as shops, chemistry classes, physical education or coaching activities. Of course, in those states which have not abrogated immunity nor have a save harmless law, the entire burden of an action in tort rests on the shoulders of the teacher, administrator, or other employee, personally.

## § 12.8 EDUCATIONAL MALPRACTICE

Several courts in recent years have issued opinions on cases that fall under a general classification of educational malpractice. Such cases are not a separate area of law, but rather represent an expansion of the traditional tort law concept as applied to the educational setting. Basically, educational malpractice is an attempt to apply tort law to educational outcomes in such a way as to compensate a student in damages for knowledge deficiencies allegedly created by some substandard treatment of the student during the educational process.

Evidence to support an allegation of intentional tort would seem to be very difficult to support unless one could show that an educator, for some malicious purpose, set out to prevent a child from obtaining an education. The possibility of maintaining an action for intentional tort was recognized by a Maryland court when it stated: "It is our view that where an individual engaged in the educational process is shown to have wilfully and maliciously injured a child entrusted to his educational care, such outrageous conduct greatly outweighs any public policy considerations which would otherwise preclude liability so as to authorize recovery." Hunter v. Board of Education (Md.1982).

The more common application of tort to redress a student's educational deficiencies is found in negligence. Here it is maintained that educators failed to act reasonably in administering to a student's educational needs. Such actions, though, have met with little or no success as the courts have established an imposing array of precedents denying students damages. The courts have generally denied such remedies for three reasons: "the absence of a workable rule of care against which defendant's conduct may be measured, the inherent uncertainty in determining the cause and nature of any damages, and the extreme burden which would be imposed on the already strained resources of the public school system to say nothing of the judiciary."

The first reason given is related directly to the tort of negligence. But this type of action involved several legal questions including the following. How can a court enunciate a standard of care without a clear determination of the actual duty owed the student? Does the educator have a duty to fill the vessel of the student's mind with a given amount of knowledge, and if the vessel remains half-full, does the educator, student, parent, or society bear the blame?

The problem of delineating an actionable duty was recognized by a California court in Peter W. v. San Francisco Unified School District (Cal.App.1976), when it explained: "The 'injury' claimed here is plaintiff's inability to read and write. Substantial professional authority attests that the achievement of literacy in the schools, or its failure, is influenced by a host of factors which affect the pupil subjectively, from outside the formal teaching process, and beyond the control of its ministers. They may be physical, neurological, emotional, cultural, environmental; they may be present but not perceived, recognized but not identified."

In such a situation, the court could not find that the student had suffered injury within the meaning of negligence law, nor could it identify a workable "rule of care" that could be applied. Neither could the court find a causal relationship between any perceived injury and the alleged negligent commission or omission by the defendant. A New York court had drawn a similar conclusion to that of *Peter W.* and further maintained that judicial interference in this area would constitute a "blatant interference" with the administration of the public school system. In agreement with these courts, the court in *Hunter*, said that "to allow petitioners asserted negligence claims to proceed would in effect position the courts of this state as overseers of both the day-to-day operation of our educational process as well as the formulation of its governing policies. This responsibility we are loath to impose on our courts." Other courts have likewise rejected plaintiffs' tort claims in negligence actions of educational malpractice.

## § 12.9 CONSTITUTIONAL TORTS

Although the foundation of constitutional torts is grounded in the Civil Rights Act of 1871, codified as Title 42 of the United States Code, Section 1983, the majority of litigation is of recent origin. The basic concept extends personal liability to public officials who violate the statutory or constitutional rights of an individual, such as a student or teacher.

The statute was enacted during the Reconstruction Era after the Civil War to protect the rights of blacks and was commonly referred to as the Ku Klux Act. In March of 1871, President Grant sent a message to Congress requesting they use their power under the Fourteenth Amendment to pass legislation to protect individuals from state officials who were abusing their power and violating the natural rights of those individuals. The President further pleaded that legislation was needed to protect the life, liberty, and property and enforcement of laws at all levels of government. Congress responded by passing the 1871 Civil Rights Act which states: "Every person who, under color of any statute, ordinance, regulation, custom, or usage, of any State or Territory, subjects, or causes to be subjected, any citizen of the United States or other person within the jurisdiction thereof to the deprivation of any rights, privileges or immunities secured by the Constitution and laws, shall be liable to the party injured in an action at, law, suit in equity, or other proper proceeding for redress." 42 U.S.C.A. § 1983.

This statute was the subject of very little litigation from the time of passage until the 1960s. With the expansion of the civil rights movement, this Act was used as a weapon to hold state officials personally liable if they violated the rights of another.

## § 12.91 Definition of Person

The Act provides that liability shall be for "every person" who infringes on the rights of another. Plaintiffs attempted to have "person" interpreted to mean an institution as well as an individual. Since an institution has more fiscal resources than the individual, greater resources would be available to pay damages. In Monroe v. Pape (S.Ct.1961), the Supreme Court determined policemen were personally liable as individuals, but the City of Chicago was not a person and, therefore, was not liable. Some seventeen years later in Monell v. New York City Department of Social Services (S.Ct.1978), the Supreme Court overturned *Monroe* and declared the word "person" included local government or institution.

## § 12.92 Absolute Immunity

The Supreme Court, in a series of cases, determined that absolute immunity was available as a defense for prosecutors in initiating and presenting the state's case,

Imbler v. Pachtman (S.Ct.1976), and state legislators. Tenney v. Brandhove (S.Ct.1951).

## § 12.93 Qualified or Conditional Immunity

Prosecutors and legislators have absolute immunity; therefore, it may appear other state officials have absolute immunity. But in Scheuer v. Rhodes (S.Ct.1974), the Supreme Court declared the Governor of Ohio and other state officials have only qualified or conditional immunity. Qualified or conditional immunity from civil liability means individuals would not be liable as long as they are acting clearly within the scope of their authority for the betterment of those they serve. If they venture outside the scope of their authority, and, in doing so, violate someone's rights, then they may be personally liable. The Supreme Court granted qualified immunity to the superintendents of state hospitals in O'Connor v. Donaldson (S.Ct.1975), and for local school board members in Wood v. Strickland (S.Ct.1975).

## § 12.94 Good Faith Immunity

Although individuals may assert good faith as a defense in a constitutional tort action, a municipality has no immunity and may not assert a good faith defense. Owen v. City of Independence (S.Ct.1980).

## § 12.95 Actual and Punitive Damages

Generally, actual damages will be allowed, but not punitive damages. The Supreme Court "... had indicated that punitive damages might be awarded in appropriate circumstances in order to punish violations of constitutional rights..." Carey v. Piphus (S.Ct.1978). "...

but it never suggested that punishment is as prominent a purpose under the statute as are compensation and deterrence." City of Newport v. Fact Concerts, Inc. (S.Ct. 1981).

# CHAPTER 13

# STUDENT RECORDS, DEFAMATION, AND PRIVACY

## § 13.1 INTRODUCTION

By the very nature of the educational process, educators are constantly dealing in sensitive matters involving students' private and personal affairs. Schools routinely collect and process information that can materially affect the student's life and prosperity. Personal information that is carelessly released may attach a stigma to a student's image in the community or may detract from the student's success in both future education and employment. The incorrect recording of a grade or idle gossip in inappropriate places can permanently cast a very damaging shadow over one's reputation.

The law protects the student in three ways. First, school districts are required to handle and process student records in a careful and prescribed manner by federal statute, failure of which can result in the loss of federal funds. A number of states have statutes mandating procedures in protecting the student's right of privacy. Second, it allows the student protection through judicial precedents which form the law of defamation. Third, the student has a right of privacy protected by the common law right against invasion of privacy.

## § 13.2   BUCKLEY AMENDMENT

The Family Educational Rights and Privacy Act (FER-PA) of 1974, more popularly known as the Buckley Amendment (see Appendix B), prescribes standards for schools to follow in handling student records. 20 U.S.C.A. § 1232g. Parents are given the right to inspect all records that schools maintain on their children and are extended the opportunity to challenge the accuracy of the records. Parents must consent before the school can release the student's records to agencies outside designated educational categories. Consent may also be given by the student, in lieu of the parent, to release his or her own records upon the attainment of age eighteen or upon entry to postsecondary school. School districts which do not follow the procedures required risk losing federal funds administered by the United States Department of Education. A school may release the records to the parent(s) of a dependent student if such parent(s) are financially supporting the student as provided under the Individual Revenue Code of 1986.

## § 13.21   Pre–Buckley

Before the Buckley Amendment, twenty-four states had statutes which gave parents or students access to records kept by the school. Only five of these states explicitly granted the right to challenge, correct, or expunge faulty information in the student files. See Katherine Cudlipp, *"The Family Educational Rights and Privacy Act Two Years Later,"* University of Richmond Law Review, Vol. 11, No. 1, Fall 1976, pp. 33–49.

Generally, prior to 1974, it was difficult for students to obtain access to their records. This was true, in spite of the fact that some courts had held that parents had a right of access to records unless such access was detrimental to the public interest. This right was assured by a New York court in 1961 when it ruled that "absent constitutional, legislative, or administrative permission or prohibition, a parent had the right to inspect the records of his child maintained by school authorities as required by law." Van Allen v. McCleary (N.Y.1961). This court's rationale was based on the common law rule that a person with an interest in public records is entitled to inspect them.

Too, as far back as 1961, a federal district court in Alabama recognized that in dismissal cases students had a due process right of access to school records and to challenge errors and inaccuracies in them. Dixon v. Alabama State Board of Education (5th Cir.1961). Following *Dixon* other due process cases established requirements for access to student records. In *Mills*, the famous handicap case, the court clearly stated that the parents had a right to "examine the child's records before the hearing, including any texts or reports upon which the proposed action may be based." Mills v. Board of Education (D.D.C.1972).

In other cases, students were upheld in their attempts to have items removed from their records or communicated to third parties. In each instance, however, litigation was required to obtain redress for the parent or the student. School districts were generally without precedents of law or other guidelines on which they could rely. School districts tended to devise their own rules which generally suited ethical considerations of the individual teachers or administrators who were in charge. The Buckley Amendment thereafter introduced a required uniformity to the handling of student records both among school districts and institutions of higher education.

## § 13.22 Requirements of the Act

Under the Family Educational Rights and Privacy Act (FERPA) each school district is required to publish a pupil records policy. Parents and students over age 18 must receive annual notification of this policy. The act requires that each agency or institution establish procedures for granting access to school records within a reasonable period of time after the parental request. The reasonable period of time cannot exceed forty-five days. The Act provides that "directory" information, date and place of birth, major field of study, participation in activities and sports, weight and height of members of athletic teams, dates of attendance, degrees and awards and most recent educational institution attended by the student, may be released by the school district without written consent of parents. But the act also provides the school district must give notice of what categories are included in directory information. After the public notice, a parent may inform the school "... that any or all of the information designated should not be released without the parent's prior consent." Parental consent is not required for release of education records to: (1) other school officials and/or teachers in the school system who have legitimate educational interests, (2) officials of other schools or school systems in which the student seeks to enroll upon the condition that the student's parents are notified of the transfer of records, are given a copy, and have an opportunity to challenge the record, (3) authorized representatives of government including state education authorities, (4) financial aid officers in connection with a student's application for financial aid, (5) state and local officials collecting information required by state statutes adopted before November 19, 1974, (6) organizations conducting studies for, or on behalf of, educational agencies if personal identification of students is destroyed after no longer needed for the study, (7) accrediting organizations, (8) parents of a dependent student as defined by statute, and (9) the Secretary of Education for the purpose of maintaining regulations pertaining to the health and welfare of the student.

The policy of the school district must also accommodate other requirements of the act including several musts:

1. Records of individual students, containing "personally, identifiable information," must be kept confidential and cannot be released by the school without written consent of the parent or consent from the student if the student is over the age of 18.

2. Parents and guardians of students under age 18, and those students over 18 must have the right to inspect all school records concerning that student.

3. The school district record-keeping system must be described in sufficient detail for parents to locate their child's records.

4. School district staff members with access to student records must be identified by title.

5. Each child's file must include a record of access, which must be signed by each staff member whenever they withdraw that student's file.

6. Parents must have a right to appeal anything in a student's file that is considered incorrect, and if

the school is not willing to delete the challenged material, the parents may request a hearing and/or provide a written statement to be attached to the challenged material.

In addition, treatment records "made or maintained by a physician, psychologist, or other recognized professional or paraprofessional acting in his or her professional capacity or assisting in a paraprofessional capacity" and used in the treatment of an eligible student may be excluded from the definition of "education records" in federal law and are not automatically accessible to the student.

An exception to the student record act (FERPA) is recognized for disclosures that were required by state statutes before enactment of the act. Further, "personal notes" that are defined as "not education records" are exempted from parental access. Personal notes are notes kept by an individual, such as a guidance counselor, to "jog the memory" when the child is counseled at a later date. These personal notes are not accessible to other school staff members and are available only to substitutes of the original note-writers.

Grades under the federal statute may only be challenged to insure they are not inaccurate, mathematically incorrect or do not reflect what the grader intended. Tarka v. Cunningham (5th Cir.1990). See John K. v. Board of Education for Sch. Dist. No. 65 (Ill.App.1987) (based on the Illinois Student Record Act).

## § 13.23 Posting of Grades

It is a common practice to post student grades on the school door or to list them in other ways. In a recent case where a parent sought to compel a board of education to release all student grades in a third-grade class containing seventy-five students, the court held that disclosure of test scores if scrambled and with names deleted would sufficiently protect the privacy of students as required under the Buckley Amendment. In this case the parents wanted to compare scores and were not interested in the grades being in any particular order. Relying on this rationale, it appears that teachers and school officials can continue to post grades so long as they cannot be identified by individual.

In a case, a conflict was created between the parent's right to view public records under the state's Freedom of Information Law and the Buckley Amendment. The public records act required school districts to release public information, while the Buckley Amendment requirements are that school districts keep individual, personal student information private except upon request of the student's parent. This conflict was resolved by the definition of what is public as opposed to that which is private and personal. According to this decision, information that is not personally identifiable may be released under public records acts. Kryston v. Board of Education, East Ramapo, etc. (N.Y.1980).

## § 13.3  DEFAMATION

Anyone, a teacher, administrator, parent, or student, is capable of incurring liability by defaming other persons. Words are defamatory if they impute to another dishonesty, immorality, vice or dishonorable conduct which engenders an evil opinion of one in the minds of others in the community. Defamation is generally understood to be injury by calumny or by false aspersion of another's reputation. Defamation is anything which tends to injure one's character or reputation.

The distinction between "criticism" and "defamation" is that criticism is addressed to public matters and does not follow a person into his or her private life. A true critic never indulges in personal ridicule but confines his or her comments to the merits of the particular subject matter under discussion.

Defamation is not a legal cause of action but encompasses the twin torts of libel and slander. Libel is written defamation and slander is spoken. Speaking defamatory words to a newspaper reporter may ultimately involve both slander and libel if the speaker intends his words to "be embodied forthwith in a physical form" and the words do, in fact, appear in a newspaper article. Tallent v. Blake (N.C.App.1982).

## § 13.31  Libel

Libel is an accusation in writing or printing against the character of a person which affects his or her reputation and tends to hold him or her up to shame or disgrace. Stevens v. Wright (Vt.1935). Libel must be false, unprivileged, and malicious to be actionable. Publication is required for libel to exist. This does not mean publication in the mass media, but may be constituted by written communication which tends to harm one's reputation in the community. A note written to a third party or a secretary typing and reading a letter may constitute publication.

Communication sufficient to establish libel may be conveyed by sign, mark, movie reel, video tape, picture, or effigy. The communication may be actionable if it holds a person up to ridicule, contempt, disgrace, obloquy, or shame in the eyes of the community.

## § 13.32   Slander

Slander is the speaking of base and defamatory words tending to create an unfavorable impression in the mind of a third party. To constitute slander there must be conveyance by words of disparagement of character of one to a third party. Plaintiff must show that there was a third party communication. Words spoken only to the offended party cannot constitute slander. If a third party overhears defamatory words, slander may be established.

There are two types of slander, slander *per se* and slander *per quod*. Words which in and of themselves, without extrinsic proof, injure one's reputation are defamatory *per se*. Defamation *per se* does not require proof of actual damage. With defamation *per se*, the plaintiff's cause of action is complete when he or she proves that the words have been articulated and conveyed. The plaintiff is not required to prove actual injury or out-of-pocket monetary loss, but rather must merely show that the words were of such a kind as to impair one's reputation or standing in the community or to cause personal anguish, suffering or humiliation. The plaintiff need not prove that he or she suffered special harm of direct loss.

Under American common law today, an action for defamation *per se* will lie without proof of special harm (damage) where there exists (1) imputation of a criminal offense punishable by imprisonment, or imputation of guilt of a crime involving moral turpitude; (2) imputation of venereal or other loathsome or communicable disease; (3) imputation of conduct, characteristics, or a condition incompatible with proper conduct of lawful business, trade, or profession, or a public or private offense; and/or (4) imputation of unchastity of a woman.

If the plaintiff is unable to bring his or her case under one of these categories, he or she must resort to proving special harm or actual damages by the communication of defamation *per quod*.

Defamation *per quod* requires that the plaintiff prove actual damage. The plaintiff must show that publication of the defamation was the legal cause of special harm. The distinction between defamation *per se* and *per quod* may rest on whether a crime is imputed. For example, the law holds that it is defamation *per quod* and special damages must be proven if the words imputed to a teacher appear to harm the teacher's reputation, but do not relate to conduct of a crime, moral turpitude, unchastity, or damage the teacher in his or her profession. To say that a male teacher seduced a female student would, of course, be defamation *per se*. On the other hand, where a defendant had accused a headmaster of committing adultery with the school custodian's wife, the court found that the words had not been uttered in the context of the school nor in reference to the plaintiff as schoolmaster, and thus, the charge could not be defamation *per se*. A showing of special and actual damage was necessary, a burden the plaintiff could not sustain. Yet because a teacher's reputation among students and the community is so vital to performance of his or her professional responsibilities, it is easy to see how, in the majority of cases, false imputations against a teacher could fall into the category of defamation *per se*.

## § 13.33 Public Officials/Public Figures

Since New York Times v. Sullivan (S.Ct.1964), a 1964 United States Supreme Court decision, the law of defamation as it pertains to freedom of speech and press has changed considerably. This case, and subsequent ones, hold the interest of the publisher to be of vital importance to a free and informed society. In *Sullivan*, a paid advertisement in the New York *Times* signed by a number of prominent individuals criticized the behavior of the Montgomery, Alabama, police in dealing with racial unrest. The police chief, Sullivan, claimed that the derogatory reference to police behavior amounted to defamation of him personally. The Alabama State Supreme Court held that the publication was libel *per se* and that the New York *Times* was liable for one-half million dollars without the plaintiff showing special damage or fault on the part of the *Times*.

The United States Supreme Court reversed the lower court, holding that the guarantee of free speech under the First Amendment prohibits a *public official* from recovering damages for a defamatory falsehood relating to his *official* conduct, unless he proves that the statement was made with malice and that the statement was made with knowledge that it was false or in reckless disregard of whether it was false or not. This protection extended to both the newspaper and to the private persons who paid for the advertisement and signed it. Plaintiffs in the case were unable to show that the New York *Times* actually had knowledge of the falsity of portions of the statement. A major question is whether the individual is a public official. The determination is made on a case by case situation. The Supreme Court in Sullivan said "We have no occasion here to determine how far down into the lower ranks of government employees the 'public official' designation would extend for purposes of this rule, or otherwise to specify categories of persons who would or would not be included."

Shortly after the *Sullivan* case, the United States Supreme Court expanded the definition of *"public officials"* to include *"public figures"* in Curtis Publishing Co. v. Butts (S.Ct.1967). Butts, a former University of Georgia football coach, was accused by a major news magazine of giving away football secrets to the University of Alabama football coach. The Supreme Court concluded that public figures who commanded "a substantial amount of public interest at the time of publications in question" were subject to the same burden of proof as public officials. A public figure is someone who injects himself into an ongoing public controversy and tries to impact the outcome of that controversy. Thus, the plaintiff must show malice and knowledge of or reckless disregard for the falsity of the publication. The law requires proof of knowledge or conscious indifference to falsity when imputations are made denigrating either public officials or public figures.

Where a private person is offended by the press, liability may be incurred by merely showing that the statement was untruthful, not that it was made with malice nor that the newspaper knew that it was false so long as liability is not imposed without *fault*. Whenever liability is imposed against the press for false publication, the damages must be limited to the actual injury sustained; general or punitive damages are not available.

The definition of "fault" is very important here because its use incurs a different standard than the traditional rule that "Whenever a man publishes he publishes at his peril." King v. Woodfall (Eng.1774). "Fault" in this regard means that the published derogatory information was intended and directed at a certain private individual. The old view was that references in books or newspapers to fictional persons which were taken by a few readers to refer to the plaintiff were libelous *per se*. This meant that the publisher was not actually at fault, but suffered the consequences anyway.

The modern view is that it must be shown that the plaintiff was the private person for whom the defamation was intended. This being established, the private individual can recover against the publisher actual damages.

The courts are split as to whether a teacher is a public official with a slight majority ruling they are not. It is a most important issue since the teacher does not need to prove malice if they are not a public official. As stated in *Sullivan* "a public figure may not recover damages for a defamatory falsehood without clear and convincing proof that the false statement was made with 'actual malice'— that is, with knowledge that it was false or with reckless disregard of whether it was false or not." Imputations against teachers by the student press would be actionable if the teacher shows that the student publisher was at fault by directing the defamation toward the teacher. Similarly, students cannot attack other students or school administrators personally without potential consequences. Yet, a former school board member running in a school board election is considered to be a public figure under the *Sullivan* precedent. Fisher v. Larsen (S.Ct. 1982).

The courts are split on whether a principal is a public official but the majority have ruled that a principal is a public official. In Ellerbee v. Mills (Ga.1992), the Su-

preme Court of Georgia ruled a high school principal
"... is not a public official under the standard of *New
York Times, Co. v. Sullivan* ..." nor is he a public figure
as defined by Gertz v. Robert Welch, Inc. (S.Ct.1974).
This decision is in contrast to Johnson v. Robbinsdale
Ind. Sch. Dist. No. 281 (D.Minn.1993), where the court
found an elementary principal to be a public figure. The
*Johnson* court decision is in agreement with Palmer v.
Bennington School Dist. (Vt.1992); Kapiloff v. Dunn
(Md.App.1975); Reaves v. Foster (Miss.1967); and Jun-
ior–Spence v. Keenan (Tenn.App.1990).

## § 13.34  Truth

Defamation constitutes harm of reputation by denigrating a person in the minds of others by falsehood.
Falsification is the basic ingredient of the tort of defamation.  It follows then that conveyance of truth is not
defamation.  In some states courts have held that truth
is a defense for libel only when published with good
motives and justifiable ends.  Farnsworth v. Tribune Co.
(Ill.1969), ruled that a person will not be allowed to
resurrect a long forgotten mistake of another and repub-
lish it.  The prevailing view is, though, that truth of a
defamatory statement affords a complete defense to defamation regardless of whether ill will or malice is present.
"One who publishes a defamatory statement of fact is
not subject to liability for defamation if the statement is
true."  Restatement 2d, Torts, § 581A (1977).

Under common law tort where the plaintiff is a private
person, a defamatory statement is presumed to be false
and the defendant must prove that the statement was
true.  The burden of proof is on the defendant.

As explained above, if the plaintiff is a "public official" or "public figure," the burden of proof shifts. The "public person" must present clear and convincing proof to the court that defendant published false, defamatory information with knowledge of its falsity or with reckless disregard for the truth.

Thus, if a teacher has been the brunt of a defamatory statement, then the burden of proving truth is on the defendant because a teacher is generally a private person. If, for example, a parent or student published defamatory information about a teacher, the burden would be on the parent or student to prove the statement is true.

One may conceive of a situation where a teacher could be a public figure if he or she had won fame for some reason, but this is generally not the case. Such fame may be localized, however, several courts have ruled high school coaches are public figures because of the athletic publicity. So long as the teacher does not acquire the status of a public personage, the burden of proving truth would be on the defendant if the publication did harm to the teacher.

## § 13.35 Absolute Privilege

Public policy requires that certain persons or officials in society be afforded absolute privilege against liability for defamation. Judges, attorneys, witnesses in court, legislators, and certain other public officials are vested with absolute protection for utterances or writings which are given in the course of conduct of public affairs and include: (1) judicial proceedings, (2) legislative proceedings, and (3) executive proceedings. See Laurence H.

Eldredge, *The Law of Defamation* (The Bobbs–Merrill Company, Inc., Charlottesville, Va.), pp. 339–532.

## § 13.36 Conditional Privilege

Courts have found it necessary to extend limited privileges to other persons in society where the public interest requires such protection. Such *conditional* or *qualified* privileges are extended to teachers and school administrators as well as to other public servants who are charged with duties which require them to handle sensitive information, which is important not only to the individual but to the public generally. Rationale for such protection may be stated as follows: "In order that the information may be freely given, it is necessary to afford protection against liability for misinformation given in an appropriate effort to protect or advance the interest in question. If protection were not given, true information that should be given or received would not be communicated because of fear of the persons capable of giving it that they would be held liable in an action of defamation if their statements were untrue." Restatement 2d, Torts, § 592A at 258, Topic 3, Scope Note.

The degree of protection afforded by the conditional or qualified privilege is determined by the courts in weighing on "one hand society's need for free disclosure without fear of civil suit, and, on the other hand, an individual's right to recover for damage to his reputation...." Weissman v. Mogol (N.Y.1983).

The conditional privilege negates any presumption of implied malice emanating from the defamatory statement, and places the burden on the plaintiff to show proof of actual malice. *Weissman v. Mogol,* supra. One can easily see that teachers would be hesitant to convey any information at all about students if no privilege existed. Without such conditional privilege school reports, both academic and disciplinary, would hold great potential for legal actions against teachers.

In order for the privilege of the teacher or administrator to withstand challenge, the communication must have been made (1) in good faith, without malice, and within the scope of the students, teachers, or public's interest in the good conduct of the school; (2) in the honest belief that the information conveyed was true, with knowledge that any communication brought about a student was made with reasonable, and probable grounds; and (3) in response to a legitimate inquiry by one with the right to know about a student's educational or personal qualifications, the answer must not go beyond that which is required to satisfy the inquiry.

Parents have a qualified privilege to speak publicly before a school board regarding teacher's instruction of his or her children. It is within the right of parents to oversee their children's education to make statements pertaining to a teacher's competency or inefficiency in the classroom. If, however, the statements are untrue and made with "actual or express malice, then the privilege is destroyed." Nodar v. Galbreath (Fla.1984).

In a case where a parent, who was also a teacher, informed the school principal about male teachers allegedly fondling girl students, the court said the teacher/parent had a qualified privilege. No malice was found because the parent/teacher had been told by girls of the alleged events and written statements were obtained to that effect. Desselle v. Guillory (La.App.1981).

## § 13.37   Malice

Malice is indicated where the defendant conveys false information which is not reasonably germane to the subject matter of the occasion; then the scope of the conditional privilege has been exceeded. For example, a teacher's privilege does not extend to communication about a student's personal love life outside of school if it has no bearing on his or her school conduct. In such instances, technically, a teacher does not abuse his or her privilege but, instead, exceeds the protection of the privilege. Volunteering excessive information not bearing on the school's or the student's interests is hazardous.

## § 13.38   Belief in Truth

Where a teacher conveys erroneous information about a student but believes the communication is truthful, then the privileged occasion of the teacher will not be foregone. Statements by teachers must be motivated by a desire to protect the interest of the student or the school and, if so taken, then an honest belief that the communication is true will be protected. The fact that the teacher is unintentionally mistaken is, in this case, immaterial. Too, the teacher may be compelled to show that reasonable or probable grounds were available to support the truthfulness or belief in the truthfulness of the communication.

## § 13.39   Legitimate Inquiry

Legitimate inquiry regarding a student's educational performance may be made by other teachers, school administrators within the same school or school districts, as well as by educational and employment agencies outside the school or school district proper. The Buckley Amendment discussed above in this chapter gives good guidelines in this regard. At common law, a teacher is protected if communication is given in response to proper inquiry.

If information were to be given about a student to a third party who had no legitimate interest in the student, then, if the communication is defamatory, the teacher may be liable. Thus, a teacher may abuse and lose the conditional privilege by carelessly releasing false information about students.

## § 13.4 RIGHT OF PRIVACY

A legal question of privacy, however, may arise beyond statute or common law defamation. Invasion of privacy may be a separate and independent tort. As a new area of law, invasion of privacy has come into focus in recent years from hundreds of cases which have emerged in which a person's privacy has been invaded and their private lives have become subject to unwanted public exposure.

According to Prosser in his *Handbook of the Law of Torts* (3rd ed. 1964), Ch. 22, p. 832, the common law right of privacy is "not one tort, but a complex of four. The law of privacy comprises four distinct kinds of invasion of four different interests of the plaintiff, but otherwise have almost nothing in common except that each represents an interference with the right of the plaintiff 'to be let alone.'" The four different kinds of invasion of privacy are: "(a) unreasonable intrusion upon the seclusion of another, ... (b) appropriation of the other's name or likeness, ... (c) unreasonable publicity given to

the other's private life, . . . (d) publicity which unreasonably places the other in a false light before the public,
. . . ." Restatement 2d, Torts, § 652A, 1967. Invasion
of the right of privacy may result from any of the four or
there may be overlapping or concurrent invasion.

The law of privacy was relied on by plaintiffs in a
Maryland case where parents claimed that the release of
their child's psychological records to another school upon
transfer subjected the child to unreasonable publicity
and unreasonably placed her in a false light before the
public. Klipa v. Board of Education of Anne Arundel
County (Md.App.1983). Parents had asked that the
girl's records be transferred, but had specifically requested that the psychological portion of the records not be
sent. Parents had signed a consent form to transfer the
records in which no reference was made to psychological
records. The school psychologist had agreed not to send
the psychological records, but due to a clerical error of
another employee, the records were mailed anyway.

The court in ruling for the defendant school district
held that the fact that parents had signed a consent form
for the records, but had not specifically released the
psychological records, was irrelevant because the school
district had no legal obligation to obtain parental consent
for the transfer. The evidence made it clear that the
records were mailed directly to the principal of the school
to which the girl transferred and were delivered by him
to the custody of the chief school guidance counselor,
thereafter the records remained under lock and key.
Further, no evidence was presented which indicated that
the student was exposed to unwarranted publicity. In
applying the four legal conditions under which invasion
of privacy can occur, the court found that there was no

invasion of something secret, secluded or private, as required by the first and second types of invasion. The school had validly obtained the information in the first instance. There was no publicity as required under the third and fourth types of invasion and there was no falsity or fiction involved as required under the third kind of invasion. Neither was the information used for the defendant's advantage as is required by the fourth condition. On the contrary, the information regarding the student's psychological background and prior behavioral pattern was vital and necessary for the school to plan for an appropriate educational program, and to address the student's social and emotional needs.

# CHAPTER 14

# STUDENT TESTING

## § 14.1 INTRODUCTION

The state has the authority to set standards for promotion and graduation in public school programs and to establish criteria by which students are to be evaluated. One of the most commonly used criteria is, of course, some type of examination. A federal court has said that boards of education have the right, if not a positive duty, to develop reasonable means to determine the effectiveness of their educational programs with respect to all individual students to whom they issue diplomas, and that tests are a reasonable means of accomplishing this purpose. Brookhart v. Illinois State Board of Education (7th Cir.1983). Public schools may set standards and require adherence to those standards. Bester v. Tuscaloosa City Board of Education (11th Cir.1984).

## § 14.2 JUDICIAL REVIEW

The courts have been reluctant to substitute their judgment in academic matters for that of school officials. The United States Supreme Court has distinguished between judicial review of academic and disciplinary measures taken by school authorities saying that "Courts are particularly ill-equipped to evaluate academic performance." Board of Curators, University of Missouri v. Horowitz (S.Ct.1978).

The inappropriateness of judicial intervention in student evaluations has long been documented by judicial precedent. In 1913 a Massachusetts court refused to substitute its judgment for that of school authorities who had not allowed a student to continue in school because of his poor academic performance. "The care and management of schools which is vested in the school committee includes the establishment and maintenance of standards for the promotion of pupils from one grade to another and for their continuance as members of any particular class. So long as the school committee acts in good faith their conduct in formulating and applying standards and making decisions touching this matter is not subject to review by any other tribunal." Barnard v. Inhabitants of Shelburne (Mass.1913).

Pupil evaluation is essential to the conduct of schools and testing is considered to be an appropriate means of determining educational effectiveness of the school and the achievement of the pupil. Unless the school enunciates a level of academic attainment for the student and measures student progress toward that level "no certification of graduation can have any meaning whatsoever." *Brookhart v. Illinois State Board of Education*, supra.

The general view of the courts was set out in Gaspar v. Bruton (10th Cir.1975), where it was said that "the courts are not equipped to review academic records based upon academic standards within the particular knowledge, experience, and expertise of academicians.... The court may grant relief, as a practical matter, only in those cases where the student presents positive evidence of ill will or bad motive." See also Clements v. Nassau County (2d Cir.1987).

## § 14.3　LIMITATIONS ON THE SCHOOL

A child's constitutional rights, however, may place limitations on the school's prerogatives in employing tests as standards of academic attainment. In recent years states have begun to use competency tests to gauge students' progress. Such tests have been used as the criterion by which students are advanced, remediated or placed in special educational programs. Courts have always exercised their power to overturn the determinations of school boards where a student could show that an academic decision was arbitrary or capricious or was motivated by bad faith or ill will unrelated to academic performance. The burden of proof, however, has heretofore been on the plaintiff to show that the action was taken without due regard for the welfare of the student.

More recently the Due Process and Equal Protection Clauses of the Constitution have been applied to competency tests when a student's movement from grade to grade would be affected or when graduation would be delayed or denied.

## § 14.4　COMPETENCY TESTS

Recent state legislation requiring educational accountability for minimal competency tests has been the impetus for litigation challenging testing. The purpose of such test legislation is to assure that (a) students have mastered certain skills, (b) students with deficiencies have been identified and (c) students are provided the appropriate types of classroom instruction. Passage of a minimum competency test means that a student has reached the prescribed level of proficiency on a series of skills.

Legislation requiring competency tests generally assumes that tests are an appropriate method of measuring the attainment of the required skills. Such tests have been used as the prerequisite for obtaining a high school diploma, promotion from grade to grade, and placement of students in remedial programs. The failure to progress normally through school or the denial of a diploma may be of such importance as to invoke strict judicial scrutiny if the student's constitutional rights are threatened. The constitutional rights which may be at stake include substantive due process and/or equal protection. Debra P. v. Turlington (5th Cir.1981).

## § 14.5 DUE PROCESS INTERESTS

The United States Supreme Court has made it clear that a high school diploma is of such personal importance that its denial may be tantamount to denial of "liberty or property" under the Fourteenth Amendment. The Court observed in Board of Regents v. Roth (S.Ct.1972), that property interests are not bestowed lightly. "To have a property interest in a benefit, a person clearly must have more than an abstract need or desire for it. He must have more than a unilateral expectation of it. He must, instead, have a legitimate claim of entitlement to it."

The interest must be founded on a state created benefit which is available to all persons in the same circumstance. Such interests emanate from "rules and understandings that secure certain benefits and that support claims of entitlement to those benefits."

A person's interest in receiving a public education is beyond a mere "unilateral expectation," it is essential to success in today's society. A high school diploma is a means to social and economic mobility. Also, the high school diploma is a prerequisite to admission to higher education. Thus, public education which culminates in the all important diploma may be viewed as an entitlement to every citizen.

However, even though a person has a property interest in public education and, ultimately, in a high school diploma, this interest can be denied if a student does not perform to expectations. Public education and the diploma can be denied by following judicial requirements of procedural due process.

The student, likewise, has a liberty interest which has implications for competency testing. A "liberty" interest has at least two aspects. First, the state may not impose a stigma on a student which will effectively denigrate the student's future. Failure to achieve a certain level on a test may result in a student being branded as an intellectual inferior or even a functional illiterate. Where the potential for damage to a person is so great as to risk peer ridicule or possible public scorn, a liberty interest may well be at issue. Second, a person has an interest in pursuing further education and to be gainfully employed in a chosen field. *Goss v. Lopez*, supra. Any indication on a student's record that he or she is intellectually inferior "imposes a stigma ... that forecloses freedom to take advantage of other opportunities." Greenhill v. Bailey (8th Cir.1975). Thus, the presence of both property and liberty interests requires constitutional restraints of due process be accorded. Kelley v. Johnson (S.Ct.1976).

The Supreme Court in Board of Curators of the University of Missouri v. Horowitz (S.Ct.1978), refused to extend procedural due process rights to a medical student before she was dismissed from school because of less than adequate clinical performance. The Court stated: "Academic evaluations of a student, in contrast to disciplinary determinations, bear little resemblance to the judicial and administrative factfinding proceedings to which we have traditionally attached a full-hearing requirement. In *Goss*, the school's decision to suspend the students rested on factual conclusions that the individual students had participated in demonstrations that had disrupted classes, attacked a police officer, or caused physical damage to school property. The requirement of a hearing, where the student could present his side of the factual issue, could under such circumstances 'provide a meaningful hedge against erroneous action.' The decision to dismiss respondent [Horowitz], by comparison, rested on the academic judgment of school officials that she did not have the necessary clinical ability to perform adequately as a medical doctor and was making insufficient progress toward that goal. Such a judgment is by its nature more subjective and evaluative than the typical factual questions presented in the average disciplinary decision. Like the decision of an individual professor as to the proper grade for a student in his course, the determination whether to dismiss a student for academic reasons requires an expert evaluation of a cumulative information and is not readily adapted to the procedural tools of judicial or administrative decisionmaking."

"Under such circumstances, we decline to ignore the historic judgment of educators and thereby formalize the academic dismissal process by requiring a hearing. The educational process is not by nature adversary; instead it centers around a continuing relationship between faculty and students, 'one in which the teacher must occupy many roles—educator, adviser, friend, and, at times, parent-substitute.' ... In *Goss*, this Court concluded that the value of some form of hearing in a disciplinary context outweighs any resulting harm to the academic environment. Influencing this conclusion was clearly the belief that disciplinary proceedings, in which the teacher must decide whether to punish a student for disruptive or insubordinate behavior, may automatically bring an adversary flavor to the normal student-teacher relationship. The same conclusion does not follow in the academic context. We decline to further enlarge the judicial presence in the academic community and thereby risk deterioration of many beneficial aspects of the faculty-student relationship."

While the Supreme Court answered the question of whether procedural due process applies in academic matter it did not address the substantive due process issues. In 1985 this question was answered. The Court stated: "In ... Horowitz ... we assumed, without deciding, that federal courts can review an academic decision of a public educational institution under a substantive due process standard." The Court assumed that the student had a substantive property right under the due process clauses to continued enrollment. This right could not be taken away for an arbitrary reason, but " ... university faculties have a wide range of discretion in making judgments as to academic performance of students." Regents of University of Michigan v. Ewing (S.Ct.1985).

The courts, however, have held that the nature of substantive due process review does not apply to subjective judgments about academic qualifications.

# § 14.6   EQUAL PROTECTION

Beyond due process, students are also entitled to constitutional protection against unjustified discrimination. If a test is racially discriminatory, its use is violative of the Equal Protection Clause of the Fourteenth Amendment. In 1967, a federal judge in Washington, D.C., held that the use of tests for "tracking" of students was unconstitutional. Hobson v. Hansen (D.D.C.1967). The court had found that the use of tests to assign students to ability groups resulted in black students being relegated to lower curricular levels and little opportunity was provided them to improve their position by moving upward from level to level. The court concluded with regard to testing that "teachers acting under false assumptions because of low test scores will treat the disadvantaged student in such a way as to make him conform to their low expectations ... creating a self-fulfilling prophecy based on false assumptions that black students are intellectually inferior."

A similar decision in California in 1972 found that the use of non-validated I.Q. tests to evaluate students for placement in classes for the educable mentally retarded violated federal statutes and the equal protection clauses of the United States and California Constitutions. The school administrators could not show that there was a relationship between the I.Q. tests and the intellectual capabilities of the black students. P. v. Riles (N.D.Cal. 1972).

In 1984 the Ninth Circuit reversed the decision on the federal and state constitutional issue but affirmed on statutory grounds. Larry P. By Lucille P. v. Riles (9th Cir.1984). The court stated that "... provisions of the Rehabilitation Act and the Education for All Handicapped Children Act [were violated] (1) by not insuring that the tests were validated for the specific purpose for which they were used, and (2) by not using the variety of statutorily mandated evaluation tools." To determine whether the children's rights under Title VI of the 1964 Civil Rights Act were violated, the court applied the "discriminatory *effect* analysis." A disproportionate number of black children were placed in the EMR class and the school could not prove the disproportionate placements were required by an educational necessity.

The court found that there was not proof of discriminatory intent which would be required to establish a violation of constitutional rights.

## § 14.61  Effect vs. Intent

The *Hobson* and *Larry P.* cases, referred to above, rested on the judicial assumption that if the "effect" of a test was to create a racially disparate placement of students, the use of the tests was unconstitutional unless school officials could show that the test measured what it was supposed to measure, was not biased and was required by an educational necessity.

The "effect" standard is used when statutory violations are analyzed. The United States Supreme Court decision in 1976, Washington v. Davis (S.Ct.1976), established a higher standard when analyzing a constitutional violation and this is that the plaintiff must prove discriminatory intent. In this case the Court upheld a written test of verbal knowledge used to select recruits for the District of Columbia police force even though the test resulted in disqualification of a much higher percentage of black applicants than whites. The Court found that racially disparate results alone were not enough to invalidate selection based on test scores for a constitutional violation. The standard adopted by the Court was one of "intent"; plaintiffs must show that government has a racially discriminatory intent or purpose in order to have the test set aside. (See Chapter 18, Employee Testing.)

## § 14.62   Academic Grouping

In applying the intent test, the courts have held that tests may be constitutionally appropriate academic tools for measuring achievement. The U.S. Court of Appeals for the Eleventh Circuit has held that the use of achievement tests for the purpose of academic grouping does not violate the Equal Protection Clause. Georgia State Conference of Branches of NAACP v. State of Georgia (11th Cir.1985).

"[T]he practice of achievement grouping is not, *per se*, unconstitutional. Under proper circumstances, courts have approved the practice. Indeed, in some cases, courts have directed the use of special groups, particularly where concentrated remedial counseling is required to overcome language difficulties." The mere fact that scholastic achievement tests result in the placement of a disproportionately greater number of white students than black in advance placement courses does not indicate racial discrimination. If a school district has operated a unitary school system and can, thus, show that the ability grouping is not caused by past discrimination, then the black students' rights are not violated. Montgomery v. Starkville Municipal Separate School District (5th Cir.1988).

## § 14.7 DEBRA P.

In 1978, the Florida Legislature enacted a law requiring that public school students pass a functional literacy examination in order to receive a high school diploma. Shortly afterward students challenged the test maintaining that it violated both the due process and equal protection clauses of the Fourteenth Amendment. A federal district court held for the students and enjoined the use of the test to withhold diplomas until the 1982–83 school year. Debra P. v. Turlington (M.D.Fla.1979). On appeal the Fifth Circuit Court of Appeals affirmed the lower court's findings. Debra P. v. Turlington (5th Cir.1981). The Circuit Court, however, remanded the case for further factual findings on two key issues, (a) the instructional validity of the test (the Florida Student State Assessment Test, Part II) and (b) the vestiges of racial discrimination questions.

## § 14.71 Teaching What Is Tested

The validity issue was succinctly stated by the court as being whether the "test is a fair test of that which was taught." Accordingly, if the test was not fair, then it could not be rationally related to a legitimate state interest and therefore would be violative of the Equal Protection Clause. The state presented evidence showing that the subjects tested parallelled the curricular goals of the state. Instructional programs of all the school districts addressed the skills for which the test was designed and the state-approved instructional materials were used in all districts to implement the state prescribed curricular objectives. Further, local school districts reported that the skills required to pass the test were included in their curriculum and that a substantial number of public school teachers responded to a questionnaire and stated that they actually taught the prescribed curriculum. The court held that this intensive verification of instructional validity was sufficient to withstand constitutional challenge.

The court rejected the plaintiff's argument that the state must show that each teacher individually actually teaches the prescribed curriculum. "What is required," the court said, "is that the skills be included in the official curriculum and that the majority of the teachers recognize them as being something they should teach." Debra P. v. Turlington (M.D.Fla.1983). The court further elaborated in rejecting plaintiff's contentions, that "It strains credibility to hypothesize that teachers, especially remedial teachers, are uniformly avoiding their responsibilities at the expense of their pupils."

Tests that are not validated for the purpose for which they are used may violate the Equal Protection Clause or Title IX of the 1972 Education Amendments. This was the situation in New York where the Scholastic Aptitude Test (SAT) was used to award scholarships to college. Such use of the test was challenged by female students who claimed that the test discriminated because females won disproportionately fewer scholarships. The legislature defended the use of the test by maintaining that the tests were a valid means of determining superior high school achievement. The court held for the female students. Upon examining the evidence, the court found that the SAT had been statistically validated to predict college academic performance, but had never been validated as a means of past high school academic achievement. The court in holding against the state ruled that the state must show that the SAT does, in fact, measure high school performance if the test is to be used as a device to reward such performance. Without showing such a relationship, the test is invalid. Sharif v. New York State Education Department (S.D.N.Y.1989).

§ 14.71a   Vestiges of Segregation

Concerning the vestiges of racial discrimination issue, the court had originally deferred the effective date of the test until 1983 because Florida public schools had not been fully integrated until 1970, and the court wanted to assure that all black students would have had the opportunity to attend integrated schools for a full twelve years. With regard to racial segregation, the court enunciated the rule that the use of a particular test "can be enjoined only if it perpetuates the effects of past school segregation or if it is not needed to remedy those effects." In applying this standard the court was unable to find that the tests were offensive to equal protection; on the contrary, because the tests identified students who did not have the necessary skills and provided remedial instruction for them, the court was of the opinion that use of the basic literacy test was an important factor in eradicating vestiges of past racial discrimination.

Thus, competency tests are acceptable instruments to measure student performance, even if the effect is for higher percentages of black students than white to fail. According to *Debra P.*, however, the state must be prepared to go to substantial lengths to document the validity of the tests given and provision must be made for those students failing the test to be given remedial assistance in overcoming their deficiencies.

As yet the United States Supreme Court has not ruled on the extent of the burden which a state must bear in showing test validity for students. The range of options, at this time, extend from the strict adherence to the intent standard as espoused in *United States v. South Carolina*, supra, where the state must merely show that its test is rationally related to a legitimate state objective, to the more restrictive standard of *Debra P.* where the state must bear a substantial burden of proof to document instructional validity and to show that the test does not perpetuate and augment the vestiges of racial discrimination.

# CHAPTER 15

# TERMS AND CONDITIONS OF
# TEACHER EMPLOYMENT

## § 15.1 INTRODUCTION

In order to qualify for employment as a public school teacher, a person must be certified or licensed by the state. Certification signifies that an individual is competent to teach. The assurance of teacher competency was to some degree a response to compulsory attendance laws; if the state compelled children to attend school, then it would be logical, and indeed rational, if they were to be supervised and taught by qualified or certified teachers.

## § 15.2 CERTIFICATION

Education is a state responsibility; consequently, certification differs in each state depending on the statutory provisions and regulations. Each state has the responsibility for certification or decertification (revocation of license) and in normal circumstances this responsibility is delegated to the State Board of Education and/or the Department of Education. These agencies administer the certification process and promulgate rules and regulations. The certification process is generally less involved than decertification. A teacher who is decertified has a right to know the cause of revocation and the opportunity for a hearing since constitutional issues may be present and generally are a factor.

Most states require all teachers to have a college degree as a condition precedent to certification. Some states have made provisions for qualified or conditional certification where teachers have completed only a specified number of college units that have to be upgraded within a specified period of time. College credits usually are required in the subject area (i.e., history) in which the teacher plans to teach. Concomitantly, states usually require the appropriate professional curriculum and methodology classes. In addition to higher education training, states require individuals to be: (1) of good moral character, (2) a specified age (usually 18 or older), and (3) a citizen of the United States, or if not already a citizen, the applicant must intend to become a citizen. Some states require pledging loyalty to the Constitutions of the state and United States. In recent years, some states have instituted a teacher examination. By 1989–90, the number of states requiring state-prescribed standardized tests as a condition for entering the teaching profession numbered 39. All 50 states approve the content of Teacher Education programs conducted by colleges and universities. If individuals meet all of the state established standards, then they are eligible for certification or licensing, and the certifying body may not arbitrarily or capriciously refuse certification.

Some states require further academic training after initial certification in order to maintain certification, while other states endorse teachers for life. If certification requirements are changed, grandfather clauses often cover those already certified and the new regulations apply to new applicants only.

In most states, certifying agencies are vested with some discretionary authority. This discretion is particularly important when applying the elusive standard of good, moral conduct or appropriate and good behavior. In one case, an Oregon policeman was convicted of breaking and entering and grand larceny. Afterward, serving his term, he completed all the college requirements to apply for a teaching certificate but was denied. The crux of the question was whether he had overcome his questionable past. State certification standards required that an individual be of good moral character. It was the determination of the State Board of Education that he had not overcome his past indiscretions and therefore, he was denied certification. The courts generally refuse to question the discretion of a Board's decisions unless it can be shown that the board members acted arbitrarily or capriciously. Bay v. State Board of Education (Or.1963).

## § 15.21  Tests

In recent years, states have reinstituted examinations as conditions to certification, with several states employing the National Teacher Examination. Some teachers have objected, maintaining that the "effect" of the tests is to exclude a higher percentage of blacks than of whites. These tests do not violate the Fourteenth Amendment if they were not designed with the "intent" to discriminate. To challenge the test under the Fourteenth Amendment, the teachers must bear the burden of proving discriminatory intent. The tests have also been challenged under Title VII, Civil Rights Act of 1964, and have been upheld if the state can show that they are reasonably related to the knowledge one needs to teach. In a key decision dealing with Title VII, the court said: "[a]lthough the NTE were not designed to evaluate experienced teachers, the State could reasonably conclude that the NTE provided a reliable and economical means for measuring one element of effective teaching—the degree of knowledge possessed by the teacher." United States v. State of South Carolina (D.S.C.1977).

In other litigation involving the testing of teachers, the Texas legislature passed a law which required all teachers and administrators to pass an examination to continue certification. The test was challenged claiming it (1) impaired the contracts of the educators who were already certified, and (2) violated due process. The court held a teaching certificate is not a contract, therefore the constitutional prohibition against impairment of contracts was not violated. Accordingly, the court concluded that a teaching certificate is a license subject to future reasonable restrictions by the state. With regard to due process, the court said teachers who failed the test may retake the test and appeal to a state commission before revocation of their certificate. The court concluded that such provision gave the teachers ample due process. State v. Project Principle, Inc. (Tex.1987).

## § 15.22  Aliens

Can states legally deny teacher certification to persons who are not citizens of the United States? The answer is yes. A New York statute provided that a teaching certificate would be denied any individual who was not a United States Citizen or who had not manifested an intention to apply for citizenship. In 1979, the United States Supreme Court upheld the New York statute. In doing so, the court relied on a 1978 case which upheld the exclusion of individuals who wanted to be policemen because of the special nature of the governmental obligation, Foley v. Connelie (S.Ct.1978). The Supreme Court held that there was a rational governmental interest in requiring teachers to be either citizens or be in the process of becoming naturalized citizens. Ambach v. Norwick (S.Ct.1979).

## § 15.23  Revocation

Teaching certificates may be revoked for unprofessional conduct, which may include the violation of state law, false swearing to loyalty oaths, incompetency, and immorality. If a state plans to revoke or decertify a teacher, it may consider not only classroom ability and performance but also outside activity. The California Supreme Court upheld the decertification of a teacher who belonged to a "swingers" club and engaged in public sexual acts with numerous men and had appeared on television in disguise, espousing nonconventional sexual behavior. Pettit v. State Board of Education (Cal.1973).

Although teachers may have their certificates revoked for good and valid reasons, the revocation may not be for an unconstitutional reason. It is unconstitutional to deny teachers freedom of speech or expression unless the actions of the teacher disrupt the educational process. Reasonable questions related to job performance must be answered by teachers.

Teaching certificates may be revoked only for serious offenses that are detrimental to students or the teaching profession. The following are examples of such serious nature that have led to revocation of teaching certificates. Certification was revoked where a classroom teacher physically attacked the district superintendent and the superintendent was cut, bloodied and bruised. Everett v. Texas Education Agency (Tex.App.1993).

Where a "transcript of victim's trial testimony describing rape [by the teacher] was sufficient evidence of teacher's immorality and misconduct in office to support license revocation." Ulrich v. State (Ind.App.1990). Where a teacher falsified welfare records for six years and received approximately $43,000 in welfare benefits revocation was justified. Stelzer v. State Bd. of Ed. (Ohio App. 3 Dist.1991). And where a male teacher engaged in sexual conduct with male students certification withdrawal was deemed appropriate by the court. Stedronsky v. Sobol (N.Y.1991).

## § 15.3  LOCAL  BOARD  PREROGATIVES  FOR EMPLOYMENT

Teacher certification does not guarantee employment. State legislatures delegate the authority to employ personnel to local school boards. Although the final authority over employment rests with the school board, some states provide that a school board may employ personnel only if the superintendent has recommended the person to the board for employment. Wide latitude is vested in the board so long as the board does not violate one's constitutional or statutory rights such as sex, race, or religion, or if the board acted arbitrarily, capriciously or in bad faith.

## § 15.31  Certification as a Minimum Standard

A local school board may promulgate reasonable rules and regulations relating to employment even though the teacher has already met minimum certification standards. A board may require additional training more advanced than that required for certification, such as having a Master's degree before employment. Also, a board may require a teacher to take additional courses or be involved in staff development training after employment. A teacher may be required, as a part of the employment relationship, to obtain higher levels of academic training as long as the school board policy requirements are not discriminatory.

## § 15.32　Residency Requirement

A board may require a teacher to establish residency in the school district. In recent years, urban school districts have utilized this authority to prevent mass movement of teachers out to the suburbs. Teachers have challenged the residency requirements as violation of their liberty rights. The courts have upheld the policies as rational. The courts have accepted the school boards' rationale that teachers who live in the district have a better understanding of the students and the community and, therefore, are more likely to be committed to the school district, and more involved in community activities. They also would be local taxpayers and, therefore, more personally interested in the quality of education offered in the districts. Some school districts have established policies that allow teachers, who lived outside of the district prior to the implementation date of the residency policy, to be exempt from the policy. These "grandfather" provisions have been attacked by new teachers claiming discrimination, but the courts have upheld the policies as reasonable if they are applied in a nondiscriminatory manner. Wardwell v. Board of Education (6th Cir.1976); McClelland v. Paris Public Schools (Ark.1988).

## § 15.33  Outside Employment

Some school boards have formulated policies forbidding teachers to engage in other employment during the school year. The courts have given wide latitude to local school boards in establishing such employment rules and have upheld these policies. Such policies though must be applied uniformly and consistently to all teachers in like classification.

## § 15.34  Health and Physical Requirements

Within the boundaries of federal and state statutes and regulations, a local school board may adopt reasonable health and physical condition requirements for teachers. These standards are generally viewed favorably by the courts if they are applied uniformly. But, a board has to be especially cognizant of the protections and prohibitions with regard to those persons who may be classified under various federal and state provisions as disabled. Health and physical requirements must be rationally related to job performance and should not be promulgated to disenfranchise otherwise qualified persons. In a New York case, the court said "From this constitutional authority the right of government agencies to adopt such 'health' standards may be inferred provided such standards are reasonably and rationally related to ability to perform...." Parolisi v. Board of Examiners of the City of New York (N.Y.1967).

In another case shedding light on this issue, a teacher was advised to visit a dentist, to improve condition and appearance of his teeth, and he was also advised to lose weight and develop adequate body tone. The teacher sued and the court ruled the superintendent had taken no steps to compel compliance with the suggestions, therefore no rights were violated. The teacher was, though, required to undergo a physical examination as authorized by statute. Mermer v. Constantine (N.Y. 1987).

## § 15.35 Assignment of Teaching Duties

A school board generally has the authority to transfer and assign teachers to best benefit the educational program of the school district. Such assignments are contingent on the certification of the teacher. If a teacher is certified to teach in the primary grades, then the teacher may only be assigned to primary courses. A teacher has no right to demand a particular grade or teaching position within a school district. A local board may adopt reasonable rules and regulations regarding transfer, but once established they cannot be violated. To transfer a teacher for purposes of punishment or to make life so uncomfortable as to force the teacher's resignation is, of course, considered to be arbitrary and violative of the teacher's rights.

In a case illustrating the extent of school board prerogative, a court ruled that a guidance counselor, who refused to supervise the school campus before school, could be dismissed for refusing to obey the request. Jones v. Alabama State Tenure Commission (Ala.Civ. App.1981). In contrast a West Virginia court has ruled that librarians and guidance counselors could not be used on a regular basis as substitute teachers but could only be assigned as regular substitutes for a reasonable time if a financial emergency existed. Randolph County Bd. of Ed. v. Scalia (W.Va.1989).

## § 15.36  Extracurricular Duties and Activities

In the absence of specific contractual terms, a school board may assign reasonable extracurricular duties to a teacher. These duties may constitute such responsibilities as supervising study halls, directing a school play, coaching intramurals, conducting field trips and supervising athletic events. School officials may not assign bus driving duty, crossing guard duty or janitorial duties to teachers. Such duties are not reasonably related to the professional responsibilities of teachers. Extracurricular assignments must be related to the instructional activities for which the teacher is certified.

## § 15.4  RIGHT TO REMAIN SILENT

In Beilan v. Board of Public Education (S.Ct.1958), the United States Supreme Court ruled that a teacher must answer questions posed by school officials if those questions are relevant to the terms of employment. In this case, the teacher was dismissed because of refusal to answer relevant questions posed by the school superintendent regarding teaching responsibilities.

However, questions posed by a legislative committee or in a judicial proceeding may not be used as a basis for dismissing teachers. Board of Public Education School District of Philadelphia v. Intille (Pa.1960). Any questions asked must be balanced against the teacher's constitutional rights. The United States Supreme Court has recognized the unique position and interest teachers have in speaking out on educational issues that are matters of public concern. Thus, the political rights and prerogatives of teachers are protected and any state or local encroachments on those political freedoms are unconstitutional. Pickering v. Board of Education (S.Ct. 1968).

## § 15.5 CONTRACTS

A teacher contract contains the basic elements of regular contract law. The basic elements for a valid contract are: (1) offer and acceptance; (2) competent parties; (3) consideration; (4) legal subject matter; and (5) proper form. Each of these elements are elaborated below as pertaining to teacher contracts.

### § 15.51 Offer and Acceptance

Only a school board may make a valid offer to contract with a teacher. The offer has to be made to the teacher and within a reasonable time; the teacher may only accept the offer that has been tendered. If a school board tenders an offer for a specific salary and the teacher accepts the offer but requests the salary be increased, then there is no valid offer and there cannot be a valid acceptance. In essence, the teacher has made a counter offer. There has been no meeting of the minds as to conditions and terms of the contract, thus no contract can be formed without further action by the school board.

### § 15.52 Competent Parties

Both parties must have the legal capacity to contract. A school board is a legal party under the authority vested in it by the legislature. A person is not legally competent to contract as a teacher if he/she is without certification. Thus, certification makes a teacher competent to contract.

## § 15.53 Consideration

Consideration is an essential element of a contract. By definition, consideration is something of value received for performing an act or services for another party. In most teacher contracts, consideration constitutes the paying of a salary for the teaching services rendered. Consideration may be divided into three categories: (1) a valuable; (2) a good; and (3) a promise for an act. A teacher's salary falls into the category of a "valuable". An example of good consideration would be love and affection, although important to teaching is not normally considered to be applicable to a teaching contract. This category is normally not found in public school board transactions. The third category may be a promise to act for good consideration.

## § 15.54 Legal Subject Matter

The contract must be for a legal subject matter. Contracting for a teacher to teach a prescribed curriculum would fall in this category. If a board enters into a contract that is not of legal subject matter (such as conducting rooster fights or selling drugs) or is beyond the scope of its authority, the contract would be invalid or voidable.

## § 15.55 Legal Form

The contract must be in the legal form required by state statutes or regulations. Most states require contracts to be written and to include specific provisions. However, there are instances when an oral agreement may be legally binding. Teacher contracts, however, must be in writing and approved in public action by the board, and recorded in its minutes.

## § 15.6  TENURE

Tenure is a privilege bestowed upon the teaching profession by the legislature. This privilege may be prospectively altered by legislative action, but not by local school boards. In 1927, the Indiana legislature used the word contract in the tenure statute and this created a contract between the tenured teachers and the state. The United States Constitution, Article I, Section 10, provides that the obligation of a contract may not be impaired, and the United States Supreme Court invoking this provision ruled that subsequent Indiana legislatures could not alter the contractual relationship. If a tenure statute is written so as not to create a contractual relationship, it may be altered or abolished by the state legislature. Indiana ex rel. Anderson v. Brand (S.Ct. 1938).

Many reasons have been given as to why tenure was established. Some of these are: (1) to remove political abuse from the profession; (2) to prevent arbitrary interference by boards; (3) to provide a permanent, competent teaching force; and (4) to protect the competent, experienced professional, thereby providing job security.

Most states have established statutory provisions which grant tenure, or continuing contracts. These statutes provide that a teacher, after serving a specified probationary period, cannot be removed from a position unless the school board has established good and just cause and provided the teacher with procedural due process. The specific causes for removal vary from state to state depending on the statutory language, but include such causes as immorality, insubordination, incompetence, misconduct, neglect of duty, or other good and just cause. (See Chapter 17, Teacher Dismissal.) Generally, the tenure statutes provide specific procedures that must be followed before a teacher may be removed. Tenure is a statutory right and not a constitutional right, but once tenure is granted a "property" right is created and by virtue of that right procedural due process is required before removal.

Before teachers are awarded tenure status they must serve a probationary period. States require from two to five years of probation, with the majority of states requiring three years. After serving the specified period, a local school board has the discretion of granting tenure or not renewing the probationary teacher's contract. If a school board chooses not to renew a probationary teacher's contract during the probationary period, the board is not required to give reasons unless statute so requires. Even if reasons are given by the board, and they are not constitutionally impermissible reasons, the board has no obligation to provide the teacher with a removal hearing.

Tenure may or may not be transferred from district to district, within a particular state, depending on the construction of the state statute. Some states allow at the discretion of the local school board the granting of tenure immediately upon moving from one district to another. In other states, an experienced teacher may be required to serve a partial probationary period such as one year rather than a full probationary period of three years.

Tenure is granted for teaching and not for extracurricular assignments such as coaching. Supplementary contracts have been interpreted by the courts to be outside tenure statutes. This rule, though, is not uniform. Not only are teaching positions encompassed by tenure laws, but statutes in a number of states provide tenure status for administrative personnel such as principals, assistant superintendents, superintendents and others.

## § 15.7   REDUCTION IN FORCE

In recent years, in many districts, there has been a decline in the student population. This has necessitated a corresponding reduction in the number of professional employees. As mentioned previously, teachers and other professionals who have acquired tenure may be dismissed for reasonable cause only. Where there are declining enrollments, teachers may be laid-off as a result of a work force reduced. Legitimate reduction in force may be caused by such factors as enrollment decline, fiscal restraints, reorganization, or elimination of positions or programs. Most state tenure laws provide local school boards the flexibility to reduce the work force due to financial exigency. The local school board has within its discretion the authority to adopt procedures to reduce the work force, absent contractual obligations created by statutory or collective bargaining agreements.

## § 15.71   Rationale for Reduction in Force

The courts will look closely at whether or not a reduction in force is necessary or rather is an attempt to circumvent statutory protections of employees. Whether a board has a real financial exigency requiring lay-off becomes an essential question. The burden is upon the board or institution to establish that a financial exigency exists. In *American Association of University Professors*

v. Bloomfield College (N.J.Super.1974), Bloomfield College abolished tenure for all faculty, then dismissed eleven tenured faculty members. The union requested that the college sell a golf course to obtain funds for re-employment. The court found that the college had a true financial crisis and need not dispose of assets to obtain funds to continue faculty employment.

## § 15.72   Positions to be Eliminated

After it has been determined that a financial crisis exists, school boards then must decide who and what positions are to be eliminated. In the absence of statutory or collective bargaining provisions, tenured teachers are in most states given priority over non-tenured teachers in consideration of dismissal. Seniority is generally given substantial weight. However, there have been some court decisions to the contrary in which other standards besides seniority have been upheld. The courts, though, require that these standards be rational, job related, and established prior to the incident of their implementation. Underwood v. Henry County School Board (Va.1993).

A board in deciding which positions are to be eliminated may not act in an arbitrary or capricious manner. A board cannot abolish a position, and terminate the employee, then transfer the responsibilities of the former employee to another position. This type of shift in responsibilities may circumvent tenure laws and if it does is illegal.

## § 15.73  Intent of the Board

A board must act in good faith and may not terminate a teacher under the guise of need to reduce the teaching force. Some cases have arisen over whether a true financial exigency existed or whether the teacher's position was eliminated because of some teacher action that offended the board. In Zoll v. Eastern Allamakee Community School District (8th Cir.1978), a teacher had written letters to a local paper criticizing the school board. A jury determined the real reason for elimination of the position was something the teacher had said. The board was unable to show that a financial crisis existed and because the teacher had been outspoken, the court suspected that the dismissal was motivated by the teacher's speech and not financial exigency. Thus the teacher prevailed. In Hagarty v. Dysart–Geneseo Community School District (Iowa 1979), the court said "... we could not countenance a subterfuge by which an unscrupulous school board would use a fictitious necessity for staff reduction as a pretext for discharging a teacher."

## § 15.74  Seniority Displacement

As previously mentioned, generally, tenured teachers take precedence over non-tenured teachers in reduction in force. School board rules, however, may provide for "bumping" procedures if reduction in force is necessary. In the absence of such rules, a school board generally would take into consideration not only seniority but also certification. If a teacher is certified in a specific area where teachers are needed, then he or she may be able to replace someone with less seniority.

# CHAPTER 16

# CONSTITUTIONAL RIGHTS OF TEACHERS

## § 16.1 INTRODUCTION

Teachers' lives and activities have always been subject to close public scrutiny. Because teachers are entrusted with the responsibilities of educating the children and legally stand *in loco parentis*, they are expected to provide a role model for youth. Earlier, teachers' contracts included provisions that prohibited the use of alcoholic spirits, smoking, and in many cases required dismissal of female teachers who had the temerity to get married while employed as a teacher. There were also other restrictions forbidding attendance at theaters, dating, keeping late hours, and divorce. In some instances, teachers were required to teach Sunday School and perhaps more importantly, teachers were also prohibited from speaking out on political issues that might be construed as criticism of individuals in authority.

## § 16.2 TEACHERS' FREEDOMS OF SPEECH AND EXPRESSION

At the aforementioned point in our nation's constitutional development, public employment was viewed as a privilege and not a right. The basis for this logic, that public employees could not fully retain their political freedoms and concurrently hold public employment, was justified by Justice Holmes' in his often-quoted assertion, in 1892, that "The petitioner may have a constitutional right to talk politics, but he has no constitutional right to be a policeman."

Many earlier cases involving public school teachers followed this philosophy, holding that the contract provisions between the board and the teacher could prohibit the exercise of various rights and freedoms by teachers; and, if the teacher violated the provisions of the contract, even though they were repressive of the teacher's rights, dismissal could be upheld.

Although the courts were generally split and relatively uncertain as to the personal freedoms of teachers, the privilege-right dichotomy continued to exist. Where teachers did prevail, the courts based their conclusions on common-law reasonableness and not on constitutional rights or freedoms. The teacher employment relationship with the school board was largely defined by common-law reasonableness, contract law, and statutory and regulatory provision of the state. It did not clearly reach to constitutional rights and freedoms until 1968.

## § 16.3  PICKERING AND POLITICAL FREEDOM

The watershed case in application of constitutional standards to teacher employment came in 1968 in Pickering v. Board of Education (S.Ct.1968), the U.S. Supreme Court held that freedom of speech, while not absolute in all circumstances, is nevertheless sufficiently strong to require the state show a "compelling state interest" in order to overcome a teacher's right to speak out on issues of public importance. In so doing the Court equated the teachers' right of free speech with

that of other members of the general public to criticize
and comment on public policies and issues. Any linger-
ing doubt about the legal dichotomy of privileges versus
rights was extinguished by this case, and the dictum of
Justice Holmes was repudiated.

In *Pickering* the Supreme Court held that "a teacher's
exercise of his right to speak on issues of public importance may not furnish the basis for his dismissal from
public employment." In this particular case a teacher
sent a letter to a local newspaper attacking a proposed
tax increase by the Board of Education. The letter
contained partially erroneous information and the teacher was dismissed by the board because the letter "im-
pugned" the "motives," "honesty" and "integrity" of
board and administration. The Court, acknowledging
that a balance must be maintained regarding such political activity, gave the following guideline: "... It cannot
be gainsaid that the State has interests as an employer in
regulating the speech of its employees that differ significantly from those it possesses in connection with regulation of the speech of the citizenry in general. The
problem in any case is to arrive at a balance between the
interests of the teacher, as a citizen, in commenting upon
matters of public concern and the interest of the State,
as employer, in promoting the efficiency of the public
services it performs through its employees."

The Court pointed out that a school board may be
justified in dismissal of an employee if the statements or
activities are of such a nature as to be detrimental to the
actual operation of the schools. The Court further concluded that the activity was not inhibitive in any manner
to the educational performance of the school. It was not
shown that the teacher's letter had any impact on the

proposed tax increase nor was it shown that the false statements were made recklessly or knowingly. The Court said: "On such a question free and open debate is vital to informed decision-making by the electorate. Teachers are, as a class, the members of a community most likely to have informed and definite opinions as to how funds allotted to the operation of the schools should be spent. Accordingly, it is essential that they be able to speak out freely on such questions without fear of retaliatory dismissal."

## § 16.31 Teacher Speech and the *Connick* Rule

After *Pickering*, the courts developed a flexible rule that provided for balancing the public's interests against the private interest of the employee in each circumstance. This balancing, however, did not remove all state restraint on teacher activities; on the contrary, the courts have reflected a strong belief that because of their sensitive position in the classroom, teachers must be held accountable for certain activities both internal and external to the school. The interest of the public is to a great extent dependent on the teachers' status, appearance, and stature in the community. The courts have maintained that the school board must preserve the integrity of the learning processes of the school. Thus, an important equilibrium must be maintained between the private and the public interests.

The balancing of these interests with regard to freedom of speech was given new clarity by the U.S. Supreme Court in Connick v. Myers (S.Ct.1983). *Connick* explains that First Amendment free speech is protected when the employee speaks out on "matters of public concern."

Implicitly, speech or expression exercised by a public employee concerning matters of private or personal interest and not as a citizen upon matters of public concern is not protected by the First Amendment.

*Connick* and *Pickering* combined to form a free speech test that is a two-step process. First, the initial inquiry is whether the speech is a matter of public concern; in this regard *Connick* states: "When employee expression cannot be fairly considered as relating to any matter of political, social, or other concern to the community, government officials should enjoy wide latitude in managing their offices, without intrusive oversight by the judiciary in the name of the First Amendment."

Second, if the speech is found to be a matter of public concern, the court then must apply the *Pickering* balancing test. The interest of the public employee as a citizen in commenting on matters of public concern must be weighted against the interests of the state, as an employer, to promote effective and efficient public service.

## § 16.32  Dismissal When Constitutional Issues Are Involved

A board may dismiss or not renew a teacher's contract even if constitutional protections are involved if there are other valid and legitimate reasons for termination. In other words, if a board, in deciding to dismiss a teacher, would have reached the same decision, even if the free speech issue had not occurred, then dismissal would not have infringed on the constitutional rights of the teacher. This rule is termed the mixed motive test where there are both constitutional and non-constitutional issues involved. If the constitutional right were set aside, would the employee be dismissed for the non-constitutional action? If the answer is yes, then the employee is dismissed for the non-constitutional action and not the constitutional free speech.

In Mount Healthy City Sch. Dist. Bd. of Ed. v. Doyle (S.Ct.1977), a non-tenured teacher telephoned a local radio station and criticized a dress and appearance policy unilaterally issued to teachers by the administration. The teacher, Doyle, was also involved in a number of other incidents such as: a physical altercation with another teacher, an argument with school cafeteria employees, swearing at students and making obscene gestures to female students. Doyle's contract was subsequently not renewed and he requested the reasons for non-renewal. In response to Doyle's request, the superintendent referred to "a notable lack of tact in handling professional matters which leave much doubt as to your sincerity in establishing good school relationships," then, he specifically referred to the radio station incident. The teacher challenged the dismissal as violative of his First and Fourteenth Amendment rights. The Sixth Circuit Court of Appeals reasoned that the telephone call was a matter of public concern and therefore protected free speech and it also was the major reason for Doyle's dismissal and ordered reinstatement. The United States Supreme Court remanded the case back to the lower court to determine if the board had substantial and legitimate reasons for not renewing Doyle's contract, other than those of protected free speech. "A borderline or marginal candidate should not have the employment question resolved against him because of constitutionally protected conduct. But that same candidate ought not to be able, by engaging in such conduct, to prevent his employer from assessing his performance record and reaching a decision not to rehire on the basis of that record, simply because the protected conduct makes the employer more certain of the correctness of its decision."

The mixed motive test was used in *Connick v. Myers*. In *Connick*, a public employee (Assistant District Attorney Sheila Myers), when informed she would be transferred to another area in the district attorney's office, opposed this personnel decision. In response, Myers passed out a questionnaire to other fellow assistant district attorneys, soliciting information about office morale and pressure to work in political campaigns. Myers was told the questionnaire constituted insubordination, and her employment was terminated. The Supreme Court upheld Myers' dismissal, finding that the matter was basically of a personal nature and not a matter of public concern of any particular weight or magnitude. Though one question on Myers' questionnaire did fall under the rubric of "public concern," Myers' First Amendment interest was outweighed by the disruptive nature of the other questions. The beliefs by the state that Myers' actions would disrupt the office, undermine authority, and destroy the close working relationships within the office were reasonably taken in view of the evidence. The fact that Myers issued the questionnaire immediately after the transfer dispute lent weight in balancing the scales on behalf of the state that her actions were of a personal nature and not a matter of public concern. In so holding, the Court rejected Myers' contention that the state must bear the burden of clearly demonstrating that the discharge was necessary because the speech "substantially interfered" with the operation of the office.

## § 16.33  Private Criticism

A teacher's freedom of speech is protected in private communication with an employer.  In Givhan v. Western Line Consolidated School District (S.Ct.1979), a junior high school English teacher met privately with the principal and criticized the policies of the school on racial discrimination.  The principal alleged that the criticism involved "petty and unreasonable demands and were presented in an insulting, loud, hostile and arrogant manner."  The Fifth Circuit Court of Appeals upheld the dismissal, citing *Pickering*, supra, and *Mount Healthy*, supra.  The United States Supreme Court reversed the decision and rejected the argument that the First Amendment did not protect the teacher's private criticism of the school principal.  A teacher's First Amendment rights are not lost when the teacher ". . . arranges to communicate privately with his employer rather than to spread his views before the public."

The court refused to grant a lesser protection to private speech than to public speech, but emphasized that the teacher could be dismissed if either private or public speech impeded the proper performance of classroom duties.  It was recognized that public speech is contingent upon content, whereas the impact of private speech might be judged on the time, place, and manner of the comments.

## § 16.34  Political Activity

*Pickering*, as discussed above, tells us that teachers may speak out on political issues as citizens.  Political rights are protected by the First Amendment.  Thus, a school administrator may not use punitive measures such as transferring, dismissing or demoting a teacher for protected political activities. On the other hand, a teacher may not be involved in political activities which disrupt the educational process. A school board may reasonably expect a teacher not to use his or her position to promote a particular political outcome, or to use the classroom for political purposes, or to be involved in any activity that will interfere with or disrupt the educational environment of the school, or detract from job performance.

A California court upheld the suspension of a teacher for using the classroom for political activity. Goldsmith v. Board of Education (Cal.App.1924). The teacher chose to comment on the election of the superintendent and said, "I think he would be more helpful to our department than a lady, and we need more men in our schools. Sometimes your parents do not know one candidate from another; so they might be glad to be informed. Of course, if any of you have relatives or friends trying for the same office, be sure and vote for them."

Some states have passed legislation modeled after the Federal Hatch Act which prohibits participation in partisan politics. United States Civil Service Commission v. National Ass'n of Letter Carriers (S.Ct.1973). The United States Supreme Court in Broadrick v. Oklahoma (S.Ct.1973), upheld an Oklahoma statute prohibiting public employees from participating in partisan politics. These statutes usually limit activities such as direct fund raising for partisan candidates, becoming a candidate, starting a political party, or actively managing a campaign.

## § 16.35  Political Office

It is well settled that a teacher, as a citizen of the United States, has a right to run for political office, but there is a difference between the right to run for public office and the right to continue public employment after being elected.  Common law provisions stipulate that a public employee may not hold positions simultaneously that are incompatible, and may not have a conflict of interest, or be in violation of the separation of powers of government.  These prohibitions have been determined to be of "compelling state interest," and, therefore, do not infringe on the basic political rights of teachers. Whether or not a teacher may hold political office and serve as a teacher depends on these provisions and individual state statutes.  Some states have "conflict of interest" statutes which provide that teachers may not serve as a state legislator while employed as a public teacher.  But, if a state does not have a statutory provision prohibiting teachers from serving in the legislature, then, the courts have held, they may serve.

## § 16.4  PERSONAL APPEARANCE

School boards have promulgated dress codes, not only for students, but sometimes for teachers as well.  These regulations have sometimes been challenged as violations of teachers' rights of free speech, expression, privacy and liberty.  There is a distinct difference between the privacy rights of a governmental employee and the privacy rights of a member of the general public.  The United States Supreme Court in Kelley v. Johnson (S.Ct.1976), ruled that hair-grooming of police officers could be regulated.  "The constitutional issue to be decided by the courts is whether petitioner's determination that such regulations should be enacted is so irrational that it may be branded 'arbitrary,' and therefore a deprivation of respondent's 'liberty' interest in freedom to choose his own hairstyle."

Similarly, where a Louisiana school board expanded its student dress code to prohibit employees from wearing beards, Domico v. Rapides Parish School Board (5th Cir.1982), the Fifth Circuit Court of Appeals recognized the liberty interest of the individual in choosing how to wear his hair. Yet, this court ruled that the school board had made a rational determination in establishing the rule as "... a reasonable means of furthering the school board's undeniable interest in teaching hygiene, instilling discipline, asserting authority, and compelling uniformity." This court clearly distinguished a difference between high school and college environments where hair regulations of faculty and students, in institutions of higher education, could not be justified, absent exceptional circumstances.

In Miller v. School District No. 167, Cook County, Illinois (7th Cir.1974), the Seventh Circuit Court held that a school board "... undoubtedly may consider an individual's appearance as one of the factors affecting his suitability for a particular position. If a school board should correctly conclude that a teacher's style of dress or plumage has an adverse impact on the educational process, and if that conclusion conflicts with the teacher's interest in selecting his own life style, we have no doubt that the interest of the teacher is subordinate to the public interest."

The Second Circuit Court in East Hartford Education Association v. Board of Education, etc. (2d Cir.1977), recognized the liberty interest of an individual's personal appearance, but said that these liberty interests are "less weighty" than those of "procreation, marriage, and family life." The school board had instituted a rule requiring male classroom teachers to wear a jacket, shirt and tie and female teachers a dress, skirt, blouse and pantsuits except where other teaching assignments would require more appropriate apparel, i.e., gym teachers, to this the court responded, "[w]e join the sound views of the First and Seventh Circuits, and follow *Kelley* by holding that a school board may, if it wishes, impose reasonable regulations governing the appearance of the teachers it employs."

## § 16.5 RIGHT OF PRIVACY

The word "privacy" is not mentioned in the Constitution nor in the Bill of Rights, yet, the right of privacy is so basic and fundamental to individual freedom that it is assumed to emanate implicitly from the Constitution.

Justice Douglas in Griswold v. Connecticut (S.Ct.1965), stated that there is a broad right of privacy which may be inferred from several provisions of the Bill of Rights. He said that the various guarantees of the constitution "create zones of privacy." Justice Douglas elaborated on the areas where privacy is found in the constitution saying that "The right of association contained in the penumbra of the First Amendment is one.... The Third Amendment in its prohibition against the quartering of soldiers 'in any house' in time of peace without the consent of the owner is another ... The Fourth Amendment explicitly affirms the 'right of the people to be secure in their persons, houses, papers, and effects, against unreasonable searches and seizures.' The Fifth Amendment in the Self–Incrimination Clause enables the citizen to create a zone of privacy beyond which government may not encroach. The Ninth Amendment provides: 'The enumeration in the Constitution, of certain rights, shall not be construed to deny or disparage others retained by the people.' "

The right of privacy also finds basis in the substance of liberty of the Due Process Clause of the Fourteenth Amendment. This was the basis for the Supreme Court's decision in Roe v. Wade (S.Ct.1973). The connection between personal privacy and liberty is reinforced by the earlier U.S. Supreme Court precedents of Pierce v. Society of Sisters (S.Ct.1925), and Meyer v. Nebraska (S.Ct.1923).

It is the confluence and implication of these specified constitutional rights and freedoms that create the penumbras that Justice Douglas spoke of in *Griswold*. Because privacy is a fundamental right governmental restraint can be justified only by a showing of a "compelling state interest."

## § 16.51 Teacher's Mental and Physical Examinations

Teachers have always served as role models for pupils, and school boards expect high moral standards consistent with this status. The courts have generally upheld school boards in regulating the personal conduct of teachers within reasonable limits. Litigation, though, may result when teachers allege that certain school rules invade their privacy.

Teachers' use of the right of privacy has become more frequent in recent years, as schools have required teachers to take tests and be subject to various examinations. In one such case, a federal district judge rejected the privacy claim of a female teacher who refused to submit to a physical examination by a male physician employed by the school district. The court, in holding against the teacher, said that there was no right of privacy at stake, but rather a personal predilection against male physicians. Gargiul v. Tompkins (N.D.N.Y.1981). See also Hoffman v. Jannarone (D.N.J.1975).

In another case, a school principal's privacy claim was found to give way to the public interest where the school superintendent had reason to believe that the principal needed psychiatric attention. The principal had gotten into three near physical altercations with other administrators and a student. Daury v. Smith (1st Cir.1988). Thus, school districts may require teachers or administrators to be examined to determine their physical, mental or intellectual fitness to teach so long as the tests conducted are reasonable and related to job performance.

## § 16.52 Drug Testing

In 1990 the Georgia General Assembly passed a number of bills aimed at dealing with the problems of drugs in society. One of these acts required all state employment applicants to submit to urine testing to determine the presence of illegal drugs. In Skinner v. Railway Labor Executives' Ass'n (S.Ct.1989), the U.S. Supreme Court stated "[b]ecause it [is] clear that the collection and testing of urine intrudes upon expectations of privacy that society has long recognized as reasonable ... these intrusions [are] searches under the Fourth Amendment." It was established in National Treasury Employees Union v. Von Raab (S.Ct.1989), that there are times when Fourth Amendment intrusion serves a special government interest as to whether it is impractical to require a search warrant or have a particularized individual suspicion. *Von Raab* concerned the drug testing of Custom Service employees who because of their duties were required to carry fire arms and had access to classified information. The Court found the need compelling for first line drug enforcement officials to be drug free. Being drug free was therefore paramount to the performance of their official duties. This case is factually different from the Georgia case because Georgia justified the testing on a *generalized* governmental interest of maintaining a drug-free work place. In contrast the drug testing in *Von Raab* was job specific.

Therefore drug testing appears to be permissible if specific governmental reasons are articulated, having to do with particularized job performance which impacts the health and safety of the public. The government or school district may require a drug test if they have particularized reasonable suspicion concerning the actions of a specific teacher. A broad sweep of testing all employees is not permissible. Thus, the court in the Georgia case found the act violated the Fourth and Fourteenth Amendments because the "... state's generalized interest in insuring [the] work force was not sufficiently compelling to outweigh applicants' right to privacy...." Georgia Association of Educators v. Harris (N.D.Ga.1990).

## § 16.6 FREEDOM OF RELIGION

All persons have the right of religious freedom as guaranteed by the First Amendment. However, religion, as with other freedoms, is not without limits. For example, in Palmer v. Board of Education of the City of Chicago (7th Cir.1979), a teacher refused to carry out certain aspects of the approved curriculum because of personal religious beliefs. The court acknowledged the teacher's right to freedom of belief, but also recognized a compelling state interest in the proper education of all its children. The court stated that education "cannot be left to individual teachers to teach the way they please." Teachers have "no constitutional right to require others to submit to [their] views and to forego a portion of their education they would otherwise be entitled to enjoy." (See Chapter 18, Employee Discrimination.)

A teacher's religious freedom may extend into several aspects of the educational program. For example, if the tenets of a teacher's religion are violated by the Pledge of Allegiance to the American flag, the teacher cannot be compelled to recite the pledge, but, the teacher, in accordance with school board rules, must conduct the pledge ceremony for student participation. Religious freedom of teachers will be sustained by the courts so long as the exercise of the freedom does not encroach on the rights of students or is not deleterious to the good conduct of the school.

A New Jersey court held unconstitutional a teacher-negotiated agreement that allowed for paid leaves of absences for religious believers, but made no allowance for non-believers. According to the court, the rule violated the First Amendment's free exercise clause. Hunterdon Central High School Board of Ed. v. Hunterdon Central High School Teachers' Ass'n (N.J.Super.1980).

## § 16.61 The 1964 Civil Rights Act and 1972 Amendment (Title VII)

The Civil Rights Act of 1964, Title VII, 42 U.S.C.A. § 2000e et seq., prohibits any employer from discriminating against an individual because of religion. The 1972 Amendment states: "[t]he term religion includes all aspects of religious observance and practice, as well as belief, unless an employer demonstrates that he is unable to reasonably accommodate an employee's or prospective employee's religious observance or practice without undue hardship on the conduct of the employer's business." One of the key questions is, what does an employer need to do to accommodate the religious beliefs of an employee.

In Ansonia Board of Education v. Philbrook (S.Ct. 1986), the employee and employer each proposed a reasonable accommodation. The Supreme Court stated, "An employer has met its obligations under § 701(j) when it demonstrates that it has offered a reasonable accommodation to the employee. The employer need not further show that each of the employee's alternative accommodations would result in undue hardship. The extent of undue hardship on the employer's business is at issue only where the employer claims that it is unable to offer any reasonable accommodation without such *hardship* " (emphasis added).

As to what constitutes "hardship," the issue was addressed in Trans World Airlines, Inc. v. Hardison (S.Ct. 1977). In this case, Hardison, an employee, was working in a maintenance division under a negotiated agreement that allowed employees, with greater seniority, to choose what days they would work. Because of his seniority, Hardison chose not to work on Saturdays, his day of religious observance.  Later, at his own request, he was transferred to another work assignment.  Hardison had little seniority in his new position, and, therefore, he could not take Saturday off.  Hardison challenged the collective bargaining agreement and the seniority rule claiming that his religious beliefs took precedence over such provisions.  Justice White said that Title VII did not require TWA "... to carve out special exemptions." "To require TWA to bear more than a *de minimis* cost, in order to give Hardison Saturdays off, is an undue hardship."

Thus, relying on *Hardison* as applicable precedent, it would appear that the burden of proof is on the teacher or individual to establish that religion was a primary determinant in an employment decision.  If the teacher sustains the burden and shows the employer's primary motivation was religiously related, then the burden of proof shifts to the school board or employer to show that it made a good faith effort to accommodate the employee and, if this is unsuccessful, then it must be demonstrated that the employer (board) was unable to reasonably accommodate the employee's religious beliefs without undue hardship.

Another case that sheds light on the employer-employee relationship is Wangsness v. Watertown School District No. 14–4, etc. (D.S.D.1982), wherein an employee requested seven days off, without pay, to attend a religious festival.  When the request was denied, the employee attended the festival anyway and was as a result discharged from employment.  The school board claimed that a qualified teacher could not be found to serve as a substitute during the absence.  The teacher, before departing for the festival, prepared lesson plans to be used by a substitute teacher. The court determined that the classes had run smoothly, and no undue hardship was suffered by the board, therefore, the teacher was due equitable relief for a violation of Title VII.

In another similar case, a school district, through a negotiated agreement, provided each teacher with two personal leave days. A Jewish teacher claimed that she needed more than two days to celebrate religious holidays and she emphasized that Christian teachers benefitted from the structure of the school calendar citing that school was closed at Christmas and for Easter. Thus, Christian teachers could participate in religious ceremonies without being absent from school. The court ruled the school district's policy did not constitute religious discrimination against Jewish teachers merely because the Jewish teacher was required to occasionally take unpaid leave to accommodate his religious beliefs. The teacher was allowed to take unpaid leave and this was sufficient accommodation. Pinsker v. Joint District No. 28J (10th Cir.1984).

## § 16.62　Religious Garb

Whether teachers can wear religious garb of any particular church, religious order or society has been an occasional subject of contention over the years. The fact that there is no precise definition as to what constitutes religious dress does not simplify the situation. Yet, some religious dress is readily identifiable and may be of concern because teachers of public school districts, as agents of the state, should not by their various manifestations convey a particular religious belief so as to violate state neutrality toward religion.

A notable case of this type was litigated in Pennsylvania before the turn of the century in which nuns teaching in public schools wore the dress of the Sisterhood of St. Joseph. Pennsylvania state court ruled that the mere wearing of particular apparel did not constitute sectarian teaching and did not inculcate religion, thus such practice was permissible. Moreover, the court found that to deny the wearing of the religious regalia would effectively violate the teacher's religious liberty. Hysong v. School District of Gallitzin Borough (Pa.1894).

Later, however, the Pennsylvania legislature prohibited the wearing of religious garb by public school teachers and the act was upheld. The Supreme Court of Pennsylvania found that such a denial was a reasonable exercise of state authority to maintain the secular nature of public schools and to prevent sectarian establishment. The court said in justifying the legislative action that the legislation "is directed against acts, not beliefs, and only against acts of the teacher while engaged in the performance of his or her duties as such teacher." Commonwealth v. Herr (Pa.1910).

Most recently, in a definitive analysis of the issue, the Supreme Court of Oregon held that a teacher's certificate could be revoked for wearing religious garb. The teacher wore white clothes and a Sikh Hindu turban. In so holding, the court observed the legislature had a legitimate objective in maintaining the neutrality of the public schools. While the denial of the wearing of religious garb could be interpreted by some as an impingement on the teacher's personal religious freedom, it could just as logically be maintained the state's condoning of such garb favors a particular religion, and, in fact, places the imprimatur of the state behind that particular religious sect. The Oregon court said "the teacher's appearance in religious garb may leave a conscious or unconscious impression among young people and their parents that the school endorses the particular religious commitment of the person (teacher)." Cooper v. Eugene School District No. 4J (Or.1986).

The issue arose again in Pennsylvania; this time involving a devout Muslim teacher who insisted on wearing traditional Muslim dress. The Pennsylvania statute prohibiting religious attire was again challenged. The teacher claimed discrimination under Title VII of the Civil Rights Act and violation of religious liberty and sought an injunction preventing the school board from enforcing the statute. The U.S. Court of Appeals, Third Circuit, held for the school board ruling that the state had a compelling interest in maintaining religious neutrality in the public schools. With specific regard to Title VII, the court held that the compelling interest of the state in protecting the religious liberty of the public school students in the classroom was clearly an interest of such magnitude to overcome any claimed religious right of the teacher to wear the attire. United States v. Board of Education for the School District of Philadelphia (3d Cir.1990).

The Pennsylvania and Oregon cases appear to reflect the prevailing view of the courts with regard to teacher religious attire. A contrary opinion, however, is expressed by the Supreme Court of Mississippi where it upheld the right of a teacher to wear an African Hebrew Israelite head-wrap as an expression of religious and cultural heritage beliefs. The Mississippi court said that the wearing of the head-wrap was grounded in a sincerely held religious belief protected by the First Amendment. Mississippi Employment Security Commission v. McGlothin (Miss.1990).

# CHAPTER 17

# TEACHER DISMISSAL

## § 17.1 INTRODUCTION

Conditions of employment are controlled by state statute. Whether a teacher has permanent employment, continuing contract, or tenure the conditions are defined by legislative enactment. Procedures for nonrenewal of a probationary teacher or the dismissal of a tenured or permanent teacher are also determined by statute.

There is a distinction between nonrenewals and dismissals. With nonrenewal a probationary teacher is simply not offered a new term of employment at the end of the contract period. The school board has the discretion to decide the employee's services are no longer needed. State statute stipulates the date of notification for the nonrenewal. Dismissal, on the other hand, occurs within the term of the contract period, not at the end. A dismissal may occur during the period of an annual contract or during the period of tenure or continuing contract.

With dismissal, a teacher is removed from employment during a statutory period of probation or during the term of the permanent contract or tenure. A school board, in dismissing a tenured teacher, must prove good cause and afford the individual an opportunity to refute the reasons for dismissal alleged by the board. To dismiss requires full procedural process, whereas nonrenewals generally require only that the individual be notified of nonrenewal by a specific time.

Teachers' rights are guaranteed by the Federal Constitution. The Fourteenth Amendment provides no state shall "... deprive any person of life, liberty, or property, without due process of law; ...." The first ten amendments may all impact upon teacher employment. If a school board contravenes the constitutional rights of an employee (tenured or non-tenured) such as freedom of speech, then procedural due process must be afforded the employee.

## § 17.2 DUE PROCESS OF LAW

As noted more extensively elsewhere in this book, due process of law has two important aspects: (1) procedural and (2) substantive. Procedural due process is the actual legal procedure that must be adhered to when a court or administrative tribunal holds a hearing to ascertain the guilt or innocence of an individual. Procedural due process itself has been acknowledged in Anglo–American law since 1215 and Magna Charta. Two elements are essential to procedural due process: (a) fairness of hearing, and (b) an impartial tribunal.

Substantive due process, on the other hand, does not involve the actual hearing process, but, rather, is the extent and nature of the content of due process. The substance of due process emanates from the expanded definition of liberty and property. Liberty is more than simply a right to be free from incarceration and property rights extend far beyond simply the right to obtain and hold physical property. (See Chapter 3.)

## § 17.21 Procedural Due Process

The basic concept of procedural due process is an opportunity to be heard, in a manner that promotes fairness and establishes the accuracy of the charges. Procedural due process is a flexible concept and has been referred to by the courts as "fundamental fairness." An individual has a right to refute the charges brought against him by government, before a liberty or property right is taken away. The more serious the deprivation, the more formal the procedure for due process. Therefore, an administrative hearing to remove a teacher from his/her position is not as serious as a criminal offense and would require less stringent procedural due process.

The procedures to be followed in dismissing a teacher are generally specified by statute. Some of the elements of procedural due process are: There must be fair and reasonable notice of the charges; there must be an opportunity for a hearing; the hearing must be conducted by an impartial tribunal; there must be sufficient time to prepare for the hearing; the decision should be based on the evidence presented at the hearing; and there must be an opportunity to appeal a negative decision.

Although the specific elements of hearings are not set forth, the hearing must adhere to the minimal requirements of fair play to allow the teacher the opportunity to refute the charges. The Supreme Court of Missouri in Valter v. Orchard Farm School District (Mo.1976), suggested these minimal elements for a hearing. They may not necessarily be the same as provided for students since circumstances may be quite different. According to *Valter* the requirements for teachers are:

1.　The opportunity to be heard.

2.　The opportunity to present evidence to refute the charges.

3.　The opportunity to present witnesses.

4.　Representation by legal counsel.

5.　The opportunity to cross-examine witnesses.

6.　Access to all evidence, such as written reports, in advance.

School boards, generally, are the tribunal hearing the evidence and making the decision to dismiss or retain a teacher. This procedure has been challenged as a violation of due process because the school board is said not to be an impartial tribunal and therefore, fundamental fairness of procedural due process is allegedly hindered.

The Supreme Court addressed this issue of impartiality in Hortonville Joint School District No. 1 v. Hortonville Education Association (S.Ct.1976). Negotiations between teachers and the school board failed to produce an agreeable contract and the teachers went on strike. Wisconsin statutes prohibited teacher strikes, and, after a period of time, when the teachers were asked to return to work and did not, they were notified that disciplinary hearings would take place. The teachers appeared before the board, as a group, with counsel. The day after the hearing, the board terminated the teachers, but invited any who wished to reapply for a teaching position. A teacher reapplied and was rehired. The teachers claimed the Due Process Clause of the Fourteenth Amendment was violated because the board was not sufficiently impartial. The Supreme Court found that board members who were public servants, and who had no personal or financial stake in the negotiations had no conflict of interest. In the words of the Court, "[M]ere familiarity with the facts of a case gained by an agency in the performance of its statutory role does not, however, disqualify a decisionmaker."

## § 17.22 Liberty and Property Interests

Teachers have been granted certain liberty and property interests by the Constitution and the extent of these rights has been frequently interpreted by the courts. The United States Supreme Court has recognized that liberty and property are "broad and majestic" terms and society demands that if one of these rights is denied, then due process is required. Property rights have been recognized when the teacher has tenure or a permanent contract, as provided by the legislature. Also, the contractual agreement the employee has with the employer is a property right and cannot be breached during the contract period. A property right is created if the individual has a legitimate claim of entitlement to continued employment as created by state law or by the policies and procedures of a local board.

Liberty interests are involved if the employer stigmatizes the employee and jeopardizes one's opportunities for future employment. Stigmatizing the individual's good name or reputation is a violation of a teacher's liberty interest and will require due process of law. The following cases are landmarks in establishing and setting the parameters for teacher liberty and property rights.

## § 17.23 *Board of Regents v. Roth*

*Roth* provides the definitive statement as to the meaning of property and liberty interests. In Board of Regents v. Roth (S.Ct.1972), a professor was hired by the University of Wisconsin for a fixed term of one academic year. He subsequently was notified his contract would not be renewed for a second year. Wisconsin statute provided that after four years, tenure could be acquired and, at that time, procedural safeguards, such as due process, were by law provided. *Roth* claimed the university had deprived him of his Fourteenth Amendment rights by not giving him reasons for his nonrenewal. He further alleged the true reason for his nonretention was his public criticism of the university administration. The Supreme Court was presented with the question of whether a probationary teacher, without tenure protection, was entitled to procedural due process for nonrenewal.

The Supreme Court observed that the Fourteenth Amendment requires an opportunity for a hearing if a "property" or "liberty" interest is jeopardized. The Court said: "the range of interests protected by procedural due process is not infinite," but liberty and property are " ... broad and majestic terms that are ... purposely left to gather meaning with experience...." "Property interests ... are not created by the Constitution. Rather they are created and their dimensions are defined by existing rules or understandings that stem from an independent source such as state law—rules or understandings that secure certain benefits and that support claims of entitlement to those benefits."

Property interests therefore may be established: (1) by tenure statute, (2) by contract, or (3) if the individual has a legitimate and objective expectation of reemployment.

With regard to liberty, the Supreme Court said that a liberty interest arises if charges are made against an individual "... that might seriously damage his standing and associations in his community." If, for example, a school district makes charges that would implicate guilt of dishonesty, or immorality, then a liberty interest would arise. A charge of dishonesty or immorality would damage one's "good name, reputation, honor, or integrity," and if such were leveled against a teacher, then a hearing to refute the charges would be required. A liberty interest arises if a school district places a "stigma" upon the individual that forecloses his or her freedom to pursue employment opportunities in the chosen profession. The Court found, however, that Roth had not been deprived of his property or liberty interests and was not entitled to procedural due process.

## § 17.24 *Perry v. Sindermann*

On the same day that *Board of Regents v. Roth* was rendered, the Supreme Court also handed down Perry v. Sindermann (S.Ct.1972). This case further elaborated the property rights of individuals engaged in public employment. Sindermann had been employed in the State of Texas college system for ten years, the last four as a junior college professor at Odessa Junior College. His employment had been based on a series of one year contracts. The college of his current employment, Odessa, had not adopted a tenure system.

During his term of employment, he had had public disagreements with the board of regents. In particular, he had advocated that the junior college be expanded to a four year institution. This was opposed by the governing board. The college board elected not to renew his contract and issued a press release alleging insubordination on the part of the plaintiff. Sindermann brought suit, claiming his nonrenewal was based on his public criticism, a violation of his free speech rights, and he claimed that he should be granted a due process hearing. Although Sindermann did not have a property interest derived from a formal tenure system because the college had none, he claimed *de facto* tenure.  To substantiate his claim of *de facto* tenure he pointed out that the faculty handbook stated that as long as the teacher is performing satisfactorily, the administration "wishes the faculty member to feel that he has permanent tenure." In deciding the case, the United States Supreme Court reiterated its statement made in *Roth* that "property" denotes a broad range of interests that are secured by "existing rules and understandings" that may be created by conditions of statute, rules, or regulation.  Therefore, the faculty handbook rules constituted a legitimate claim of entitlement which created an objective expectancy of employment on behalf of the plaintiff;  he could have reasonably expected to have continued employment. The Court, thus, ruled that Sindermann had a right to procedural due process if his employment was to be terminated.

The *Roth* and *Sindermann* cases established that probationary teachers have no right to a hearing unless they can demonstrate a deprivation of liberty or property interests.  A property interest may be established by state statute, policies, rules, or regulations.  A property interest may be gained by either direct or *"de facto"* obligations.  A liberty interest may be established if the institution stigmatizes the individual, damaging his good name and reputation.

## § 17.25  Stigmatizing Reasons

A person's constitutional liberty rights are impacted when the state jeopardizes his/her "good name, reputation, honor or integrity," or forecloses the freedom to take advantage of other employment. Courts have ruled that charges such as "immorality, dishonesty, alcoholism" or "lying and/or misrepresentation of facts" were stigmatizing.

## § 17.26  Public Charges

The courts have established that as long as reasons for nonrenewal are not made public, then no stigma or infringement of a liberty interest exists. In Bishop v. Wood (S.Ct.1976), the Supreme Court further explained what constituted a stigma. In *Bishop*, a probationary policeman was told, in private, by his superior, he would not be reemployed because of his failure to follow orders, his poor attendance, his having and causing low morale among fellow workers and other conduct inappropriate to being a policeman. Testimony indicated that all of the reasons given for his dismissal were false.

The two issues litigated were: (1) whether the employee had a property interest, and (2) if the explanations for dismissal were false, did this deprive the employee of his liberty rights? The Court answered both of these in the negative. The policeman had relied on an ordinance for providing him a property right. The Supreme Court stated "A property interest in employment can ... be created by ordinance.... [H]owever the sufficiency of the claim of entitlement must be decided by reference to state law. The North Carolina Supreme Court has held that an enforceable expectation of continued employment

... can exist only if the employer, by statute or contract, has actually granted some form of guarantee." The Supreme Court, therefore, accepted the state court's interpretation of a property interest and concluded the employee "held his position at the will and pleasure of the city." Therefore, no liberty interest had been infringed upon since the reasons for dismissal were communicated in private. Because the reasons were given in private, their truth or falsity was irrelevant and did not create a liberty interest. Therefore, if reasons for dismissal of a probationary teacher are given in private, then no stigma is placed upon the individual and no deprivation of liberty occurs. The Supreme Court stated "The due process clause of the Fourteenth Amendment is not a guarantee against incorrect or ill-advised personnel decision of public employees."

### § 17.27  Incompetence, Insubordination, Neglect of Duty

In some cases, nontenured teachers have sought to have the nonrenewal of their employment overturned by alleging that they have been stigmatized by the district's charges of incompetence, inadequacy, and insubordination. In one such case, Gray v. Union County Intermediate Education District (9th Cir.1975), an employee was charged with insubordination, incompetence, hostility toward authority and aggressive behavior. The court stated, "[n]early any reason assigned for dismissal is likely to be to some extent a negative reflection on an individual's ability, temperament, or character. But not every dismissal assumes a constitutional magnitude. The concern is only with the type of stigma that seriously damages an individual's ability to take advantage of other employment opportunities.... These allegations certainly are not complimentary and suggest that [the teacher] may have problems in relating to some people, but they do not import serious character defects such as dishonesty or immorality ... as contemplated by *Roth*." Other courts have held that neglect of duty, failure to maintain discipline, improper teaching techniques, tardiness, and failure to follow orders, do not invoke liberty interests. These reasons for dismissal do not reflect so negatively on the teacher's reputation or honor as to harm the teacher's future employability.

## § 17.28 Stigma of Racism

Accusations of racism may be stigmatizing. In a Minnesota Community College case a nontenured professor's contract was not renewed and he claimed he had been stigmatized because of remarks accusing him of being a "racist." Charges of racism had been forwarded to the college by various campus groups, and had been entered into the teacher's personnel file. The Court of Appeals for the Eighth Circuit held that these charges were a deprivation of a liberty interest, reflecting on the teacher's reputation and good name. Therefore, a hearing would be required before he could be terminated, despite his nontenured status. Wellner v. Minnesota State Junior College Board (8th Cir.1973).

## § 17.29 Emotional Stability

Charges that a teacher lacks mental or emotional stability may attach a stigma. In a 1981 case, a school board announced the reasons for nonrenewal of a teacher were for "... apparent emotional instability, resentment of authority, ..." and her failure to follow orders. The court ruled that charges of emotional instability constituted a stigma. The emotional instability charge went beyond job related comments and, thereby, stigmatized the teacher. Such a charge implied a serious personal defect and, therefore, was a violation of the teacher's liberty rights. The other reasons were not found to be stigmatizing. Bomhoff v. White (D.Ariz.1981).

Similarly, public comment about mental state or psychiatric condition have also been held to stigmatize the teacher. See Stewart v. Pearce (9th Cir.1973).

## § 17.3 BURDEN OF PROOF FOR NONTENURED TEACHERS

If a nontenured teacher's contract is not renewed and no reasons are given by the board, the teacher's constitutional rights are not offended. If the teacher does not challenge the board and allege denial of a due process right, the board has no responsibility to institute such a hearing of its own volition. An Alabama court, citing *Roth*, stated that the employee must assert himself to protect his rights and institute the process whether school board procedures are established for such procedure or not. Stewart v. Bailey (N.D.Ala.1975).

If a teacher claims his or her contract has not been renewed because of constitutionally impermissible reasons, the burden of establishing the deprivation rests upon the teacher. The teacher must establish a *prima facie* case that a constitutionally offensive reason was the motivating factor for the nonrenewal. If the teacher establishes that an impermissible reason for dismissal is involved, the burden shifts to the school board to show, by a preponderance of evidence, "that [the board] would have reached the same decision as to [plaintiff's] reemployment even in the absence of the protected conduct." Mount Healthy City School Board of Education v. Doyle (S.Ct.1977). Courts have noted that a nontenured teacher may be nonrenewed for good reasons, no reasons, bad reasons, even false reasons, but not unconstitutional reasons.

## § 17.4  DISMISSAL OF TENURED TEACHERS FOR INCOMPETENCY

Incompetency has been given broad definition by the courts. Legal incompetency may be "want of physical, intellectual, or moral ability; insufficiency; inadequacy; specific want of legal qualifications or fitnesses," (Webster's New International Dictionary) Beilan v. Board of Education, School District of Philadelphia (S.Ct.1958). Incompetency generally concerns a fitness to teach encompassing a broad range of factors. The courts have included in the definition of incompetency, lack of knowledge of subject matter, lack of discipline, unreasonable discipline, unprofessional conduct, and willful neglect of duty. Where incompetency exists, some states' statutes require that teachers be given an opportunity to improve or to remediate themselves. If a statute requires remediation before dismissal for incompetency can be effectuated, the school board must show that remediation was attempted or that the situation was irremediable.

A teacher who has been certified by the state is assumed to be competent and it is the responsibility of the school board to prove incompetency. As long as a school board's actions are not arbitrary or capricious, the courts will generally not interfere. The Fifth Circuit Court of

Appeals has stated that "[f]or sound policy reasons, courts are loathe to intrude upon the internal affairs of local school authorities in such matters as teacher competency." Blunt v. Marion County School Board (5th Cir.1975).

Incompetency may be evidenced by poor classroom decorum. In one instance, a school district dismissed a tenured teacher on grounds of incompetence because she was unable to maintain order in her classroom, the classroom was littered with sunflower seeds, paper, and "junk," and the furniture and walls were covered with graffiti. Moreover, the teacher had not planned her lessons or given students proper directions; the court was, therefore, not hesitant to uphold dismissal for incompetency. Board of Education of the School District of Philadelphia v. Kushner (Pa.Cmwlth.1987).

The manner of offering evidence in incompetency cases is generally through testimony. Both the quantity and quality of evidence is important. The courts have liberally allowed opinions of principals, curriculum supervisors, and other supervisory personnel to stand as expert testimony. Other testimony by students and parents may be important as well, but the actual observations, by supervisors, of what transpired in the classroom, are very significant. One court said, "This court, in absence of proof of an abuse of discretion, cannot substitute its opinion for the decision of the school board and of the district court where both of these tribunals were presented with substantial evidence upon which to base their decisions." Frank v. St. Landry Parish School Board (La.App.1969).

## § 17.41  Incompetency Not Proven

Teachers, though, cannot be dismissed for incompetency for nebulous and uncertain evaluations.  For example, a case on this point reveals the following factual situation.  A tenured teacher of 13 years who had received satisfactory evaluations requested and was granted a one-year unpaid leave of absence.  The board of trustees instituted a new policy that all teachers seeking positions or teachers seeking voluntary transfers must participate in a structured interview.  When the teacher returned from leave, she participated in the structured interviews and did poorly.  The trustees dismissed her for incompetency.  The court held that after 13 years of apparently satisfactory teaching, the structured interviews were not sufficient to meet the burden of proof necessary to dismiss a tenured teacher.  Trustees, Missoula County School District No. 1 v. Anderson (Mont.1988).

## § 17.42  Failure to Maintain Discipline

Although failure to maintain discipline has been a major factor in dismissing teachers for incompetency, it is usually coupled with other charges.  In either case, however, a teacher's inability to conduct the classroom behavior with decorum and maintain a studious atmosphere is good grounds for dismissal.  In one case where a teacher's dismissal notification listed fourteen specific reasons and included inadequate maintenance of discipline during class, excessive and ineffective use of films, ineffective classroom teaching, and failure to cooperate with school administrators, the court upheld the dismissal because the preponderance of evidence showed that the teacher's students were disruptive, daydreamed in

class, wandered around the room, and left the room
without permission. The evidence also showed that
these same students behaved properly in other classes.
Board of Directors of Sioux City School Dist. v. Mroz
(Iowa 1980).

In Louisiana, a teacher was charged with failure to
keep classroom discipline and to prepare lesson plans.
The teacher exhibited a negative attitude and did not
institute suggested strategies to improve teaching. The
failure to maintain discipline was confirmed by the principal, the supervisor of child welfare, the coordinator of
special education, and another teacher. The children
were allowed to roam around the room and read aloud
when the teacher was attempting to read. The assistant
principal testified that the teacher did an adequate job
and the disciplinary problems arose because of the disparity of student ages in the room. Even so, the court
said, "[o]ur review of the record convinces us there is no
foundation for holding that the action of the School
Board was arbitrary, capricious or an abuse of the
Board's discretion." Mims v. West Baton Rouge Parish
School Board (La.App.1975).

## § 17.43  Excessive Discipline

Dismissal of a tenured teacher for excessive discipline
has been upheld where it was shown that the teacher
punished students by making them stay in the bathroom,
pulling their hair, pinching them, and pulling their ears.
Gwathmey v. Atkinson (E.D.Va.1976). Another teacher's dismissal was upheld for incompetency when he
administered excessive physical punishment without authority to do so. Kinsella v. Board of Education, etc.
(N.Y.1978).

Inappropriate discipline may take many forms. Unreasonable teacher conduct in administering punishment constitutes strong evidence supporting a teacher's removal. Where a teacher was dismissed for striking students in the genitals for disciplinary purposes, the court in ruling against the teacher stated the obvious "... a teacher's intentional striking of a student's genitals lacks any positive educational aspect or legitimate professional purpose." Mott v. Endicott School District No. 308 (Wash.1986).

## § 17.44  Teacher's Ability

Incompetence may also include a lack of knowledge of subject matter, using incorrect English, poor teaching methods, and failure to follow the required pedagogy methodology. For example, the U.S. Court of Appeals for the Fifth Circuit upheld the dismissal of a teacher who had been teaching for twenty-five years and was discharged for incompetency for using poor grammar, both written and spoken, making spelling errors, including misspelled words on the blackboard, which students copied, having instructional deficiencies in math, English (phonics) and reading, and using poor writing techniques. The teacher also attempted to teach spelling before the children had mastered the alphabet. Three supervisors presented substantial and credible evidence that the teacher lacked the necessary academic skills to teach and was hostile toward criticism aimed at improvement. Blunt v. Marion County School Board (5th Cir. 1975).

In Louisiana, a teacher was held properly discharged for incompetency where the specific charges were made that she could not adapt to the new instructional pro-

gram, and misspelled and mispronounced words. Moreover, she lacked the ability to organize and carry out
constructive instructional programs and had serious discipline problems in class. Jennings v. Caddo Parish
School Board (La.App.1973).

The courts have allowed the dismissal of teachers for
acts inappropriate to the educational environment or
where there was evidence of unfitness to teach. As
noted earlier, some states, through statute, require that
teachers be given a chance to improve or remediate
themselves before dismissal. If a state statute requires
remediation, the school board must show that a good
faith effort has been made to improve the instructional
capabilities of the teacher before proceeding with dismissal. In Gilliland v. Board of Education of Pleasant
View (Ill.1977), a teacher was charged with incompetency
for allegedly ruining pupils' attitudes toward school,
lacking rapport with pupils, and giving irregular homework assignments. Charges of cruelty were also alleged
because the teacher had grabbed childrens' hair, arms
and shoulders, and had hit one child with a book. The
teacher claimed she should be allowed to remediate the
problems, but the court disagreed and stated "... many
causes, when standing alone, may be remediable, whereas those same causes in combination with others may
well be irremediable. Here, we think it clear that the
combination of a number of causes plus the continuous
nature of the conduct were sufficient bases for a finding
of irremediability."

Although one act may be remediable, another act may
be irremediable, particularly if it is of a nature that
offends the senses of the community or endangers the
health and safety of children. Where a sixth grade

tenured teacher used high amperage batteries in a cattle prod to discipline children, the court was not convinced that the teacher deserved a second chance and said the "manifest weight of evidence" showed the actions of the teacher were irremediable. Rolando v. School Directors of District No. 125 (Ill.App.1976).

## § 17.5 DISMISSAL OF TENURED TEACHERS FOR INSUBORDINATION

Courts have defined insubordination as "constant or continuing intentional refusal to obey a direct or implied order, reasonable in nature, and given by and with proper authority." In re Proposed Termination of James E. Johnsons' Teaching Contract (Minn.App.1990); See also School District No. 8, Pinal County v. Superior Court (Ariz.1967). Some courts have found insubordination in a single incident, while other courts have required a constant or persistent course of conduct. Generally, though, insubordination can be substantiated by the seriousness of the single action if the act is of substantial magnitude in bearing on the ability of the teacher to perform his or her duties. Charges of insubordination are not supportable if: "(1) the alleged misconduct was not proved; (2) the existence of a pertinent school rule or a superior's order was not proved; (3) the pertinent rule or order was not violated; (4) the teacher tried, although unsuccessfully, to comply with the rule or order; (5) the teacher's motive for violating the rule or order was admirable; (6) no harm resulted from the violation; (7) the rule or order was unreasonable; (8) the rule or order was invalid as beyond the authority of its maker; (9) the enforcement of the rule or order revealed possible bias or discrimination against the teacher; or (10) the enforcement of the rule or order violated the First Amendment rights to free speech or academic freedom." (78 ALR 3d 83, 87).

## § 17.51    Insubordination Not Proven

As observed above, insubordination may be refusal or repeated refusal to follow directions. In a case where a teacher was charged with insubordination for inappropriate punishment of students and allowing card games to be played in study hall, the court ruled that there was no insubordination, though the conduct was highly questionable. Evidence was presented to the court showing that the teacher no longer continued the activities after being admonished by the principal. Thompson v. Wake County Board of Education (N.C.App.1976), see Thompson v. Wake County Board of Education (N.C.1977).

In another insubordination case a teacher was told not to use J.D. Salinger's "Catcher in the Rye" in his classroom and had agreed not to do so. Later, he started to use the novel again and was requested to meet with the principal concerning the situation. The teacher walked out of the meeting after five minutes and was charged with two counts of insubordination: (1) breaking the previous agreement, and (2) walking out of the conference. The school board upheld the charges and dismissed the teacher. Upon appeal, the court determined the dismissal was too severe. Although the courts will not generally review administrative sanction, in this instance the court found that the dismissal was disproportionate to the offense and was not fair since students were not harmed and there was no indication of lack of fitness to teach. Harris v. Mechanicville Central School District (N.Y.1978).

## § 17.52   Insubordination Proven

Insubordination may be manifested by a teacher's willful disregard for school policies. Three cases may be cited to illustrate the point. In the first case, a teacher of twenty-four years requested leave for five days to attend an out-of-state reading conference. The board denied the request, whereupon the teacher obtained a well qualified substitute and attended the conference. The teacher was charged with insubordination and dismissed. The act was held to be irremediable because of the damage done to the faculty and school district by willful violation of a reasonable rule. Christopherson v. Spring Valley Elementary School Dist. (Ill.App.1980).

A second case involved a tenured teacher who informed the superintendent she planned to take a week off to take a trip to Jamaica with her husband. The superintendent denied the leave and when the teacher did not appear at school, the superintendent recommended she be dismissed for insubordination. After a hearing, the school committee dismissed the teacher, whereupon the teacher filed suit. The court stated, "[i]n wake of plaintiff's conduct come grave doubts among school administrators, recriminations and jealousy among teachers, and an attitude of laxity and self-indulgence, possibly affecting the entire school community. These are consequences which the law does not require school administrators to condone." Fernald v. City of Ellsworth Superintending School Committee (Me.1975).

A third illustrative case involved a repetition of conduct that had been prohibited by the school. In this case a coach was repeatedly told not to let noncertified volunteers coach at games in violation of school policy. The coach did so and the court upheld his dismissal. King v.

Elkins Public Schools (Ark.App.1987). See also Gaylord v. Board of Education, Unified School District No. 218 (Kan.App.1990); Board of Education of Laurel County v. McCollum (Ky.1986).

## § 17.6 DISMISSAL OF TENURED TEACHERS FOR IMMORALITY

Immorality is specified by statute in numerous states as grounds for dismissal. Although the term immorality has been attacked as unconstitutionally vague, Kilpatrick v. Wright (M.D.Ala.1977) it generally has been upheld by the courts, especially when it relates to fitness to teach and where there is a rational nexus between the prohibited activity and the individual's position as a teacher. Immorality may include both heterosexual and homosexual activities, but does not pertain exclusively to sexual activities. In Horosko v. Mount Pleasant Township School District (Pa.1939), immorality was defined as "[a] course of conduct as offends the morals of the community and is a bad example to the youth whose ideals a teacher is supposed to foster and elevate."

Lying is considered to be immoral. Where a tenured teacher was denied permission to attend a conference, she left anyway, and upon her return submitted a request for excused absences because of illness. The board dismissed her based on immorality. The court upheld the board and said: "questions of morality are not limited to sexual conduct, but may include lying." Bethel Park School District v. Krall (Pa.Cmwlth.1982).

### § 17.61 Heterosexual Conduct

#### § 17.61a With Students

Because of the exemplary nature of teaching, the courts have left little question about the seriousness of sexual involvement with students. Teachers must be pure in motivation and act when dealing with students. In one instance, a tenured teacher, while on a field trip, tickled and touched female students on various parts of their bodies including between the legs. He was observed lying on a motel bed with one of the female students, watching television. The teacher made sexual remarks and innuendos to the female students and was subsequently dismissed for immorality. Upon being charged with immorality, the teacher responded that the activities were "good natured horseplay." Later, some students apologized to the field trip coordinator because they considered their behavior was "pretty gross." The teacher, who had enjoyed a reputation as a good teacher with excellent student rapport, contended there was no nexus between his classroom effectiveness and his conduct. The court determined his activities constituted unfitness to teach and his dismissal was upheld. Weissman v. Board of Education of Jefferson City School District (Colo.1976).

Another teacher had females sit between his legs, kissed them on the cheek, stuck his tongue in one's ear, and placed his hand on another's breast. Although the teacher testified he did not touch the students, the girls accusations were corroborated by a male student. The court upheld the dismissal as supported by evidence. Lombardo v. Board of Education of School District No. 27 (Ill.App.1968). See also Strain v. Rapid City School Board (S.D.1989).

Dismissal for immoral conduct has been upheld where a teacher placed his hand inside the jeans of a student in the area of her buttocks and on another occasion squeezed the breast of a female student. The court determined the conduct to be immoral and irremediable. Fadler v. Illinois State Bd. of Education (Ill.App.1987).

### § 17.61b　With Nonstudents

The courts, when dealing with cases of sexual activity by teachers with nonstudents, attempt to determine if there has been an impact on the teacher's fitness to teach and whether the activities were public or private. In a California case, a 48 year old elementary school teacher had her life certificate revoked by the State Board of Education for immorality. The teacher had been arrested at a private club by an undercover police officer after he watched her commit three separate acts of oral copulation, a violation of the California Penal Code. After plea bargaining, the charges were reduced to a misdemeanor, outraging public decency. The teacher and her husband had also appeared previously on television, in disguise, discussing non-conventional sexual life styles. Even though the teacher introduced into evidence her classroom evaluations, which were satisfactory, and a contract from the local board offering to rehire her, the court held that the state board was correct in revoking her certificate. The evidence showed that the sex acts were witnessed by several strangers in a semi-public atmosphere and "[p]laintiff's performance certainly reflected a total lack of concern for privacy, decorum or preservation of her dignity and reputation." The court said a teacher " . . . in the public school system is regarded by the public and pupils in the light of an exemplar, whose words and actions are likely to be followed by children coming under her care and protection." Obviously participation in sex orgies fell short of this standard. Pettit v. State Board of Education (Cal. 1973). See also Ross v. Springfield School District No. 19 (Or.1986).

In a Florida case, a teacher who had an unblemished record performed cunnilingus with his 9 year old step-daughter and was dismissed by the school board for immorality. Although expert testimony stated it was an isolated act, and would probably never happen again, the court upheld the dismissal and said that the act reflects a "... perverse personality which makes (the teacher) a danger to school children and unfit to teach them." Tomerlin v. Dade County School Board (Fla.App.1975).

The mores of a small rural community are usually quite different than large metropolitan areas. The norms and expectations of the community have much to do with acceptability of teacher conduct. In a South Dakota case, a teacher's boyfriend moved in to live with her about two months after she became a teacher in a small rural community. The community became aware of the situation and several persons became offended. School officials, trying to stem the initial protest, sought to resolve the situation by talking to the teacher at which time she advised the school officials that her living arrangements were private. The school officials then sought to dismiss her for gross immorality and incompetence. The teacher responded that the dismissal violated her rights of privacy and freedom of association, as well as substantive due process and equal protection of the Fourteenth Amendment. The court ruled for the school board concluding that the state is entitled to maintain a "properly moral scholastic environment" and in this circumstance the dismissal was proper. Sullivan

v. Meade Independent School District No. 101 (8th Cir. 1976).

### § 17.61c   Unwed Pregnant Teachers

School boards have attempted to dismiss unwed pregnant teachers on charges of immorality and teachers have challenged such actions, basing their claims on right of privacy, denial of due process and equal protection, contravention of Title VII of the 1964 Civil Rights Act, and violation of Title IX of the Education Amendments Act of 1972.

Pregnancy is not proof *per se* of immorality. In a case involving equal protection a pregnant, unmarried, elementary, remedial reading teacher was discharged for immorality because the school board felt that being unwed and pregnant is proof *per se* of immorality. Since the school board offered no proof to support the contentions, the court held the dismissal was in violation of the teacher's equal protection rights. Avery v. Homewood City Board of Education (5th Cir.1982). See also Ponton v. Newport News School Board (E.D.Va.1986). (See Pregnancy, Chapter 18, Employment Discrimination.)

In another case where the superintendent learned, through rumor, that a teacher was pregnant and unmarried, the school board dismissed her for immorality. "The Board made no findings that [the teacher's] claimed immorality had affected her competency or fitness as a teacher, and no such nexus was developed in the evidence. No 'compelling interest' ... was established by the evidence which would justify the invasion of [the teacher's] constitutional right of privacy." Drake v. Covington County Board of Education (M.D.Ala.1974).

In yet another case where a teacher was dismissed for being pregnant and unwed, but no action had been taken against other pregnant and unmarried teachers who were employed in the district, the court held that the board had acquiesced in allowing unwed pregnant teachers to remain employed and, therefore, was foreclosed from arguing that unwed pregnant teachers were unfit to teach. New Mexico State Board of Education v. Stoudt (N.M.1977).

## § 17.62  Homosexuality

Two factors are considered by the courts when a school board takes action to dismiss a teacher for homosexuality:  (1) the degree to which the teacher's sexual preferences have become public knowledge;  and (2) the recognition that an individual is a practicing homosexual, even if there is no specific act.  In matters of sexual misconduct, both homosexual and heterosexual, the courts have attempted to determine if a school board can establish a rational nexus between the private activity and the professional responsibility, and if the private activity manifests an unfitness to teach.

### § 17.62a  Public Homosexual Acts

Dismissal of a teacher who had his teaching certificate revoked because he was convicted of disorderly conduct for having touched and rubbed another man's genitalia on a public beach was upheld by a California court because the action demonstrated unfitness to teach.  The court held that a nexus did exist between the act and the teacher's professional responsibilities.  Sarac v. State Board of Education (Cal.App.1967).  Where a male teacher was having sex with another male in a booth in an "adult bookstore," the Supreme Court of Oregon stated,

"Privacy is a well-known requirement of society for
sexual activity. Engaging in sexual intercourse publicly
is universally condemned." Ross v. Springfield School
District No. 19 (Or.1986).

### § 17.62b    Private Homosexual Acts

In determining fitness to teach, the nexus between the
homosexuality and teaching, a number of questions must
be considered: (1) Are the students and other teachers
adversely affected? (2) Could one anticipate a high degree of adversity from the situation? (3) Was the conduct or act of a recent nature or substantially in the
past? (4) What type of teaching certificate does the
teacher hold: elementary, secondary, etc.? (5) Are there
any extenuating factors surrounding the situation? (6)
What were the motives of the individual? (7) What is
the probability of the situation being replicated? and (8)
Are any constitutional rights involved? All of these
factors are important when considering the teacher's
impact on the students and the educational environment,
the necessary nexus. The school board must balance the
constitutional interests of the teacher against the right
to have an orderly and appropriate educational environment for the school children.

The nexus issue is illustrated in a case where a teacher
was not a practicing homosexual and had engaged in only
one such act, with another teacher, and the state board
of education revoked his certificate. The revocation took
place three years after the incident and two years after
the teacher had voluntarily related the incident to the
school superintendent. The court held that the certificate must be restored unless the board could show actual
unfitness to teach. Morrison v. State Board of Education
(Cal.1969).

In another case where nexus was shown, a former student told the vice-principal he believed a teacher to be a homosexual. The teacher was dismissed because he was an active member of a homosexual society, had responded to blind advertisements for homosexual company, and had actively sought out other males. The court held that the teacher's homosexuality must be considered within the context of his position as a teacher, the necessary nexus, and it would be unreasonable to assume that his ability as a teacher was not damaged or impaired. The court concluded that the school board does not have to wait for an overt act before exercising fiduciary responsibilities for the children and the school district. Gaylord v. Tacoma School Dist. (Wash.1977).

## § 17.63 Transsexuality

The rule of law with regard to transsexuals is the same as with homosexuals, that is, if it is detrimental to the educational environment, the transsexual teacher can be dismissed. In one such case, a 54 year old tenured, male elementary teacher, who was married with three children, requested leave for surgery in early spring. Upon returning in May, after surgery, he had become a she. The board, on becoming aware of the situation, had a series of meetings with the teacher, and submitted a proposal to the teacher, including, *inter alia*, teaching electives at the high school and resigning after one more year. The teacher rejected these options. Although testimony presented by psychiatrists conflicted, as to the psychological harm the teacher would cause to children in the school, the court concluded that the "... teacher's presence in the classroom would create a potential for psychological harm to the students, the teacher is unable properly to fulfill his or her role and his or her incapacity has been established within the purview of the statute". The court emphasized the conclusions only related to teaching in that specific district, but expressed no opinion on fitness to teach elsewhere, under different circumstances. In re Grossman (N.J.Super.1974).

## § 17.7 PUBLIC LEWDNESS

Public lewdness is, of course, objectionable behavior in civilized society and is generally presumed to be inappropriate behavior for a school teacher. In a case where a tenured teacher caressed, undressed and made lewd gestures with a mannequin in a well-illuminated vacant lot and the activity became public knowledge and was observed by the school superintendent; the teacher claimed his private conduct is constitutionally protected and his psychiatrist testified that although he had a personality disorder, it would not impair his classroom effectiveness. The court held that because the actions had already gained notoriety it was likely the conduct would damage his effectiveness as a teacher and "his working relationship within the educational process." The court said that: "The right to be left alone in the home extends only to the home and not to conduct displayed under the street lamp on the front lawn." Wishart v. McDonald (1st Cir.1974).

## § 17.8 CRIMINAL CONVICTION

A number of state statutes provide that teachers can be dismissed for "a felony or a crime of moral turpitude." A felony is "[a] crime of a graver or more atrocious nature than those designated as misdemeanors

...." *Black's Law Dictionary,* Fourth Edition (West Publishing Company), p. 744. See State v. Parker (N.J. 1991).

## § 17.81 Felony

It is not necessary for a teacher to be convicted of an offense in order for a school board to dismiss the teacher for the same act. A teacher may be unfit to teach, but may not have been convicted of a crime. In a case where a teacher was charged with a criminal act of engaging in oral copulation with another man and was acquitted of criminal charges, the school board dismissed the teacher for immorality and unfitness. The state code provided that school boards may dismiss teachers for sex offenses. The court held for the board and said that it was the responsibility of the board to determine the fitness of the employee even if they had been acquitted of criminal charges. The key, again, is whether the act is a detrimental influence to the pupils of the district. Board of Education v. Calderon (Cal.App.1973). See also Matter of Freeman (N.C.App.1993).

Yet, if a teacher's dismissal rests on violations of statute *per se* and not on the actual act as detrimental to teaching performance, then dismissal will succeed or fail on statutory grounds. In a California case where a teacher pleaded guilty to possession of narcotics and was placed on probation for two years for the conviction of a felony, the school board placed him on indefinite suspension and started dismissal proceedings. By the time his dismissal had reached the courts, his probation had ended and his charges had been reduced to a misdemeanor. However, during this time the California legislature significantly reduced the criminal penalty for possession of marijuana. The Supreme Court said: "since the school board's authority to dismiss the teacher rests solely on statutory grounds and the statute no longer existed the teacher could not be dismissed." Governing Board of Rialto Unified School District v. Mann (Cal.1977).

Guilt of criminal conduct though, itself, may constitute immorality and cause for dismissal. Where a teacher was arrested and charged with two counts of harassment, the teacher was convicted. The teacher had made approximately 35 telephone calls to a board member in the early morning hours; the calls were related to a protracted labor dispute between the board and the teacher's union. The school board brought charges of immorality against the teacher because of the criminal conviction for harassment. The court said "guilty verdict of criminal conduct will support a finding of immorality." Covert v. Bensalem Township School District (Pa.Cmwlth.1987).

## § 17.82   Moral Turpitude

Moral turpitude is "[a]n act of baseness, vileness, or depravity in the private and social duties which a man owes to his fellow men, or to society in general, contrary to the accepted and customary rule of right and duty between man and man." (*Black's Law Dictionary*, p. 1160). Moral turpitude is difficult to clearly define because it is premised on the moral standards of the community.

Growing of marijuana in violation of law may constitute moral turpitude. In Florida, revocation of the teaching certificate of two teachers for growing 52 marijuana plants in a greenhouse has been upheld. The court concluded that since teachers are in a leadership capacity, and are obligated to maintain a high moral standard in the community, the possession of marijuana plants, and the ensuing publicity, seriously impaired their abilities to be effective teachers. Adams v. State, Professional Practices Council (Fla.App.1981). In an earlier decision, a teacher was found not to be guilty of moral turpitude where he was cultivating only one marijuana plant out of curiosity. Board of Trustees v. Judge (Cal.App.1975). Conviction for mail fraud constitutes moral turpitude justifying revocation of teaching certificate. Startzel v. Commonwealth (Pa.Cmwlth.1989).

### § 17.83  Misdemeanor

Teachers may also be dismissed in certain circumstances for misdemeanors. Misdemeanors are "[o]ffenses lower than felonies and generally those punishable by a fine or imprisonment otherwise than in a penitentiary." (*Black's Law Dictionary,* p. 1150). Improprieties in public that reflect on the school, even though relatively minor, may be grounds for dismissal.

In a case where a tenured teacher was arrested and charged with " . . . disturbing the peace by being under the influence of intoxicants, attempting to fight, and display of a gun," his dismissal was upheld for good and just cause and the board's action was held not to be arbitrary, irrational or unreasonable. Williams v. School District No. 40 of Gila County (Ariz.App.1966).

### § 17.84  Drugs

Several cases have arisen in recent years where teachers have been dismissed for possession and use of controlled substances. Because state statutes usually do not require dismissal for use of drugs, teachers who have been involved with drugs have, alternatively, been dismissed under statutory provisions for fitness to teach, moral turpitude, immorality, misdemeanor, and felony convictions, plus other good and sufficient cause.

An example is found in Georgia where a tenured teacher was arrested for possession of cocaine, glutethimide, and marijuana and pleaded guilty to violating that state's Controlled Substances Act. Because it was a first offense, the teacher was placed on probation. In order to reduce the impact of bad publicity, she was transferred to two other teaching positions during the remainder of the year. Finally, the board dismissed her for "immorality" and "other good and sufficient cause" based on her guilty plea. The court said, "the proven fact of the teacher's possession of three dangerous drugs is evidence from which 'immorality' may be inferred, even in the absence of criminal purpose or intent." Dominy v. Mays (Ga.App.1979). A similar result was reached in Chicago Board of Education v. Payne (Ill.App.3d 1981).

A different result, however, was reached in a case where a teacher was charged with sale and possession of a controlled substance. The teacher pleaded guilty and was charged by the school board with misconduct. A hearing panel recommended the teacher merely be reprimanded and the teacher brought suit, claiming the reprimand was excessive. The court felt to simply reprimand the teacher, instead of imposing a more severe penalty, was far too lenient and not commensurate with the teacher's offense. The court remanded the case back to the administrative agency for reconsideration and a determination which would impose a more rigorous penalty on the teacher. The court said, "[T]his penalty is so disproportionate to the misconduct proved by the evidence in the record, an abuse of discretion is manifest and the determination may not stand." Riforgiato v. Board of Education of City of Buffalo (N.Y.1982).

## § 17.9  GOOD AND JUST CAUSE

Both common law and statute usually provide for dismissal of tenured teachers for "cause" or "good cause." Where statutes delineate the causes for dismissal, a teacher cannot be dismissed for causes beyond those specified. People v. Maxwell (N.Y.1904); School City of Elwood v. State ex rel. Griffin (Ind.1932). If, however, no causes are specified and the statute merely provides for dismissal for cause, then what constitutes cause is subject to broader interpretation.

Financial problems of a school district may constitute "just cause" for dismissal. In an Iowa case, just cause was given as the reason for release of a tenured teacher with 17 years of experience. "Just cause" was found in budgetary considerations, declining enrollments, and need to make more efficient use of staff. The decline in enrollment had caused a loss of state revenues. Also, evidence was submitted to the court showing that the district was overstaffed. The court upheld the dismissal based on just cause. Pocahontas Community School District v. Levene (Iowa App.1987).

Where a tenured teacher applied for and received sabbatical leave to pursue graduate work and continued his absence even though he was not admitted to graduate school, the court found the teacher breached his professional responsibilities and such constituted "good cause" for dismissal. Stansberry v. Argenbright (Mont.1987). "Good cause" has been established supporting dismissal where a tenured teacher (1) cohabitated with a female teacher, (2) used a human fetus in the classroom when discussing abortion, (3) talked about abortion, and (4) spoke to his classes about his personal living arrangements.  Yanzick v. School District No. 23, Lake County, Montana (Mont.1982).

Violation of school policy may constitute "cause."  Dismissal of a tenured teacher was upheld for violating a school policy, which stated that "the board of education does not encourage corporal punishment."  Over a four-year period the teacher had kicked a student, struck another in the face, knocked a female to the floor, and committed other similar acts.  Tomczik v. State Tenure Commission (Mich.App.1989).

Refusal to accede to school rules prohibiting teaching of religious beliefs in the classroom may constitute legal "cause" for dismissal.  After a tenured teacher was warned numerous times to stop religious activities such as writing "God is truth and truth is God" on the blackboard, the board dismissed him.  The teacher did not deny the allegations, and said he would not stop because "he was a Christian and that part of his mission was a sense of evangelism."  His actions and refusal to comply with school rules constituted grounds for dismissal.  Rhodes v. Laurel Highlands School District (Pa. Cmwlth.1988).

Cause for dismissal may also be evidenced by violation of policy prohibiting corporal punishment.  In a case where a teacher grabbed a child and kneed him in the back, causing him to cry, and shoved another child to the floor, the court found sufficient cause.  Ortbals v. Special School District (Mo.App.1988).

"Reasonable and just cause" for dismissal has been found where a tenured teacher was discharged for inviting two females from his driver's education class to a party where they drank beer and smoked marijuana. Barcheski v. Board of Education of Grand Rapids Public Schools (Mich.App.1987).

# CHAPTER 18

# EMPLOYMENT DISCRIMINATION

## § 18.1  INTRODUCTION

The social and political upheavals experienced in the United States after World War II brought about tremendous changes in employment practices. These movements have spawned both federal and state legislation that have attempted to overcome the effects of past discrimination against minorities and to ensure against the reemergence of discrimination. This chapter discusses precedents grounded in statutes, court decisions, and regulations bearing on race, sex, age, religion, and handicap discrimination that have influenced employment practices in public education.

## § 18.2  RACE DISCRIMINATION

Since Brown v. Board of Education (S.Ct.1954), numerous employment issues have been litigated regarding discrimination in the public sector. Many cases have challenged hiring and testing practices, reduction of staff resulting in nonretention of minority employees, and reverse discrimination. Most of these cases have invoked the Equal Protection Clause of the Fourteenth Amendment and Title VII of the Civil Rights Act of 1964.

## § 18.21  Equal Protection

The standards under the Equal Protection Clause are not the same as under the various statutory provisions that have been designed by Congress to eradicate discrimination.  The equal protection standard as developed in the school desegregation cases prohibits discrimination that can be ultimately traced to a racially motivated purpose.  Remedial action to overcome segregation is not required by the courts under the Equal Protection Clause unless it can be shown that segregation was caused by official actions, the *purpose* and *intent* of which were to discriminate.  To show merely that the *effect* of the employer's policy results in adverse impact on racial minorities is insufficient to prove a violation of the Equal Protection Clause.

If plaintiffs cannot show that segregation was a result of discriminatory purpose or intent, the state need only show that its actions were not irrational.  On the other hand, if discriminatory intent is shown, the state must bear the burden of showing a compelling reason to act as it did.  In contrast, Title VII imposes a more rigorous standard on the state.  Under Title VII, Congress provides that where employment practices are concerned, discriminatory intent need not be proved; rather, the plaintiff need only show that the effect of the policy was to discriminate.

The Supreme Court has set out evidentiary guidelines that plaintiffs must sustain in supporting claims of a discriminatory intent under the Equal Protection Clause.  These are (1) historical background, (2) specific sequence of events leading to the passage or implementation of the practice, (3) departure from accepted practices and normal procedures, (4) substantial departures, and (5) legislative and administrative history. In commenting on these, the Supreme Court has said: "Determining whether invidious discriminatory purpose was a motivating factor demands a sensitive inquiry into such circumstances and direct evidence of intent as may be available." The *impact* of the official action may be one aspect of the proof of *intent* to discriminate. Washington v. Davis (S.Ct.1976).

## § 18.22 Title VI

Title VI of the Civil Rights Act prohibits discrimination in federally assisted programs based on race, color, or national origin. With Title VI, Congress provided a statutory remedy against discrimination that could be administered by federal agencies in their regulatory capacity. The ultimate enforcement weapon given the federal agencies under this law is the denial of federal funds. It was under Title VI that Adams v. Richardson (D.C.Cir.1973), originated, maintaining that the United States Department of Health, Education, and Welfare had been derelict in its enforcement responsibilities. In that case, a federal court assumed the responsibility for monitoring enforcement of federal regulations promulgated by the department pursuant to Title VI. The regulations require desegregation of faculty, administration, and other personnel positions in public schools and universities.

An area of substantial complexity and some uncertainty in the application of Title VI lies in whether officials are required to redress *de jure* segregation only, or whether they have an obligation to correct racial imbalance caused by *de facto* segregation as well. In the Regents of University of California v. Bakke (S.Ct.1978), case, Justice Powell, writing for a splintered majority, said that Title VI requirements were coterminous with those of the Equal Protection Clause, that neither required school officials to correct unintended racial imbalances. On the other hand, four justices, while agreeing with Powell's general disposition of the case, disagreed with his interpretation of Title VI, maintaining that congressional intent was to prohibit discrimination, regardless of intent. Writing for these four judges, Justice Stevens said that "the meaning of the Title VI ban on exclusion is crystal clear: Race cannot be the basis of excluding anyone from participation in a federally funded program." He further maintained that it was not necessary to liken Title VI to the Equal Protection Clause, since Title VI's origins emanated from its own legislative intent and history. Having said this, however, the Court did not resolve the fundamental issue of whether Title VI requires affirmative administrative action to correct unintended segregation.

Some clarification of the intent questions under Title VI did come forth in 1983 in the case of Guardians Association v. Civil Service Commission of New York (S.Ct.1983). In this case, the Court held that a private person may be compensated for a state agency's violation of his or her Title VI rights, but only if the person is able to show intent to discriminate. In other words, as now written, intent must be shown to exist before Title VI is violated and federal funds can be withheld.

## § 18.23  Title VII (Race)

When Title VII was first enacted in 1964, it did not extend to discriminatory employment practices in educational institutions. In 1972, however, the law was amended, eliminating this exemption. As a result, it is now Title VII that is used most often to challenge discrimination in employment in public schools.

An area of much importance in applying Title VII has been employee testing for purposes of hiring and promotion. The position of the United States Supreme Court concerning employee testing was enunciated in 1971 in Griggs v. Duke Power Co. (S.Ct.1971). In this case, the Court found that Title VII of the Civil Rights Act prevented an employer from rejecting black job applicants on the basis of lack of completion of high school or on the results of a general intelligence test. Duke Power Company was unable to show that the general standards it had established were related to job performance. The Court said: "The facts of this case demonstrate the inadequacy of broad and general testing devices as well as the infirmity of using diplomas or degrees as fixed measures of capability. Nothing in the Act precludes the use of testing or measuring procedures; obviously they are useful. What Congress has forbidden is giving these devices and mechanisms controlling force unless they are demonstrably a reasonable measure of job performance."

After *Griggs*, several lower courts invalidated the use of the Graduate Record Examination and the National Teachers Examination because the examinations were not job related. School districts, in these instances, were unable to shoulder the burden of showing job relatedness in the face of the high percentage of black teachers who were disqualified. Under *Griggs*, once the plaintiff shows, under Title VII, that the effect or impact of an employment practice is the cause of racial imbalance, the burden shifts to the defendant to justify the particular practice by showing that the imbalance is justified in terms of job requirements.

In a later testing case, the United States brought suit against the State of South Carolina for alleged violations of Title VII. The allegation was made pursuant to discrimination against minorities who had failed the National Teacher Examination (NTE) which was used to certify teachers and determine salary levels. The plaintiffs claimed there was a disparate racial impact on minorities which violated Title VII.

The court determined that since the plaintiffs had established a disparate impact, then it should be determined whether the tests were job related. The government had to establish a rational relationship between the test and the legitimate objectives of government. A group of four hundred fifty-six individuals, with professional credentials, assessed the content validity of the National Teacher Examination. This group reviewed the curriculum of South Carolina to determine if the test measured what was being taught. "The design of the validity study is adequate for Title VII purposes." The Supreme Court made clear once again citing Washington v. Davis, supra, that "a content validity study that satisfies professional standards also satisfies Title VII." United States v. State of South Carolina (D.S.C.1977).

## § 18.24  Disparate Treatment and Disparate Impact

The Supreme Court has attempted to clarify Title VII by creating a distinction between "disparate treatment" and "disparate impact" cases and has explained the two terms in this way: Disparate treatment is the most easily understood type of discrimination. Here, the employer simply mistreats some people because of their race, color, religion, sex, or national origin. "Proof of discriminatory motive is critical, although it can in some situations be inferred from the mere fact of differences in treatment.... Undoubtedly disparate treatment was the most obvious and Congress had it in mind when it enacted Title VII.... Claims of disparate treatment may be distinguished from claims that stress 'disparate impact.' The latter involves employment practices that are facially neutral in their treatment of different groups but in fact fall more heavily on one group than another and cannot be justified by business necessity.... Proof of discriminatory motive, we have held, is not required under a disparate impact theory."

Disparate treatment cases generally occur when a plaintiff challenges a particular practice that is detrimental to him or her personally. For example, a faculty member's claim that her promotion in a particular academic department was denied because of bias must be brought as a disparate treatment issue. The nature of the facts do not lend themselves to a showing of impact. On the other hand, disparate impact may be more easily shown in cases involving a number of persons who are affected by a particular employment practice, such as a requirement that all employees pass a test as noted above in the *United States v. South Carolina* case.

When a plaintiff shows evidence to substantiate a claim of disparate impact, the employer may then bear the burden of showing that the particular employment practice was justified as a "business necessity" or that it was "related to job performance."

In 1991 the United States Congress passed the Civil Rights Act of 1991, Public Law 102–166, 105 Stat. 1071.

The passage of this act was in response to the perceived weakening of the scope and effectiveness of civil rights protections by the Supreme Court in Wards Cove Packing Co. v. Antonio (S.Ct.1989). This Act overturned the Wards Cove decision which had placed a greater burden on the plaintiff to prove disparate impact. Congress stated the purposes of the Act were: "(1) to provide appropriate remedies for intentional discrimination and unlawful harassment in the workplace; (2) to codify the concept of 'business necessity' and 'job related' enunciated by the Supreme Court in *Griggs* ... and in the other Supreme Court decisions prior to *Wards Cove* ...; (3) to confirm statutory authority and provide statutory guidelines for adjudication of disparate impact suits under Title VII ...; and (4) to respond to recent decisions of the Supreme Court by expanding the scope of relevant civil rights statutes in order to provide adequate protection to victims of discrimination."

Also, the 1991 Act allowed the plaintiff to recover compensatory and punitive damages under Title VII. The Act had as its basic purpose to "strengthen and improve federal civil rights laws, to provide damages in cases of intentional employment discrimination, to clarify provisions regarding disparate impact actions...." This Act includes the rights of victims of sexual discrimination to sue for damages ranging from $50,000 for companies with 100 or fewer workers to $300,000 for employers with more than 500 workers. These damages are recoverable when "unlawful intentional discrimination 'occurred' not [when] a practice is unlawful because of disparate impact."

## § 18.25 *Prima Facie* Case

Because of the difficulties of proving intent, most litigation has been concerned with disparate impact under Title VII. The plaintiffs, in establishing a *prima facie* case must show four basic factors are true: "(i) that he belongs to a racial minority; (ii) that he applied and was qualified for a job for which the employer was seeking applicants; (iii) that, despite his qualifications, he was rejected; and (iv) that, after his rejection, the position remained open and the employer continued to seek applicants from persons of complainant's qualifications." McDonnell Douglas Corp. v. Green (S.Ct.1973).

The *McDonnell Douglas* standards for establishing a *prima facie* case are flexible. Facts will vary from case to case and specifications for *prima facie* proof will not necessarily be the same in every aspect. "A prima facie case under *McDonnell Douglas* raises an inference of discrimination only because we [the Courts] presume these acts, if otherwise unexplained, are more likely than not based on the consideration of impermissible factors." Furnco Construction Corp. v. Waters (S.Ct.1978).

Therefore, to dispel the adverse inference from a *prima facie* showing, all the employer needs to do is "articulate some legitimate, nondiscriminatory reason for the employee's rejection." *McDonnell Douglas v. Green*, supra. After the employer has articulated some legitimate reason, the plaintiff must be afforded the opportunity to present evidence that this is no more than a pretext for discrimination.

## § 18.26  Affirmative Action

Affirmative action in employment is a voluntary plan adopted by a school district in an effort to remediate past discrimination in that system. The Supreme Court has said that we must be mindful of "this Court's and Congress' consistent emphasis on 'the value of voluntary efforts to further the objectives of the law.' " Yet, affirmative action in employment plans, if not justified, may result in unlawful reverse discrimination. The lawfulness of such plans has been tested under Title VII, Title VI, and the Equal Protection Clause.

Title VII attempts to make hiring practices neutral and does not require affirmative action that favors anyone over another. The Act states specifically that "Nothing contained in [Title VII] shall be interpreted to require any employer ... to grant preferential treatment to any individual or any group because of the race, color, religion, sex or national origin of such individual or group...." Under Title VII, affirmative action may, however, be voluntary. In McDonald v. Santa Fe Trail Transportation Co. (S.Ct.1976), the Supreme Court stated: "Title VII, whose terms are not limited to discrimination against members of any particular race, prohibits racial discrimination in private employment against white persons upon the same standards as racial discrimination against nonwhites."

Affirmative action has been imposed by the courts upon employers as a judicial remedy. But this court remedy has only been used when the defendant is proven to have had a pattern of intentional, egregious violations of the law.

An *affirmative action* employment plan adopted by a school district will not be unlawful *reverse discrimination* under Title VII if (a) there exists a statistical disparity between the races or sexes in a particular job category, (b) if the institution was guilty of discrimination in the past, (c) the plan does not "unnecessarily trammel" the rights of nonminority employees, (d) the plan does not stigmatize nonminority employees, and (e) the plan is temporary in nature and is scheduled to terminate upon the achievement of a racially or sexually integrated work force.

In 1979, in the case of United Steelworkers, etc. v. Weber (S.Ct.1979), employees of a steel company claimed reverse discrimination, citing Title VII. The United Steelworkers and Kaiser Aluminum had negotiated an agreement that included a provision for the elimination of racial imbalance at the Kaiser Aluminum plant. The agreement provided that craft-training positions would be reserved for minorities until the percentage of blacks in the craft work force equaled the percentage of blacks in the local labor market. In the first year of the agreement, thirteen individuals were selected for craft training, seven blacks and six whites. The most senior black of the group had less seniority than a number of white workers who were not selected. The white workers who were not selected filed suit. The Supreme Court ruled that the mutually agreed-upon contract did not violate Title VII because not all private, voluntary, race-conscious, affirmative action plans instituted by companies are prohibited.

In the case of The Regents of the University of *California v. Bakke*, supra, the university's medical school admissions program was challenged by a student applicant named Bakke. The school had established two admission programs. The first, the regular admission program, which had eighty-four (84) slots, considered the applicant's grade point average, scores on the Medical College Admissions Test, and other requirements, such as recommendations. This plan applied to both minorities or nonminorities. The second admissions program, which had sixteen (16) positions available, was designated for blacks, Chicanos, Asians, and American Indians. Such candidates were screened on similar standards as those in the regular admissions process but were given special consideration because of their disadvantaged backgrounds. Minority candidates who did not qualify for the regular program were considered for admission under the special admission program.

Bakke, a white applicant, sued the medical school, charging reverse discrimination based on the Equal Protection Clause of the Fourteenth Amendment and Title VI of the Civil Rights Act of 1964. Bakke stated that he was only allowed to apply for one of eighty-four positions, while a minority candidate could apply for one of the regular eighty-four slots and, if not successful in the regular process, could apply for one of the sixteen reserved positions. The Supreme Court decided the case on Title VI grounds and did not address the equal protection issue. The Court found that the use of "quotas" was not permitted and that the admission system was quota based. According to the Court, race may be used as a factor in admission programs, and it may even be "weighted" more heavily, but it cannot be the sole and decisive factor.

In other cases, the Supreme Court has provided some guidance as to the boundaries between affirmative action and reverse discrimination under the Equal Protection Clause. In Wygant v. Jackson Board of Education (S.Ct.

1986), the school board, because of racial tension in the community, negotiated with the union a new provision in the collective bargaining agreement. This provision allowed tenured non-minority teachers to be laid off before non-tenured minority teachers were. The rationale was based on a role model theory. The Supreme Court ruled the agreement violated Equal Protection because the "Board's layoff plan is not sufficiently narrowly tailored. Other, less intrusive means of accomplishing similar purposes—such as the adoption of hiring goals—are available." *Wygant* can be distinguished from *Weber*, although both involved collective bargaining agreements. In *Wygant* a governmental agency, a public school, was involved, whereas in *Weber* all parties were in the private sector. Following *Wygant*, the Court of Appeals, Seventh Circuit, held that a "no minority layoff" clause in a collective bargaining agreement violated both Equal Protection and Title VII. This court found that the plan, which laid off 48 white teachers with greater seniority than black teachers who were retained on the job, constituted an absolute racial preference and was not "narrowly tailored" to serve any remedial affirmative action purpose. Britton v. South Bend Community School Corporation (7th Cir.1987).

Thus, affirmative action plans may be found to be discriminatory if they are justified only on very broad grounds of correcting discrimination alone and/or are too vague to serve the specified remedial purpose of removing the vestiges of past discrimination. In order to have a valid plan to remediate past discrimination, there must be convincing evidence of prior discrimination by the particular governmental unit and "[s]ocietal discrimination alone is insufficient to justify a racial classification."

## § 18.3  SEX DISCRIMINATION

Sex-based discrimination in affecting working conditions, compensation, prerequisites for employment, and work-related benefits has been of such magnitude historically that Congress responded by passing legislation to prohibit such discrimination. Lawsuits has been filed under the Equal Protection Clause of the Fourteenth Amendment, the Equal Pay Act of 1963, Title VII of the Civil Rights Act of 1964, and Title IX of the Education Amendment of 1972, challenging such sex discrimination.

## § 18.31  Title VII

Sex discrimination in employment is prohibited by Title VII. In part, the Act provides that it shall be unlawful for an employer "to fail or refuse to hire or to discharge an individual or otherwise to discriminate against any individual, ... because of such individual's race, color, religion, *sex* or national origin." The plaintiff is required to show, as with racial discrimination, that: (1) he or she is a member of a class protected by Title VII; (2) he or she applied and was qualified for the position; (3) despite such qualifications, plaintiff was rejected; and (4) after plaintiff's rejection, the position remained open and the employer continued to seek similarly qualified applicants. If plaintiff sustains this *prima facie* case of sex discrimination, then the burden falls on the defendant to show the employment decision was based on a legitimate nondiscriminatory reason.

If a teacher establishes a *prima facie* case of discrimination, the school board must show that its rationale for the employment decision was based on nondiscriminary reasons. Where a school board defends its decision not to promote a black female teacher on the subjective factors of her "lack of interpersonal and management skills which are necessary for an administrator to have" as well as "abrasive" personality, the court found that these reasons "articulated legitimate nondiscriminatory reasons" for the board's decision. If plaintiff establishes by direct evidence that an employer acted with discriminatory intent, the defense will fail unless the employer can show "that the same decision would have been reached absent illegal motive." Where a female plaintiff presented direct evidence of discrimination, the board's defense in showing that "she would not have been promoted if she were a man" provided the defendants with a complete defense to plaintiff's charges. In other words, the employment decision must be gender neutral or that gender was irrelevant to the determination. McCarthney v. Griffin–Spalding County Board of Education (11th Cir.1986).

In considering sex discrimination, the court must determine, based on proof, the determinants of the employer's decision. Was the decision based on considerations that were legitimate, illegitimate, or a mixture of the two? The Supreme Court in considering the dilemma of a mixture of the two has held that the language of Title VII which states, in part, *"because of* such individual's sex," means if the evidence is insufficient to discern the causal significance between legitimate and illegitimate considerations, then the court must conclude that the employment decision was made "because of" sex. According to the Court, plaintiffs should be spared the extremely difficult burden of precisely distinguishing causality as to the employer's motives. Therefore, if gender is not a discernible aspect of an array of reasons for a decision, the Court will assume that neutrality has not been maintained. In this way Title VII "forbids employers to make gender an indirect stumbling block to employment opportunity." The Supreme Court has concluded with regard to the plaintiff's burden of proof that "[i]t is difficult for us to imagine that, in the simple words 'because of' Congress meant to obligate plaintiff to identify the precise causal role played by legitimate and illegitimate motivations in the employment decisions she challenges. We conclude, instead, that Congress meant to obligate her to prove that the employer relied upon sex-based considerations in coming to its decision." Price Waterhouse v. Hopkins (S.Ct.1989).

Sexual stereotyping is prohibited. The employer cannot have different standards or demand different levels of performance for one gender but not the other. The courts have ruled that a no-children rule applied only to women and discharging a female for extra-marital relations, but tolerating it for male workers, violated the law. Phillips v. Martin Marietta Corp. (S.Ct.1971); Thomas v. Metroflight, Inc. (10th Cir.1987).

In *Price*, supra, a female was refused a partnership in an accounting firm. The individual was described as "macho," "overcompensated for being a woman," "a lady using foul language." She was also advised to "walk more femininely, dress more femininely, wear make-up, have her hair styled and wear jewelry" to improve her chances for a partnership. The court held this to be sex discrimination, that of measuring a female against male perceived expectations.

## § 18.32 Pregnancy

Discrimination based on pregnancy is prohibited under the Pregnancy Discrimination Act of 1978 (PDA), an amendment to Title VII, 42 U.S.C.A. § 2000e(k). The Act has been interpreted to require employers to treat pregnancy as any other disabling illness. Health and leave benefits extended to employees for disabling illnesses must also be extended to pregnancy. Proof in establishing discrimination applies to pregnancy allegations in the same manner as to other aspects of Title VII. Plaintiffs must establish a *prima facie* case of disparate treatment and, if successful, the institution must articulate legitimate nondiscriminatory reasons for the employment decision.

The Supreme Court has held that "... Congress intended the PDA (Pregnancy Discrimination Act) to be a floor beneath which pregnancy disability benefits may not drop—not a ceiling above which they may not rise." Therefore, the PDA does not prohibit employment practices that favor pregnant women. California Federal Savings and Loan Association v. Guerra (S.Ct.1987).

## § 18.33 Benefits

The actuarial tables used by insurance companies indicate that females live longer than males. Because of this fact, females have either been charged more at the initial pay-in stage of pension plans or receive smaller monthly payments at the pay-out stage. These types of programs have been challenged as a form of sex discrimination under Title VII. The U.S. Supreme Court held in *Manhart* in 1978 that a pension plan that required female employees to make larger contributions than males for equivalent monthly benefits upon retirement violated Title VII because the difference in treatment was based strictly on sex. Los Angeles Dept. of Water and Power v. Manhart (S.Ct.1978).

The State of Arizona developed a different approach with the differential at the pay-out as opposed to the pay-in stage. Employees were offered a deferred annuity plan and could select from three options: (1) a single lump-sum payment upon retirement, (2) payments at a specified amount for a fixed period of time, or (3) monthly annuity payments for the remainder of the employee's life. The first two options treated males and females equally and therefore were not in dispute. The third option was determined by sex-based morality tables and therefore in violation of Title VII. All benefits provided by an employer must be gender neutral. Arizona Governing Committee v. Norris (S.Ct.1983).

## § 18.34  Equal Pay Act

In 1963, the Fair Labor Standards Act of 1938 (See Appendix B) was amended to include what is commonly called the Equal Pay Act. The intent of the Act was to eliminate discrimination in wages based on sex where equal work, equal skills and effort are performed under the same working conditions, 29 U.S.C.A. § 206(d)(1). The Act provided for exceptions when differential pay is based on: (1) a seniority system; (2) a merit system; (3) where quantity and quality of production is a factor; and (4) where pay differences are based on any factor except sex.

Title VII of the Civil Rights Act of 1964, 42 U.S.C.A. § 2000e–2(h), was amended to incorporate the Equal Pay

Act. The language of Title VII is similar to that of the Equal Pay Act, except that race, color, religion and national origin as well as sex is covered. Title VII provides: it is not unlawful to provide different compensation, "or different terms, conditions, or privileges of employment pursuant to a bona fide seniority or merit system, or a system which measures earnings by quantity or quality of production or to employees who work in different locations, provided that such differences are not the result of an intention to discriminate because of race, color, religion, sex or national origin," 42 U.S.C.A. § 2000e–2(h).

When a claim of unequal pay for equal work is litigated, the standard is essentially the same for the Equal Pay Act and Title VII. "To establish a claim of unequal pay for equal work a plaintiff has the burden to prove that the employer pays different wages to employees of opposite sexes for equal work on jobs the performance of which requires equal skill, effort and responsibility, and which are performed under similar working conditions." Odomes v. Nucara, Inc. (6th Cir.1981); see Corning Glass Works v. Brennan (S.Ct.1974). It was not the intent of Congress that the jobs must be identical. To effectuate the Equal Pay Act and its remedial remedies, "only substantial equality of skills, effort, responsibility and working conditions is required." *Odomes*, supra. Whether the work is equal must be established on a case by case basis. In the *Odomes* case, it was shown by the plaintiff nurse's aide's uncontradicted testimony, that orderlies do little or nothing that the nurse's aide did not do, therefore, equal pay should be received.

Once the plaintiff has established that he or she is being paid unequally for the same work "the burden shifts to the employer to show that the differential [pay scale] is justified under one of the Act's four exemptions." *Corning Glass Works v. Brennan*, supra.

In Usery v. Columbia University (2d Cir.1977), the Secretary of Labor commenced an action against the university for discriminating against female "light cleaners" who receive lower pay than male "heavy cleaners." The district judge declared that the Secretary had not sustained the burden of proof since heavy cleaners exerted greater effort than light cleaners. On appeal, the circuit court applied the criterion of "equal effort." The "mere fact that two jobs call for effort different in kind will not render them unequal, nor will effort expended on additional tasks assigned to male employees necessarily suffice to justify pay differential; if additional tasks do not consume significant total amount of all employee's time, or if female employees also perform duties which require additional effort or if third persons who perform additional tasks as their primary job are paid less than male employees in question, in these situations additional effort is insufficient to differentiate male positions under the Act." Since the heavy cleaners job required substantially more effort, the unequal pay was justified under the Equal Pay Act.

## § 18.35  Title IX

In 1972, Title IX of the Education Amendments (Appendix B) was enacted to prohibit sex discrimination in educational programs or activities receiving federal funds. Title IX was closely patterned after Title VI of the Civil Rights Act of 1964. Title IX in its original form stated: "No person in the United States shall, on the basis of sex, be excluded from participation in, be denied the benefits of, or be subjected to discrimination under any educational program or activity receiving Federal financial assistance, ...."

Because Title IX is patterned after Title VI, and covers students in educational institutions, some courts ruled that Title IX did not cover employees. But the Supreme Court, in North Haven Board of Education v. Bell (S.Ct. 1982), stated, "[W]hile section 901(a) does not expressly include or exclude employees within its scope, its broad directive that 'no person' may be discriminated against on the basis of gender includes employees as well as students."

Further controversy over the application of Title IX occurred as a result of the federal government's requirement that a private college, Grove City College, supply assurance of compliance. The college refused, and the United States Department of Education cut off the students' federal financial assistance. The U.S. Supreme Court in Grove City College v. Bell (S.Ct.1984), held that Title IX applied only to "programs" receiving federal assistance and not to the entire institution. Under a narrow interpretation of the statute, the Court held that the college was obliged to submit assurance of compliance for the office responsible for administration of student federal financial aid only, and not for the college as a whole.

This decision was the impetus for the Congress to amend Title IX with the Civil Rights Restoration Act of 1987, 20 U.S.C.A. § 1687, correcting the loophole identified in the Grove City case. Effectively, Grove City not only narrowed the coverage of Title IX, but of Title VI of the Civil Rights Act of 1964, § 504 of the Rehabilitation Act of 1973, and the Age Discrimination in Employment

Act of 1975 as well. The Civil Rights Restoration Act of 1987 restored institution-wide application of these laws. The 1987 law added no new language to the coverage or fund termination provisions of the four acts, but amended each of the affected statutes by adding a section defining the phrase "program or activity" and "program" to make it clear that discrimination is prohibited throughout the entire institution or agency if any part is the recipient of federal financial assistance.

The new Act provides that the entire institution or system is covered and not just the program receiving federal assistance. If federal aid is distributed to any part of a public school district, the entire school system is subject to compliance requirements. Private education corporations are also covered if they receive federal funding.

In 1992 in Franklin v. Gwinnett County Public Schools (S.Ct.1992), the Supreme Court drastically changed the enforcement of Title IX and other anti-discrimination statutes by unanimously allowing monetary damages for intentional violations of Title IX. Until *Franklin*, there was very little litigation under Title IX, but since *Franklin* there has been an explosion of cases. Monetary damages are available to the plaintiff.

## § 18.36    Sexual Harassment

Employees are protected from sexual harassment in the workplace by Title VII of the Civil Rights Act of 1964 and Title IX, Education Amendments of 1972. Sexual harassment may range from verbal innuendo to an overt act, and the definition must be broad enough to encompass the diversity of behavior. In 1980 the Equal Employment Opportunity Commission (EEOC) promulgated regulations prohibiting sexual harassment. These regulations state: "Harassment on the basis of sex is a violation of Sec. 703 of Title VII. Unwelcome sexual advances, requests for sexual favors, and other verbal or physical conduct of a sexual nature constitute harassment when (1) submission to such conduct is made explicitly or implicitly a term or condition of an individual's employment, (2) submission to or rejection of such conduct by an individual is used as a basis for employment decisions affecting such individual, (3) such conduct has the purpose or effect of unreasonably interfering with an individual's work performance or creating an intimidating, hostile, or offensive working environment."

The EEOC guidelines suggest two types of sexual harassment, *quid pro quo* and *non quid pro quo*. The United States Supreme Court in Meritor Savings Bank, FSB v. Vinson (S.Ct.1986), the leading case on sexual harassment, provides definition: "[T]he guidelines provide that sexual conduct constitutes prohibited 'sexual harassment,' whether or not it is directly linked to the grant or denial of an economic *quid pro quo*, where 'such conduct has the purpose or effect of unreasonably interfering with an individual's work performance or creating an intimidating, hostile, or offensive working environment *[non quid pro quo]*.' "

The Supreme Court in a 1993 case found that a hostile or abusive environment is determined by examining a number of factors and the frequency with which they occurred. These include the severity of the conduct, whether it was physically threatening or humiliating and whether it interferes with the employee's work performance. The Court also said, "To be actionable under

Title VII as 'abusive work environment' harassment, conduct need not seriously affect the employee's psychological well-being or lead the employee to suffer injury, so long as the environment would reasonably be perceived, and is perceived, as hostile or abusive...." Title VII does not require the employee to prove they have actually been harmed psychologically or otherwise. Harris v. Forklift Systems, Inc. (S.Ct.1993).

The Eleventh Circuit Court of Appeals has observed: "Sexual harassment which creates a hostile or offensive environment for members of one sex is every bit the arbitrary barrier to sexual equality at the workplace that racial harassment is to racial equality. Surely, a requirement that a man or woman run a gauntlet for the privilege of being allowed to work and make a living can be as demeaning and disconcerting as the harshest of racial epithets." Henson v. Dundee (11th Cir.1982).

The EEOC guidelines further provide that an employer is held responsible "[f]or its act and those of its agents and supervisory employees with respect to sexual harassment regardless of whether the specific acts complained of were authorized or even forbidden by the employer and regardless of whether the employer knew or should have known of their occurrence."

Also, an employer is held responsible for acts of sexual harassment between fellow employees where the employer "knows or should have known of the conduct, unless it can show that it took immediate and appropriate corrective actions." In 1992 the U.S. Supreme Court in *Franklin v. Gwinnett County Public Schools*, supra, ruled that a student may collect monetary damages for sexual harassment. Since Title IX covers employees as well as students, then an employee can hold an employer liable for damages under Title IX if sexual harassment occurs in the work place.

## § 18.37 Sexuality

Some states and municipalities have passed statutes or ordinances which prohibit discrimination on the basis of sexual orientation. These are defined as heterosexuality, homosexuality, or bisexuality. Homosexuality is not defined by the Rehabilitation Act of 1973, the American Disabilities Act, or other federal statutes. The American Disabilities Act specifically excludes from protection homosexuality, transvestism and transsexualism. See DeSantis v. Pacific Tel. & Tel. Co., Inc. (9th Cir.1979), and Ulane v. Eastern Airlines (7th Cir.1984).

## § 18.4   RELIGIOUS DISCRIMINATION

Employees' religious rights and freedoms are protected by both the First Amendment of the U.S. Constitution and Title VII of the Civil Rights Act of 1964, as amended in 1972.

The Civil Rights Act of 1964, Title VII, prohibits any employer from discriminating against an individual because of religion. The 1972 Amendment states: "The term religion includes all aspects of religious observance and practice, as well as belief, unless an employer demonstrates that he is unable to reasonably accommodate an employee's or prospective employee's religious observance or practice without undue hardship on the conduct of the employer's business." The Supreme Court in 1989 ruled that religion not only includes organized faiths such as Baptist, Judaism, etc., but also "moral or ethical beliefs as to what is right and wrong which are sincerely held with the strength of traditional religious views, . . . The fact that no religious group espouses such beliefs or the fact that the religious group to which the individual professes to belong may not accept such belief will not determine whether the belief is a religious belief of the employee or prospective employee." Frazee v. Illinois Dept. of Employment Security (S.Ct.1989). Title VII protects atheists from discrimination because of the absence of religious beliefs, EEOC v. Townley Engineering & Mfg. Co. (9th Cir.1988), but political beliefs are not included under the act. The act exempts religious organizations and religious corporations, also religion can be a bona fide occupational qualification. A professor of Catholic Theology must be a Catholic, therefore, this is a *bona fide* occupational qualification (BFOQ). Pime v. Loyola University of Chicago (7th Cir.1986).

A primary question emerges as to what the employer must do to reasonably accommodate the religious beliefs of an employee. In Trans World Airlines, Inc. v. Hardison (S.Ct.1977), the Supreme Court addressed this issue. Hardison, the plaintiff employee, challenged a company rule, claiming violation of Title VII, which prevented him from observing Saturday as his religious holiday. The U.S. Supreme Court held for the airline and said that Title VII did not require the company "to carve out special exemptions" to accommodate one's religious beliefs. To require the company, in this case Trans World Airlines, "to bear more than a *de minimis cost* " in order to give Hardison Saturdays off is an undue hardship.

As with other aspects of Title VII, the burden of proof to show religious discrimination is borne by the plaintiff, who must show that the employer's decision was religiously related. If the plaintiff sustains this burden,

then the employer must in turn show that the encroachment on the employee's religious beliefs could not be
reasonably accommodated without undue hardship to the
employer.

Employees' work schedules have also come in conflict
with religious worship in other cases. In one such case a
teacher was dismissed because of absence from the job,
without permission, to attend a religious festival. The
teacher had arranged for a substitute teacher, instructed
the substitute on lesson plans, and so on; and the classes
had in fact run very smoothly. The court determined
that to accommodate the teacher resulted in no undue
hardship to the school and rendered judgment for the
teacher. Wangsness v. Watertown School Dist. No. 14–4
(D.S.D.1982).

In a similar case, the court held that it is a violation of
one's freedom of religion to compel an employee to
choose between employment and religion. The court
said: " ... [A]n employer who punishes an employee by
placing the latter in a position in which he or she must
ignore a tenet of faith in order to retain employment
violates" Title VII. Pinsker v. Joint District No. 28J,
etc. (D.Colo.1983).

In Ansonia Board of Education v. Philbrook (S.Ct.
1986), the Supreme Court ruled a school board had met
its obligation under Title VII when it offered a reasonable accommodation to the teacher. The employee presented his preferred plan which would have given him
three additional days of paid leave for religious meetings.
The school district need not accept the employee's preferred plan but may present its own plan as long as it
reasonably accommodates the teacher.

## § 18.5  AGE DISCRIMINATION

The federal government passed the Age Discrimination in Employment Act (ADEA) in 1967 (Appendix B). This Act prohibited discrimination against individuals who are at least forty, but less than seventy years of age. The Act was amended in 1986, striking out the language "but less than seventy years of age." The effect of the amendment is to remove the maximum age limitation applicable to employees who are protected under the Act. The Act applies equally to all governmental employees, with the exception of firefighters and law enforcement officers who, by virtue of the rigors of their job requirements, are considered separately. The Act which was modeled after Title VII prohibits discrimination with respect to hiring, discharging, compensation, terms and conditions, privileges, retirement, and demotion.

Two cases decided by the Supreme Court are important in understanding mandatory retirement statutes and age discriminations. In the first case, Massachusetts Board of Retirement v. Murgia (S.Ct.1976), the Court upheld a Massachusetts statute requiring uniformed state police to retire at age fifty. The Court held that government employment was not a fundamental constitutional right, nor age a suspect classification. Therefore, the Court required that the government show a rational interest to support its policy and not bear the higher burden of showing a compelling interest to support the policy if a fundamental constitutional right were involved. Because the purpose of the statute was to assure physical preparedness by having younger troopers patrolling the highways, the policy was not unconstitutional. The rationale that younger policemen are more physically capable and can provide better protection to all of society was held to be a proper and reasonable societal objective.

In the other case, again using the rational interest test, the Supreme Court upheld a statute requiring Foreign Service employees to retire at age sixty. The Court said: "Congress ... was legitimately intent on stimulating the highest performance in the Foreign Service by assuring that opportunities for promotion would be available despite [the] limits on [the] number of personnel in the Service, and plainly intended to create [a] relatively small, homogeneous and particularly able corps of foreign service officers...." Vance v. Bradley (S.Ct.1979). This the Court found to be an acceptable objective.

Whether a *bona fide* occupational qualification (BFOQ) exemption is allowed under the ADEA depends on how narrowly the employer fashions the exemption. In Western Air Lines, Inc. v. Criswell (S.Ct.1985), the U.S. Supreme Court established a two-part test for evaluating an employer's exemption. First, the job qualifications must be reasonably necessary to the essence of the business; and second, the employer must be "compelled to rely on age as a proxy for a safety-related" job qualification by showing that there exists a factual basis for believing that all persons over a specified age are incapable of performing the duties in a safe and efficient manner, or that it is "impossible or highly impractical" to deal with older employees on an individual basis.

This test was applied to a rule for eight school bus drivers, a lower federal court ruled that to broadbrush all persons of sixty-five and older as incapable was inappropriate when the entire group of drivers was such a small number that all could have been evaluated separately. Tullis v. Lear School, Inc. (11th Cir.1989).

Thus, the reasonableness of an exemption can be large-ly determined by the practicality of application and effi-cacy of implementation. An employer may not require all employees over a certain age, such as 60, to take a mental and physical test unless all workers are given the test. Shager v. UpJohn Co. (7th Cir.1990). Standard of performance must be applied to all age groups.

The courts have held that the party claiming age discrimination will be evaluated under the same factors as established for race discrimination. If the action is a private, nonclass action: "the complainant has the bur-den of establishing a *prima facie* case, which he can satisfy by showing that (i) he belongs to a special minori-ty; (ii) he applied and was qualified for a job the employ-er was trying to fill; (iii) though qualified, he was reject-ed; and (iv) therefore, the employer continued to seek applicants with complainant's qualifications."

After establishing a *prima facie* case, the burden shifts to the employer, who must articulate legitimate, nondis-criminatory reasons for not employing the individual or individuals.

## § 18.6 DISCRIMINATION AGAINST THE DIS-ABLED

In 1990 the Congress enacted the Americans with Disabilities Act of 1990 (ADA) (Appendix B). In expand-ing on the Vocational Rehabilitation Act of 1973, § 504, which was conditioned on the receipt of federal funds, the new ADA covers all employees, in the public and private sector, who work for companies with fifteen or more employees.

The ADA covers virtually all aspects of society, includ-ing transportation, public accommodations, telecommunications, and other areas. For purposes of liability, the act specifically waives state immunity under the Eleventh Amendment. The Act's coverage is categorically delimited to exclude coverage of illegal drug use and defines "disability" as excluding "(1) transvestism, transsexualism, pedophilia, exhibitionism, voyeurism, gender identity disorders not resulting from physical impairment, or other sexual behavior disorders; (2) compulsive gambling, kleptomania, or pyromania; or (3) psychoactive substance use disorders resulting from current illegal use of drugs."

The focal point of employee litigation by disabled persons continues to be the Vocational Rehabilitation Act of 1973, § 504. Section 504 is violated if a disabled person is denied a position "solely by reason of his handicap." "The standards for determining the merits of a case under Section 504 are contained in the statute. First, the statute provides that the individual in question must be an 'otherwise qualified handicapped individual'; second, the statute provides that a qualified handicapped individual may not be denied admission to any program or activity or denied the benefits of any program or activity ... solely on the bases of handicap." If an individual is not otherwise qualified, he or she cannot be said to have been rejected solely because of handicap.

Pursuant to this Act, the Supreme Court has held tuberculosis is a physiological disorder covered by § 504. If a person is "otherwise qualified" to work, then the handicapping condition cannot be the grounds for dismissal. The Court said that "[a]n otherwise qualified person is one who is able to meet all of a program's requirements in spite of his handicap." School Board of Nassau County v. Arline (S.Ct.1987).

In a recent case that helps define the extent of protections of this statute, two school van drivers who were insulin-dependent diabetics were demoted to aide positions at a lower rate of pay because of their illness. It was determined that they were not "otherwise qualified" under Section 504 because of safety. The court stated, "Section 504 of the Rehabilitation Act provides that 'no otherwise qualified individual with a disability ... shall ... be excluded from the participation in, be denied the benefits of, or be subjected to discrimination under any program or activity receiving Federal financial assistance' solely by reason of her or his disability. An otherwise qualified individual is one who, with reasonable accommodation, can perform the essential functions of the position in question without endangering the health and safety of the individual or others. In determining what kinds of accommodations are reasonable, courts are permitted to take into account the reasonableness of the cost of any necessary workplace accommodation, the availability of alternatives therefore, or other appropriate relief in order to achieve an equitable and appropriate remedy. An unreasonable accommodation is one which would impose undue hardship on the operation of the program in question." Wood v. Omaha School District (8th Cir.1994).

In 1969 a blind English teacher who held a Professional Certificate from the Pennsylvania Department of Education was refused the opportunity to take the Philadelphia Teacher's Examination. The school district classified her as having a "chronic or acute physical defect" which included blindness. With persistence and legal assistance the teacher in 1974 was allowed to take the test which she passed. Because the school district refused to afford her seniority as of the time she properly should have been admitted to take the examination, she filed suit. The court held for the teacher, awarding her retroactive seniority. Gurmankin v. Costanzo (3d Cir. 1977). Significantly, the Court held that a handicap could not be considered a suspect classification for equal protection purposes. Thus, the issue of handicap, as an equal protection issue, must be decided under the rational relationship test, not the more rigorous compelling interest standard. The fact that handicapped persons do not form a suspect class has important bearing on the necessity for separate statutory protection as provided in § 504 and the new ADA.

In another equal protection case, bearing on the issue of suspect class, a blind teacher sued because school policy prevented him from obtaining an administrative position. The policy required that an oral and written examination be completed by each prospective administrator. The plaintiff completed the written section of the test, with the aid of a reader, and performed very poorly. A committee also rated the plaintiff very low on the oral part of the examination. The court held that because physical handicaps were not to be treated as a suspect classification, the school district needed only to show a rational relationship between its policy and reasonably state its objective. Using this test, the court determined that the plaintiff did not possess the skills and qualifications to be an administrator. The school had a legitimate, rational purpose in seeking competent individuals, and the oral and written tests were reasonable devices to assure such competence.

## § 18.7   FAMILY AND MEDICAL LEAVE ACT OF 1993

In 1993 the U.S. Congress passed the Family and Medical Leave Act (FMLA), 29 U.S.C.A. § 2601. The purpose of the Act is "to balance the demands of the workplace with the needs of families, to promote the stability and economic security of families; and to promote national interest in preserving family integrity." Also the Act is designed to "entitle employees to take reasonable leave for medical reasons, for the birth or adoption of a child, and for the care of a child, or parent who has a serious health condition."

The FMLA applies to both public and private sector employees. Private employers must have 50 or more eligible employees at any one site to be included under the Act. There is a special section for schools, stating eligible employees of any "local educational agency" and "any private elementary or secondary school" are covered. In order to be eligible an employee, which includes part-time, must have worked for at least one year providing that at least 1250 hours of service were completed during the year immediately preceding the start of leave.

The employee may request leave for the birth or adoption of a child. This provision expires one year after the birth or adoption, also care for a seriously ill child, parent or spouse. The term child includes biological, adopted, foster, step-child, legal ward with focus on the actual provider of care. The leave to which an employee is entitled is up to 12 weeks of unpaid leave within any 12 month period. The leave may be taken intermittently, an occasional day leave, or a reduced work week. Leave generally requires agreement and coordination with the employer unless it is a "medical necessity."

The FMLA has a section that addresses employees who are "principally in an instructional capacity" which impacts schools. This provision is where an employee requests leave which is "foreseeable based on planned medical treatment" and the employee would be on leave for more than 20% of the total working days during the instructional period. If this is the case, the employer may require the leave either to be taken for a particular duration not to exceed the planned medical treatment or transfer to a temporary alternative position. This is based on the need for instructional continuity. There are also rules for leave near the end of the academic term which here again are designed not to jeopardize the instructional integrity of the class.

# APPENDIX A

# SELECTED CONSTITUTIONAL PROVISIONS

## CONSTITUTION OF THE UNITED STATES

We the People of the United States, in Order to form a more perfect Union, establish Justice, insure domestic Tranquillity, provide for the common defence, promote the general Welfare, and secure the Blessings of Liberty to ourselves and our Posterity, do ordain and establish this Constitution for the United States of America.

## Article I.

Section 1. All legislative Powers herein granted shall be vested in a Congress of the United States, which shall consist of a Senate and House of Representatives.

Section 2. The House of Representatives shall be composed of Members chosen every second Year by the People of the several States, and the Electors in each State shall have the Qualifications requisite for Electors of the most numerous Branch of the State Legislature.

. . .

Section 7. All Bills for raising Revenue shall originate in the House of Representatives; but the Senate may propose or concur with amendments as on other Bills.

Every Bill which shall have passed the House of Representatives and the Senate, shall, before it become a Law, be presented to the President of the United States; If he approve he shall sign it, but if not he shall return it, with his Objections to that House in which it shall have originated, who shall enter the Objections at large on their Journal, and proceed to reconsider it. If after such Reconsideration two thirds of that House shall agree to pass the Bill, it shall be sent, together with the Objections, to the other House, by which it shall likewise be reconsidered, and if approved by two thirds of that House, it shall become a Law. But in all such Cases the Votes of both Houses shall be determined by yeas and Nays, and the Names of the Persons voting for and against the Bill shall be entered on the Journal of each House respectively. If any Bill shall not be returned by the President within ten Days (Sunday excepted) after it shall have been presented to him, the Same shall be a Law, in like Manner as if he had signed it, unless the Congress by their Adjournment prevents its Return, in which Case it shall not be a Law.

. . .

Section 8. The Congress shall have Power To lay and collect Taxes, Duties, Imposts and Excises, to pay the Debts and provide for the common Defence and general Welfare of the United States; but all Duties, Imposts and Excises shall be uniform throughout the United States;

To borrow Money on the credit of the United States;

To regulate Commerce with foreign Nations, and among the several States, and with the Indian Tribes;

. . .

To promote the Progress of Science and useful Arts, by securing for limited Times to Authors and Inventors the exclusive Right to their respective Writings and Discoveries;

. . .

Section 9.  The privilege of the Writ of Habeas Corpus shall not be suspended, unless when in Cases of Rebellion or Invasion the public Safety may require it.

No Bill of Attainder or ex post facto Law shall be passed.

. . .

Section 10.  No State shall enter into any Treaty, Alliance, or Confederation; grant Letters of Marque and Reprisal; coin Money; emit Bills of Credit; make any Thing but gold and silver Coin a Tender in Payment of Debts; pass any Bill of Attainder, ex post facto Law, or Law impairing the Obligation of Contracts, or grant any Title of Nobility.

. . .

## Article II.

Section 1.  The executive Power shall be vested in a President of the United States of America....

Section 2.  The President shall be Commander in Chief of the Army and Navy of the United States, and of the Militia of the several States, ...

He shall have Power, by and with the Advice and Consent of the Senate, to make Treaties, provided two thirds of the Senators present concur; and he shall nominate, and by and with the Advice and Consent of the Senate, shall appoint Ambassadors, other public Ministers and Consuls, Judges of the supreme Court, and all other Officers of the United States, whose Appointments are not herein otherwise provided for, and which shall be established by Law: but the Congress may by Law vest the Appointment of such inferior Officers, as they think proper, in the President alone, in the Courts of Law, or in the Heads of Departments....

Section 4. The United States shall guarantee to every State in this Union a Republican Form of Government, and shall protect each of them against Invasion; and on Application of the Legislature, or of the Executive (when the Legislature cannot be convened) against domestic Violence.

## Article III.

Section 1. The judicial Power of the United States, shall be vested in one supreme Court, and in such inferior Courts as the Congress may from time to time ordain and establish. The Judges, both of the supreme and inferior Courts, shall hold their Offices during good Behaviour, and shall, at stated Times, receive for their Services, a Compensation, which shall not be diminished during their Continuance in Office.

Section 2. The judicial Power shall extend to all Cases, in Law and Equity, arising under this Constitution, the Laws of the United States, and Treaties made, or which shall be made, under their Authority;—to all Cases affecting Ambassadors, other public Ministers and Consuls;—to all Cases of admiralty and maritime Jurisdiction;—to Controversies to which the United States shall be a Party;—to Controversies between two or more States;—between a State and Citizens of another State;—between Citizens of different States;—between Citizens of the same State claiming Lands under Grants of different States, and between a State, or the Citizens thereof, and foreign States, Citizens or Subjects.

. . .

The Trial of all Crimes, except in Cases of Impeachment, shall be by Jury; and such Trial shall be held in the State where the said Crimes shall have been committed; but when not committed within any State, the Trial shall be at such Place or Places as the Congress may by Law have directed.

## Article IV.

Section 1. Full Faith and Credit shall be given in each State to the public Acts, Records, and judicial Proceedings of every other State. And the Congress may by general Laws prescribe the Manner in which such Acts, Records and Proceedings shall be proved, and the Effect thereof.

Section 2. The Citizens of each State shall be entitled to all Privileges and Immunities of Citizens in the several States.

. . .

Section 3. New States may be admitted by the Congress into this Union; but no new State shall be formed or erected within the Jurisdiction of any other State; nor any State be formed by the Junction of two or more States, or Parts of States, without the Consent of the Legislatures of the States concerned as well as of the Congress.

. . .

## Article V.

The Congress, whenever two thirds of both Houses shall deem it necessary, shall propose Amendments to this Constitution, or, on the Application of the Legislatures of two thirds of the several States, shall call a Convention for proposing Amendments, which, in either Case, shall be valid to all Intents and Purposes, as Part of this Constitution, when ratified by the Legislatures of three fourths of the several States, or by Conventions in three fourths thereof, as the one or the other Mode of Ratification may be proposed by the Congress; Provided that no Amendment which may be made prior to the Year One thousand eight hundred and eight shall in any Manner affect the first and fourth Clauses in the Ninth Section of the first Article; and that no State, without its Consent, shall be deprived of it's equal Suffrage in the Senate.

. . .

This Constitution, and the Laws of the United States which shall be made in Pursuance thereof; and all Treaties made, or which shall be made, under the Authority of the United States, shall be the supreme Law of the Land; and the Judges in every State shall be found thereby, any Thing in the Constitution or Laws of any State to the Contrary notwithstanding.

The Senators and Representatives before mentioned, and the Members of the several State Legislatures, and all executive and judicial Officers, both of the United States and of the several States, shall be bound by Oath or Affirmation, to support this Constitution; but no religious Test shall ever be required as a Qualification to any Office or public Trust under the United States.

**Article VII.**

The Ratification of the Conventions of nine States, shall be sufficient for the Establishment of this Constitution between the States so ratifying the Same.

## AMENDMENTS TO THE CONSTITUTION OF THE UNITED STATES OF AMERICA

Articles in Addition to, and Amendment of, the Constitution of the United States of America, Proposed by Congress, and Ratified by the Several States, Pursuant to the Fifth Article of the Original Constitution

### Amendment [I.] [1791]

Congress shall make no law respecting an establishment of religion, or prohibiting the free exercise thereof; or abridging the freedom of speech, or of the press; or the right of the people peaceably to assemble, and to petition the Government for a redress of grievances.

### Amendment II. [1791]

A well regulated Militia, being necessary to the security of a free State, the right of the people to keep and bear Arms, shall not be infringed.

### Amendment III. [1791]

No Soldier shall, in time of peace be quartered in any house, without the consent of the Owner, nor in time of war, but in a manner to be prescribed by law.

### Amendment IV. [1791]

The right of the people to be secure in their persons, houses, papers, and effects, against unreasonable searches and seizures, shall not be violated, and no Warrants shall issue, but upon probable cause, supported by Oath or affirmation, and particularly describing the place to be searched, and the persons or things to be seized.

## Amendment V. [1791]

No person shall be held to answer for a capital, or otherwise infamous crime, unless on a presentment or indictment of a Grand Jury, except in cases arising in the land or naval forces, or in the Militia, when in actual service in time of War or public danger; nor shall any person be subject for the same offence to be twice put in jeopardy of life or limb; nor shall be compelled in any criminal case to be a witness against himself, nor be deprived of life, liberty, or property, without due process of law; nor shall private property be taken for public use, without just compensation.

## Amendment VI. [1791]

In all criminal prosecutions, the accused shall enjoy the right to a speedy and public trial, by an impartial jury of the State and district wherein the crime shall have been committed, which district shall have been previously ascertained by law, and to be informed of the nature and cause of the accusation; to be confronted with the witnesses against him; to have compulsory process for obtaining witnesses in his favor, and to have the Assistance of Counsel for his defence.

## Amendment VII. [1791]

In Suits at common law, where the value in controversy shall exceed twenty dollars, the right of trial by jury shall be preserved, and no fact tried by a jury, shall be otherwise reexamined in any Court of the United States, than according to the rules of the common law.

## Amendment VIII. [1791]

Excessive bail shall not be required, nor excessive fines imposed, nor cruel and unusual punishments inflicted.

## Amendment IX. [1791]

The enumeration in the Constitution, of certain rights, shall not be construed to deny or disparage others retained by the people.

## Amendment X. [1791]

The powers not delegated to the United States by the Constitution, nor prohibited by it to the States, are reserved to the States respectively, or to the people.

## Amendment XI. [1798]

The Judicial power of the United States shall not be construed to extend to any suit in law or equity, commenced or prosecuted against one of the United States by Citizens of another State, or by Citizens or Subjects of any Foreign State.

## Amendment XIII. [1865]

Section 1. Neither slavery nor involuntary servitude, except as a punishment for crime whereof the party shall have been duly convicted, shall exist within the United States, or any place subject to their jurisdiction.

Section 2. Congress shall have power to enforce this article by appropriate legislation.

## Amendment XIV. [1868]

Section 1. All persons born or naturalized in the United States and subject to the jurisdiction thereof, are citizens of the United States and of the State wherein they reside. No state shall make or enforce any law which shall abridge the privileges or immunities of citizens of the United States; or shall any State deprive any person of life, liberty, or property, without due process of law; nor deny to any person within its jurisdiction the equal protection of the laws.

Section 5. The Congress shall have power to enforce, by appropriate legislation, the provisions of this article.

## Amendment XV. [1870]

Section 1. The right of citizens of the United States to vote shall not be denied or abridged by the United States or by any State on account of race, color, or previous condition of servitude.

Section 2. The Congress shall have power to enforce this article by appropriate legislation.

. . .

## Amendment XIX. [1920]

The right of citizens of the United States to vote shall not be denied or abridged by the United States or by any State on account of sex.

Congress shall have power to enforce this article by appropriate legislation.

## Amendment XXVI. [1971]

Section 1. The right of citizens of the United States, who are eighteen years of age or older, to vote shall not be denied or abridged by the United States or by any State on account of age.

Section 2. The Congress shall have power to enforce this article by appropriate legislation.

# APPENDIX B

# SELECTED FEDERAL STATUTES

## THE CIVIL RIGHTS ACT OF
## 1871 42 U.S.C. § 1983

Section 1983 provides:

"Every person who, under color of any statute, ordinance, regulation, custom or usage, of any State or Territory, subjects, or causes to be subjected, any citizen of the United States or other person within the jurisdiction thereof to the deprivation of any rights, privileges or immunities secured by the Constitution and laws, shall be liable to the party injured in an action at law, suit in equity, or other proper proceeding for redress."

## CIVIL RIGHTS ACT OF 1964 TITLE
## VI (SELECTED PARTS) 42
## U.S.C.A. § 2000D—D-1

## FEDERALLY ASSISTED PROGRAMS

**§ 2000d. Prohibition against exclusion from participation in, denial of benefits of, and discrimination under Federally assisted programs on ground of race, color, or national origin**

No person in the United States shall, on the ground of race, color, or national origin, be excluded from participation in, be denied the benefits of, or be subjected to discrimination under any program or activity receiving Federal financial assistance.

Pub.L. 88–352, Title VI, § 601, July 2, 1964, 78 Stat. 252.

§ 2000d–1. **Federal authority and financial assistance to programs or activities by way of grant, loan, or contract other than contract of insurance or guaranty; rules and regulations; approval by President; compliance with requirements; reports to Congressional committees; effective date of administrative action**

Each Federal department and agency which is empowered to extend Federal financial assistance to any program or activity, by way of grant, loan, or contract other than a contract of insurance or guaranty, is authorized and directed to effectuate the provisions of section 2000d of this title with respect to such program or activity by issuing rules, regulations, or orders of general applicability which shall be consistent with achievement of the objectives of the statute authorizing the financial assistance in connection with which the action is taken. No such rule, regulation, or order shall become effective unless and until approved by the President. Compliance with any requirement adopted pursuant to this section may be effected (1) by the termination of or refusal to grant or to continue assistance under such program or activity to any recipient as to whom there has been an express finding on the record, after opportunity for hearing, of a failure to comply with such requirement, but such termination or refusal shall be limited to the particular political entity, or part thereof, or other recipient as to whom such a finding has been made and, shall be limited in its effect to the particular program, or part thereof, in which such noncompliance has been so found, or (2) by any other means authorized by law: *Provided*, however, That no such action shall be taken until the department or agency concerned has advised the appropriate person or persons of the failure to comply with the requirement and has determined that compliance cannot be secured by voluntary means. In the case of any action terminating, or refusing to grant or continue, assistance because of failure to comply with a requirement imposed pursuant to this section, the head of the Federal department or agency shall file with the committees of the House and Senate having legislative jurisdiction over the program or activity involved a full written report of the circumstances and the grounds for such action. No such action shall become effective until thirty days have elapsed after the filing of such report.

Pub.L. 88–352, Title VI, § 602, July 2, 1964, 78 Stat. 252.

## CIVIL RIGHTS ACT OF 1964 TITLE VII (SELECTED PARTS) 42 U.S.C.A. § 2000E—E–2

## EQUAL EMPLOYMENT OPPORTUNITIES

### § 2000e–2. Unlawful employment practices

### Employer practices

(a) It shall be an unlawful employment practice for an employer—

(1) to fail or refuse to hire or to discharge any individual, or otherwise to discriminate against any individual with respect to his compensation, terms,

conditions, or privileges of employment, because of such individual's race, color, religion, sex, or national origin; or

(2) to limit, segregate, or classify his employees or applicants for employment in any way which would deprive or tend to deprive any individual of employment opportunities or otherwise adversely affect his status as an employee, because of such individual's race, color, religion, sex, or national origin.

## Employment agency practices

(b) It shall be an unlawful employment practice for an employment agency to fail or refuse to refer for employment, or otherwise to discriminate against, any individual because of his race, color, religion, sex, or national origin, or to classify or refer for employment any individual on the basis of his race, color, religion, sex, or national origin. . . .

## Training programs

(d) It shall be an unlawful employment practice for any employer, labor organization, or joint labor-management committee controlling apprenticeship or other training or retraining, including on-the-job training programs to discriminate against any individual because of his race, color, religion, sex, or national origin in admission to, or employment in, any program established to provide apprenticeship or other training.

## Business or enterprises with personnel qualified on basis of religion, sex, or national origin; educational institutions with personnel of particular religion

(e) Notwithstanding any other provision of this subchapter, (1) it shall not be an unlawful employment practice for an employer to hire and employ employees, for an employment agency to classify, or refer for employment any individual, for a labor organization to classify its membership or to classify or refer for employment any individual, or for an employer, labor organization, or joint labor-management committee controlling apprenticeship or other training or retraining programs to admit or employ any individual in any such program, on the basis of his religion, sex, or national origin in those certain instances where religion, sex, or national origin is a bona fide occupational qualification reasonably necessary to the normal operation of that particular business or enterprise, and (2) it shall not be an unlawful employment practice for a school, college, university, or other educational institution or institution of learning to hire and employ employees of a particular religion if such school, college, university, or other educational institution or institution of learning is, in whole or in substantial part, owned, supported, controlled, or managed by a particular religion or by a particular religious corporation, association, or society, or if the curriculum of such school, college, university, or other educational institution or institution of learning is directed toward the propagation of a particular religion.

## Seniority or merit system; quantity or quality of production; ability tests; compensation based on sex and authorized by minimum wage provisions

(h) Notwithstanding any other provision of this subchapter, it shall not be an unlawful employment practice for an employer to apply different standards of compensation, or different terms, conditions, or privileges of employment pursuant to a bona fide seniority or merit system, or a system which measures earnings by quantity or quality of production or to employees who work in different locations, provided that such differences are not the result of an intention to discriminate because of race, color, religion, sex, or national origin, nor shall it be an unlawful employment practice for an employer to give and to act upon the results of any professionally developed ability test provided that such test, its administration or action upon the results is not designed, intended, or used to discriminate because of race, color, religion, sex or national origin. It shall not be an unlawful employment practice under this subchapter for any employer to differentiate upon the basis of sex in determining the amount of the wages or compensation paid or to be paid to employees of such employer if such differentiation is authorized by the provisions of section 206(d) of Title 29.

## Preferential treatment not to be granted on account of existing number or percentage imbalance

(j) Nothing contained in this subchapter shall be interpreted to require any employer, employment agency, labor organization, or joint labor-management committee subject to this subchapter to grant preferential treatment to any individual or to any group because of the race, color, religion, sex, or national origin of such individual or group on account of an imbalance which may exist with respect to the total number or percentage of persons of any race, color, religion, sex, or national origin employed by any employer, referred or classified for employment by any employment agency or labor organization, admitted to membership or classified by any labor organization, or admitted to, or employed in, any apprenticeship or other training program, in comparison with the total number or percentage of persons of such race, color, religion, sex, or national origin in any community, State, section, or other area, or in the available work force in any community, State, section, or other area.

Pub.L. 88–352, Title VII, § 703, July 2, 1964, 78 Stat. 255; Pub.L. 92–261, § 8(a), (b), Mar. 24, 1972, 86 Stat. 109.

## DISCRIMINATION BASED ON SEX TITLE IX (SELECTED PARTS) 20 U.S.C.A. § 1681

### § 1681. Sex
### Prohibition against discrimination; exceptions

(a) No person in the United States shall, on the basis of sex, be excluded from participation in, be denied the benefits of, or be subjected to discrimination under any education program or activity receiving Federal financial assistance, except that:

### Classes of educational institutions subject to prohibition

(1) in regard to admissions to educational institutions, this section shall apply only to institutions of vocational education, professional education, and graduate higher education, and to public institutions of undergraduate higher education;

### Educational institutions commencing planned change in admissions

(2) in regard to admissions to educational institutions, this section shall not apply (A) for one year from June 23, 1972, nor for six years after June 23, 1972, in the case of an educational institution which has begun the process of changing from being an institution which admits only students of one sex to being an institution which admits students of both sexes, but only if it is carrying out a plan for such a change which is approved by the Commissioner of Education or (B) for seven years from the date an educational institution begins the process of changing from being an institution which admits only students of only one sex to being an institution which admits students of both sexes, but only if it is carrying out a plan for such a change which is approved by the Commissioner of Education, whichever is the later;

## Educational institutions of religious organizations with contrary religious tenets

(3) this section shall not apply to an educational institution which is controlled by a religious organization if the application of this subsection would not be consistent with the religious tenets of such organization;

## Educational institutions training individuals for military services or merchant marine

(4) this section shall not apply to an educational institution whose primary purpose is the training of individuals for the military services of the United States, or the merchant marine;

## Public educational institutions with traditional and continuing admissions policy

(5) in regard to admissions this section shall not apply to any public institution of undergraduate higher education which is an institution that traditionally and continually from its establishment has had a policy of admitting only students of one sex;

## Social fraternities or sororities; voluntary youth service organizations

(h) this section shall not apply to membership practices—(A) of a social fraternity or social sorority which is exempt from taxation under section 501(a) of Title 26, the active membership of which consists primarily of students in attendance at an institution of higher education, or (b) of the Young Men's Christian Association, Young Women's Christian Association, Girl Scouts, Boy Scouts, Camp Fire Girls, and voluntary youth service organizations which are so exempt, the membership of which has traditionally been limited to persons of one sex and principally to persons of less than nineteen years of age;

## Boy or girl conferences

(7) this section shall not apply to—

(A) any program or activity of the American Legion undertaken in connection with the organization or operation of any Boys State conference, Boys Nation conference, Girls State conference, or Girls Nation conference; or

(B) any program or activity of any secondary school or educational institution specifically for—

(i) the promotion of any Boys State conference, Boys Nation conference, Girls State conference, or Girls Nation conference; or

(ii) the selection of students to attend any such conference;

## Father-son or mother-daughter activities at educational institutions

(8) this section shall not preclude father-son or mother-daughter activities at an educational institution, but if such activities are provided for students of one sex, opportunities for reasonably comparable activities shall be provided for students of the other sex; and

## Institution of higher education scholarship awards in "beauty" pageants

(9) this section shall not apply with respect to any scholarship or other financial assistance awarded by an institution of higher education to any individual because such individual has received such award in any pageant in which the attainment of such award is based upon a combination of factors related to the personal appearance, poise, and talent of such individual and in which participation is limited to individuals of one sex only, so long as such pageant is in compliance with other nondiscrimination provisions of Federal law.

## Preferential or disparate treatment because of imbalance in participation or receipt of Federal benefits; statistical evidence of imbalance

(b) Nothing contained in subsection (a) of this section shall be interpreted to require any educational institution to grant preferential or disparate treatment to the members of one sex on account of an imbalance which may exist with respect to the total number or percentage of persons of that sex participating in or receiving the benefits of any federally supported program or activity, in comparison with the total number or percentage of persons of that sex in any community, State, section, or other area: *Provided,* That this subsection shall not be construed to prevent the consideration in any hearing or proceeding under this chapter of statistical evidence tending to show that such an imbalance exists with respect to the participation in, or receipt of the benefits of, any such program or activity by the members of one sex.

### Educational institution defined

(c) For purposes of this chapter an educational institution means any public or private preschool, elementary, or secondary school, or any institution of vocational, professional, or higher education, except that in the case of an educational institution composed of more than one school, college, or department which are administratively separate units, such term means each such school, college, or department.

Pub.L. 92–318, Title IX, § 901, June 23, 1972, 86 Stat. 373; Pub.L. 93–568, § 3(a), Dec. 31, 1974, 88 Stat. 1862; Pub.L. 94–482, Title IV, § 412(a), Oct. 12, 1976, 90 Stat. 2234.

### EQUAL PAY ACT (SELECTED PARTS) 29 U.S.C.A. § 206

### § 206. Minimum wage
### Prohibition of sex discrimination

(d)(1) No employer having employees subject to any provisions of this section shall discriminate, within any establishment in which such employees are employed, between employees on the basis of sex by paying wages to employees in such establishment at a rate less than the rate at which he pays wages to employees of the opposite sex in such establishment for equal work on jobs the performance of which requires equal skill, effort, and responsibility, and which are performed under similar working conditions, except where such payment is made pursuant to (i) a seniority system; (ii) a merit system; (iii) a system which measures earnings by quantity or quality of production; or (iv) a differential based on any other factor other than sex: *Provided,* That an employer who is paying a wage rate differential in violation of this subsection shall not, in order to comply with the provisions of this subsection, reduce the wage rate of any employee.

(2) No labor organization, or its agents, representing employees of an employer having employees subject to any provisions of this section shall cause or attempt to cause such an employer to discriminate against an employee in violation of paragraph (1) of this subsection.

(3) For purposes of administration and enforcement, any amounts owing to any employee which have been withheld in violation of this subsection shall be deemed to be unpaid minimum wages or unpaid overtime compensation under this chapter.

(4) As used in this subsection, the term "labor organization" means any organization of any kind, or any agency or employee representation committee or plan, in which employees participate and which exists for the purpose, in whole or in part, of dealing with employers concerning grievances, labor disputes, wages, rates of pay, hours of employment, or conditions of work.

June 25, 1938, c. 676, § 6, 52 Stat. 1062; June 26, 1940, c. 432, § 3(e), (f), 54 Stat. 616; Oct. 26, 1949, c.

736, § 6, 63 Stat. 912; Aug. 12, 1955, c. 867, § 3, 69 Stat. 711; Aug. 8, 1956, c. 1035, § 2, 70 Stat. 1118; May 5, 1961, Pub.L. 87–30, § 5, 75 Stat. 67; June 10, 1963, Pub.L. 88–38, § 3, 77 Stat. 56; Sept. 23, 1966, Pub.L. 89–601, Title III, §§ 301–305, 80 Stat. 838, 839, 841; Apr. 8, 1974, Pub.L. 93–259, §§ 2–4, 5(b), 7(b)(1), 88 Stat. 55, 56, 62; Nov. 1, 1977, Pub.L. 95–151, § 2(a)-(d)(2), 91 Stat. 1245, 1246.

## FAMILY RIGHTS AND PRIVACY ACT (BUCKLEY AMENDMENT) (SELECTED PARTS) 20 U.S.C.A. § 1232G

### § 1232G. Family educational and privacy rights
Conditions for availability of funds to educational agencies or institutions; inspection and review of education records; specific information to be made available; procedure for access to education records; reasonableness of time for such access; hearings; written explanations by parents; definitions

(a)(1)(A) No funds shall be made available under any applicable program to any educational agency or institution which has a policy of denying, or which effectively prevents, the parents of students who are or have been in attendance at a school of such agency or at such institution, as the case may be, the right to inspect and review the education records of their children. If any material or document in the education record of a student includes information on more than one student, the parents of one of such students shall have the right to inspect and review only such part of such material or document as relates to such student or to be informed of the specific information contained in such part of such material. Each educational agency or institution shall establish appropriate procedures for the granting of a request by parents for access to the education records of their children within a reasonable period of time, but in no case more than forty-five days after the request has been made.

(2) No funds shall be made available under any applicable program to any educational agency or institution unless the parents of students who are or have been in attendance at a school of such agency or at such institution are provided an opportunity for a hearing by such agency or institution, in accordance with regulations of the Secretary, to challenge the content of such student's education records, in order to insure that the records are not inaccurate, misleading, or otherwise in violation of the privacy or other rights of students, and to provide an opportunity for the correction or deletion of any such inaccurate, misleading, or otherwise inappropriate data contained therein and to insert into such records a written explanation of the parents respecting the content of such records.

## Release of education records; parental consent requirement; exceptions; compliance with judicial orders and subpoenas; audit and evaluation of Federally-supported education programs; record-keeping

(b)(1) No funds shall be made available under any applicable program to any educational agency or institution which has a policy or practice of permitting the release of education records (or personally identifiable information contained therein other than directory information, as defined in paragraph (5) of subsection (a) of this section) of students without the written consent of their parents to any individual, agency, or organization, other than to the following—

(A) other school officials, including teachers within the educational institution or local educational agency who have been determined by such agency or institution to have legitimate educational interests;

(B) officials of other schools or school systems in which the student seeks or intends to enroll, upon condition that the student's parents be notified of the transfer, receive a copy of the record if desired, and have an opportunity for a hearing to challenge the content of the record;

(C) authorized representatives of (i) the Comptroller General of the United States, (ii) the Secretary, (iii) an administrative head of an education agency (as defined in section 1221e–3(c) of this title), or (iv) State educational authorities, under the conditions set forth in paragraph (3) of this subsection;

(D) in connection with a student's application for, or receipt of, financial aid;

(E) State and local officials or authorities to whom such information is specifically required to be reported or disclosed pursuant to State statute adopted prior to November 19, 1974;

(F) organizations conducting studies for, or on behalf of, educational agencies or institutions for the purpose of developing, validating, or administering predictive tests, administering student aid programs, and improving instruction, if such studies are conducted in such a manner as will not permit the personal identification of students and their parents by persons other than representatives of such organizations and such information will be destroyed when no longer needed for the purpose for which it is conducted;

(G) accrediting organizations in order to carry out their accrediting functions;

(H) parents of a dependent student of such parents, as defined in section 152 of Title 26; and

(I) subject to regulations of the Secretary, in connection with an emergency, appropriate persons if the knowledge of such information is necessary to protect the health or safety of the student or other persons.

Nothing in clause (E) of this paragraph shall prevent a State from further limiting the number or type of State or local officials who will continue to have access thereunder.

(2) No funds shall be made available under any applicable program to any educational agency or institution which has a policy or practice of releasing, or providing access to, any personally identifiable information in education records other than directory information, or as is permitted under paragraph (1) of this subsection unless—

(A) there is written consent from the student's parents specifying records to be released, the reasons for such release, and to whom, and with a copy of the records to be released to the student's parents and the student if desired by the parents, or

(B) such information is furnished in compliance with judicial order, or pursuant to any lawfully issued subpoena, upon condition that parents and the students are notified of all such orders or subpoenas in advance of the compliance therewith by the educational institution or agency.

(C) With respect to this subsection, personal information shall only be transferred to a third party on the condition that such party will not permit any other party to have access to such information without the written consent of the parents of the student.

## Students' rather than parents' permission or consent

(d) For the purposes of this section, whenever a student has attained eighteen years of age, or is attending an institution of postsecondary education the permission or consent required of and the rights accorded to the parents of the student shall thereafter only be required of and accorded to the student.

Pub.L. 90–247, Title IV, § 438, as added Pub.L. 93–380, Title V, § 513(a), Aug. 21, 1974, 88 Stat. 571, and amended Pub.L. 93–568 § 2(a), Dec. 31, 1974, 88 Stat. 1858.

## 1232h. Protection of pupil rights

## Inspection by parents or guardians of instructional material

(a) All instructional material, including teacher's manuals, films, tapes, or other supplementary instructional material which will be used in connection with any research or experimentation program or project shall be available for inspection by the parents or guardians of the children engaged in such program or project. For the purpose of this section "research or experimentation program or project" means any program or project in any applicable program designed to explore or develop new or unproven teaching methods or techniques.

## Psychiatric or psychological examinations, testing, or treatment

(b) No student shall be required, as part of any applicable program, to submit to psychiatric examination, testing, or treatment, or psychological examination, testing, or treatment, in which the primary purpose is to reveal information concerning:

(1) political affiliations;

(2) mental and psychological problems potentially embarrassing to the student or his family;

(3) sex behavior and attitudes;

(4) illegal, anti-social, self-incriminating, and demeaning behavior;

(5) critical appraisals of other individuals with whom respondents have close family relationships;

(6) legally recognized privileged and analogous relationships, such as those of lawyers, physicians, and ministers; or

(7) income (other than that required by law to determine eligibility for participation in a program or for receiving financial assistance under such program), without the prior consent of the student (if the student is an adult or emancipated minor), or in the case of unemancipated minor, without the prior written consent of the parent.

Jan. 2, 1968, P.L. 90–247, Title IV, Part C, Subpart 2, § 439, as added Aug. 21, 1974, P.L. 93–380, Title V, § 514(a), 88 Stat. 574; Nov. 1, 1978, P.L. 95–561, Title XII, Part D, § 1250, 92 Stat. 2355.

## AMERICANS WITH DISABILITIES ACT OF 1990 (SELECTED PARTS), PUBLIC LAW 101–336, 42 U.S.C. § 12101

### TITLE I—EMPLOYMENT

### § 101. Definitions

As used in this title:

(1) COMMISSION.—The term "Commission" means the Equal Employment Opportunity Commission established by section 705 of the Civil Rights Act of 1964 (42 U.S.C. 2000e–4).

(2) COVERED ENTITY.—The term "covered entity" means an employer, employment agency, labor organization, or joint labor-management committee.

(3) DIRECT THREAT.—The term "direct threat" means a significant risk to the health or safety of others that cannot be eliminated by reasonable accommodation.

(4) EMPLOYEE.—The term "employee" means an individual employed by an employer.

(5) EMPLOYER.—

(A) IN GENERAL.—The term employer means a person engaged in an industry affecting commerce who has 15 or more employees for each working day in each of 20 or more calendar weeks in the current or preceding calendar year, and any agent of such person, except that, for two years following the effective date of this title, an employer means a person engaged in an industry affecting commerce who has 25 or more employees for each working day in each of 20 or more calendar weeks in the current or preceding year, and any agent of such person.

(B) EXCEPTIONS.—The term "employer" does not include—

(i) the United States, a corporation wholly owned by the government of the United States, or an Indian tribe; or (ii) a bona fide private membership club (other than a labor organization) that is exempt from taxation under section 501(c) of the Internal Revenue Code of 1986.

(7) PERSON, ETC.—The terms "person", "labor organization", "employment agency", "commerce", and "industry affecting commerce", shall have the same meaning given such terms in section 701 of the Civil Rights Act of 1964 (42 U.S.C. 2000e).

(8) QUALIFIED INDIVIDUAL WITH A DISABILITY.—The term "qualified individual with a disability" means an individual with a disability who, with or without reasonable accommodation, can perform the essential functions of the employment position that such individual holds or desires. For the purposes of this title, consideration shall be given to the employer's judgment as to what functions of a job are essential, and if an employer has prepared a written description before advertising or interviewing applicants for the job, this description shall be considered evidence of the essential functions of the job.

(9) REASONABLE ACCOMMODATION.—The term "reasonable accommodation" may include—

(A) making existing facilities used by employees readily accessible to and usable by individuals with disabilities; and

(B) job restructuring, part-time or modified work schedules, reassignment to a vacant position, acquisition or modification of equipment or devices, appropriate adjustment or modifications of examinations, training materials or policies, the provision of qualified readers or interpreters, and other similar accommodations for individuals with disabilities.

(10) UNDUE HARDSHIP.—

(A) IN GENERAL.—The term "undue hardship" means an action requiring significant difficulty or expense, when considered in light of the factors set forth in subparagraph (B).

(B) FACTORS TO BE CONSIDERED.—In determining whether an accommodation would impose an undue hardship on a covered entity, factors to be considered include—

(i) the nature and cost of the accommodation needed under this Act;

(ii) the overall financial resources of the facility or facilities involved in the provision of the reasonable accommodation; the number of persons employed at such facility; the effect on expenses and resources, or the impact otherwise of such accommodation upon the operation of the facility;

(iii) the overall financial resources of the covered entity; the overall size of the business of a covered entity with respect to the number of its employees; the number, type, and location of its facilities; and

(iv) the type of operation or operations of the covered entity, including the composition, structure, and functions of the workforce of such entity; the geographic separateness, administrative, or fiscal relationship of the facility or facilities in question to the covered entity.

## EDUCATION OF INDIVIDUALS WITH DISABILITIES (SELECTED PARTS), 20 U.S.C. SECS. 1400–1485

### Purpose

It is the purpose of this chapter to assure that all children with disabilities have available to them, within the time periods specified in section 1412(2)(B) of this title, a free appropriate public education which emphasizes special education and related services designed to meet their unique needs, to assure that the rights of children with disabilities and their parents or guardians are protected, to assist States and localities to provide for the education of all children with disabilities, and to assess and assure the effectiveness of efforts to educate children with disabilities.

### § 1401. Definitions

(1) The term "children with disabilities" means children—

(A) with mental retardation, hearing impairments including deafness, speech or language impairments, visual impairments including blindness, serious emotional disturbance, orthopedic impairments, autism, traumatic brain injury, other health impairments, or specific learning disabilities; and

(B) who, by reason thereof need special education and related services ....

. . .

(15) The term "children with specific learning disabilities" means those children who have a disorder in one or more of the basic psychological processes involved in

understanding or in using language, spoken or written, which disorder may manifest itself in imperfect ability to listen, think, speak, read, write, spell, or do mathematical calculations. Such disorders include such conditions as perceptual disabilities, brain injury, minimal brain dysfunction, dyslexia, and developmental aphasia. Such term does not include children who have learning problems which are primarily the result of visual, hearing, or motor disabilities, of mental retardation, of emotional disturbance, or of environmental, cultural, or economic disadvantage.

(16) The term "special education" means specially designed instruction, at no cost to parents or guardians, to meet the unique needs of a child with a disability, including—

(A) instruction conducted in the classroom, in the home, in hospitals and institutions, and in other settings; and

(B) instruction in physical education.

(17) The term "related services" means transportation, and such developmental, corrective, and other supportive services (including speech pathology and audiology, psychological services, physical and occupational therapy, recreation, including therapeutic recreation and social work services, and medical and counseling services, including rehabilitation counseling, except that such medical services shall be for diagnostic and evaluation purposes only) as may be required to assist a child with a disability to benefit from special education, and includes the early identification and assessment of disabling conditions in children.

(18) The term "free appropriate public education" means special education and related services that—

(A) have been provided at public expense, under public supervision and direction, and without charge,

(B) meet the standards of the State educational agency,

(C) include an appropriate preschool, elementary, or secondary school education in the State involved, and

(D) are provided in conformity with the individualized education program required under section 1414(a)(5) of this title.

(19) The term "transition services" means a coordinated set of activities for a student, designed within an outcome-oriented process, which promotes movement from school to post-school activities, including post-secondary education, vocational training, integrated employment (including supported employment), continuing and adult education, adult services, independent living, or community participation. The coordinated set of activities shall be based upon the individual student's needs, taking into account the student's preferences and interests, and shall include instruction, community experiences, the development of employment and other post-school adult living objectives, and, when appropriate, acquisition of daily living skills and functional vocational evaluation.

(20) The term "individualized education program" means a written statement for each child with a disability developed in any meeting by a representative of the local educational agency or an intermediate educational unit who shall be qualified to provide, or supervise the provision of, specially designed instruction to meet the

unique needs of children with disabilities, the teacher, the parents or guardian of such child, and, whenever appropriate, such child, which statement shall include—

(A) a statement of the present levels of educational performance of such child,

(B) a statement of annual goals, including short-term instructional objectives,

(C) a statement of the specific educational services to be provided to such child, and the extent to which such child will be able to participate in regular educational programs, (D) a statement of the needed transition services for students beginning no later than age 16 and annually thereafter (and, when determined appropriate for the individual, beginning at age 14 or younger), including, when appropriate, a statement of the interagency responsibilities or linkages (or both) before the student leaves the school setting.

(E) the projected date for initiation and anticipated duration of such services, and

(F) appropriate objective criteria and evaluation procedures and schedules for determining, on at least an annual basis, whether instructional objectives are being achieved. In the case where a participating agency, other than the educational agency, fails to provide agreed upon services, the educational agency shall reconvene the IEP team to identify alternative strategies to meet the transition objectives.

## AGE DISCRIMINATION ACT—
### 29 U.S.C. § 621 (§ 623)

(a) It shall be unlawful for an employer—

(1) to fail or refuse to hire or to discharge any individual or otherwise discriminate against any individual with respect to his compensation, terms, conditions, or privileges of employment, because of such individual's age. . . .

(c) It shall be unlawful for a labor organization—

(1) to exclude or to expel from its membership, or otherwise to discriminate against, any individual because of his age.

(3) to cause or attempt to cause an employer to discriminate against an individual in violation of this section.

(f) It shall not be unlawful for an employer, employment agency, or labor organization—

(1) to take any action otherwise prohibited under subsections (a), (b), (c), or (e) of this section where age is a bona fide occupational qualification reasonably necessary to the normal operation of the particular business, or where the differentiation is based on reasonable factors other than age. . . .

(3) to discharge or otherwise discipline an individual for good cause.

## EQUAL EDUCATION OPPORTUNITIES
## ACT—20 U.S.C. § 1703

§ 1703 provides:

No State shall deny equal educational opportunity to an individual on account of his or her race, color, sex, or national origin, by—

(a) the deliberate segregation by an educational agency of students on the basis of race, color, or national origin among or within schools. . . .

(c) the assignment by an educational agency of a student to a school, other than the one closest to his or her place of residence within the school district in which he or she resides, if the assignment results in a greater degree of segregation of students on the basis of race, color, sex, or national origin. . . .

(d) discrimination by an educational agency on the basis of race, color, or national origin in the employment, employment conditions, or assignment to schools of its faculty or staff, except to fulfill the purposes of subsection (f) below. . . .

(e) the transfer by an educational agency, whether voluntary or otherwise, of a student from one school to another if the purpose and effect of such transfer is to increase segregation of students on the basis of race, color, or national origin among the schools of such agency; or

(f) the failure by an educational agency to take appropriate action to overcome language barriers that impede equal participation by its students in its instructional programs.

## REHABILITATION ACT OF 1973–
### 29 U.S.C. § 794 (§ 504)

The Act provides in part:

"No otherwise qualified handicapped individual . . . shall, solely by reason of his handicap, be excluded from the participation in, be denied the benefits of, or be subjected to discrimination under any program or activity receiving Federal financial assistance."

# INDEX

---

**References are to Pages**

---

483

**EVOLUTION**
See Curriculum

**EXPRESSION**
See Student Expression

**EXPULSION**
Alcohol, 114
Appropriate penalty for certain offenses, 71–72
Cross-examination of witnesses, 83
Drugs, 113
Hearsay evidence, 85
Immorality, 112
Pregnancy, 110–111, 112
Tobacco, 114

**FALSE IMPRISONMENT**
See Torts

**FAMILY AND MEDICAL LEAVE ACT OF 1993**
Coverage, 444
Leave of absence, 444
Purpose, 444
Teachers, 445

**FAMILY EDUCATIONAL RIGHTS AND PRIVACY ACT (FERPA) OF 1974**
Defamation, 319
Disclosures required by state statutes, 306
Grades,
Challenges to, 306
Posting of, 306–307
Parents' right to inspect children's records, 302
Personal notes, 306
Pupil records policy, 304–306
Release of student records, 302
State law prior to enactment, 302–303
State public records acts, 307
Treatment records, 306

**FREEDOM OF SPEECH**
See Student Expression

**HATCH ACT**
Generally, 361

**HOME SCHOOLING**
Private school instruction statutes as permitting, 21–22, 29
Religious beliefs, teaching of, as justification for, 24
Statutory authorization, 23

†